Aho-Girl

\'ahô,gərl\ *Japanese , noun*.

A clueless girl.

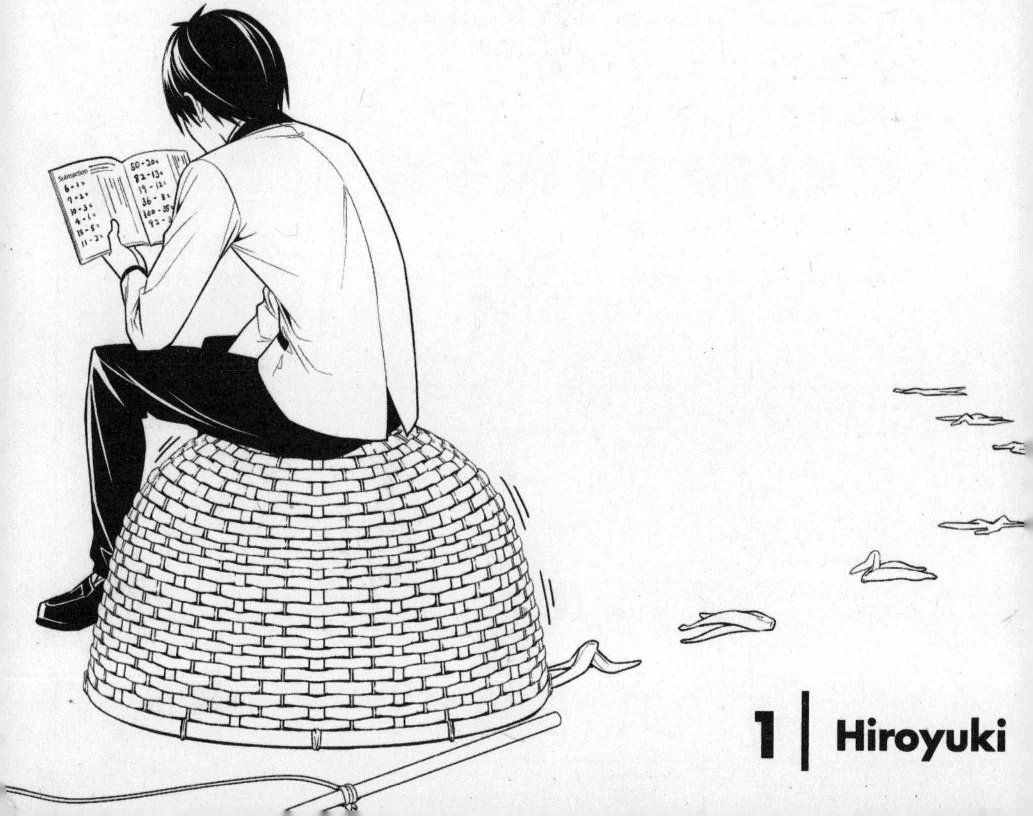
Subtraction

1 | Hiroyuki

HIROYUKI PRESENTS AHO-GIRL VOLUME.1

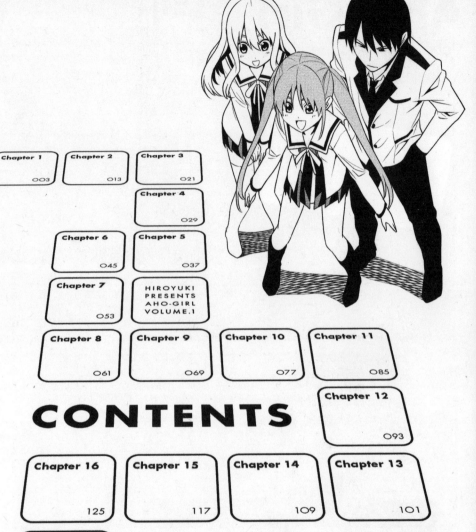

CONTENTS

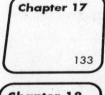

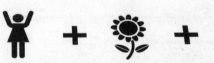

=
AHO-GIRL

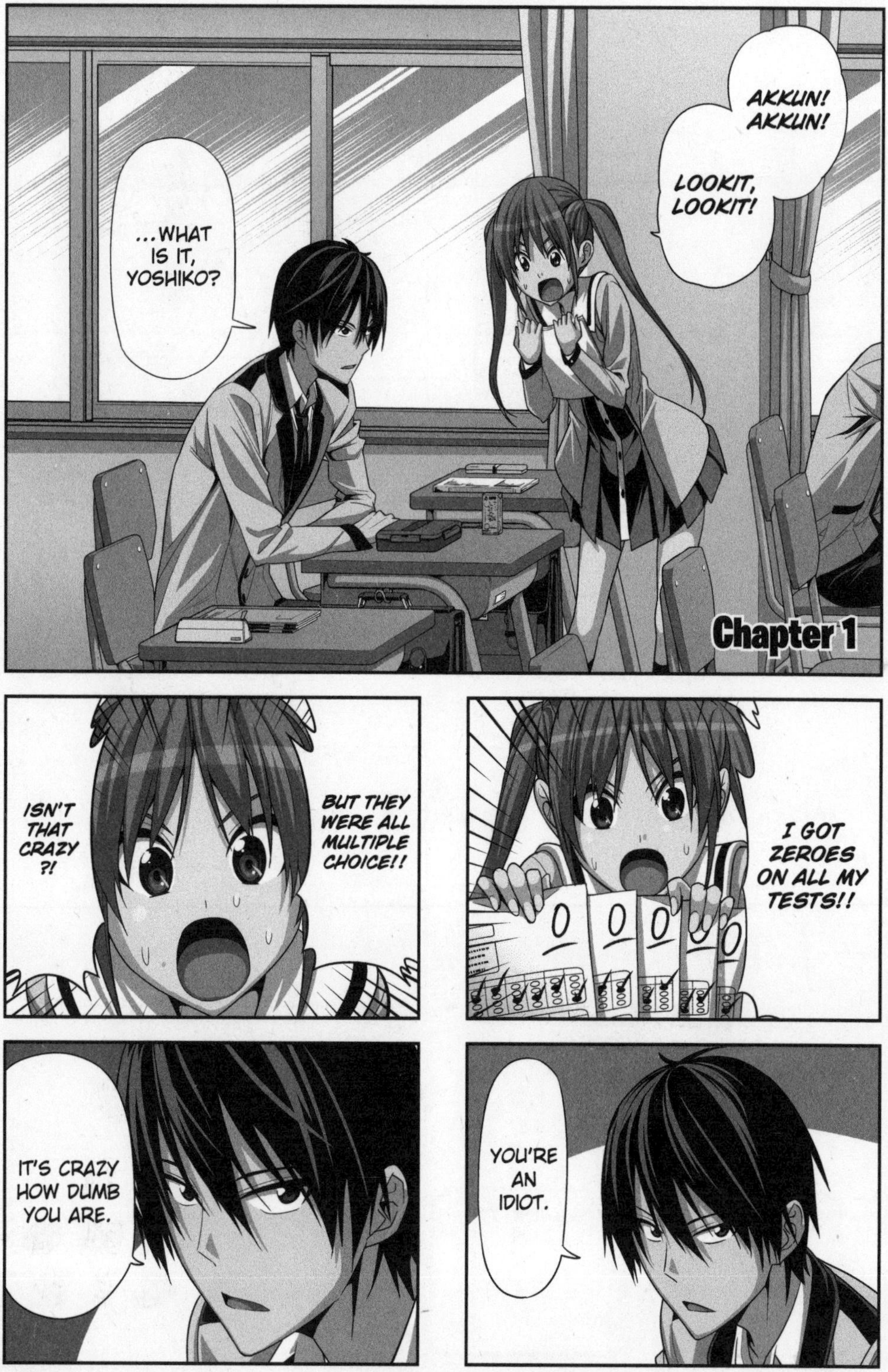
AKKUN! AKKUN!
LOOKIT, LOOKIT!
...WHAT IS IT, YOSHIKO?
Chapter 1
I GOT ZEROES ON ALL MY TESTS!!
BUT THEY WERE ALL MULTIPLE CHOICE!!
ISN'T THAT CRAZY?!
YOU'RE AN IDIOT.
IT'S CRAZY HOW DUMB YOU ARE.

Final Request

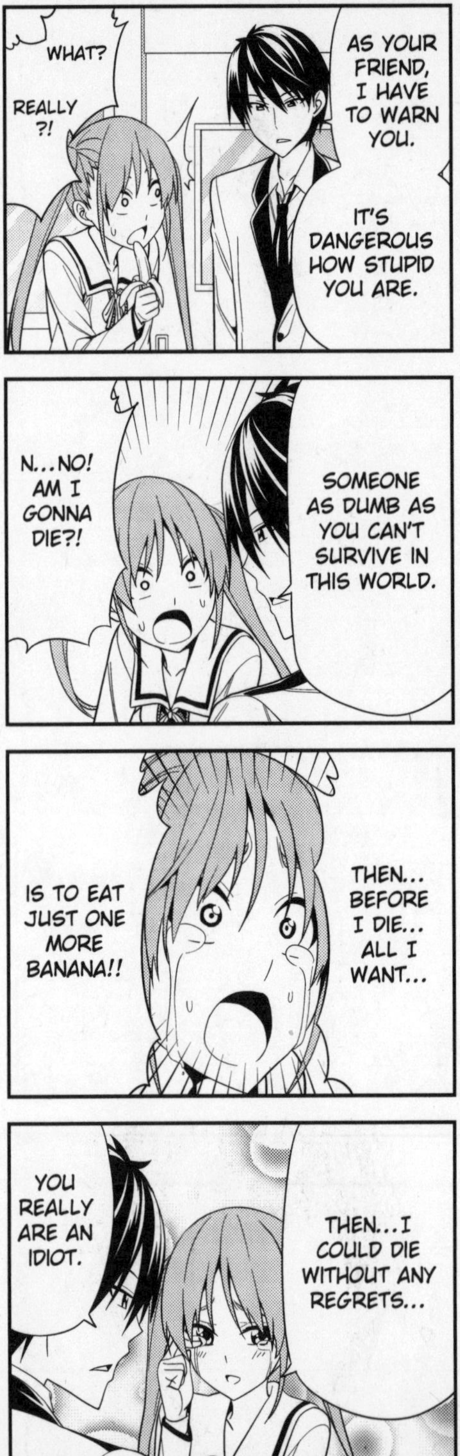
AS YOUR FRIEND, I HAVE TO WARN YOU.
IT'S DANGEROUS HOW STUPID YOU ARE.
WHAT?
REALLY?!
SOMEONE AS DUMB AS YOU CAN'T SURVIVE IN THIS WORLD.
N...NO! AM I GONNA DIE?!
THEN... BEFORE I DIE... ALL I WANT...
IS TO EAT JUST ONE MORE BANANA!!
THEN...I COULD DIE WITHOUT ANY REGRETS...
YOU REALLY ARE AN IDIOT.

But Then We Would Never Get Published!

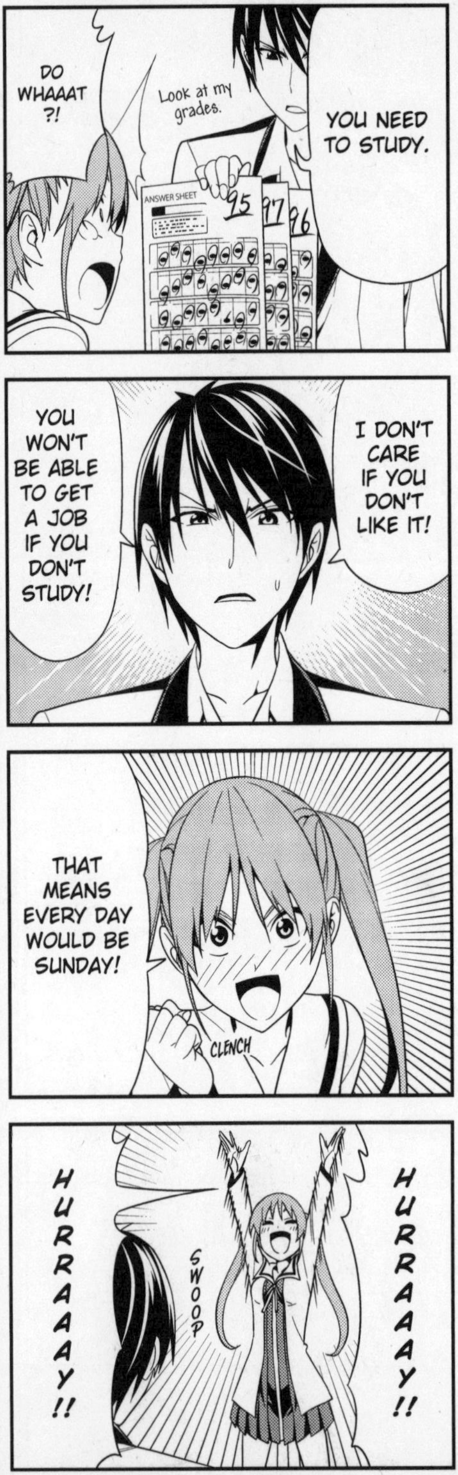
YOU NEED TO STUDY.
Look at my grades.
ANSWER SHEET
95
97
96
DO WHAAAT?!
I DON'T CARE IF YOU DON'T LIKE IT!
YOU WON'T BE ABLE TO GET A JOB IF YOU DON'T STUDY!
THAT MEANS EVERY DAY WOULD BE SUNDAY!
CLENCH
HURRAAAAY!!
SWOOP
HURRAAAAY!!

Dream Chaser

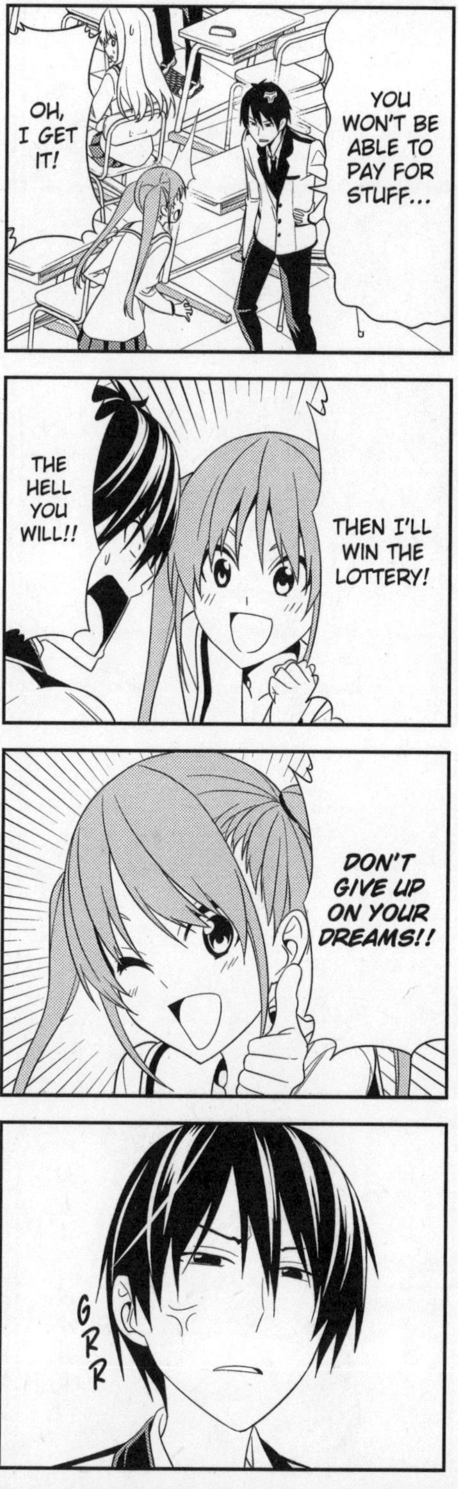
YOU WON'T BE ABLE TO PAY FOR STUFF...
OH, I GET IT!
THEN I'LL WIN THE LOTTERY!
THE HELL YOU WILL!!
DON'T GIVE UP ON YOUR DREAMS!!
GRR

There's Something in the Air(head)

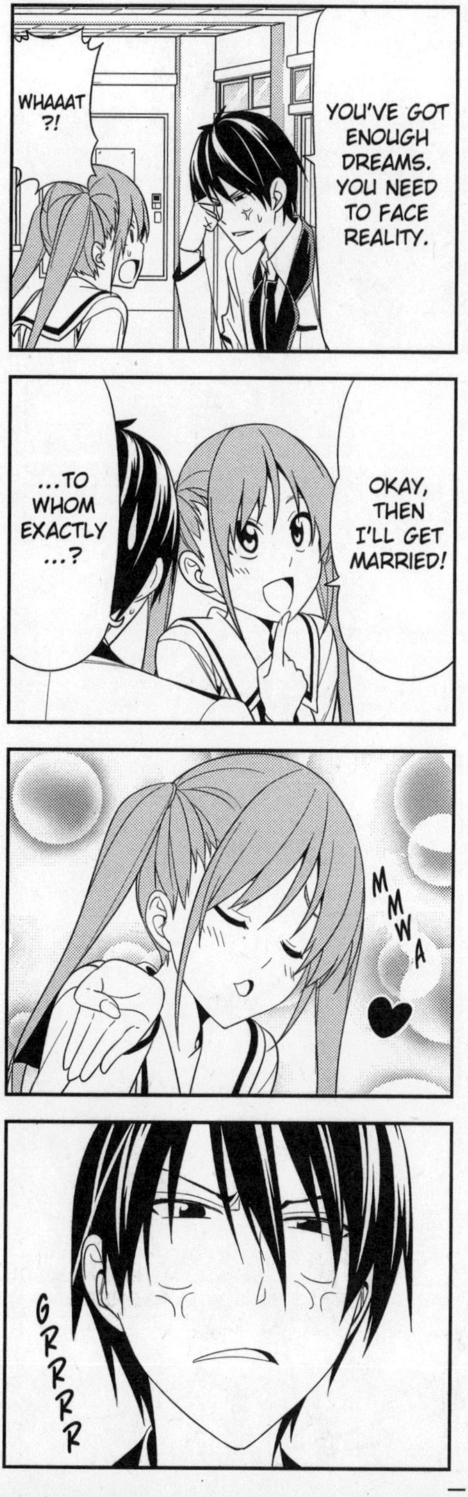
YOU'VE GOT ENOUGH DREAMS. YOU NEED TO FACE REALITY.
WHAAAT?!
OKAY, THEN I'LL GET MARRIED!
...TO WHOM EXACTLY...?
MMWA
GRRRRR

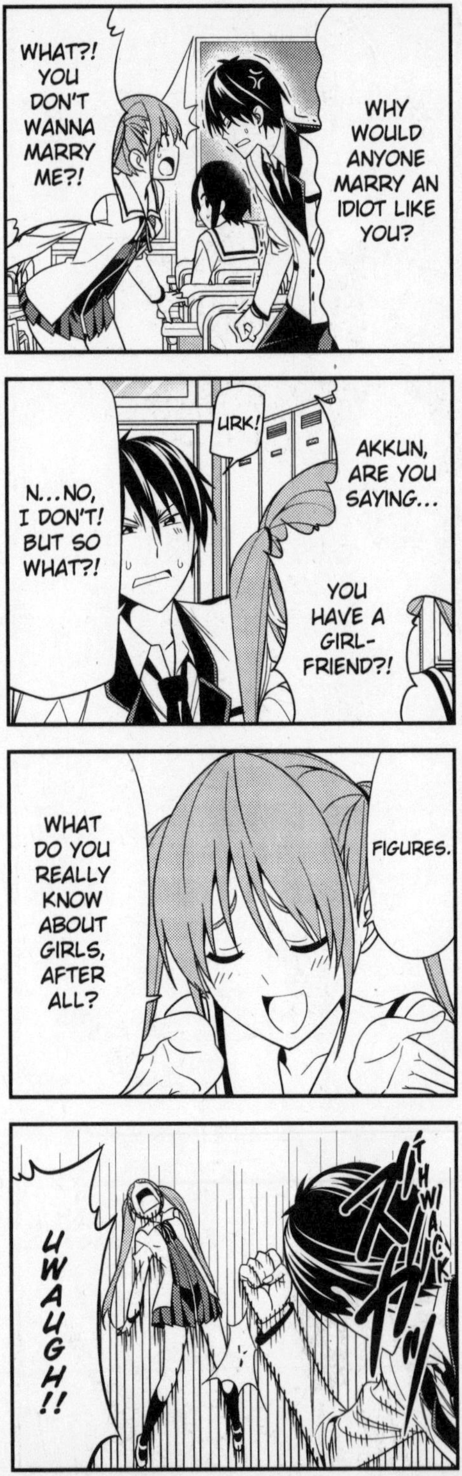
WHY WOULD ANYONE MARRY AN IDIOT LIKE YOU?
WHAT?! YOU DON'T WANNA MARRY ME?!
AKKUN, ARE YOU SAYING...
YOU HAVE A GIRL-FRIEND?!
URK!
N...NO, I DON'T! BUT SO WHAT?!
FIGURES.
WHAT DO YOU REALLY KNOW ABOUT GIRLS, AFTER ALL?
THWACK
UWAUGH!!

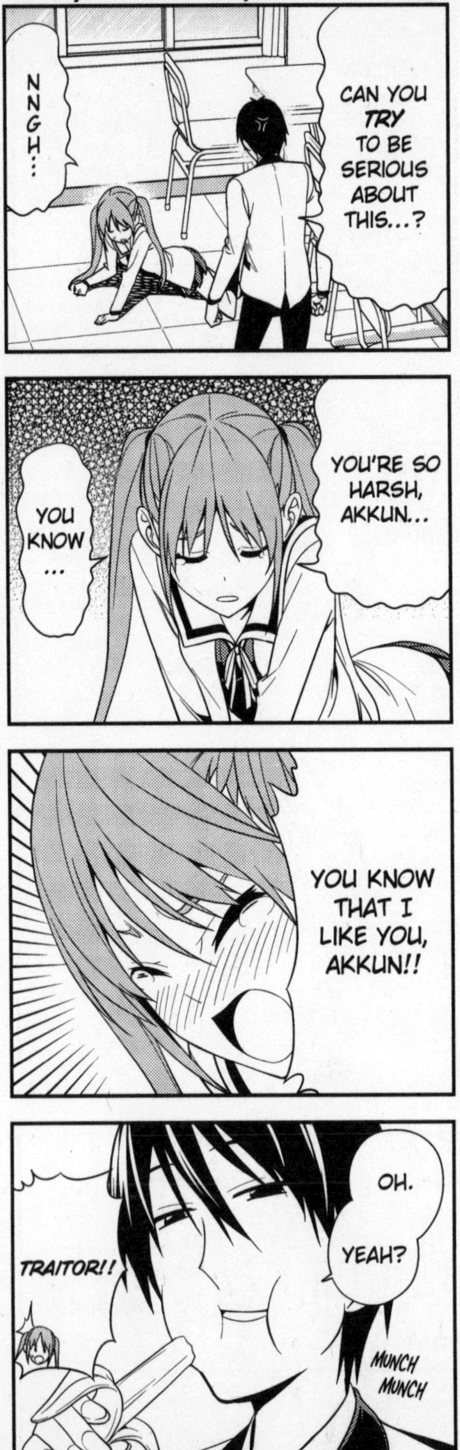
CAN YOU TRY TO BE SERIOUS ABOUT THIS...?
NNGH...
YOU'RE SO HARSH, AKKUN...
YOU KNOW...
YOU KNOW THAT I LIKE YOU, AKKUN!!
OH.
YEAH?
TRAITOR!!
MUNCH MUNCH

Why I Loved You

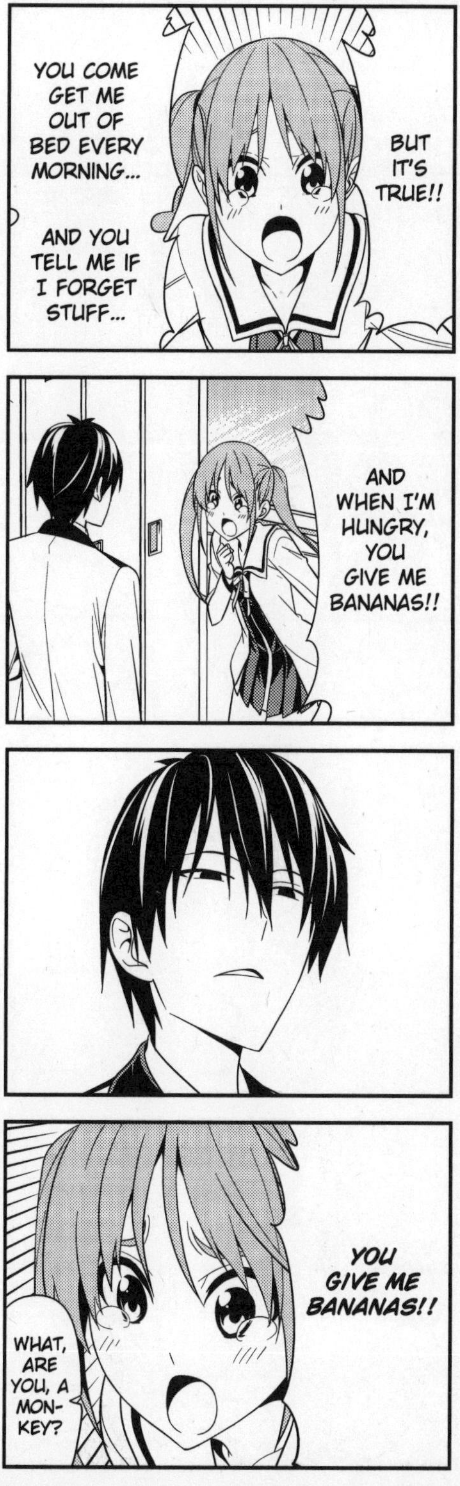
BUT IT'S TRUE!!
YOU COME GET ME OUT OF BED EVERY MORNING...
AND YOU TELL ME IF I FORGET STUFF...
AND WHEN I'M HUNGRY, YOU GIVE ME BANANAS!!
YOU GIVE ME BANANAS!!
WHAT, ARE YOU, A MONKEY?

Inscrutable

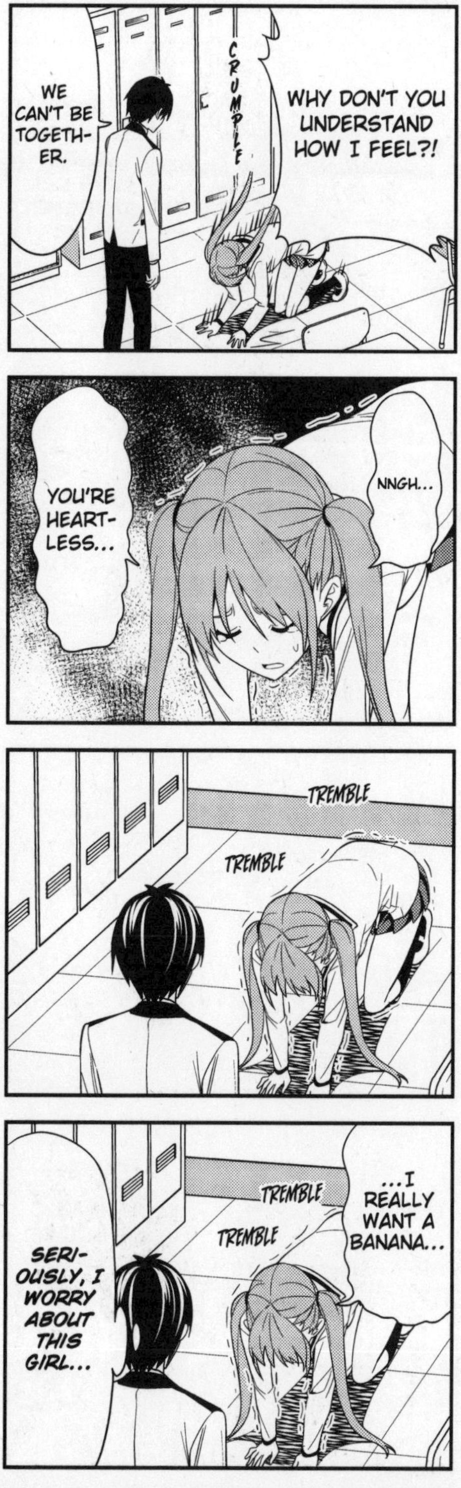
WHY DON'T YOU UNDERSTAND HOW I FEEL?!
CRUMPLE
WE CAN'T BE TOGETHER.
NNGH...
YOU'RE HEARTLESS...
TREMBLE
TREMBLE
...I REALLY WANT A BANANA...
TREMBLE
TREMBLE
SERIOUSLY, I WORRY ABOUT THIS GIRL...

Straight to Banana

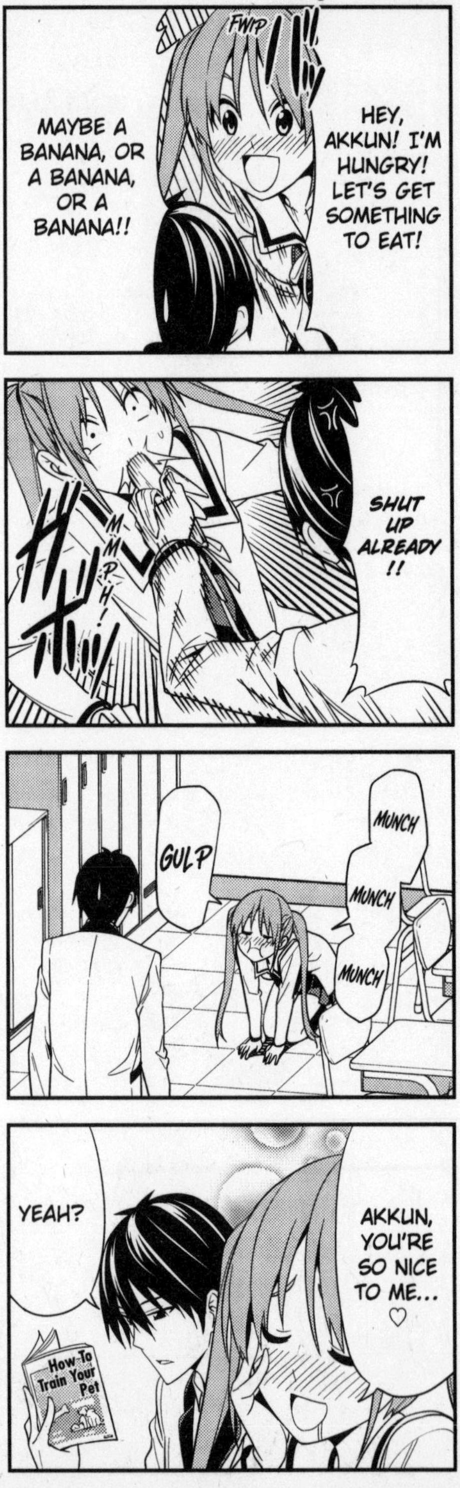
FWIP
HEY, AKKUN! I'M HUNGRY! LET'S GET SOMETHING TO EAT!
MAYBE A BANANA, OR A BANANA, OR A BANANA!!
SHUT UP ALREADY!!
MMPH!
MUNCH MUNCH MUNCH
GULP
AKKUN, YOU'RE SO NICE TO ME... ♡
YEAH?
How To Train Your Pet

All-Natural Ingredients

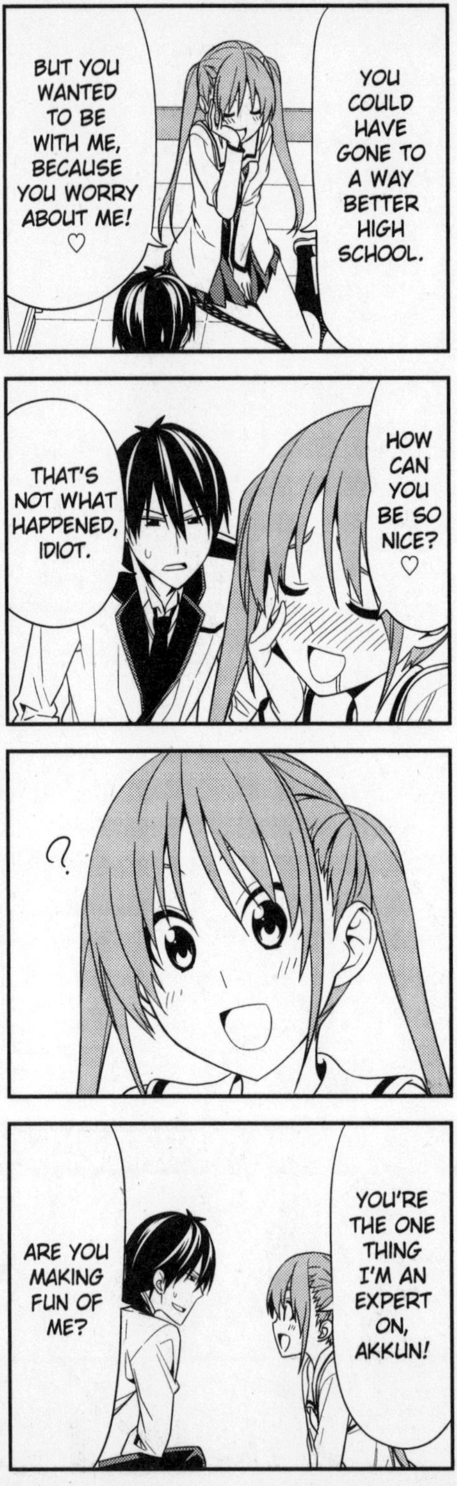
YOU COULD HAVE GONE TO A WAY BETTER HIGH SCHOOL.
BUT YOU WANTED TO BE WITH ME, BECAUSE YOU WORRY ABOUT ME! ♡
HOW CAN YOU BE SO NICE? ♡
THAT'S NOT WHAT HAPPENED, IDIOT.
?
YOU'RE THE ONE THING I'M AN EXPERT ON, AKKUN!
ARE YOU MAKING FUN OF ME?

Sometimes Prickly, Sometimes Sweet: Exhibit A

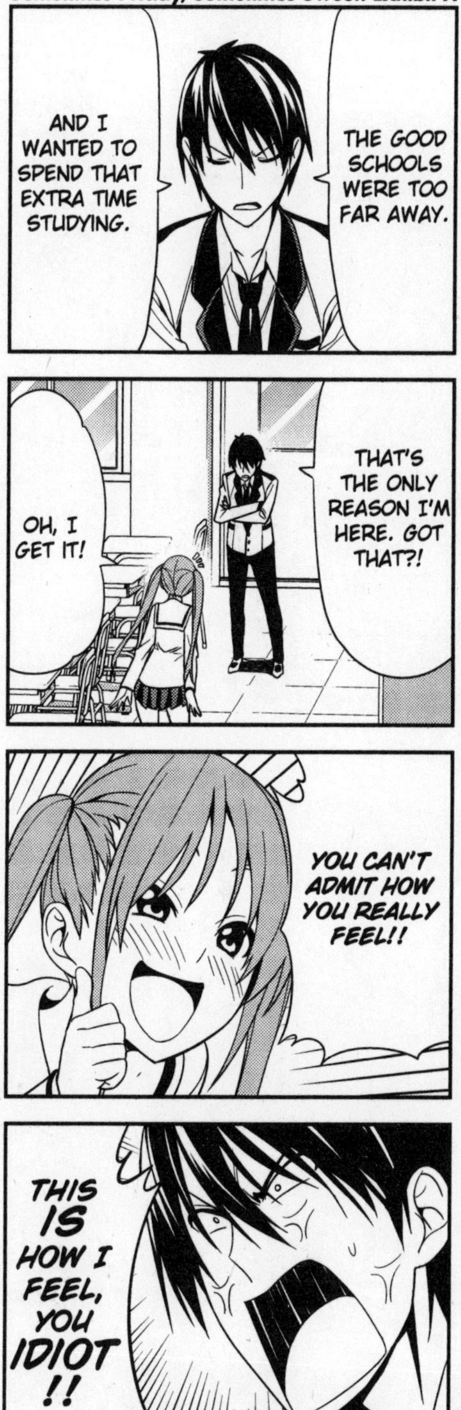
THE GOOD SCHOOLS WERE TOO FAR AWAY.
AND I WANTED TO SPEND THAT EXTRA TIME STUDYING.
THAT'S THE ONLY REASON I'M HERE. GOT THAT?!
OH, I GET IT!
YOU CAN'T ADMIT HOW YOU REALLY FEEL!!
THIS IS HOW I FEEL, YOU IDIOT!!

A Carnal Thank You

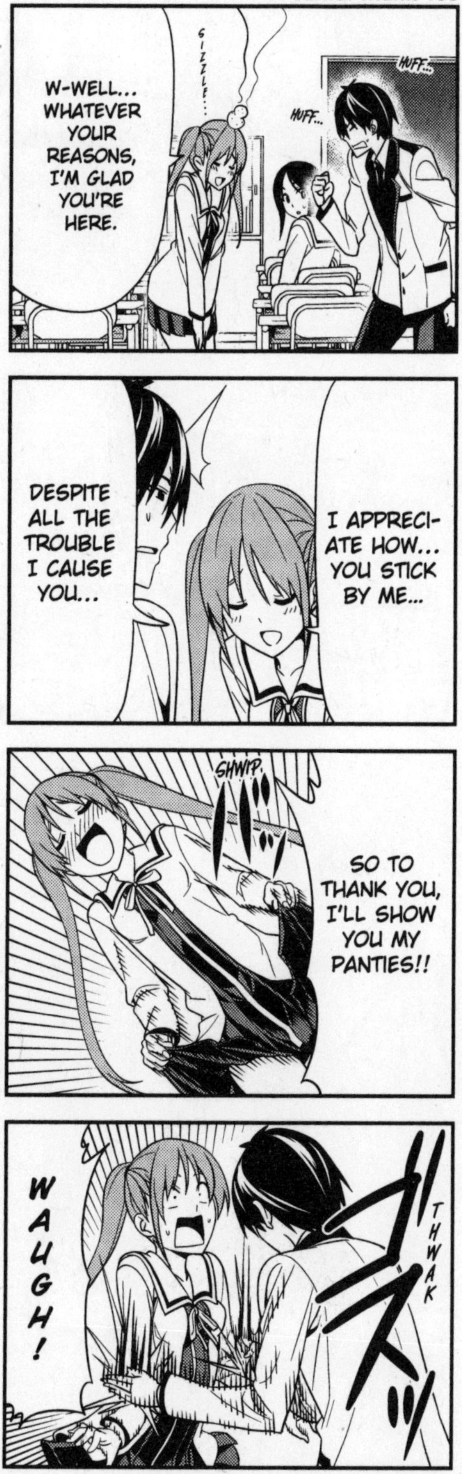
HUFF...
HUFF...
SIZZLE...
W-WELL... WHATEVER YOUR REASONS, I'M GLAD YOU'RE HERE.
I APPRECIATE HOW... YOU STICK BY ME...
DESPITE ALL THE TROUBLE I CAUSE YOU...
SHWIP
SO TO THANK YOU, I'LL SHOW YOU MY PANTIES!!
THWAK
WAUGH!

What Do You Mean, Dirty?

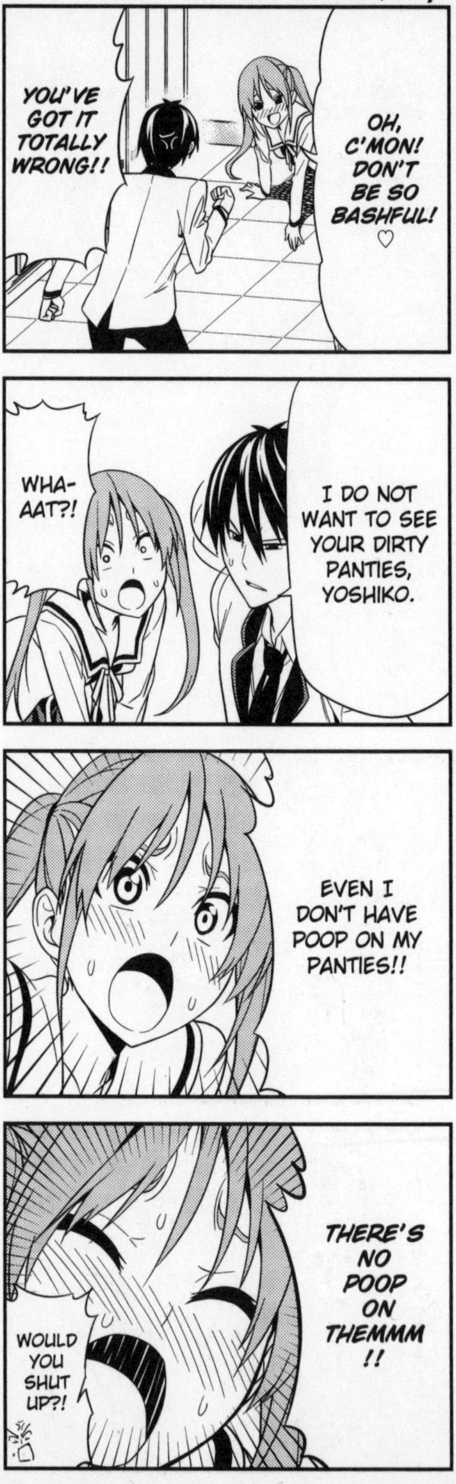
OH, C'MON! DON'T BE SO BASHFUL! ♡
YOU'VE GOT IT TOTALLY WRONG!!
I DO NOT WANT TO SEE YOUR DIRTY PANTIES, YOSHIKO.
WHA-AAT?!
EVEN I DON'T HAVE POOP ON MY PANTIES!!
THERE'S NO POOP ON THEMMM !!
WOULD YOU SHUT UP?!

A Whirlwind of Idiocy

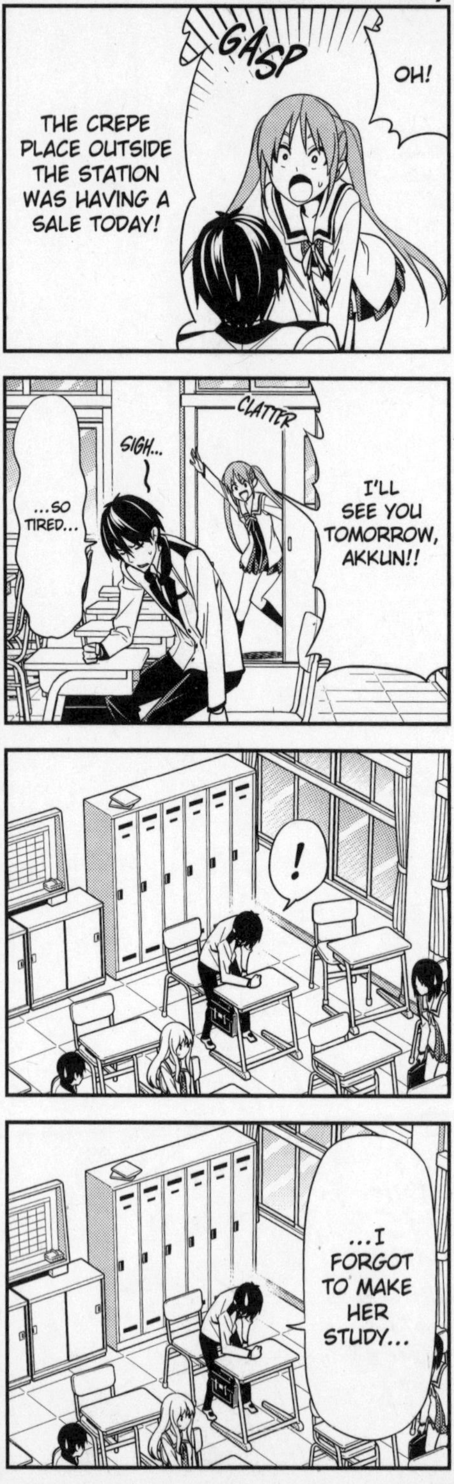
OH!
GASP
THE CREPE PLACE OUTSIDE THE STATION WAS HAVING A SALE TODAY!
I'LL SEE YOU TOMORROW, AKKUN!!
CLATTER
SIGH...
...SO TIRED...
!
...I FORGOT TO MAKE HER STUDY...

Bananas Are Great, But Crepes...

モグ
HRMMF
モグ
HRMMF
モグ
HRMMF
モグ
HRMMF
パァァ...
GLOWWW...
SO GOOD... ♡

Name	**Yoshiko Hanabatake**
Sex	
Height	**160 cm / 5'3"**
Weight	**48 kg / 106 lbs**
Blood type	**O**
Birthday	**01/01**

Memo Has been with Akkun since they were kids. Likes Akkun a lot.

Lives entirely by impulse.

Believes that whoever has the most fun in life wins.

Staple food is bananas.

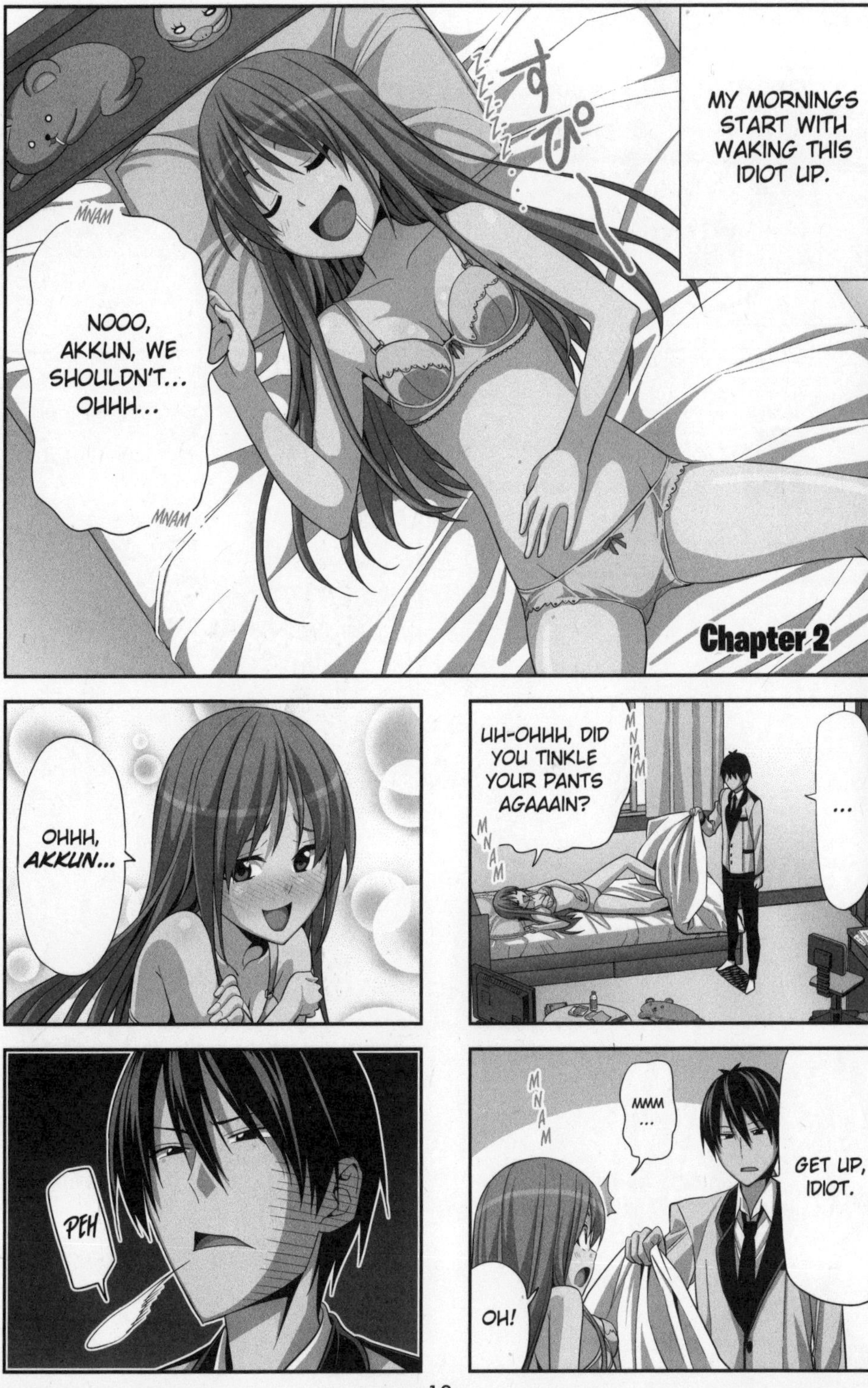
MY MORNINGS START WITH WAKING THIS IDIOT UP.
すぴ〜
MNAM
NOOO, AKKUN, WE SHOULDN'T... OHHH...
MNAM
Chapter 2
...
MNAM
UH-OHHH, DID YOU TINKLE YOUR PANTS AGAAAIN?
MNAM
OHHH, AKKUN...
GET UP, IDIOT.
MNAM
MMM ...
OH!
PEH

The Banana (-Loving Idiot) Next Door

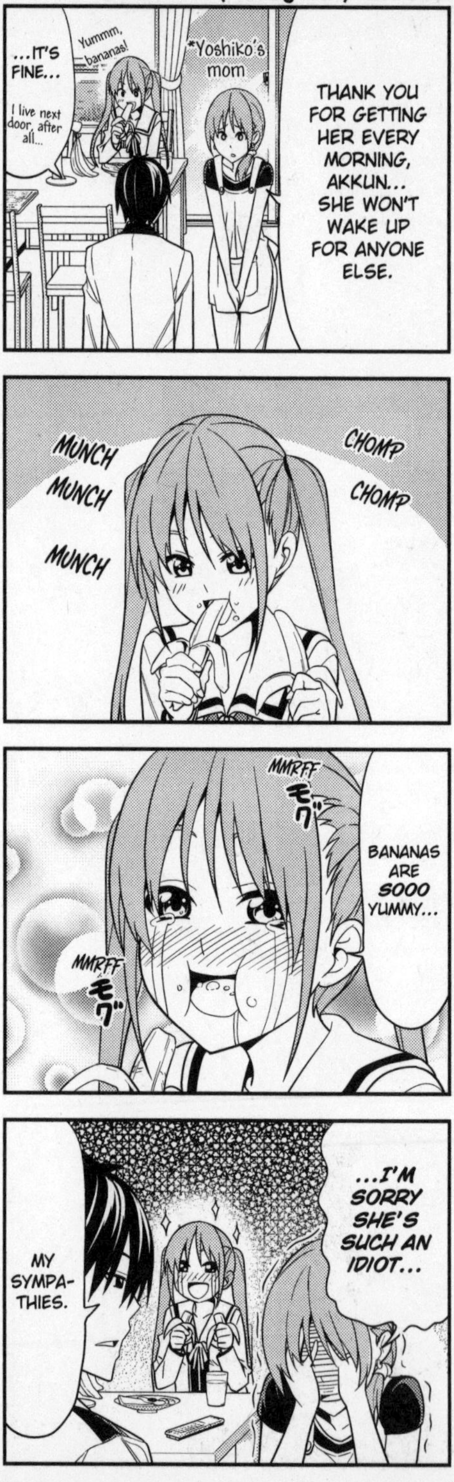
THANK YOU FOR GETTING HER EVERY MORNING, AKKUN... SHE WON'T WAKE UP FOR ANYONE ELSE.
*Yoshiko's mom
Yummm, bananas!
...IT'S FINE...
I live next door, after all...
CHOMP
CHOMP
MUNCH
MUNCH
MUNCH
MMRFF
モグ
BANANAS ARE SOOO YUMMY...
MMRFF
モグ
...I'M SORRY SHE'S SUCH AN IDIOT...
MY SYMPATHIES.

How Akkun Sees Things

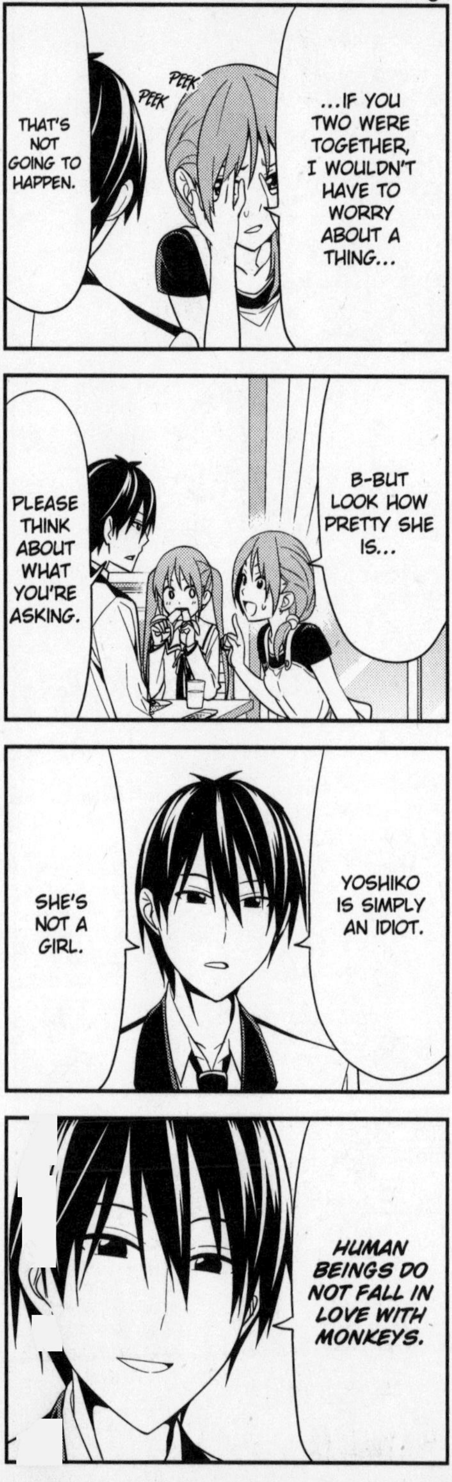
...IF YOU TWO WERE TOGETHER, I WOULDN'T HAVE TO WORRY ABOUT A THING...
PEEK
PEEK
THAT'S NOT GOING TO HAPPEN.
B-BUT LOOK HOW PRETTY SHE IS...
PLEASE THINK ABOUT WHAT YOU'RE ASKING.
YOSHIKO IS SIMPLY AN IDIOT.
SHE'S NOT A GIRL.
HUMAN BEINGS DO NOT FALL IN LOVE WITH MONKEYS.

Akkun's Plan

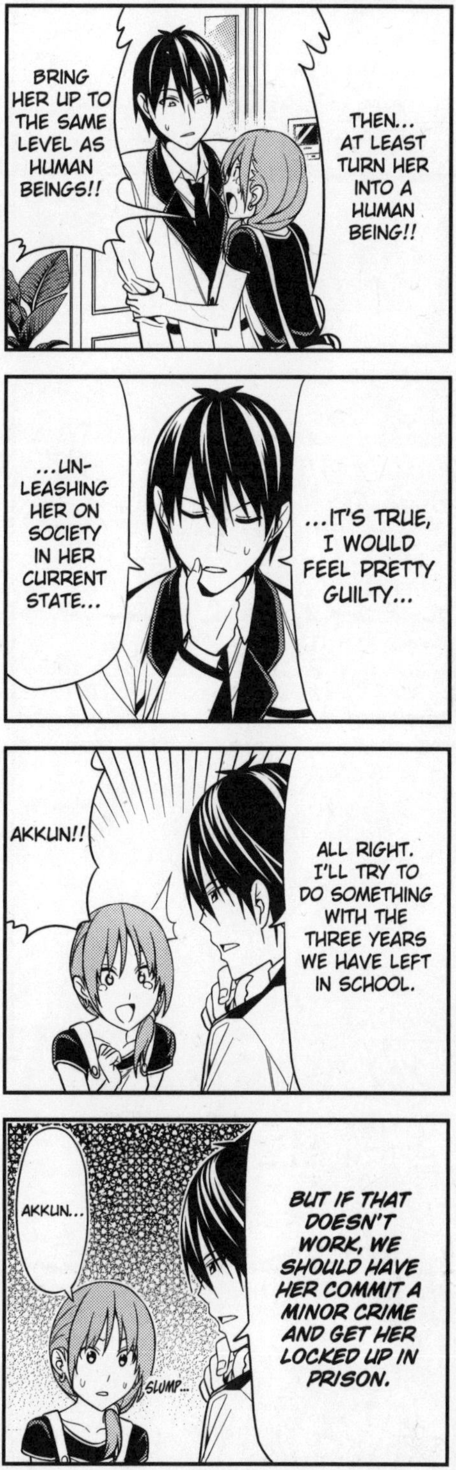
THEN... AT LEAST TURN HER INTO A HUMAN BEING!!
BRING HER UP TO THE SAME LEVEL AS HUMAN BEINGS!!
...IT'S TRUE, I WOULD FEEL PRETTY GUILTY...
...UN-LEASHING HER ON SOCIETY IN HER CURRENT STATE...
ALL RIGHT. I'LL TRY TO DO SOMETHING WITH THE THREE YEARS WE HAVE LEFT IN SCHOOL.
AKKUN!!
BUT IF THAT DOESN'T WORK, WE SHOULD HAVE HER COMMIT A MINOR CRIME AND GET HER LOCKED UP IN PRISON.
AKKUN...
SLUMP...

Akkun at Work

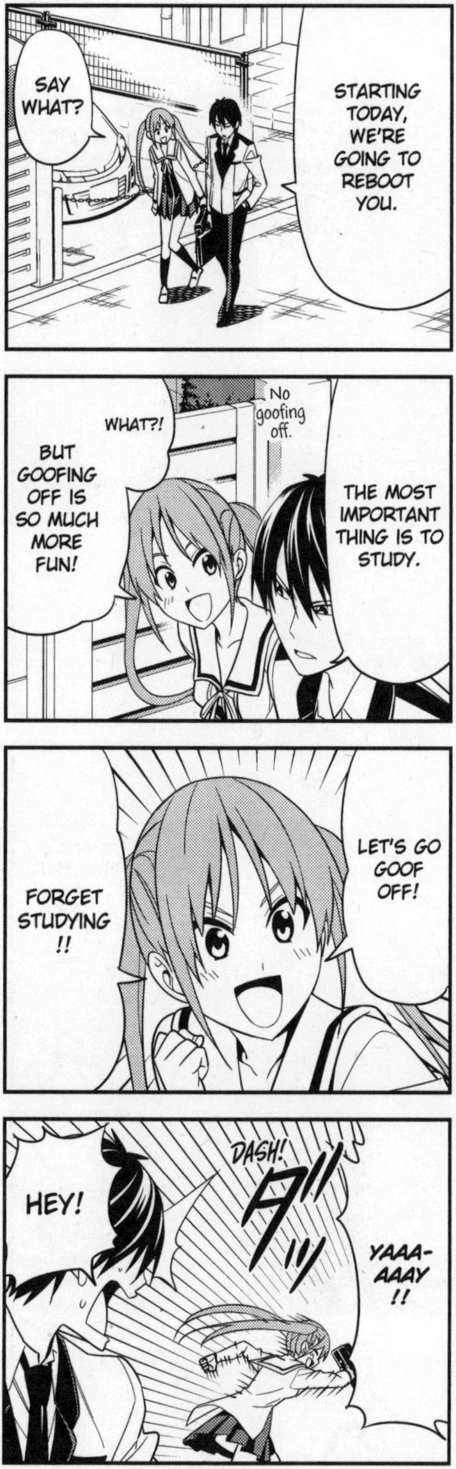
STARTING TODAY, WE'RE GOING TO REBOOT YOU.
SAY WHAT?
THE MOST IMPORTANT THING IS TO STUDY.
No goofing off.
WHAT?!
BUT GOOFING OFF IS SO MUCH MORE FUN!
LET'S GO GOOF OFF!
FORGET STUDYING !!
YAAA-AAAY !!
DASH!
HEY!

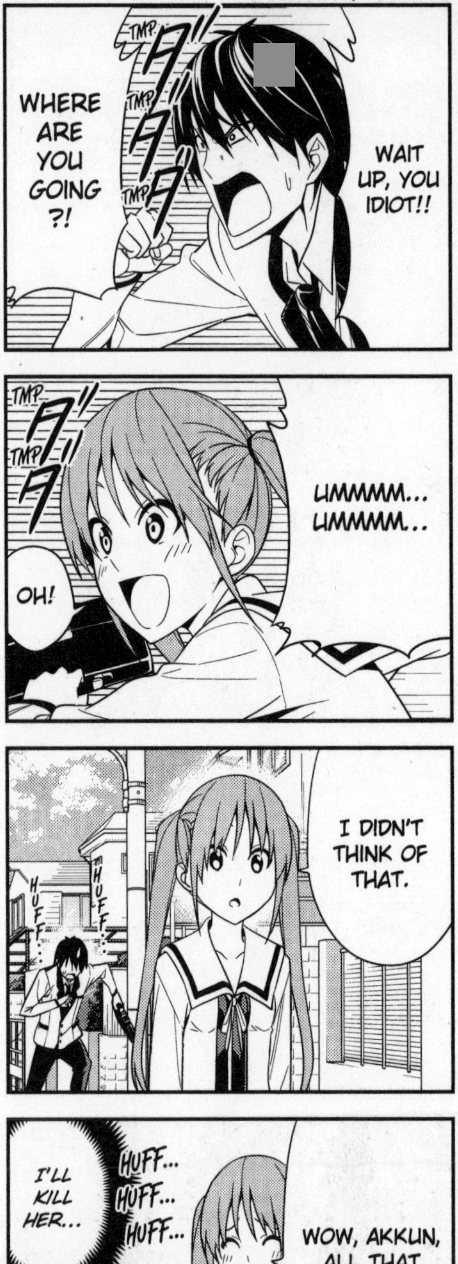
WAIT UP, YOU IDIOT!!
TMP
TMP
TMP
WHERE ARE YOU GOING ?!
UMMMM... UMMMM...
TMP
TMP
OH!
I DIDN'T THINK OF THAT.
HUFF...
HUFF...
WOW, AKKUN, ALL THAT STUDYING MADE YOU SO WEAK!
HUFF... HUFF... HUFF...
I'LL KILL HER...

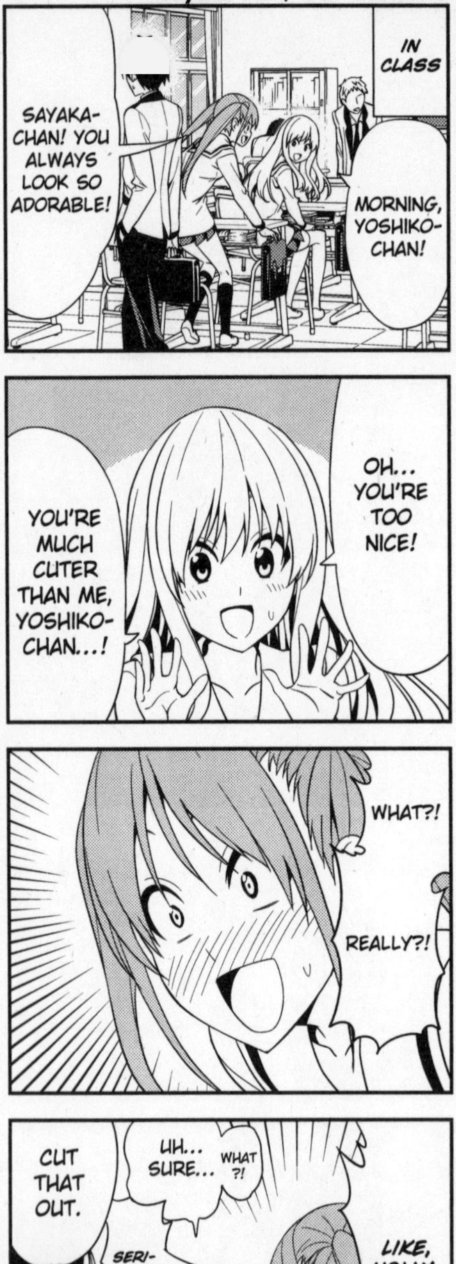
IN CLASS
MORNING, YOSHIKO-CHAN!
SAYAKA-CHAN! YOU ALWAYS LOOK SO ADORABLE!
OH... YOU'RE TOO NICE!
YOU'RE MUCH CUTER THAN ME, YOSHIKO-CHAN...!
WHAT?!
REALLY?!
LIKE, HOLLYWOOD-LEVEL ?!
WHAT ?!
UH... SURE...
SERIOUSLY?!
CUT THAT OUT.

Akkun and Sayaka-chan

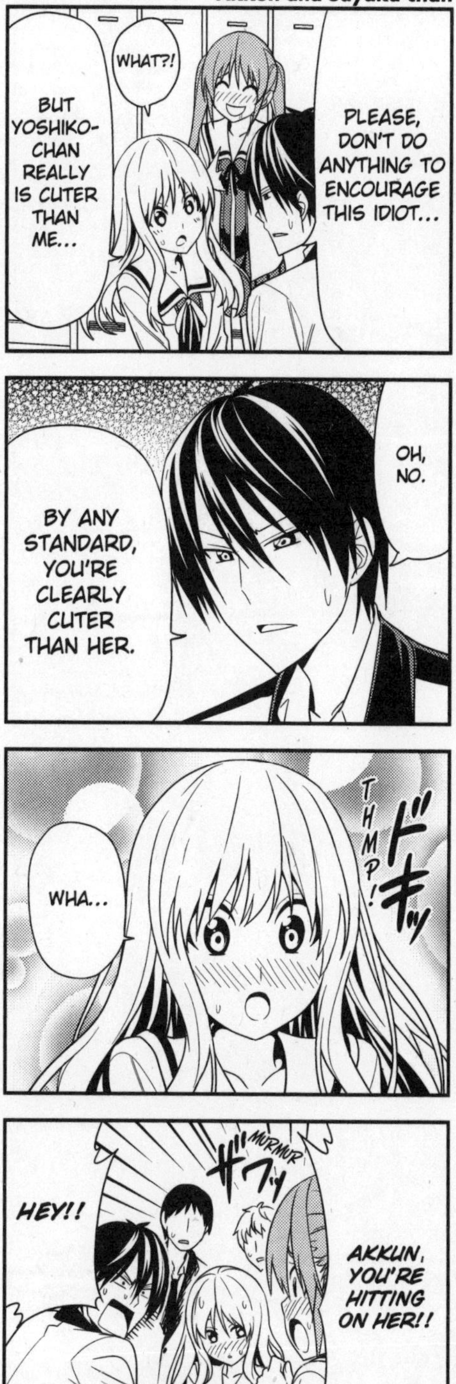

PLEASE, DON'T DO ANYTHING TO ENCOURAGE THIS IDIOT...
WHAT?!
BUT YOSHIKO-CHAN REALLY IS CUTER THAN ME...
OH, NO.
BY ANY STANDARD, YOU'RE CLEARLY CUTER THAN HER.
THMP!
ドキッ
WHA...
MURMUR
ザワッ
AKKUN, YOU'RE HITTING ON HER!!
HEY!!

Tone It Down

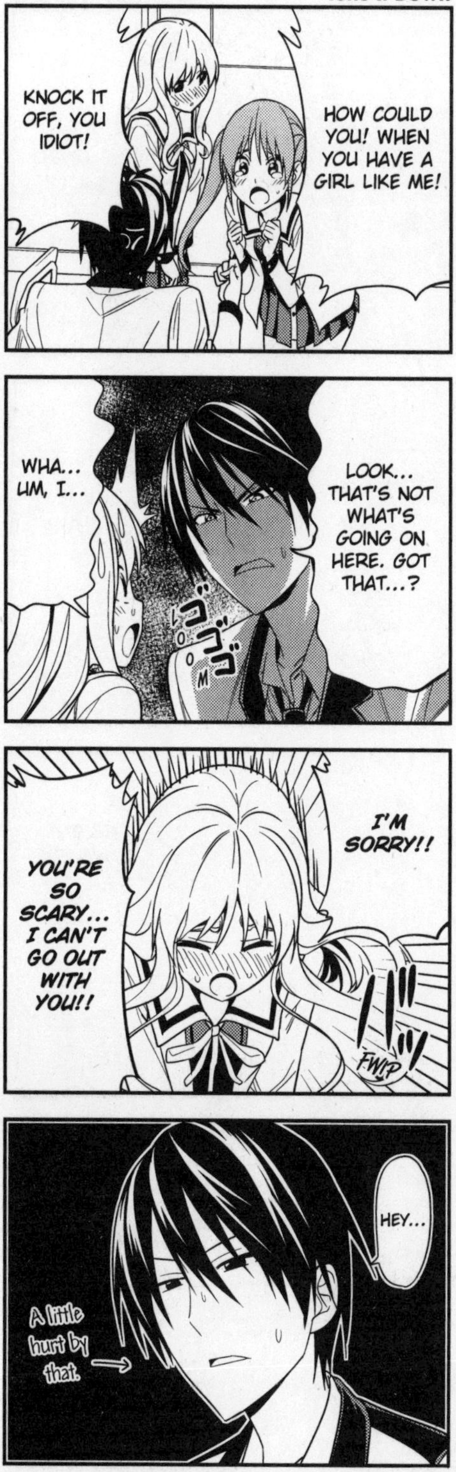

HOW COULD YOU! WHEN YOU HAVE A GIRL LIKE ME!
KNOCK IT OFF, YOU IDIOT!
LOOK... THAT'S NOT WHAT'S GOING ON HERE. GOT THAT...?
ゴゴゴ
WHA... UM, I...
I'M SORRY!!
YOU'RE SO SCARY... I CAN'T GO OUT WITH YOU!!
バッ
FWIP
HEY...
A little hurt by that.

Don't Push It

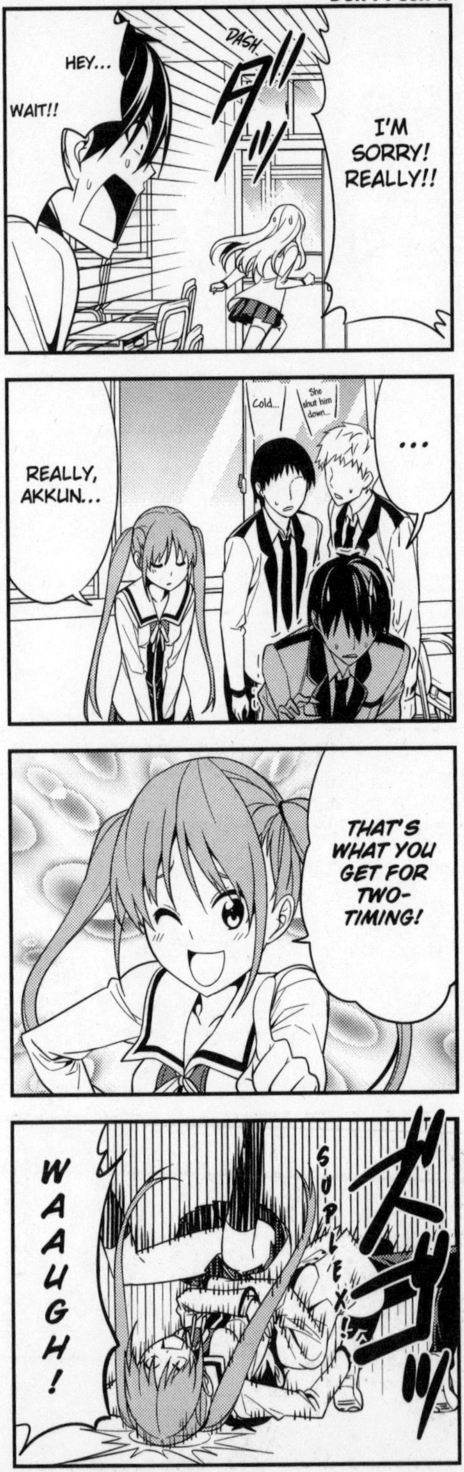
I'M SORRY! REALLY!!
DASH
HEY...
WAIT!!
...
She shut him down...
Cold...
REALLY, AKKUN...
THAT'S WHAT YOU GET FOR TWO-TIMING!
SUPLEX!!
WAAUGH!

He's Not Wrong

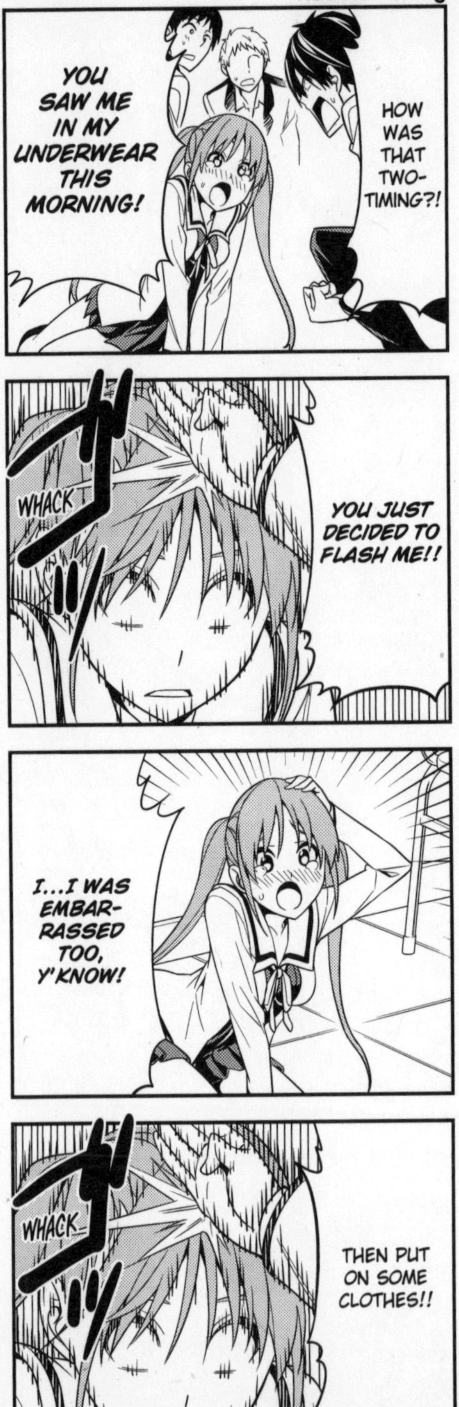
HOW WAS THAT TWO-TIMING?!
YOU SAW ME IN MY UNDERWEAR THIS MORNING!
YOU JUST DECIDED TO FLASH ME!!
WHACK
I...I WAS EMBARRASSED TOO, Y'KNOW!
THEN PUT ON SOME CLOTHES!!
WHACK

He Never Realized

HUFF!...
ハァ...
HUFF...
ハァ...
C'MON... WHAT'S SO SCARY ABOUT ME...?
YIKES...
SO SCARY.
I'M JUST A REGULAR GUY!

Name	**Akuru Akutsu**
Sex	
Height	**175 cm / 5'9"**
Weight	**60 kg / 132 lbs**
Blood type	**AB**
Birthday	**05/20**

Memo For some reason, Yoshiko took a liking to him when they were children, and he decided to try to cure her of her stupidity. It's not going well.

All told, he's pretty good at taking care of her.

He's a long-suffering person. Both his parents are often out of the house working.

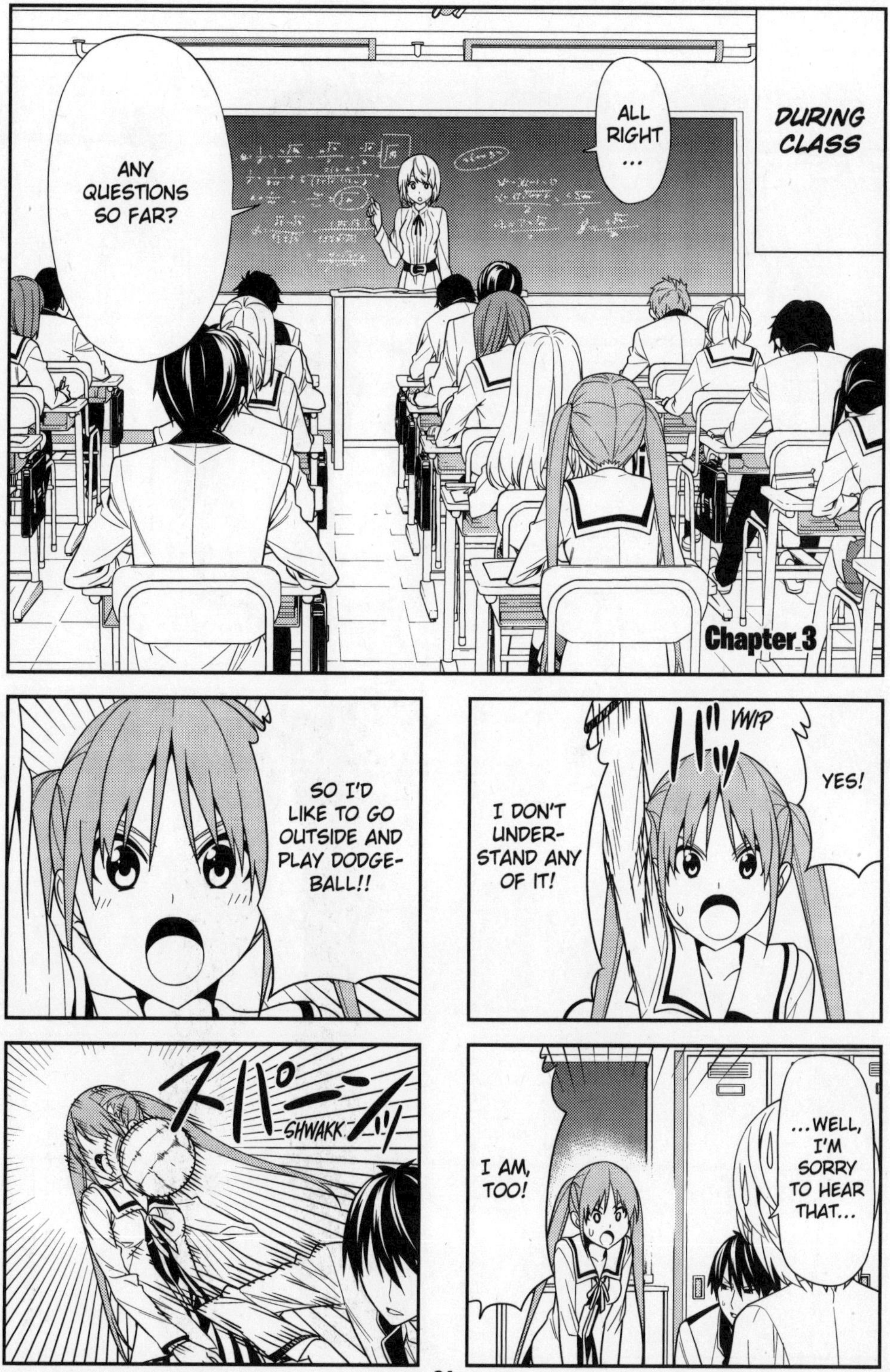
DURING CLASS
ALL RIGHT ...
ANY QUESTIONS SO FAR?
Chapter 3
VWIP
YES!
I DON'T UNDER-STAND ANY OF IT!
SO I'D LIKE TO GO OUTSIDE AND PLAY DODGE-BALL!!
...WELL, I'M SORRY TO HEAR THAT...
I AM, TOO!
スパーン!!
SHWAKK

What Path Will My Life Take?

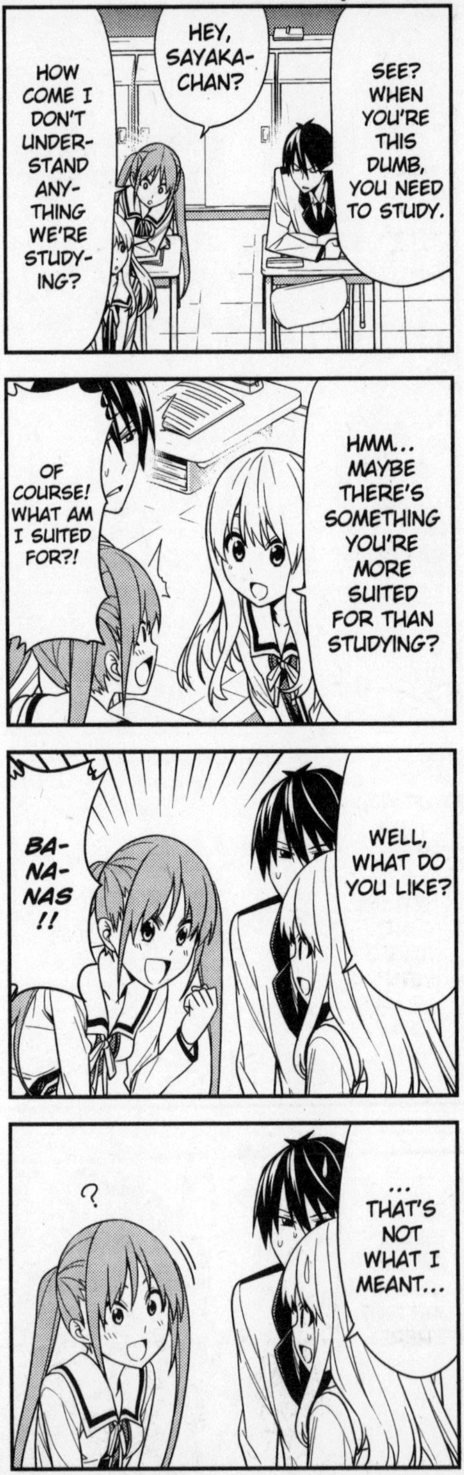
HEY, SAYAKA-CHAN?
HOW COME I DON'T UNDER-STAND ANY-THING WE'RE STUDY-ING?
SEE? WHEN YOU'RE THIS DUMB, YOU NEED TO STUDY.
HMM... MAYBE THERE'S SOMETHING YOU'RE MORE SUITED FOR THAN STUDYING?
OF COURSE! WHAT AM I SUITED FOR?!
WELL, WHAT DO YOU LIKE?
BA-NA-NAS !!
...THAT'S NOT WHAT I MEANT...
?

Way Too Idealistic!

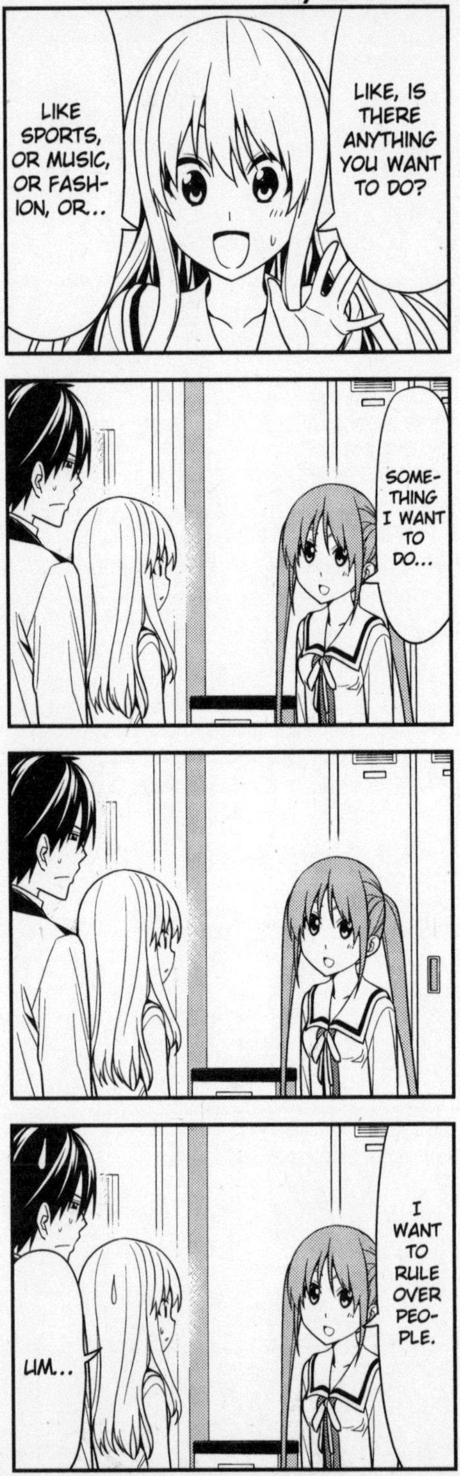
LIKE, IS THERE ANYTHING YOU WANT TO DO?
LIKE SPORTS, OR MUSIC, OR FASH-ION, OR...
SOME-THING I WANT TO DO...
I WANT TO RULE OVER PEO-PLE.
UM...

It's Okay to Laugh

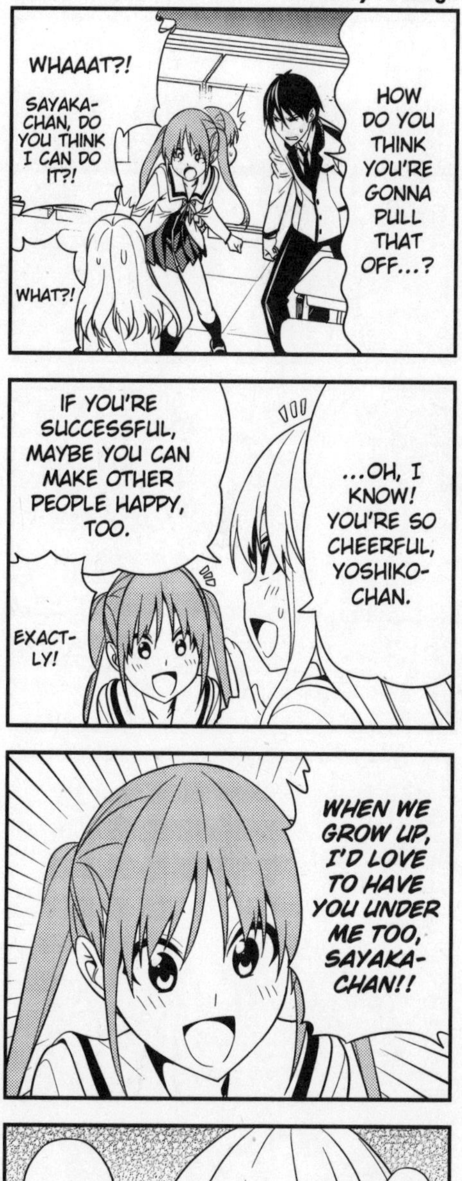
HOW DO YOU THINK YOU'RE GONNA PULL THAT OFF...?
WHAAAT?!
SAYAKA-CHAN, DO YOU THINK I CAN DO IT?!
WHAT?!
...OH, I KNOW! YOU'RE SO CHEERFUL, YOSHIKO-CHAN.
IF YOU'RE SUCCESSFUL, MAYBE YOU CAN MAKE OTHER PEOPLE HAPPY, TOO.
EXACTLY!
WHEN WE GROW UP, I'D LOVE TO HAVE YOU UNDER ME TOO, SAYAKA-CHAN!!
THAT...
...THAT'S NOT WHAT I...

Overwhelming Persuasion

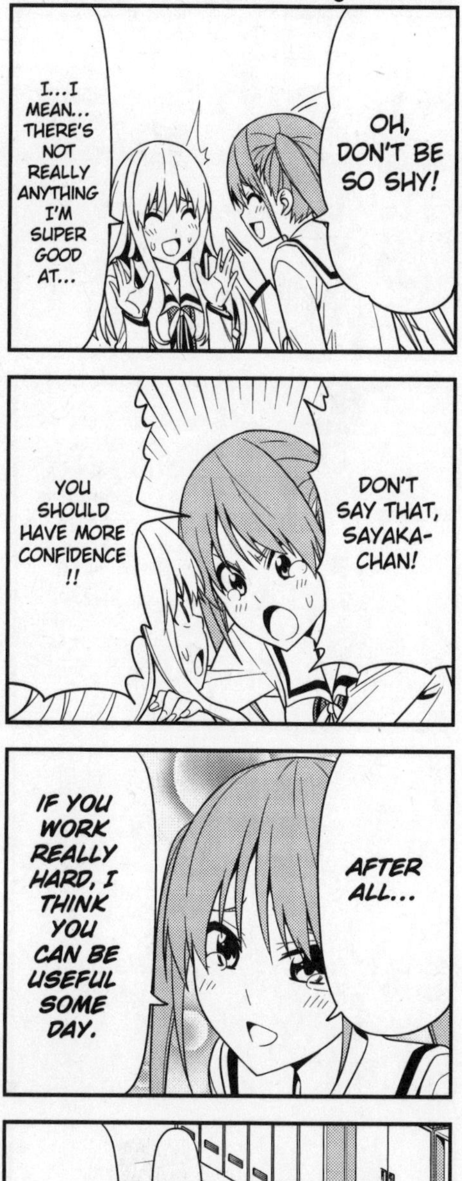
OH, DON'T BE SO SHY!
I...I MEAN... THERE'S NOT REALLY ANYTHING I'M SUPER GOOD AT...
DON'T SAY THAT, SAYAKA-CHAN!
YOU SHOULD HAVE MORE CONFIDENCE!!
AFTER ALL...
IF YOU WORK REALLY HARD, I THINK YOU CAN BE USEFUL SOME DAY.
...
Okay?
YOU CAN GET ANGRY ANYTIME HERE.

Akkun, You're Terrifying!

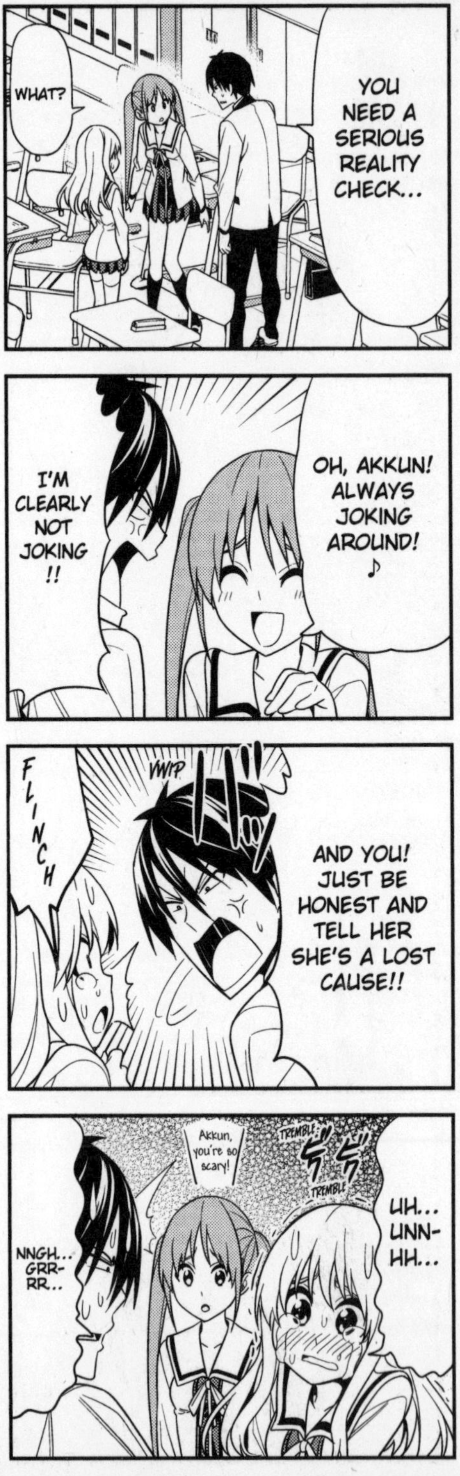
YOU NEED A SERIOUS REALITY CHECK...
WHAT?
OH, AKKUN! ALWAYS JOKING AROUND! ♪
I'M CLEARLY NOT JOKING!!
VWIP
AND YOU! JUST BE HONEST AND TELL HER SHE'S A LOST CAUSE!!
FLINCH
TREMBLE TREMBLE
UH... UNN-HH...
Akkun, you're so scary!
NNGH... GRRR-RR...

Overwhelming Agreement

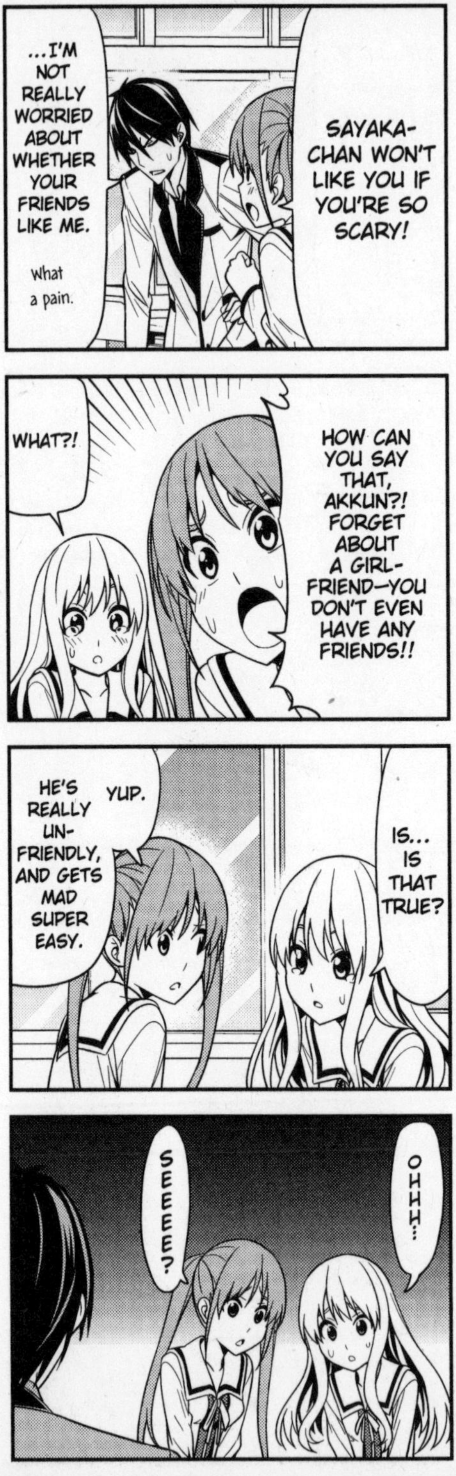
SAYAKA-CHAN WON'T LIKE YOU IF YOU'RE SO SCARY!
...I'M NOT REALLY WORRIED ABOUT WHETHER YOUR FRIENDS LIKE ME.
What a pain.
HOW CAN YOU SAY THAT, AKKUN?! FORGET ABOUT A GIRL-FRIEND—YOU DON'T EVEN HAVE ANY FRIENDS!!
WHAT?!
IS... IS THAT TRUE?
YUP.
HE'S REALLY UN-FRIENDLY, AND GETS MAD SUPER EASY.
OHHH...
SEEEEE?

Akkun, You Say Such Nice Things!

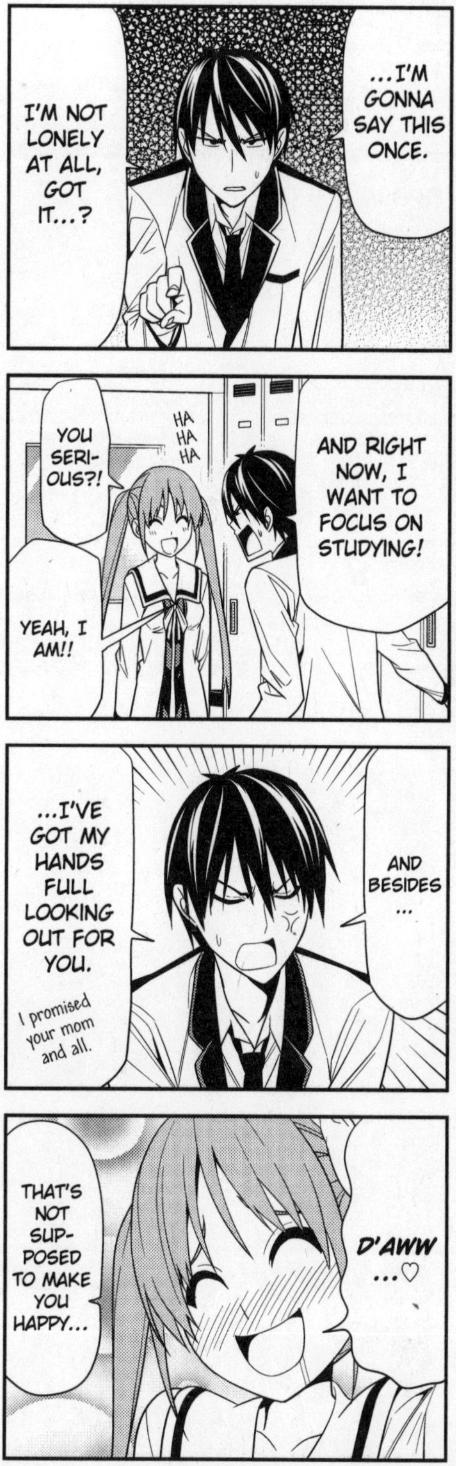
...I'M GONNA SAY THIS ONCE.
I'M NOT LONELY AT ALL, GOT IT...?
AND RIGHT NOW, I WANT TO FOCUS ON STUDYING!
HA HA HA
YOU SERI-OUS?!
YEAH, I AM!!
AND BESIDES ...
...I'VE GOT MY HANDS FULL LOOKING OUT FOR YOU.
I promised your mom and all.
D'AWW ...♡
THAT'S NOT SUP-POSED TO MAKE YOU HAPPY...

Here's the Proof

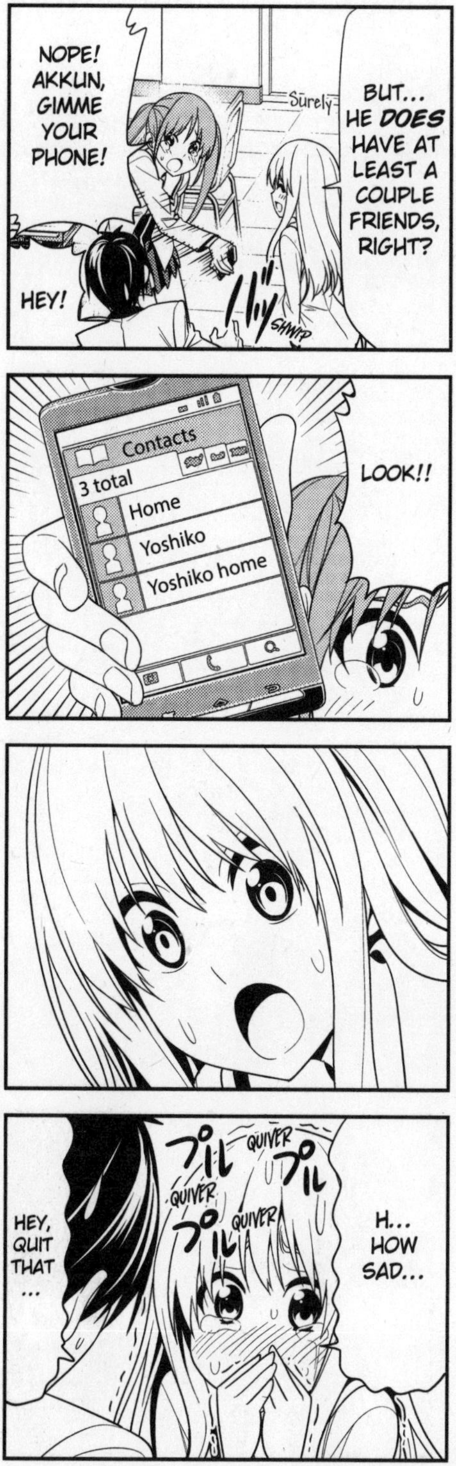
BUT... HE ***DOES*** HAVE AT LEAST A COUPLE FRIENDS, RIGHT?
Surely
NOPE! AKKUN, GIMME YOUR PHONE!
SHWIP
HEY!
LOOK!!
Contacts
3 total
Home
Yoshiko
Yoshiko home
H... HOW SAD...
プル QUIVER
プル QUIVER
プル QUIVER
HEY, QUIT THAT ...

Aww, He Made a Friend

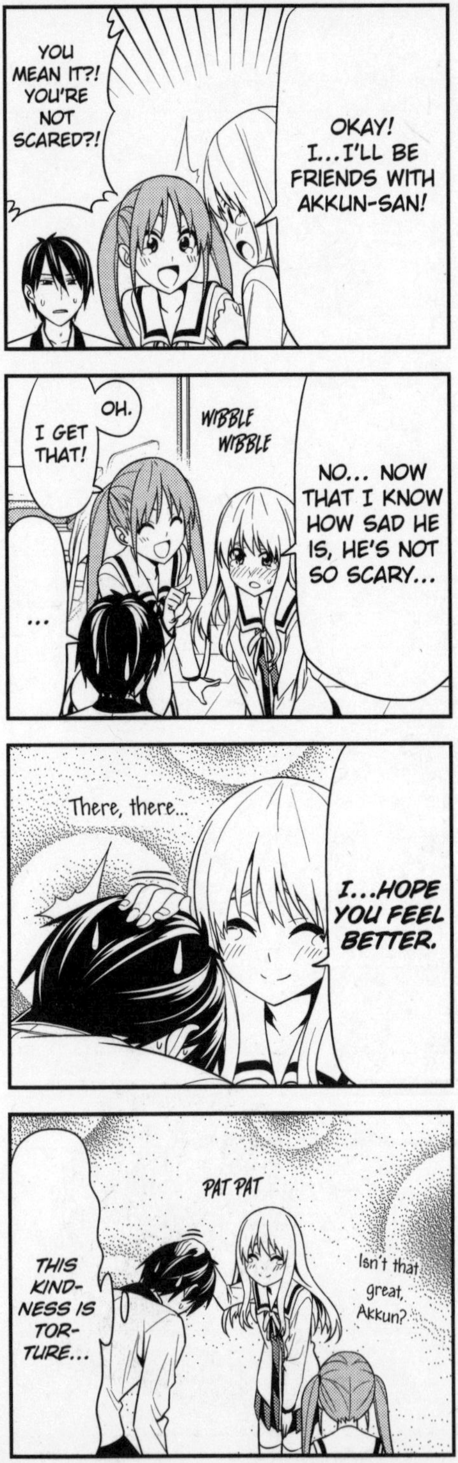
OKAY! I...I'LL BE FRIENDS WITH AKKUN-SAN!
YOU MEAN IT?! YOU'RE NOT SCARED?!
NO... NOW THAT I KNOW HOW SAD HE IS, HE'S NOT SO SCARY...
WIBBLE WIBBLE
OH.
I GET THAT!
...
I...HOPE YOU FEEL BETTER.
There, there...
Isn't that great, Akkun?
PAT PAT
THIS KINDNESS IS TORTURE...

He's Really Not Wrong

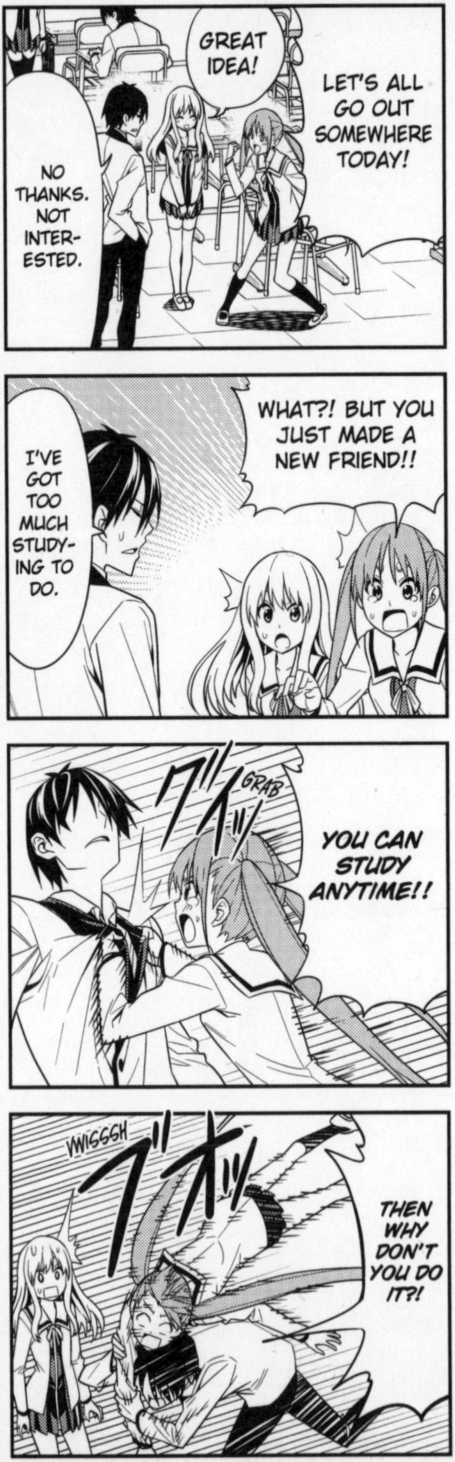
LET'S ALL GO OUT SOMEWHERE TODAY!
GREAT IDEA!
NO THANKS. NOT INTERESTED.
WHAT?! BUT YOU JUST MADE A NEW FRIEND!!
I'VE GOT TOO MUCH STUDYING TO DO.
YOU CAN STUDY ANYTIME!!
GRAB
THEN WHY DON'T YOU DO IT?!
VWISSSH

30% Growth

Contacts
4 total

Home

Yoshiko

Yoshiko home

Sayaka

A
little bit →
happy.

STARE...

Name	**Sayaka Sumino**
Sex	
Height	**153 cm / 5'**
Weight	**44 kg / 97 lbs**
Blood type	**A**
Birthday	**11/25**

Memo Became friends with
Yoshiko in high school.

She's a very kind girl, and
remains kind despite
knowing how much
trouble her kindness gets
her into.

Worries about being
boring.

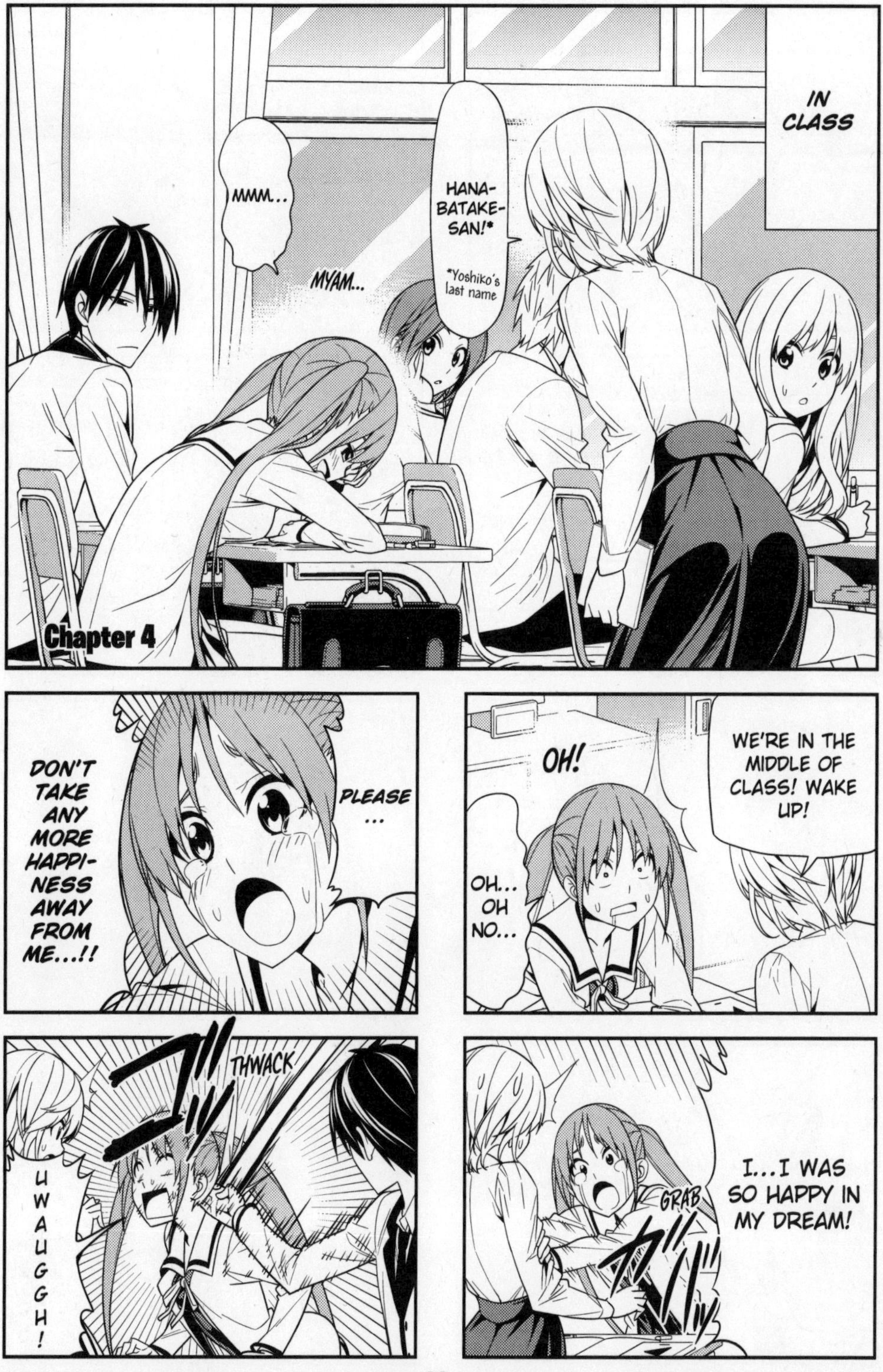
IN CLASS
HANA-BATAKE-SAN!*
MMM...
MYAM...
*Yoshiko's last name
Chapter 4
WE'RE IN THE MIDDLE OF CLASS! WAKE UP!
OH!
OH... OH NO...
PLEASE ...
DON'T TAKE ANY MORE HAPPI-NESS AWAY FROM ME...!!
I...I WAS SO HAPPY IN MY DREAM!
GRAB
THWACK
UWAUGGH!

Isn't That Kind of Old-Fashioned?

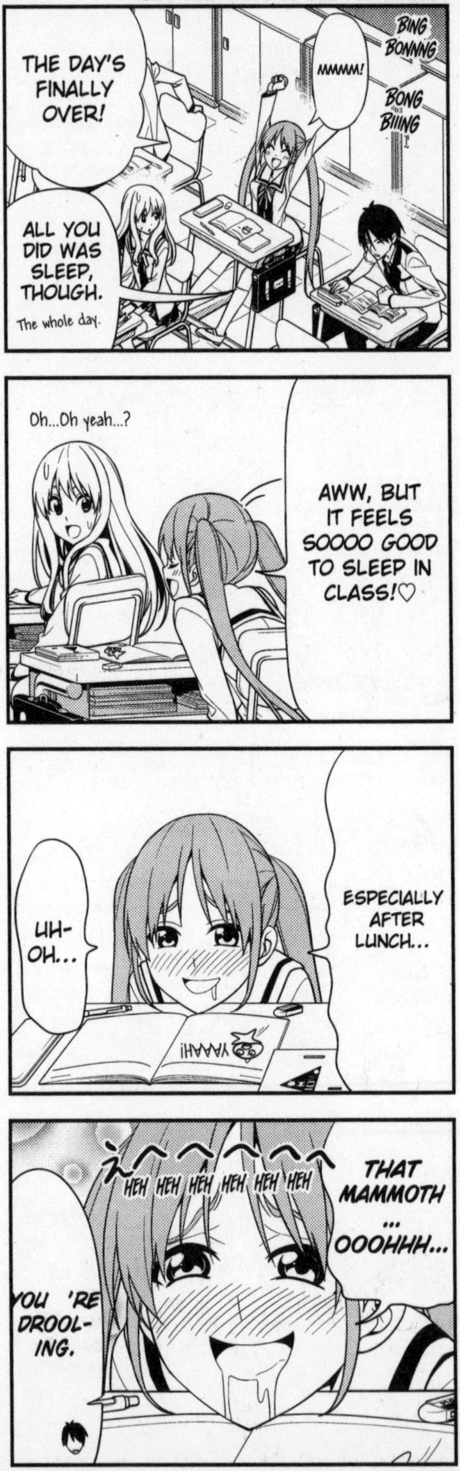
MMMM!
BING BONNNG BONG BIIING
THE DAY'S FINALLY OVER!
ALL YOU DID WAS SLEEP, THOUGH.
The whole day.
AWW, BUT IT FEELS SOOOO GOOD TO SLEEP IN CLASS!♡
Oh...Oh yeah...?
ESPECIALLY AFTER LUNCH...
UH-OH...
HEH HEH HEH HEH HEH HEH
THAT MAMMOTH ... OOOHHH...
YOU'RE DROOLING.

Don't Encourage Her

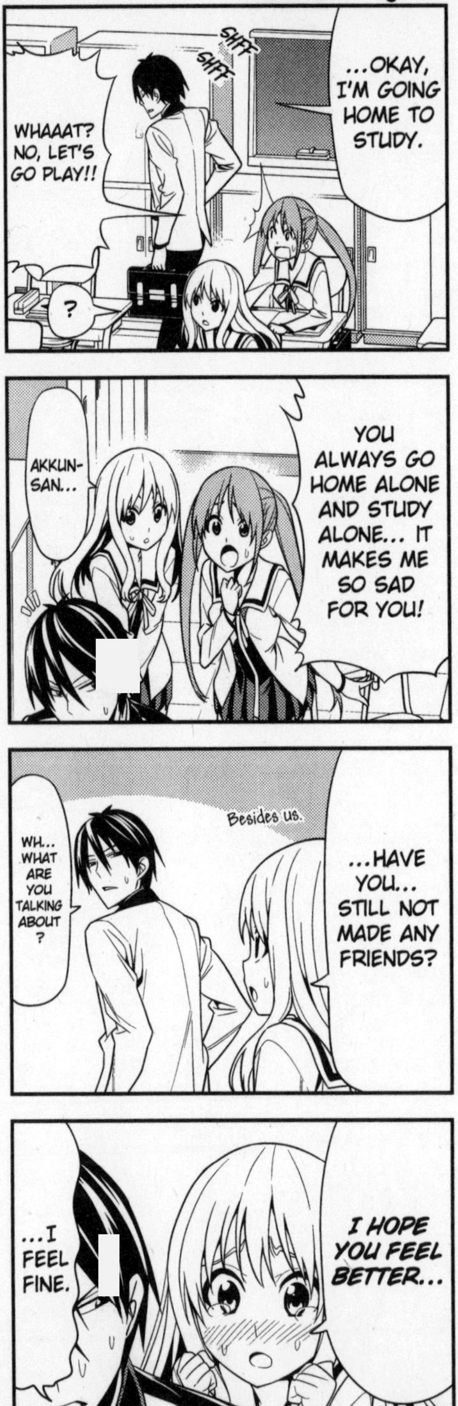
...OKAY, I'M GOING HOME TO STUDY.
SHFF SHFF
WHAAAT? NO, LET'S GO PLAY!!
?
YOU ALWAYS GO HOME ALONE AND STUDY ALONE... IT MAKES ME SO SAD FOR YOU!
AKKUN-SAN...
...HAVE YOU... STILL NOT MADE ANY FRIENDS?
Besides us.
WH... WHAT ARE YOU TALKING ABOUT?
I HOPE YOU FEEL BETTER...
...I FEEL FINE.

A Chance Meeting

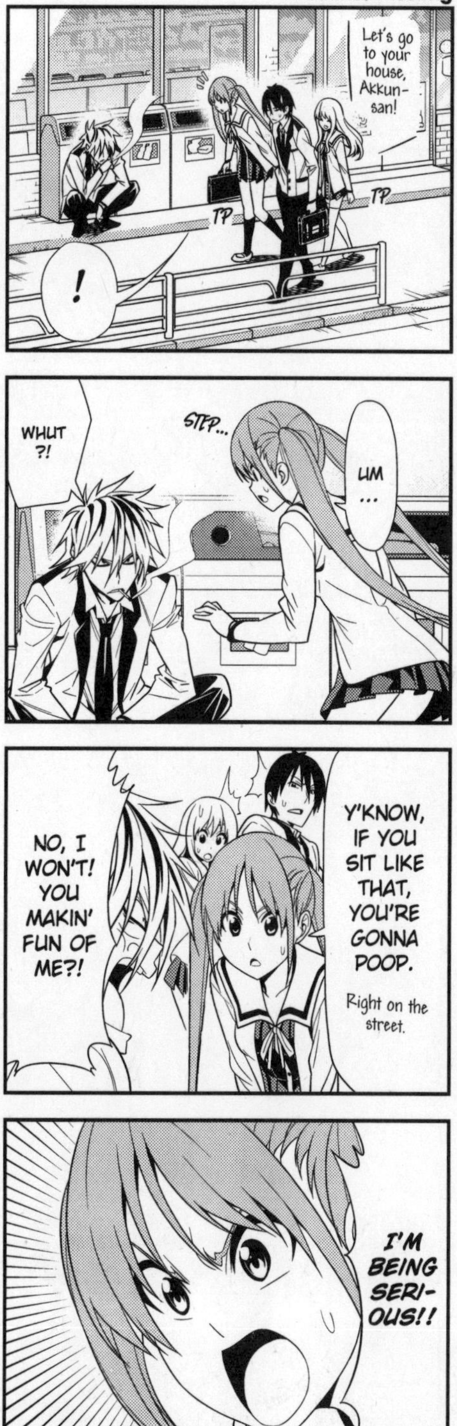
Let's go to your house, Akkun-san!
TP
TP
!
UM ...
STEP...
WHUT ?!
Y'KNOW, IF YOU SIT LIKE THAT, YOU'RE GONNA POOP.
Right on the street.
NO, I WON'T! YOU MAKIN' FUN OF ME?!
I'M BEING SERIOUS!!

We Just Barely Got to the Moral

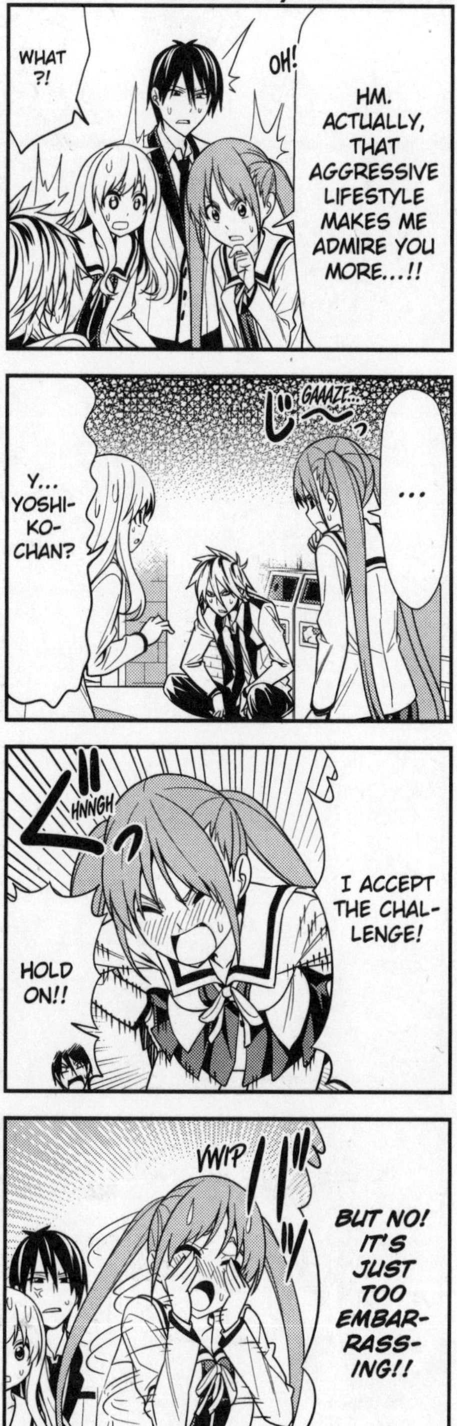
HM. ACTUALLY, THAT AGGRESSIVE LIFESTYLE MAKES ME ADMIRE YOU MORE...!!
OH!
WHAT ?!
...
GAAAZE...
Y... YOSHIKO-CHAN?
I ACCEPT THE CHALLENGE!
HNNGH
HOLD ON!!
BUT NO! IT'S JUST TOO EMBARRASSING!!
VWIP

Power Level's Only 5

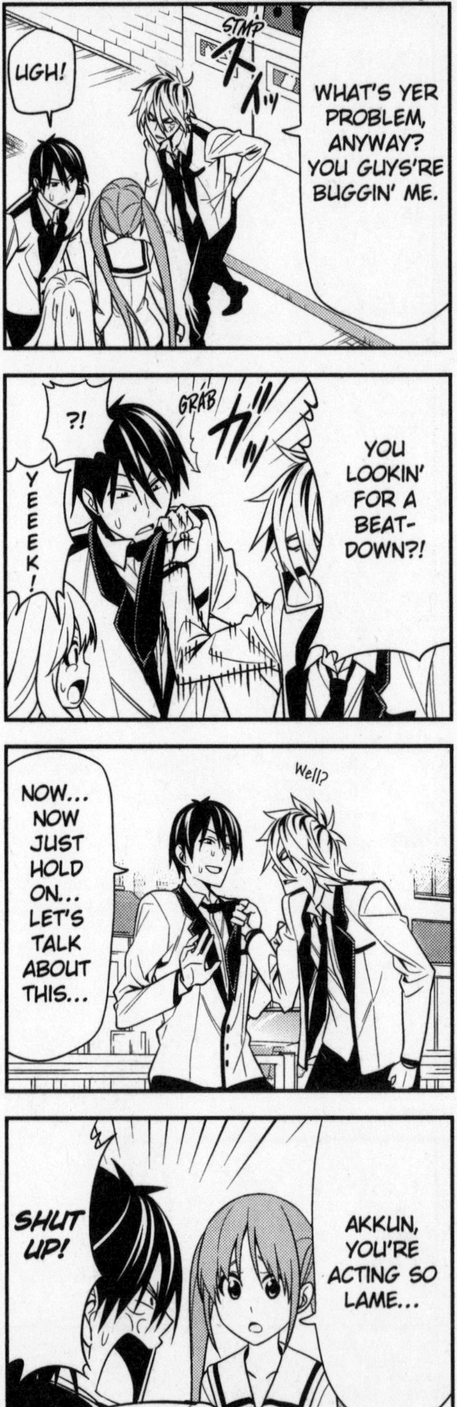
WHAT'S YER PROBLEM, ANYWAY? YOU GUYS'RE BUGGIN' ME.
STMP
UGH!
YOU LOOKIN' FOR A BEAT-DOWN?!
GRAB
?!
YEEEK!
Well?
NOW... NOW JUST HOLD ON... LET'S TALK ABOUT THIS...
AKKUN, YOU'RE ACTING SO LAME...
SHUT UP!

A Joyful Personality

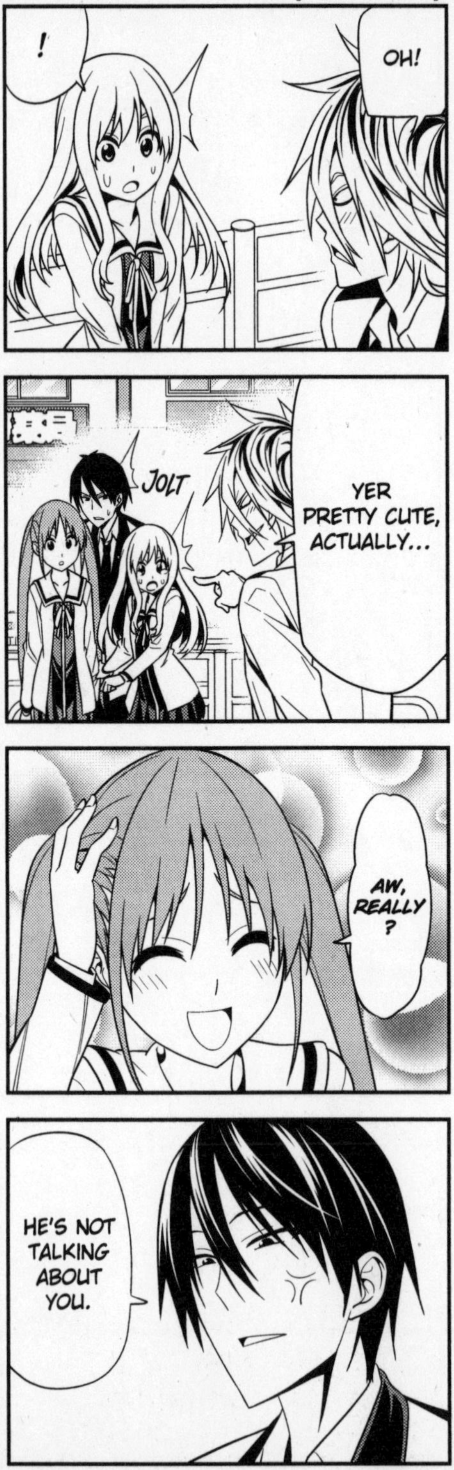
OH!
!
YER PRETTY CUTE, ACTUALLY...
JOLT
AW, REALLY?
HE'S NOT TALKING ABOUT YOU.

Not Quite a Thirst for Justice

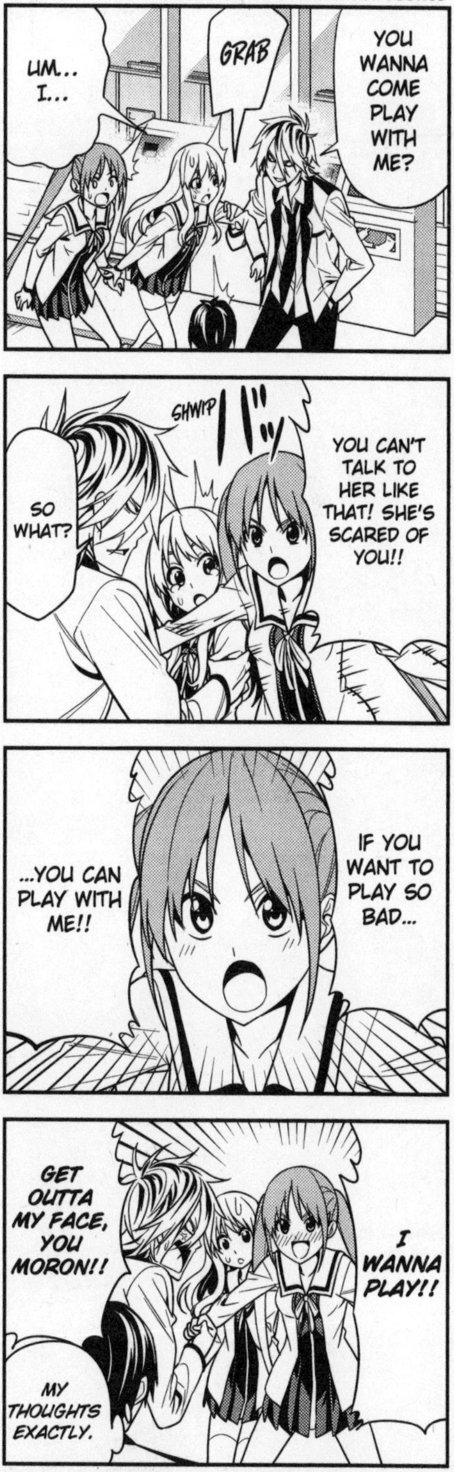
YOU WANNA COME PLAY WITH ME?
GRAB
UM... I...
YOU CAN'T TALK TO HER LIKE THAT! SHE'S SCARED OF YOU!!
SHWIP
SO WHAT?
IF YOU WANT TO PLAY SO BAD...
...YOU CAN PLAY WITH ME!!
I WANNA PLAY!!
GET OUTTA MY FACE, YOU MORON!!
MY THOUGHTS EXACTLY.

Newtype Sensitivity

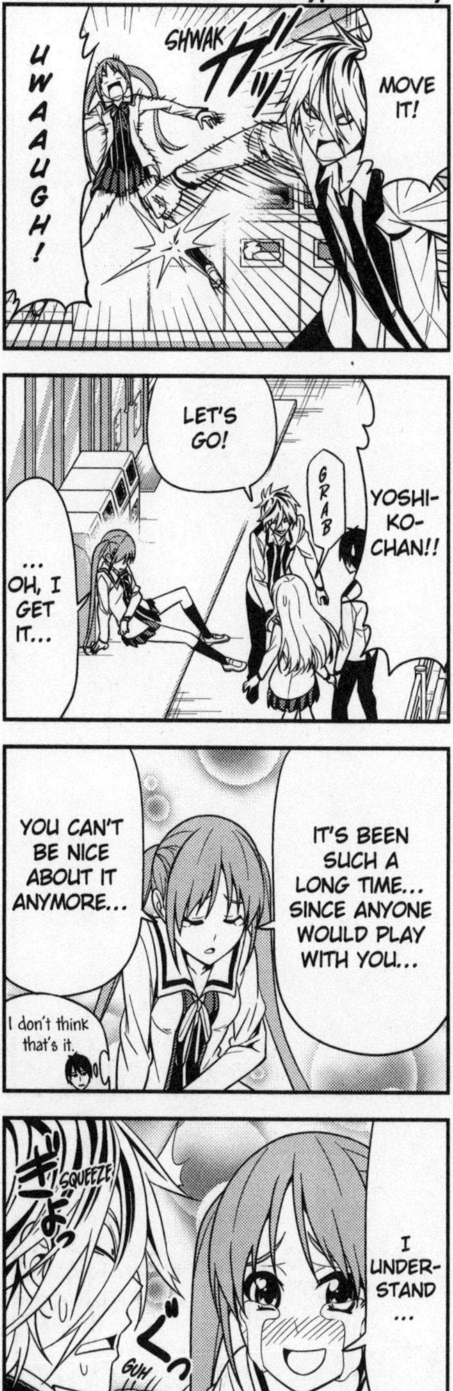
MOVE IT!
SHWAK
UWAAAUGH!
YOSHI-KO-CHAN!!
GRAB
LET'S GO!
...OH, I GET IT...
IT'S BEEN SUCH A LONG TIME... SINCE ANYONE WOULD PLAY WITH YOU...
YOU CAN'T BE NICE ABOUT IT ANYMORE...
I don't think that's it.
I UNDER-STAND...
SQUEEZE
GUH

A Generous Love

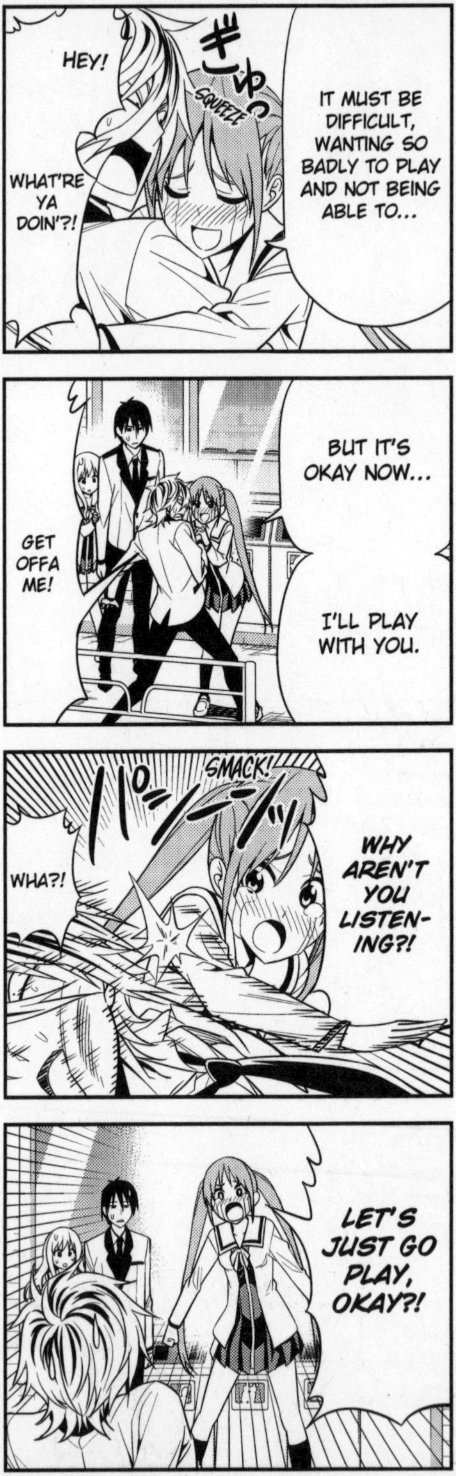
IT MUST BE DIFFICULT, WANTING SO BADLY TO PLAY AND NOT BEING ABLE TO...
ぎゅっ
SQUEEZE
HEY!
WHAT'RE YA DOIN'?!
BUT IT'S OKAY NOW...
I'LL PLAY WITH YOU.
GET OFFA ME!
SMACK!
WHY AREN'T YOU LISTEN-ING?!
WHA?!
LET'S JUST GO PLAY, OKAY?!

Bum-ba-ba-bummmm

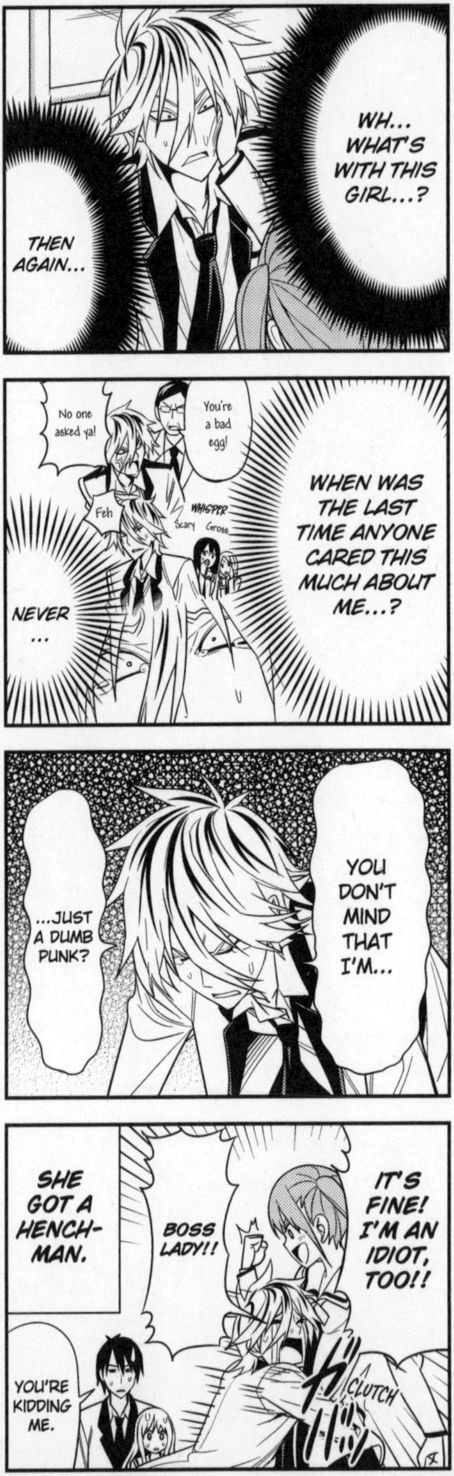
WH... WHAT'S WITH THIS GIRL...?
THEN AGAIN...
WHEN WAS THE LAST TIME ANYONE CARED THIS MUCH ABOUT ME...?
You're a bad egg!
No one asked ya!
WHISPER
Scary
Gross
Feh
NEVER...
YOU DON'T MIND THAT I'M...
...JUST A DUMB PUNK?
IT'S FINE! I'M AN IDIOT, TOO!!
BOSS LADY!!
SHE GOT A HENCH-MAN.
CLUTCH
YOU'RE KIDDING ME.

Excess Appeal

Is this for real...
STARE...
NYAHAHA!
ドヤァッ
Ugh...

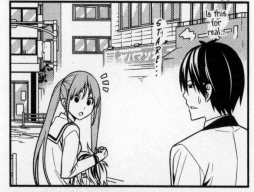

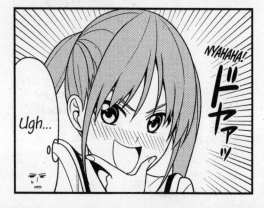

(From morning to night, she's)

Aho-Girl

\'ahô,gərl\ *Japanese , noun*.

A clueless girl.

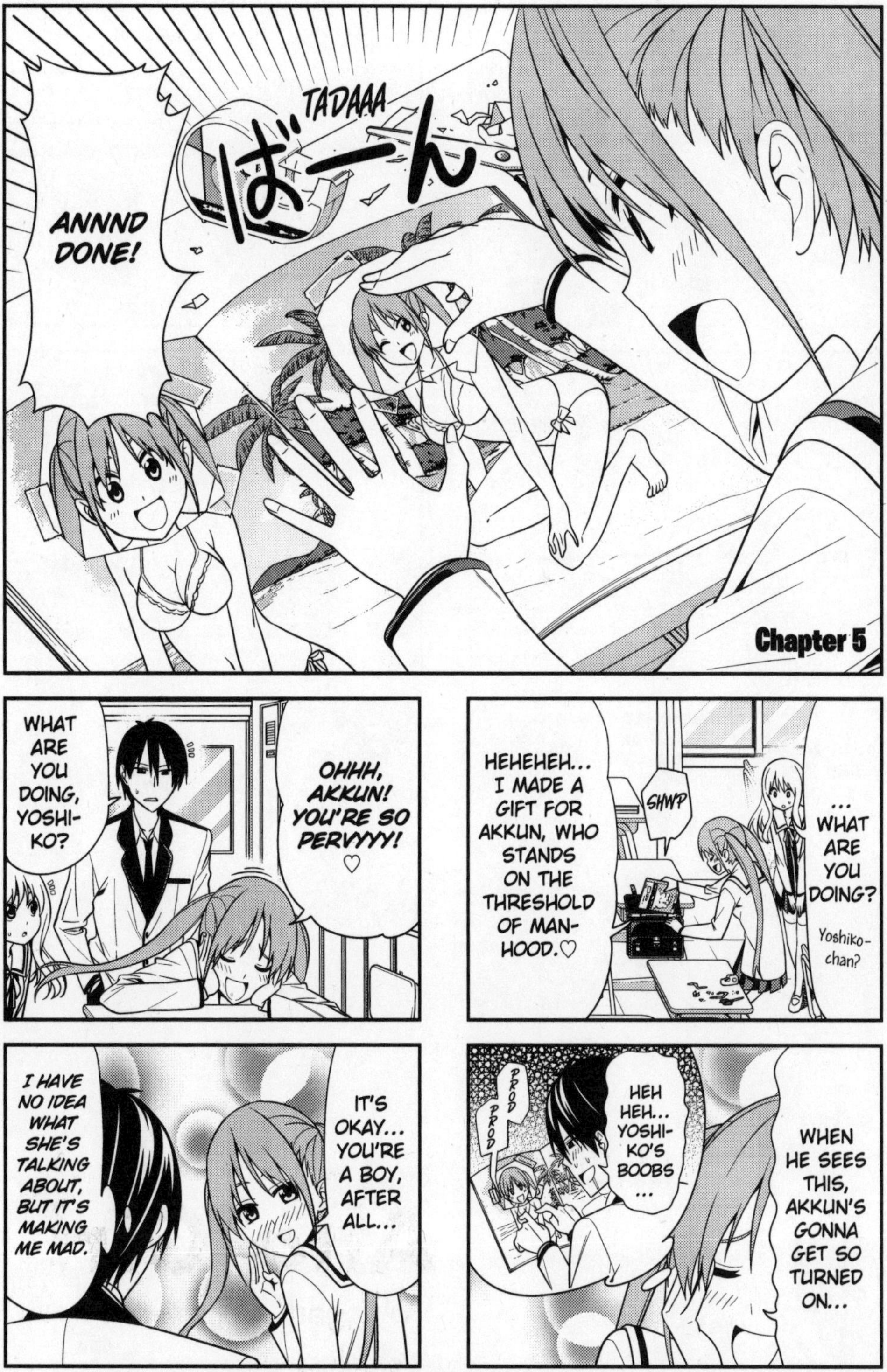
TADAAA
ばーん
ANNND DONE!
Chapter 5
... WHAT ARE YOU DOING?
Yoshiko-chan?
SHWP
HEHEHEH... I MADE A GIFT FOR AKKUN, WHO STANDS ON THE THRESHOLD OF MAN-HOOD.♡
OHHH, AKKUN! YOU'RE SO PERVYYY! ♡
WHAT ARE YOU DOING, YOSHIKO?
WHEN HE SEES THIS, AKKUN'S GONNA GET SO TURNED ON...
HEH HEH... YOSHIKO'S BOOBS...
PROD PROD
IT'S OKAY... YOU'RE A BOY, AFTER ALL...
I HAVE NO IDEA WHAT SHE'S TALKING ABOUT, BUT IT'S MAKING ME MAD.

Breaking Point

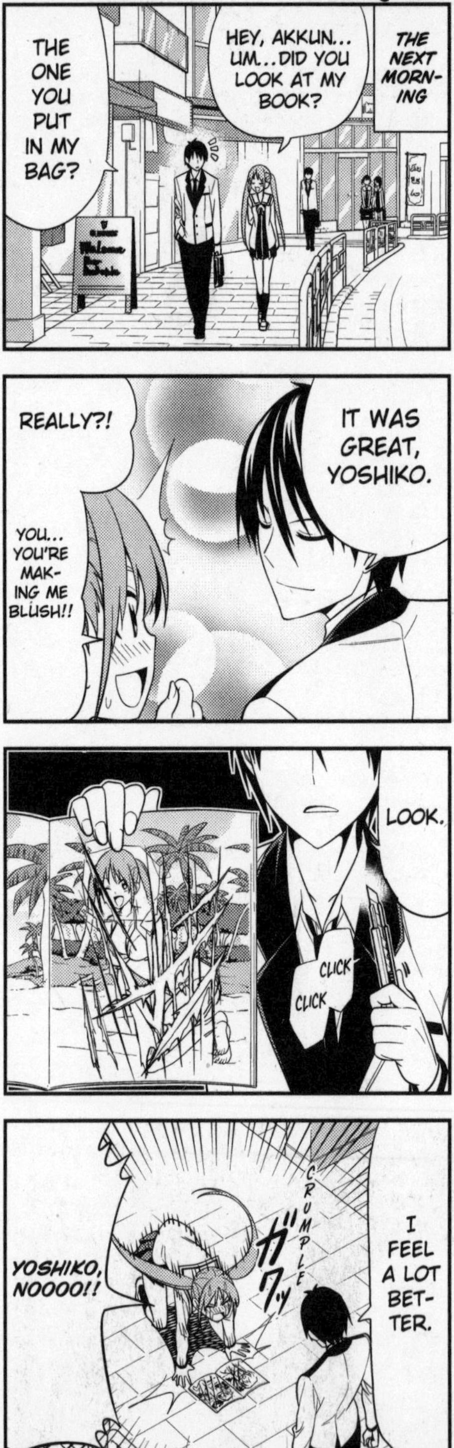
THE NEXT MORNING
HEY, AKKUN... UM...DID YOU LOOK AT MY BOOK?
THE ONE YOU PUT IN MY BAG?
IT WAS GREAT, YOSHIKO.
REALLY?!
YOU... YOU'RE MAKING ME BLUSH!!
LOOK.
CLICK
CLICK
I FEEL A LOT BETTER.
CRUMPLE
ガクッ
YOSHIKO, NOOOO!!

Bag Search

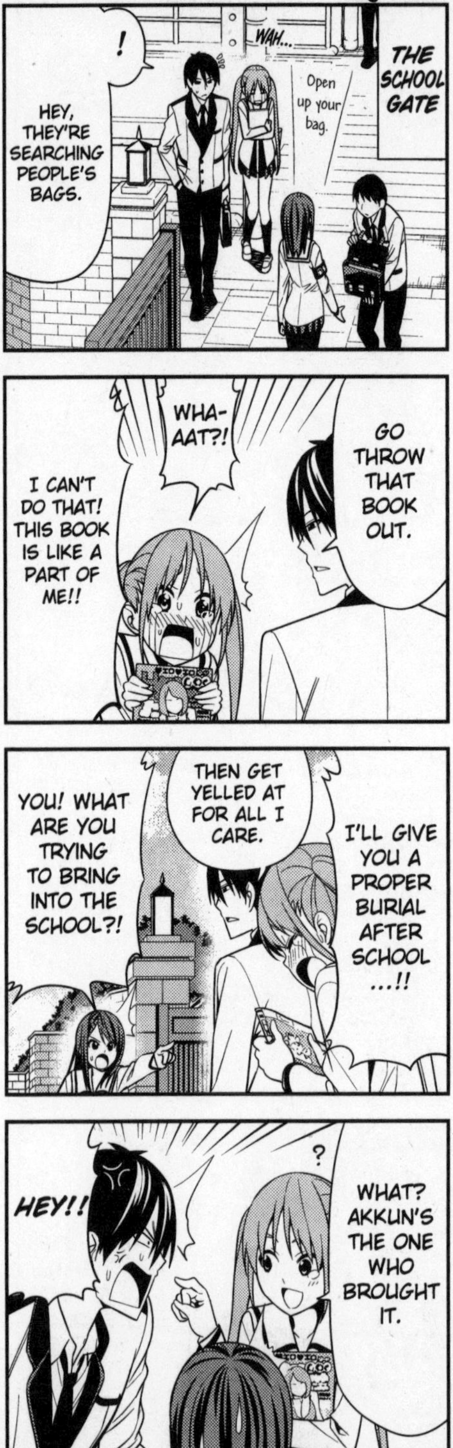
THE SCHOOL GATE
Open up your bag.
WAH...
!
HEY, THEY'RE SEARCHING PEOPLE'S BAGS.
GO THROW THAT BOOK OUT.
WHA-AAT?!
I CAN'T DO THAT! THIS BOOK IS LIKE A PART OF ME!!
I'LL GIVE YOU A PROPER BURIAL AFTER SCHOOL ...!!
THEN GET YELLED AT FOR ALL I CARE.
YOU! WHAT ARE YOU TRYING TO BRING INTO THE SCHOOL?!
WHAT? AKKUN'S THE ONE WHO BROUGHT IT.
?
HEY!!

I Don't Want to Hear It!

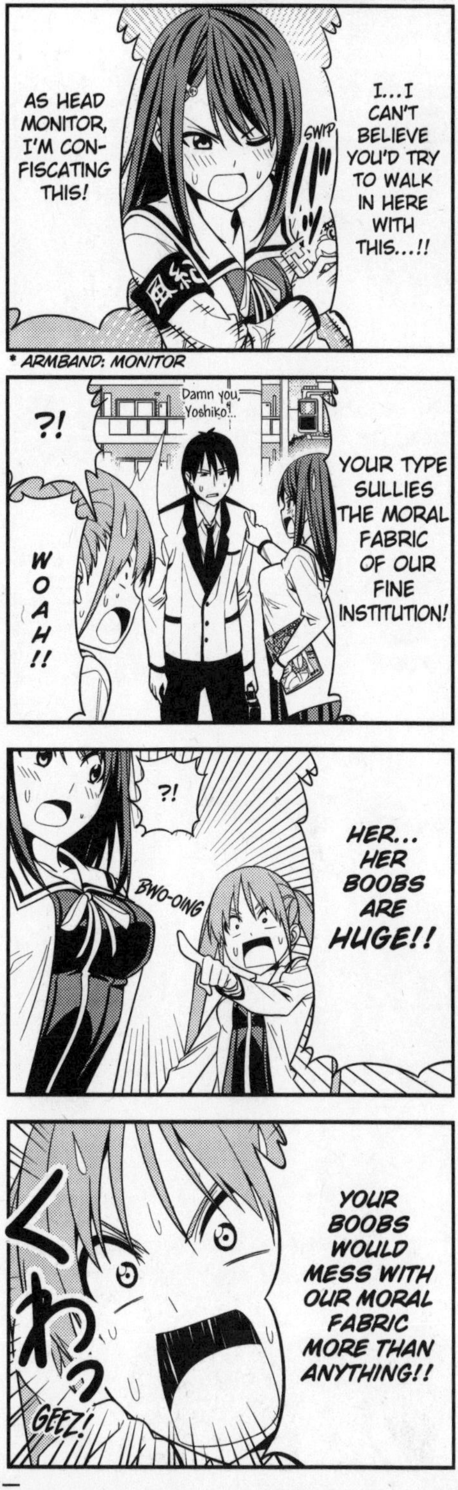
I...I CAN'T BELIEVE YOU'D TRY TO WALK IN HERE WITH THIS...!!
SWIP
AS HEAD MONITOR, I'M CON-FISCATING THIS!
YOUR TYPE SULLIES THE MORAL FABRIC OF OUR FINE INSTITUTION!
Damn you, Yoshiko...
?!
WOAH!!
HER... HER BOOBS ARE HUGE!!
?!
BWO-OING
YOUR BOOBS WOULD MESS WITH OUR MORAL FABRIC MORE THAN ANYTHING!!
くわっ
GEEZ!

* ARMBAND: MONITOR

Working the Crowd

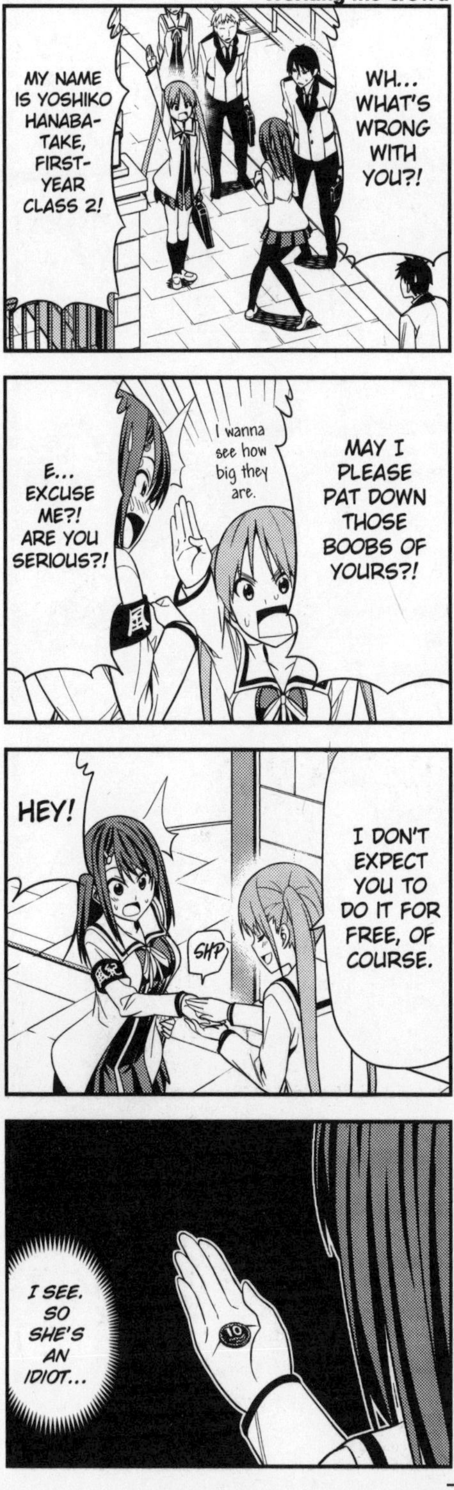
WH... WHAT'S WRONG WITH YOU?!
MY NAME IS YOSHIKO HANABA-TAKE, FIRST-YEAR CLASS 2!
MAY I PLEASE PAT DOWN THOSE BOOBS OF YOURS?!
I wanna see how big they are.
E... EXCUSE ME?! ARE YOU SERIOUS?!
I DON'T EXPECT YOU TO DO IT FOR FREE, OF COURSE.
SHP
HEY!
I SEE. SO SHE'S AN IDIOT...

Working the Crowd 2

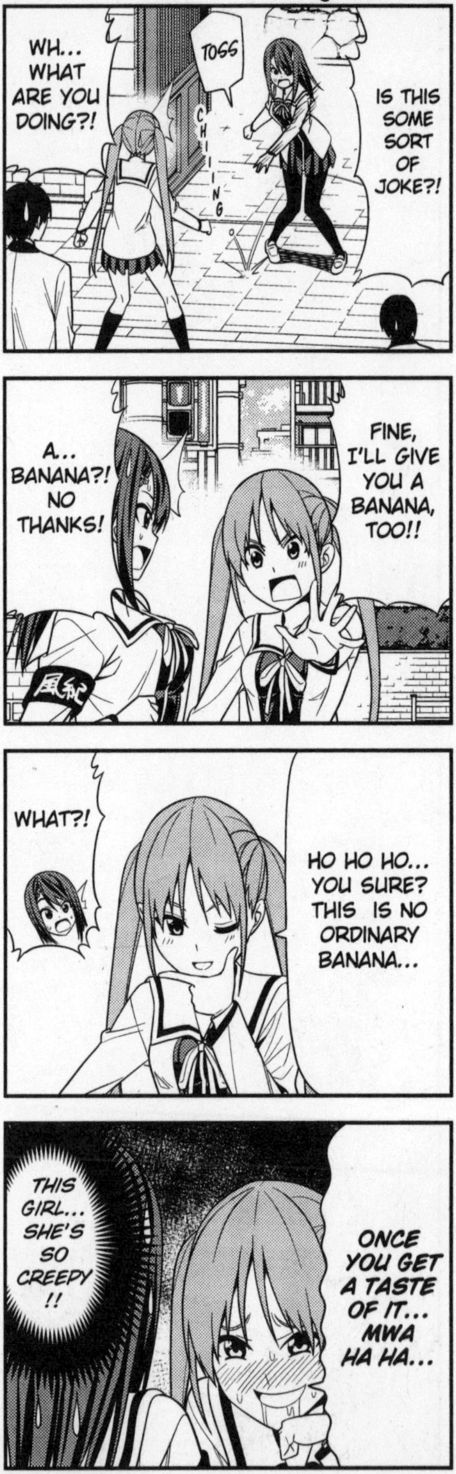
IS THIS SOME SORT OF JOKE?!
TOSS
CHIIING
WH... WHAT ARE YOU DOING?!
FINE, I'LL GIVE YOU A BANANA, TOO!!
A... BANANA?! NO THANKS!
HO HO HO... YOU SURE? THIS IS NO ORDINARY BANANA...
WHAT?!
ONCE YOU GET A TASTE OF IT... MWA HA HA...
THIS GIRL... SHE'S SO CREEPY!!

Or Maybe You Won't

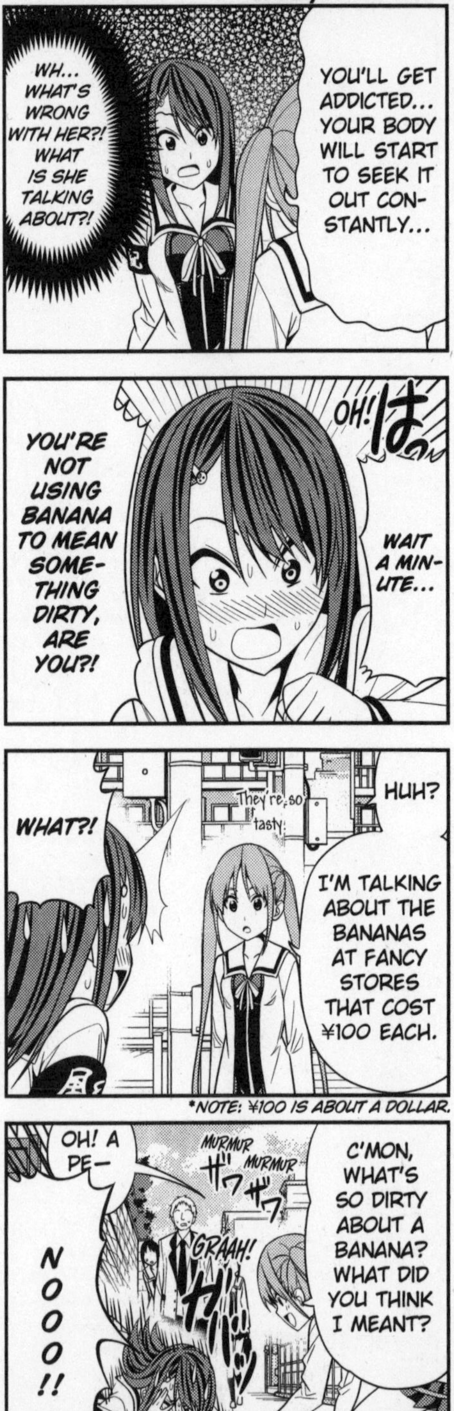
YOU'LL GET ADDICTED... YOUR BODY WILL START TO SEEK IT OUT CON-STANTLY...
WH... WHAT'S WRONG WITH HER?! WHAT IS SHE TALKING ABOUT?!
OH! はっ
WAIT A MIN-UTE...
YOU'RE NOT USING BANANA TO MEAN SOME-THING DIRTY, ARE YOU?!
HUH?
I'M TALKING ABOUT THE BANANAS AT FANCY STORES THAT COST ¥100 EACH.
They're so tasty!
WHAT?!
*NOTE: ¥100 IS ABOUT A DOLLAR.
C'MON, WHAT'S SO DIRTY ABOUT A BANANA? WHAT DID YOU THINK I MEANT?
MURMUR MURMUR ザワザワ
GRAAH!
OH! A PE—
NOOOOO!!

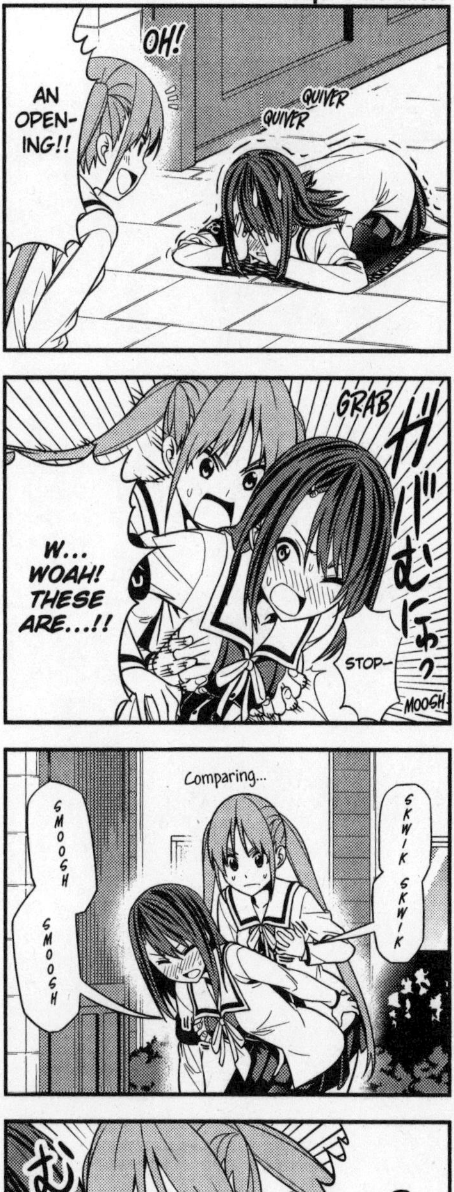
OH!
AN OPENING!!
QUIVER
QUIVER
GRAB
W... WOAH! THESE ARE...!!
STOP-
MOOSH
SKWIK SKWIK
Comparing...
SMOOSH SMOOSH
DAMMIT!!
GROPE
むにゅ むにゅ
GROPE
GROPE
むにゅーっ

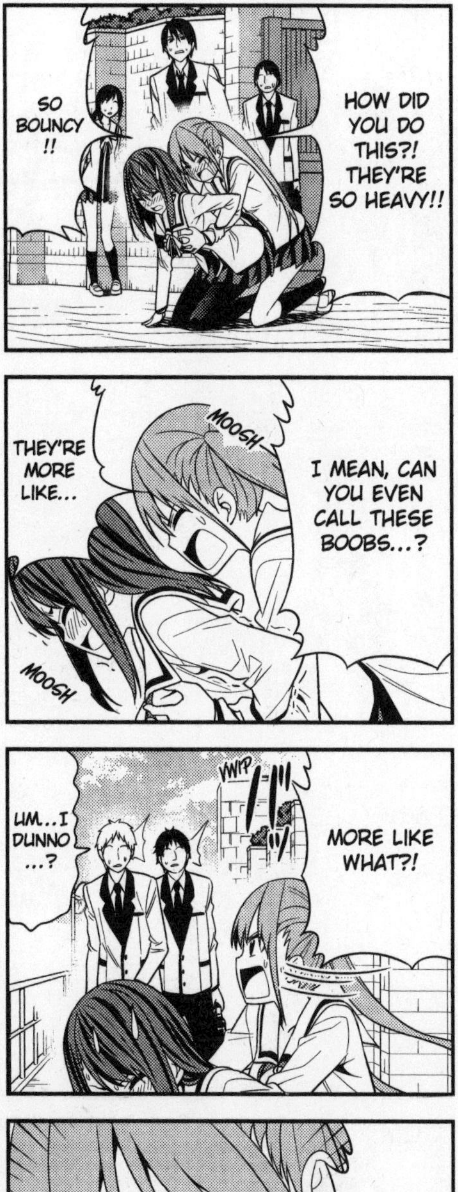
HOW DID YOU DO THIS?! THEY'RE SO HEAVY!!
SO BOUNCY !!
I MEAN, CAN YOU EVEN CALL THESE BOOBS...?
MOOSH
THEY'RE MORE LIKE...
MOOSH
MORE LIKE WHAT?!
VWIP
UM...I DUNNO ...?
WHAT ARE THEY ?!
むにゅ むにゅ〜〜
GROPE
GROPE

Temperature Difference

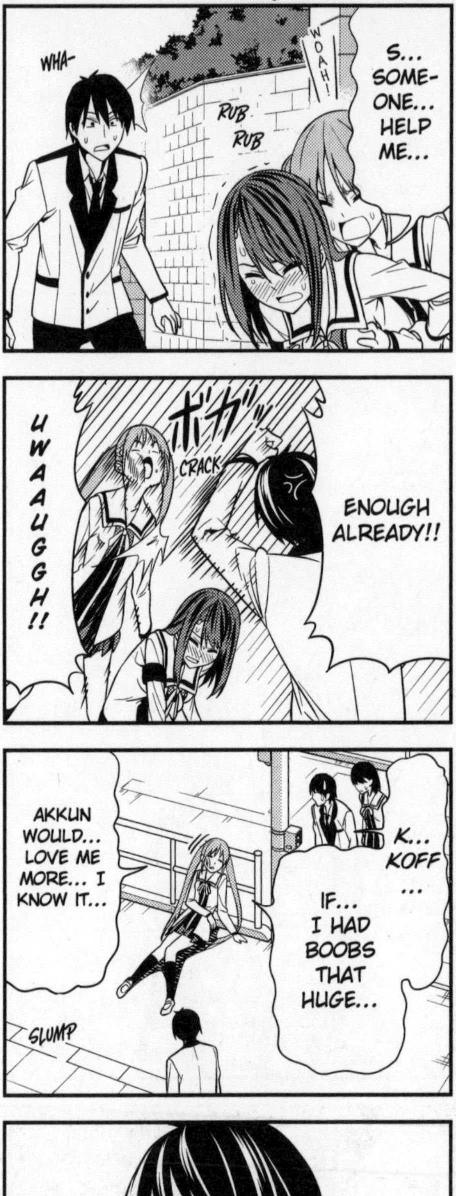
S... SOME-ONE... HELP ME...
WOAH!
RUB RUB
WHA-
ENOUGH ALREADY!!
CRACK
ボガッ
UWAAAUGGH!!
K... KOFF...
IF... I HAD BOOBS THAT HUGE...
AKKUN WOULD... LOVE ME MORE... I KNOW IT...
SLUMP
NOT A CHANCE.

Love Strikes Suddenly

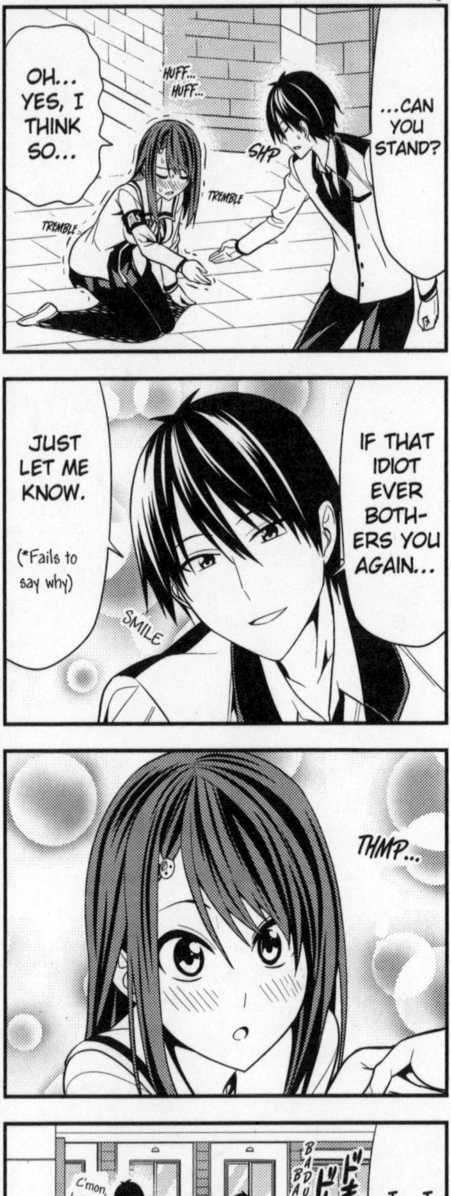
...CAN YOU STAND?
SHP
HUFF... HUFF...
OH... YES, I THINK SO...
TREMBLE
TREMBLE
IF THAT IDIOT EVER BOTHERS YOU AGAIN...
JUST LET ME KNOW.
(*Fails to say why)
SMILE
THMP...
I... I WILL...
ドキ ドキ
BADUMP BADUMP
SKFF
C'mon, let's go.

A Perverted Nature

TH... THAT BOOK HE HAD... I WONDER WHAT IT IS...

FLIP

THMP THMP

WHAT IS HE INTO?!

URK

Aho-Girl

\\'ahô͵gərl\\ *Japanese , noun.*
A clueless girl.

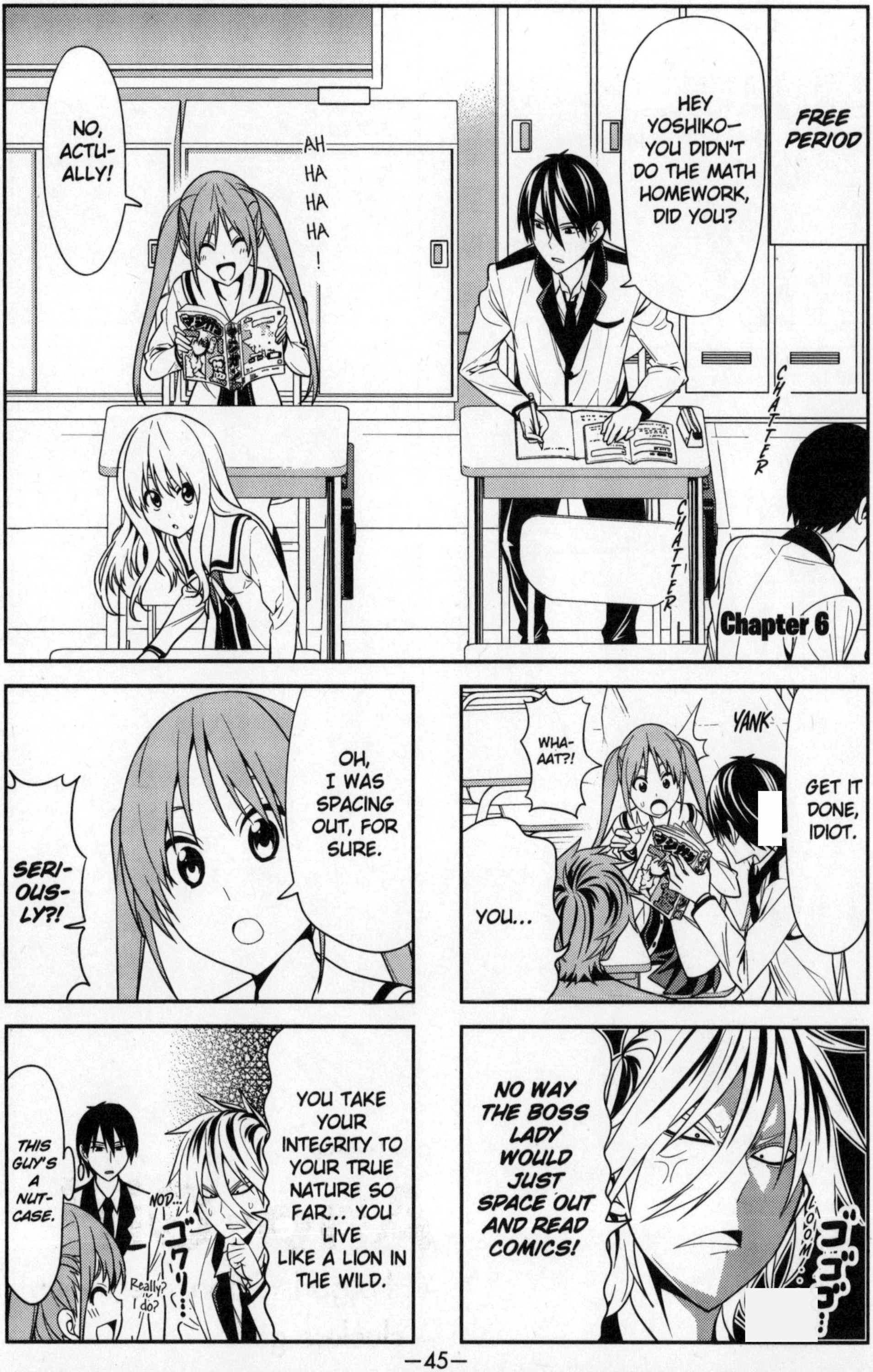
FREE PERIOD
HEY YOSHIKO— YOU DIDN'T DO THE MATH HOMEWORK, DID YOU?
CHATTER
CHATTER
AH HA HA HA!
NO, ACTU-ALLY!
Chapter 6
GET IT DONE, IDIOT.
YANK
WHA-AAT?!
YOU...
OH, I WAS SPACING OUT, FOR SURE.
SERI-OUS-LY?!
NO WAY THE BOSS LADY WOULD JUST SPACE OUT AND READ COMICS!
LOOM...
ゴゴゴ…
YOU TAKE YOUR INTEGRITY TO YOUR TRUE NATURE SO FAR... YOU LIVE LIKE A LION IN THE WILD.
NOD...
ゴクリ…
THIS GUY'S A NUT-CASE.
Really? I do?

Doctrine of Favorites

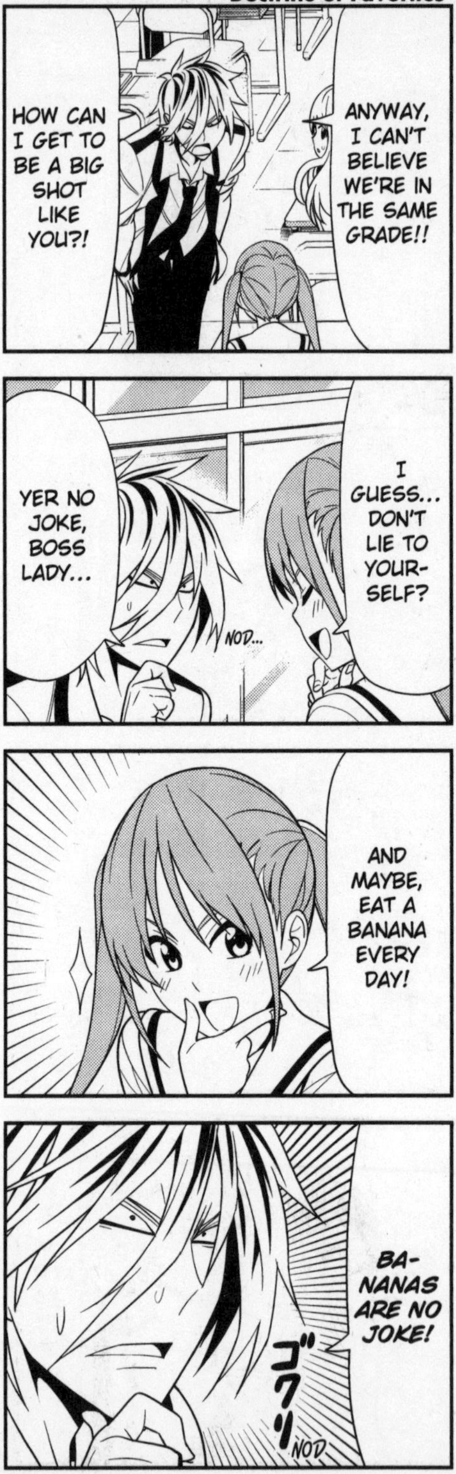
ANYWAY, I CAN'T BELIEVE WE'RE IN THE SAME GRADE!!
HOW CAN I GET TO BE A BIG SHOT LIKE YOU?!
I GUESS... DON'T LIE TO YOUR-SELF?
NOD...
YER NO JOKE, BOSS LADY...
AND MAYBE, EAT A BANANA EVERY DAY!
BA-NANAS ARE NO JOKE!
ゴクリ
NOD

Such a Nice Boy

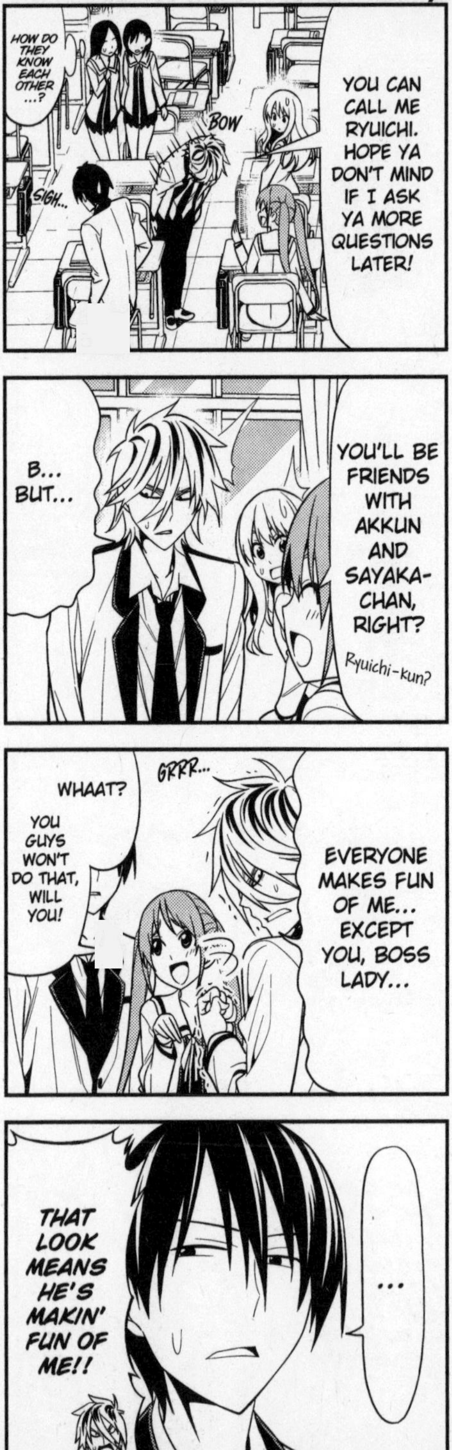
YOU CAN CALL ME RYUICHI. HOPE YA DON'T MIND IF I ASK YA MORE QUESTIONS LATER!
BOW
HOW DO THEY KNOW EACH OTHER ...?
SIGH...
YOU'LL BE FRIENDS WITH AKKUN AND SAYAKA-CHAN, RIGHT?
Ryuichi-kun?
B... BUT...
EVERYONE MAKES FUN OF ME... EXCEPT YOU, BOSS LADY...
GRRR...
WHAAT?
YOU GUYS WON'T DO THAT, WILL YOU!
...
THAT LOOK MEANS HE'S MAKIN' FUN OF ME!!

Clear out the Competition

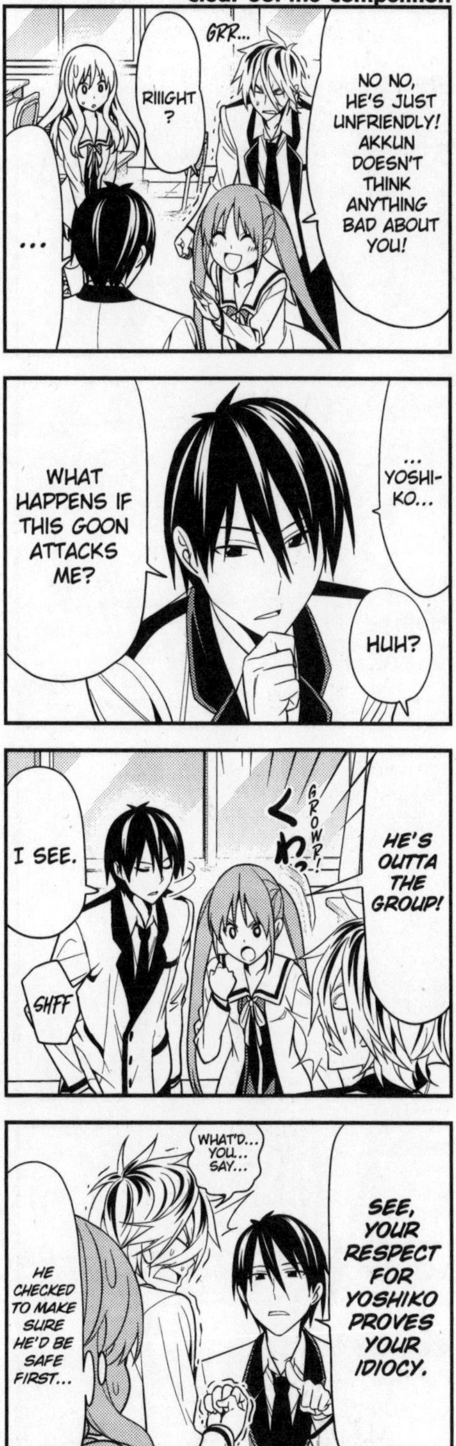
NO NO, HE'S JUST UNFRIENDLY! AKKUN DOESN'T THINK ANYTHING BAD ABOUT YOU!
GRR...
RIIIGHT?
...
... YOSHI-KO...
HUH?
WHAT HAPPENS IF THIS GOON ATTACKS ME?
HE'S OUTTA THE GROUP!
GROWR!
I SEE.
SHFF
SEE, YOUR RESPECT FOR YOSHIKO PROVES YOUR IDIOCY.
WHAT'D... YOU... SAY...
HE CHECKED TO MAKE SURE HE'D BE SAFE FIRST...

Idiot Logic

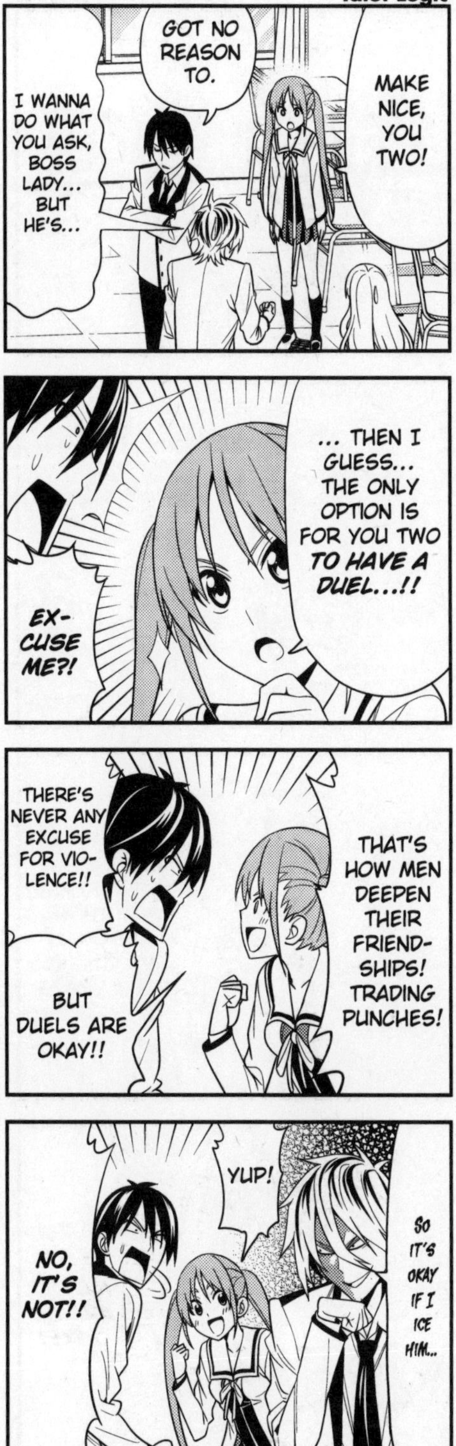
MAKE NICE, YOU TWO!
GOT NO REASON TO.
I WANNA DO WHAT YOU ASK, BOSS LADY... BUT HE'S...
... THEN I GUESS... THE ONLY OPTION IS FOR YOU TWO TO HAVE A DUEL...!!
EX-CUSE ME?!
THAT'S HOW MEN DEEPEN THEIR FRIEND-SHIPS! TRADING PUNCHES!
THERE'S NEVER ANY EXCUSE FOR VIO-LENCE!!
BUT DUELS ARE OKAY!!
SO IT'S OKAY IF I ICE HIM...
YUP!
NO, IT'S NOT!!

A Trifling Declaration

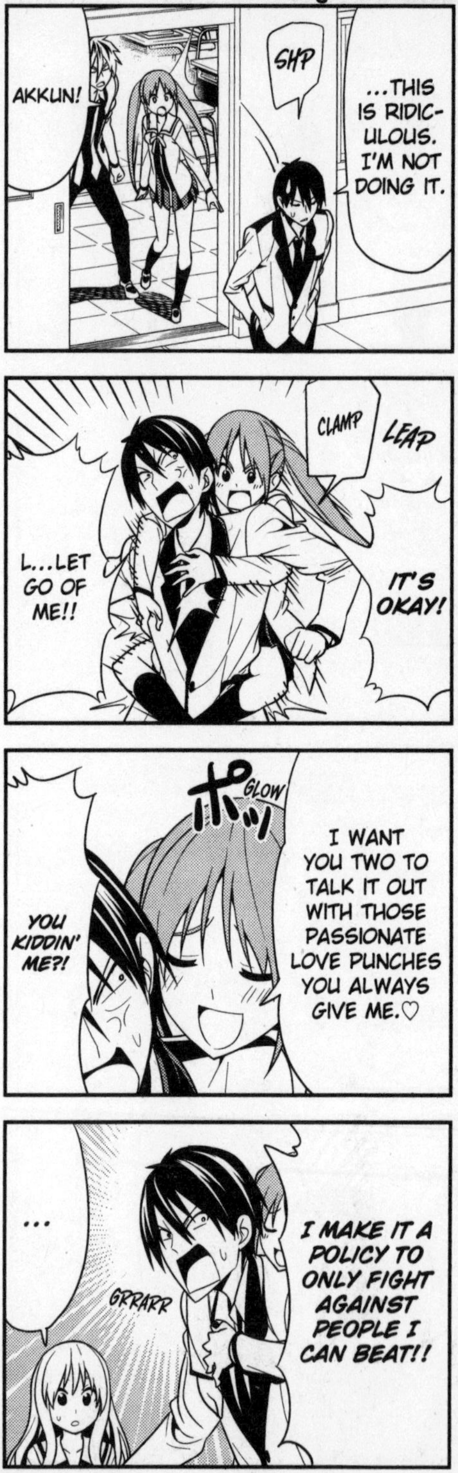
…THIS IS RIDICULOUS. I'M NOT DOING IT.
SHP
AKKUN!
LEAP
CLAMP
IT'S OKAY!
L…LET GO OF ME!!
GLOW
I WANT YOU TWO TO TALK IT OUT WITH THOSE PASSIONATE LOVE PUNCHES YOU ALWAYS GIVE ME.♡
YOU KIDDIN' ME?!
I MAKE IT A POLICY TO ONLY FIGHT AGAINST PEOPLE I CAN BEAT!!
GRRARR
…

Battle Scene out of a Shonen Story

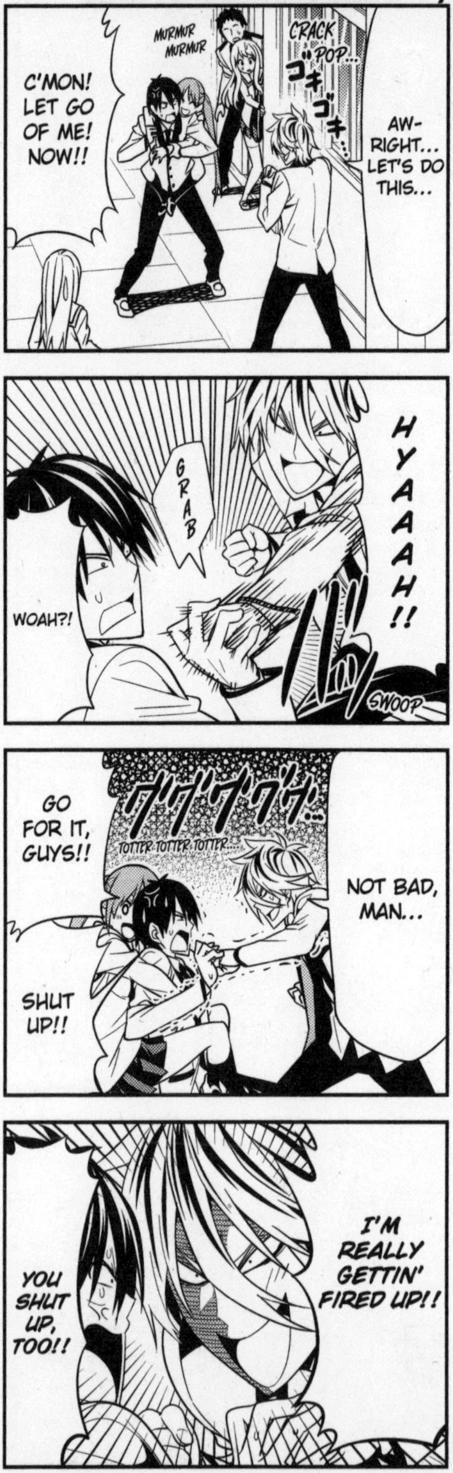
AW-RIGHT… LET'S DO THIS…
CRACK POP…
ゴキゴキ
MURMUR MURMUR
C'MON! LET GO OF ME! NOW!!
HYAAAAH!!
SWOOP
GRAB
WOAH?!
NOT BAD, MAN…
TOTTER TOTTER TOTTER…
GO FOR IT, GUYS!!
SHUT UP!!
I'M REALLY GETTIN' FIRED UP!!
YOU SHUT UP, TOO!!

That's a Low Priority

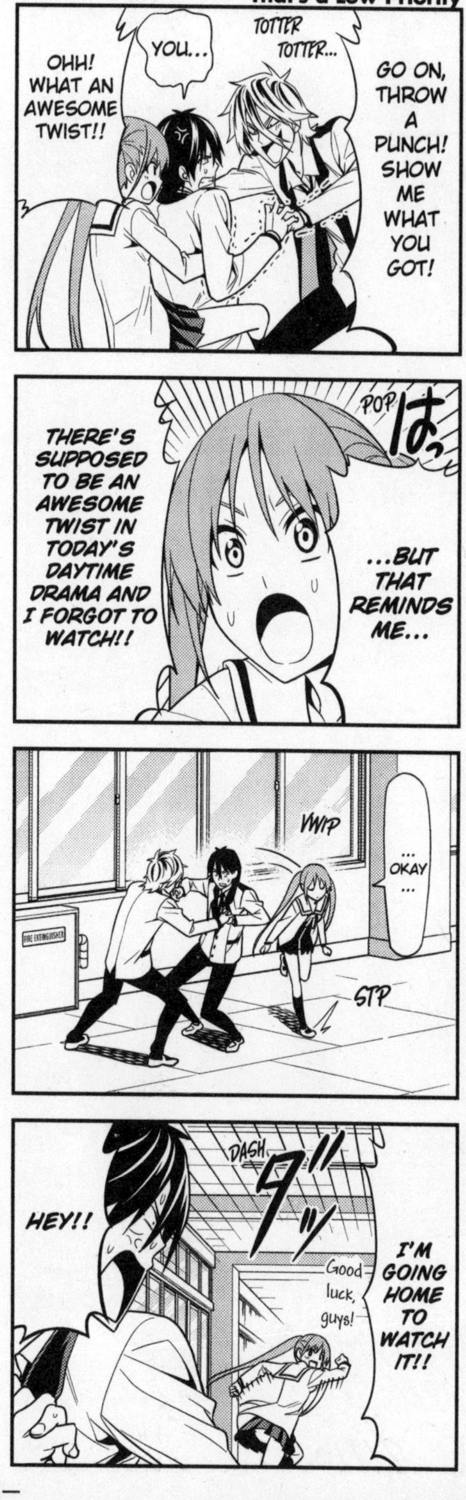
TOTTER TOTTER...
GO ON, THROW A PUNCH! SHOW ME WHAT YOU GOT!
YOU...
OHH! WHAT AN AWESOME TWIST!!
POP
はっ
...BUT THAT REMINDS ME...
THERE'S SUPPOSED TO BE AN AWESOME TWIST IN TODAY'S DAYTIME DRAMA AND I FORGOT TO WATCH!!
...OKAY...
VWIP
STP
DASH
I'M GOING HOME TO WATCH IT!!
Good luck, guys!
HEY!!

Awakening

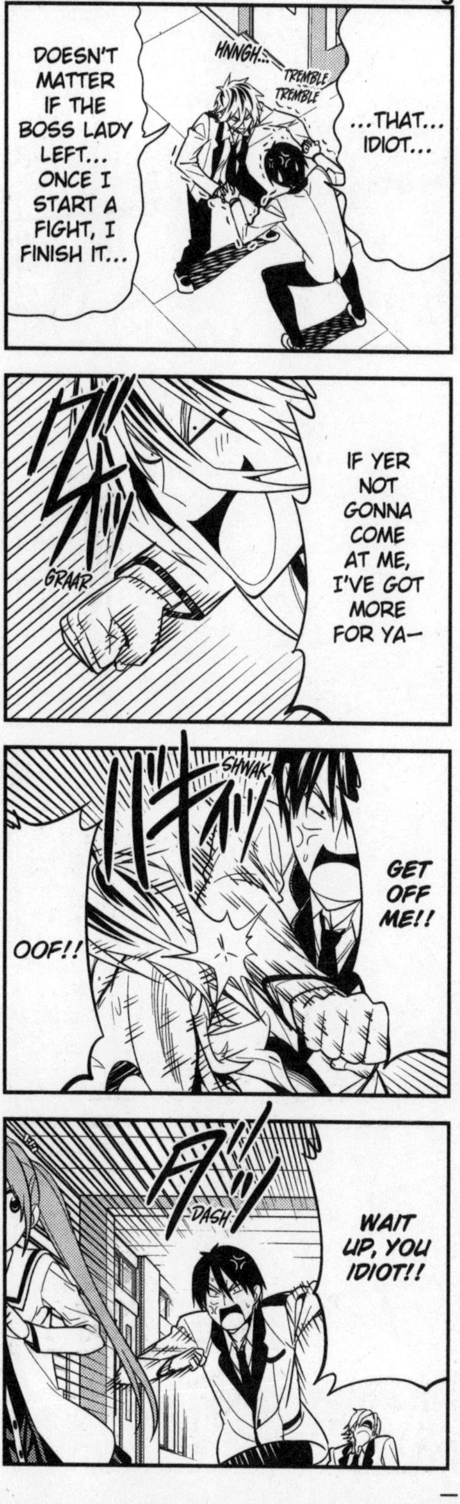
...THAT... IDIOT...
TREMBLE TREMBLE
HNNGH...
DOESN'T MATTER IF THE BOSS LADY LEFT... ONCE I START A FIGHT, I FINISH IT...
IF YER NOT GONNA COME AT ME, I'VE GOT MORE FOR YA—
GRAAR
GET OFF ME!!
SHWAK
OOF!!
WAIT UP, YOU IDIOT!!
DASH

Too Damn Fast

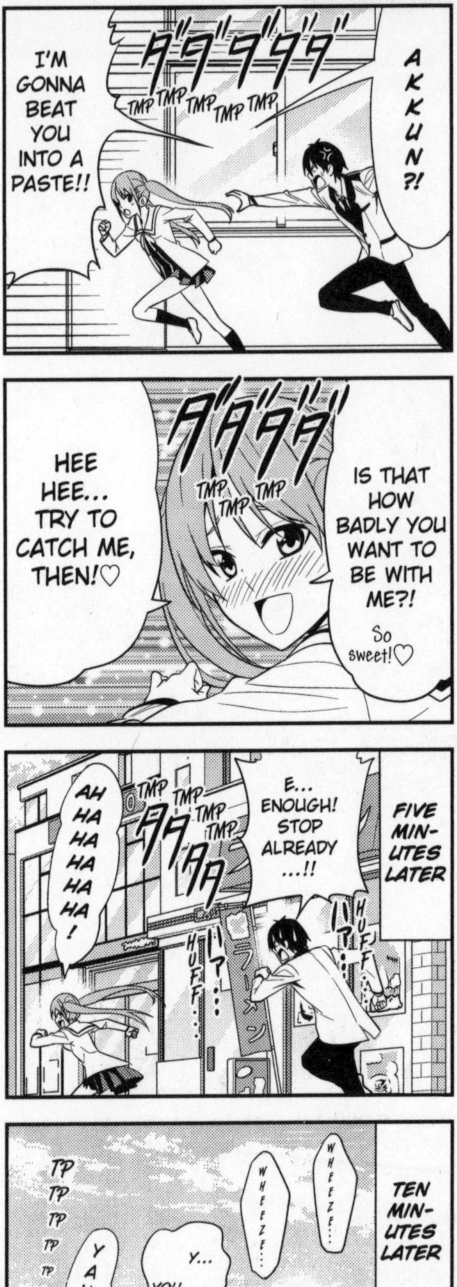
AKKUN?!
TMP TMP TMP TMP TMP
I'M GONNA BEAT YOU INTO A PASTE!!
IS THAT HOW BADLY YOU WANT TO BE WITH ME?!
So sweet!♡
TMP TMP TMP
HEE HEE... TRY TO CATCH ME, THEN!♡
FIVE MINUTES LATER
HUFF...
E... ENOUGH! STOP ALREADY...!!
TMP TMP TMP TMP
AH HA HA HA HA HA HA!
TEN MINUTES LATER
WHEEZE...
WHEEZE...
Y... YOU...
WOBBLE...
STAGGER...
WHEEZE...
YAHHOooo
TP TP TP TP TP...

Well, That's Not Good

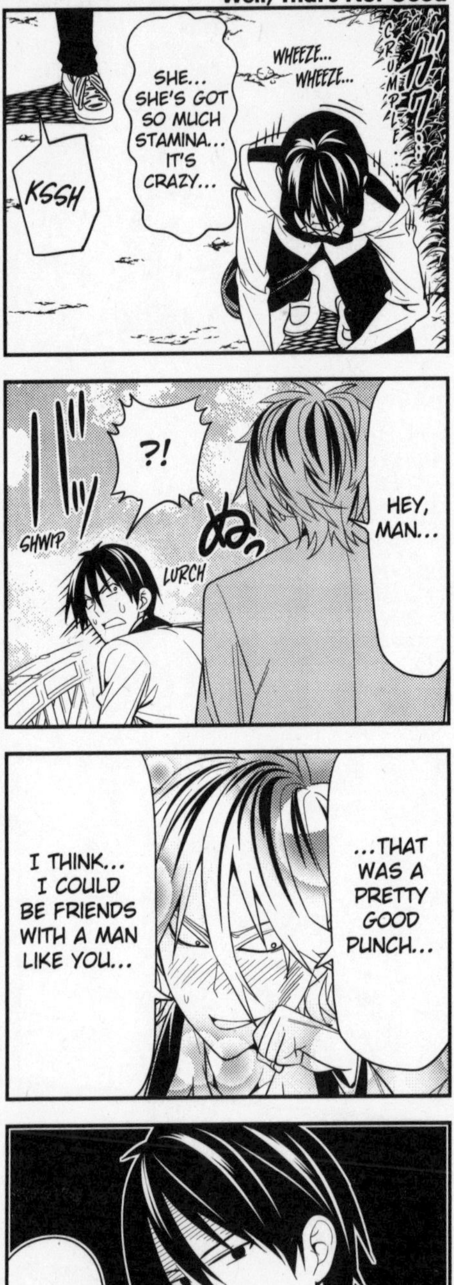
GRUMPLE
WHEEZE... WHEEZE...
SHE... SHE'S GOT SO MUCH STAMINA... IT'S CRAZY...
KSSH
HEY, MAN...
LURCH
?!
SHWIP
...THAT WAS A PRETTY GOOD PUNCH...
I THINK... I COULD BE FRIENDS WITH A MAN LIKE YOU...
...NO, I'M GOOD.

Running a Little Late

MEAN-WHILE

...

CLASS IS START-ING, YOU GUYS...

Please hand in your home-work!

Name	**Ryuichi Kurosaki**
Sex	
Height	**178 cm / 5'10"**
Weight	**64 kg / 141 lbs**
Blood type	**B**
Birthday	**12/24**

Memo A hooligan who knows nothing
of human kindness, and therefore
was easily won over by Yoshiko. Has
been alone for a long time, and so
he is reputed to be good at playing
by himself.

Seems to want to be friends with
Akkun, but there's not much hope
for that.

□RYUICHI KUROSAKI

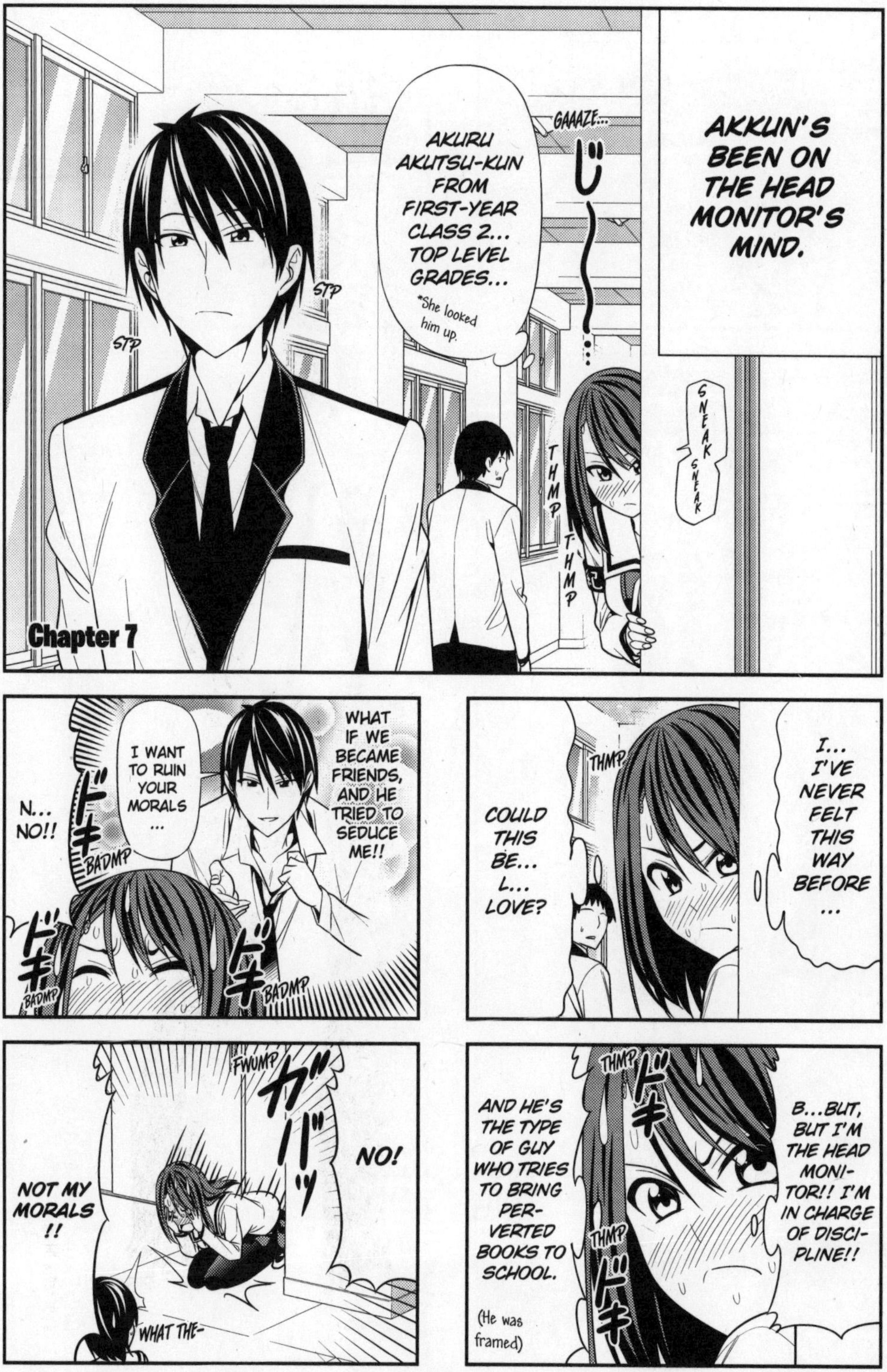
AKKUN'S BEEN ON THE HEAD MONITOR'S MIND.
GAAAZE...
じー
AKURU AKUTSU-KUN FROM FIRST-YEAR CLASS 2... TOP LEVEL GRADES...
*She looked him up.
SNEAK SNEAK
THMP THMP
STP
STP
Chapter 7
I... I'VE NEVER FELT THIS WAY BEFORE...
THMP
COULD THIS BE... L... LOVE?
WHAT IF WE BECAME FRIENDS, AND HE TRIED TO SEDUCE ME!!
I WANT TO RUIN YOUR MORALS ...
ドキ BADMP
N... NO!!
ドキ BADMP
ドキ BADMP
THMP ドキ
B...BUT, BUT I'M THE HEAD MONITOR!! I'M IN CHARGE OF DISCIPLINE!!
AND HE'S THE TYPE OF GUY WHO TRIES TO BRING PERVERTED BOOKS TO SCHOOL.
THMP ドキ
(He was framed)
FWUMP
ガバッ
NO!
NOT MY MORALS !!
WHAT THE-

Nickname

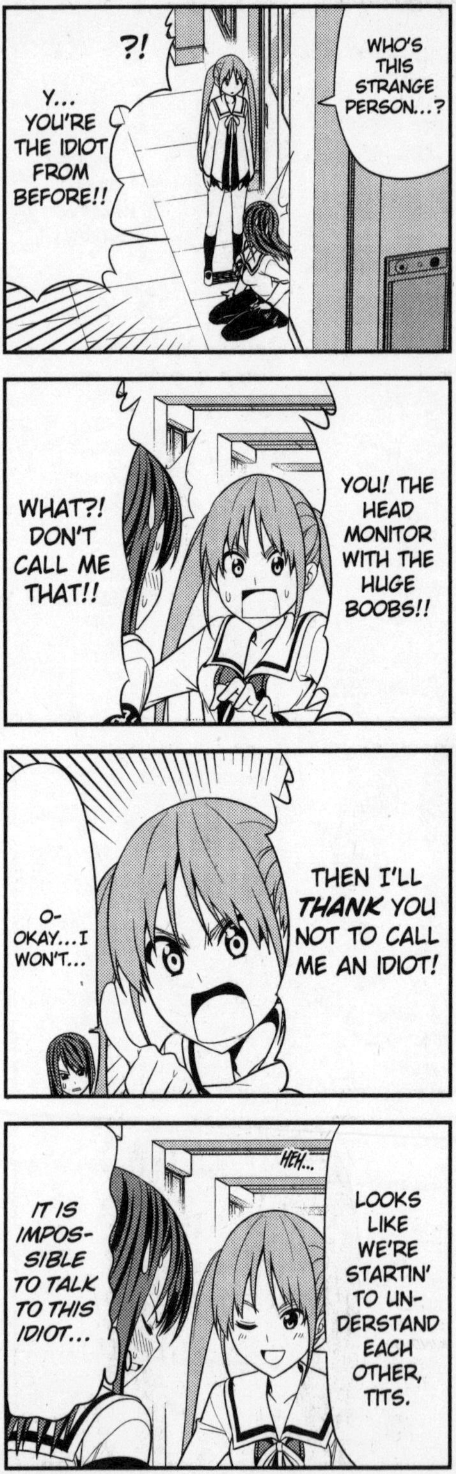
WHO'S THIS STRANGE PERSON...?
?!
Y... YOU'RE THE IDIOT FROM BEFORE!!
YOU! THE HEAD MONITOR WITH THE HUGE BOOBS!!
WHAT?! DON'T CALL ME THAT!!
THEN I'LL *THANK* YOU NOT TO CALL ME AN IDIOT!
O-OKAY...I WON'T...
HEH...
LOOKS LIKE WE'RE STARTIN' TO UNDERSTAND EACH OTHER, TITS.
IT IS IMPOSSIBLE TO TALK TO THIS IDIOT...

A Simple Girl

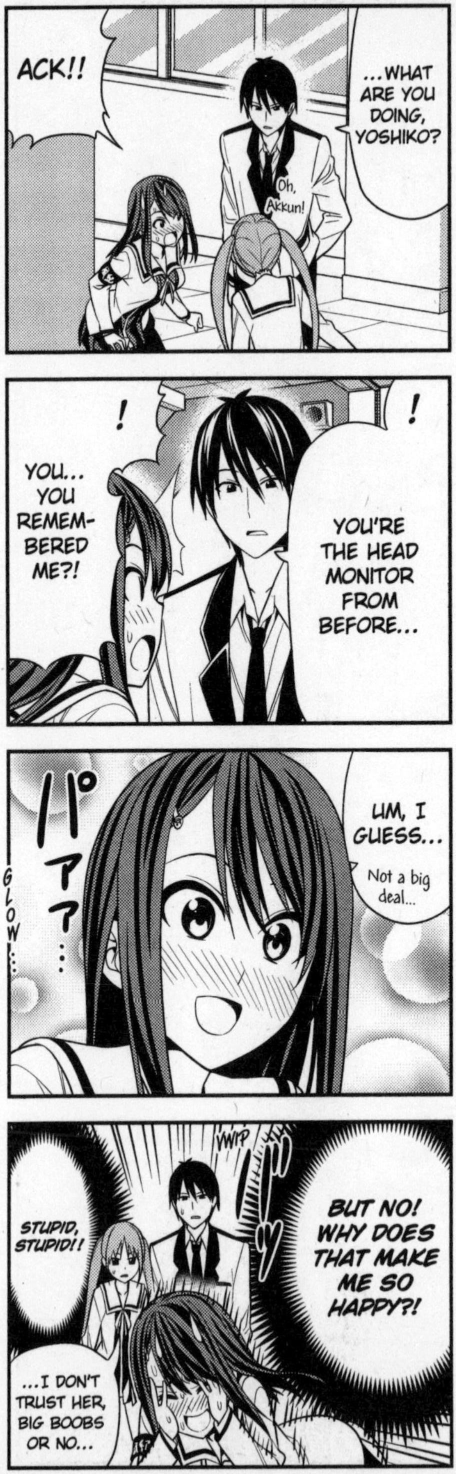
...WHAT ARE YOU DOING, YOSHIKO?
Oh, Akkun!
ACK!!
!
YOU'RE THE HEAD MONITOR FROM BEFORE...
!
YOU... YOU REMEMBERED ME?!
UM, I GUESS...
Not a big deal...
パァァ...
GLOW...
VWIP
BUT NO! WHY DOES THAT MAKE ME SO HAPPY?!
STUPID, STUPID!!
...I DON'T TRUST HER, BIG BOOBS OR NO...

Excitement

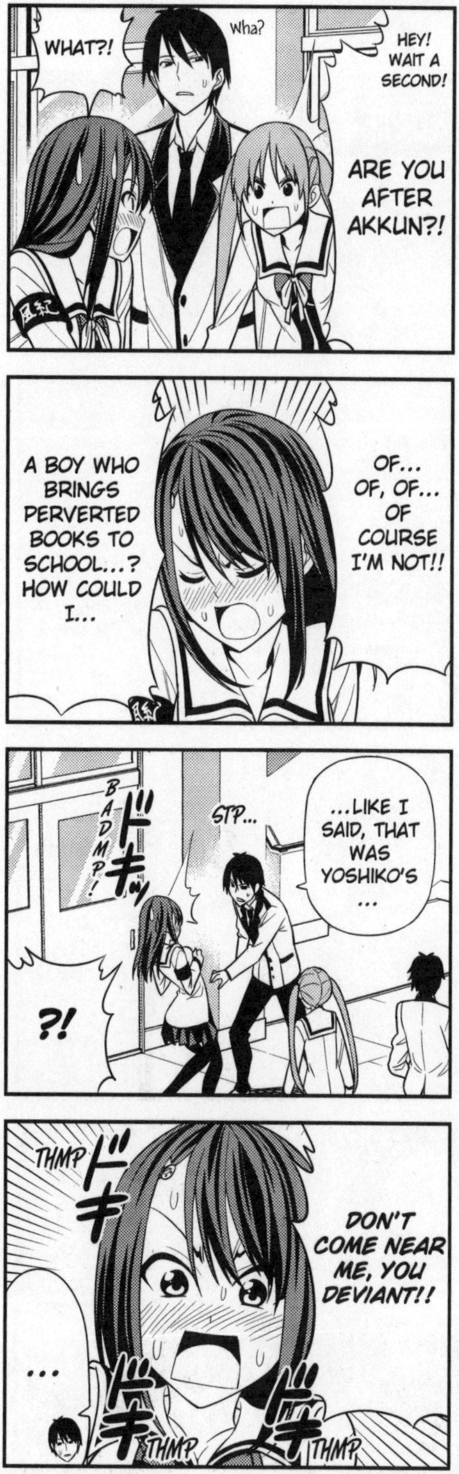
HEY! WAIT A SECOND!
Wha?
ARE YOU AFTER AKKUN?!
WHAT?!
OF... OF, OF... OF COURSE I'M NOT!!
A BOY WHO BRINGS PERVERTED BOOKS TO SCHOOL...? HOW COULD I...
...LIKE I SAID, THAT WAS YOSHIKO'S ...
STP...
BADMP!
?!
THMP
DON'T COME NEAR ME, YOU DEVIANT!!
...
THMP
THMP

Turned Down

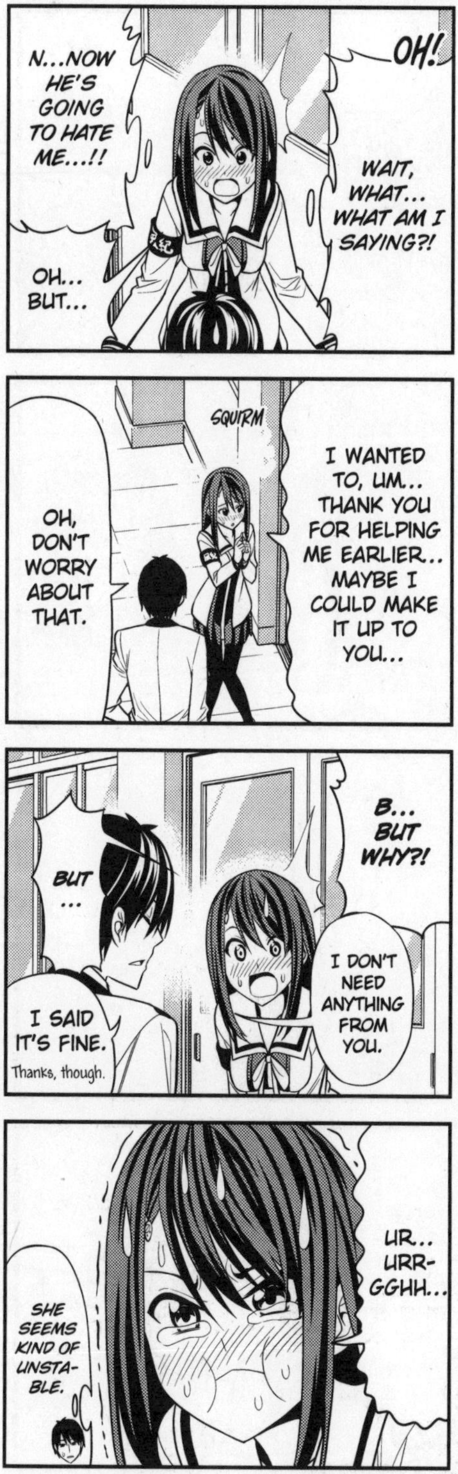
OH!
N...NOW HE'S GOING TO HATE ME...!!
WAIT, WHAT... WHAT AM I SAYING?!
OH... BUT...
I WANTED TO, UM... THANK YOU FOR HELPING ME EARLIER... MAYBE I COULD MAKE IT UP TO YOU...
SQUIRM
OH, DON'T WORRY ABOUT THAT.
B... BUT WHY?!
I DON'T NEED ANYTHING FROM YOU.
BUT ...
I SAID IT'S FINE.
Thanks, though.
UR... URR-GGHH...
SHE SEEMS KIND OF UNSTA-BLE.

Stunner

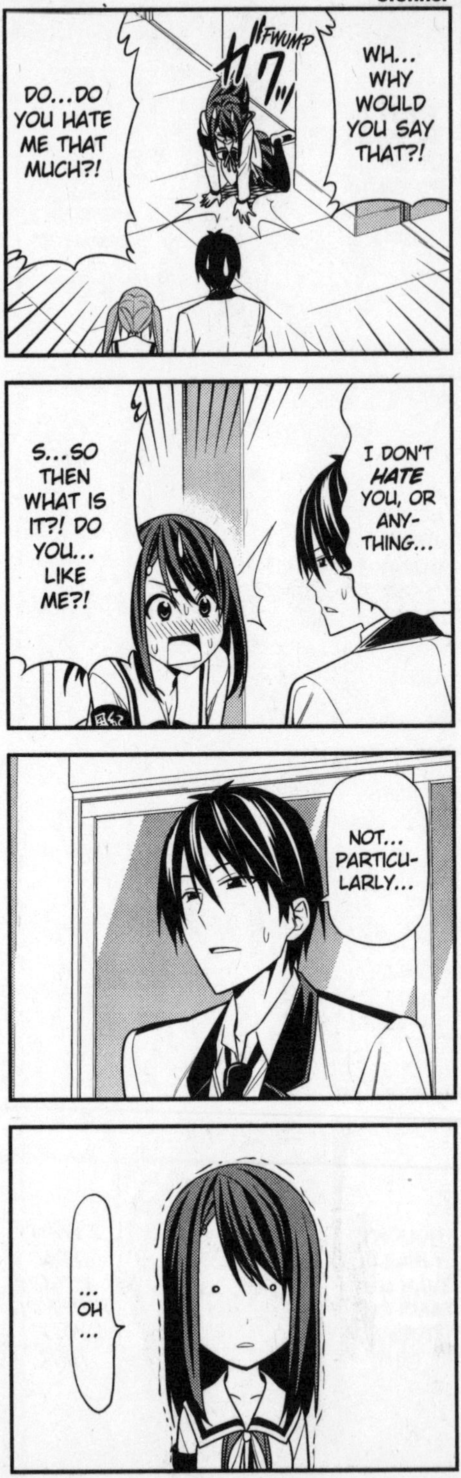
WH... WHY WOULD YOU SAY THAT?!
FWUMP
DO...DO YOU HATE ME THAT MUCH?!
I DON'T *HATE* YOU, OR ANY-THING...
S...SO THEN WHAT IS IT?! DO YOU... LIKE ME?!
NOT... PARTICU-LARLY...
...OH ...

Massive Victory

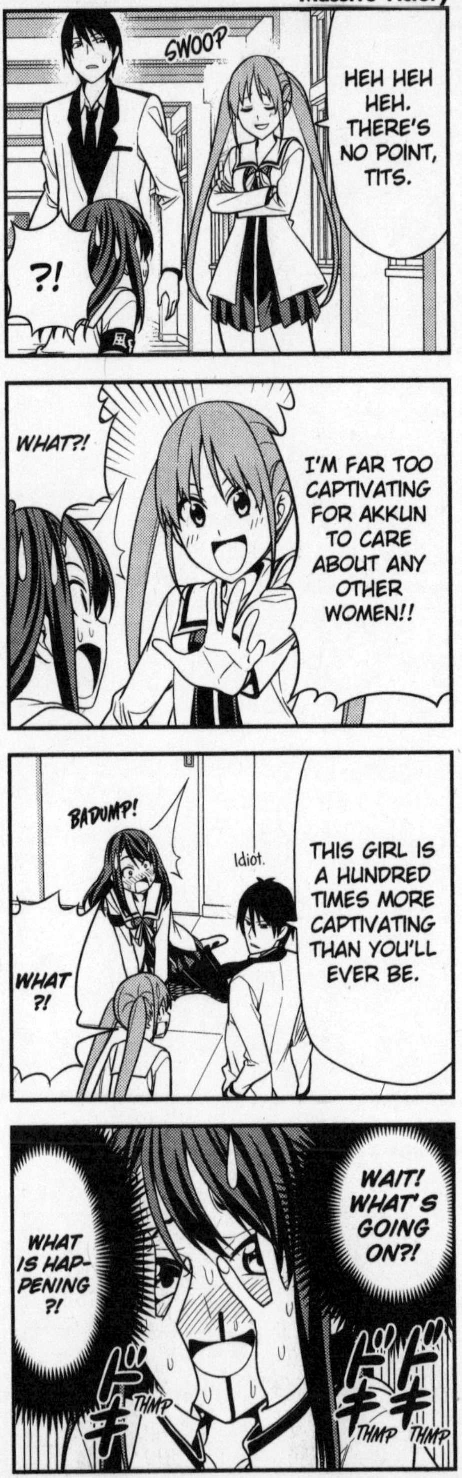
HEH HEH HEH. THERE'S NO POINT, TITS.
SWOOP
?!
I'M FAR TOO CAPTIVATING FOR AKKUN TO CARE ABOUT ANY OTHER WOMEN!!
WHAT?!
THIS GIRL IS A HUNDRED TIMES MORE CAPTIVATING THAN YOU'LL EVER BE.
Idiot.
BADUMP!
WHAT ?!
WAIT! WHAT'S GOING ON?!
THMP THMP
WHAT IS HAP-PENING ?!
THMP

Ladies' Battle

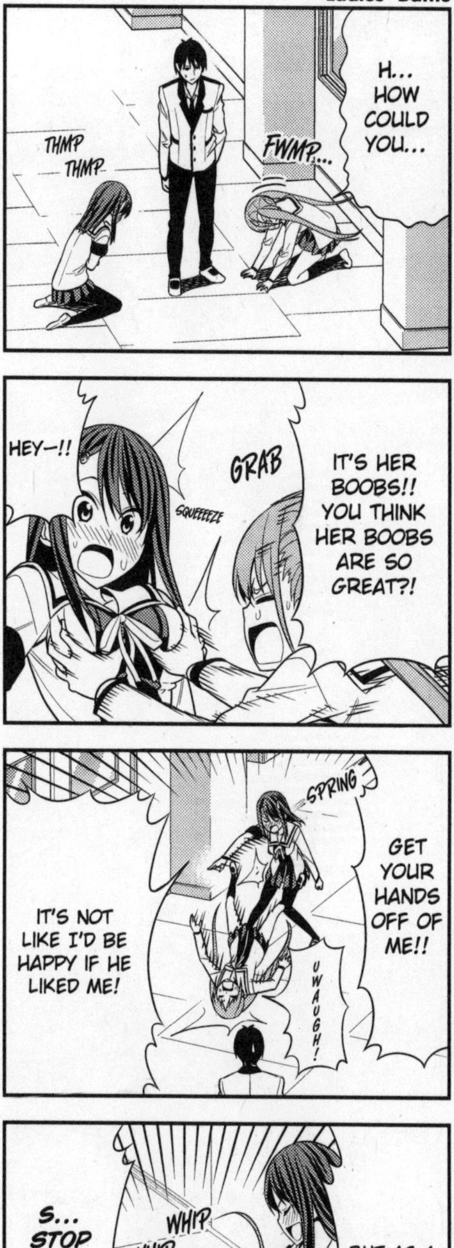
H... HOW COULD YOU...
FWMP...
THMP THMP
IT'S HER BOOBS!! YOU THINK HER BOOBS ARE SO GREAT?!
GRAB
SQUEEEEZE
HEY—!!
GET YOUR HANDS OFF OF ME!!
SPRING
UWAUGH!
IT'S NOT LIKE I'D BE HAPPY IF HE LIKED ME!
BUT AS A WOMAN, I DEFEATED YOU!
WHIP
WHIP
S... STOP IIIT!!
...

Suggestion

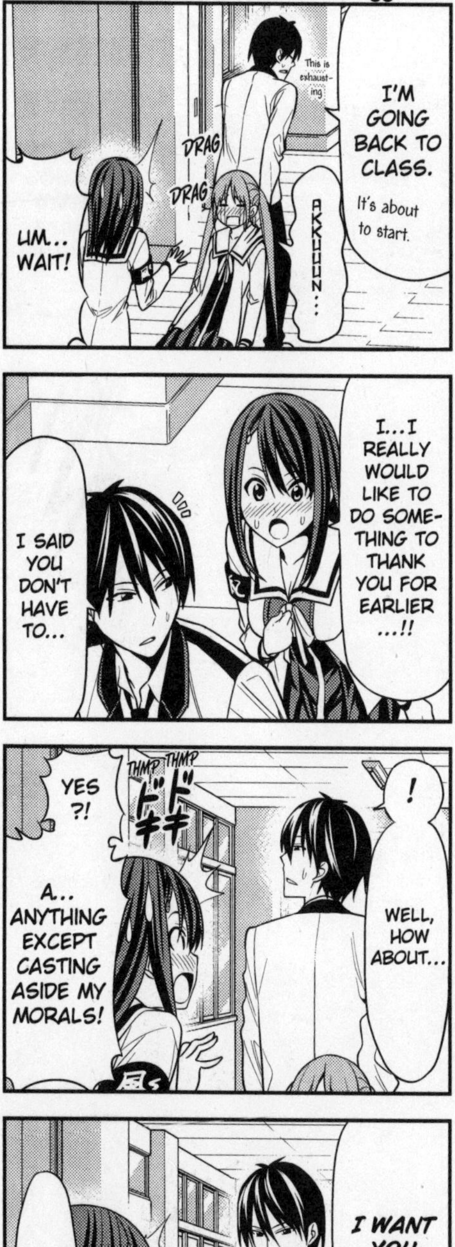
I'M GOING BACK TO CLASS.
It's about to start.
This is exhausting
AKKUUUN...
DRAG
DRAG
UM... WAIT!
I...I REALLY WOULD LIKE TO DO SOMETHING TO THANK YOU FOR EARLIER ...!!
I SAID YOU DON'T HAVE TO...
!
WELL, HOW ABOUT...
THMP THMP
YES ?!
A... ANYTHING EXCEPT CASTING ASIDE MY MORALS!
I WANT YOU TO BE FRIENDS WITH HER.
Z Z Z
*Wore herself out crying.
WHAT?

All My Power

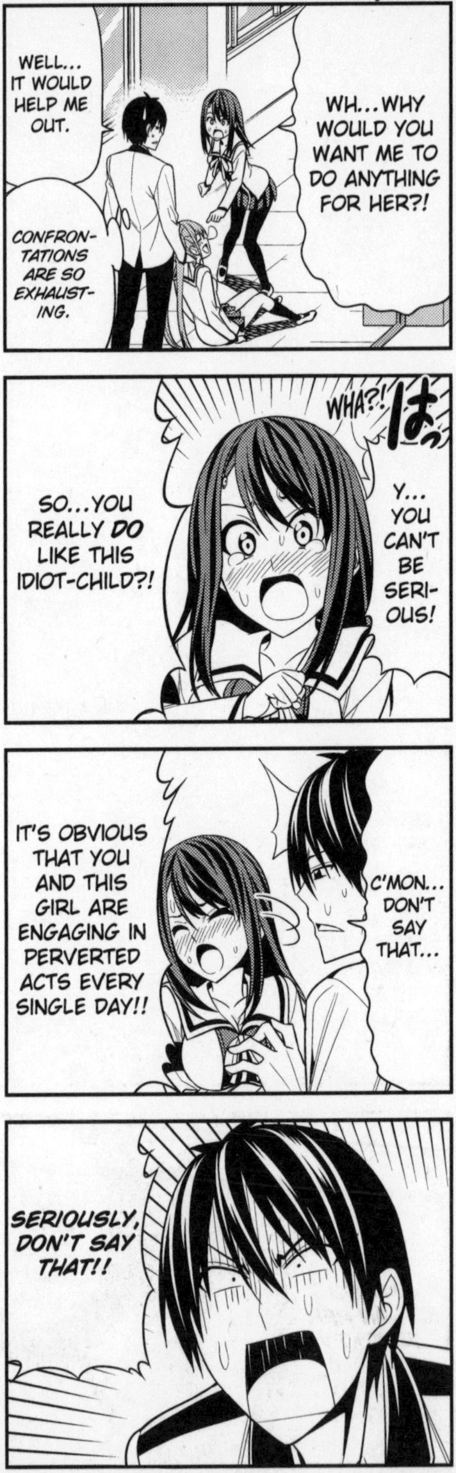
WH...WHY WOULD YOU WANT ME TO DO ANYTHING FOR HER?!
WELL... IT WOULD HELP ME OUT.
CONFRONTATIONS ARE SO EXHAUSTING.
WHA?!
はっ
Y... YOU CAN'T BE SERIOUS!
SO...YOU REALLY DO LIKE THIS IDIOT-CHILD?!
C'MON... DON'T SAY THAT...
IT'S OBVIOUS THAT YOU AND THIS GIRL ARE ENGAGING IN PERVERTED ACTS EVERY SINGLE DAY!!
SERIOUSLY, DON'T SAY THAT!!

The Body Tells the Truth

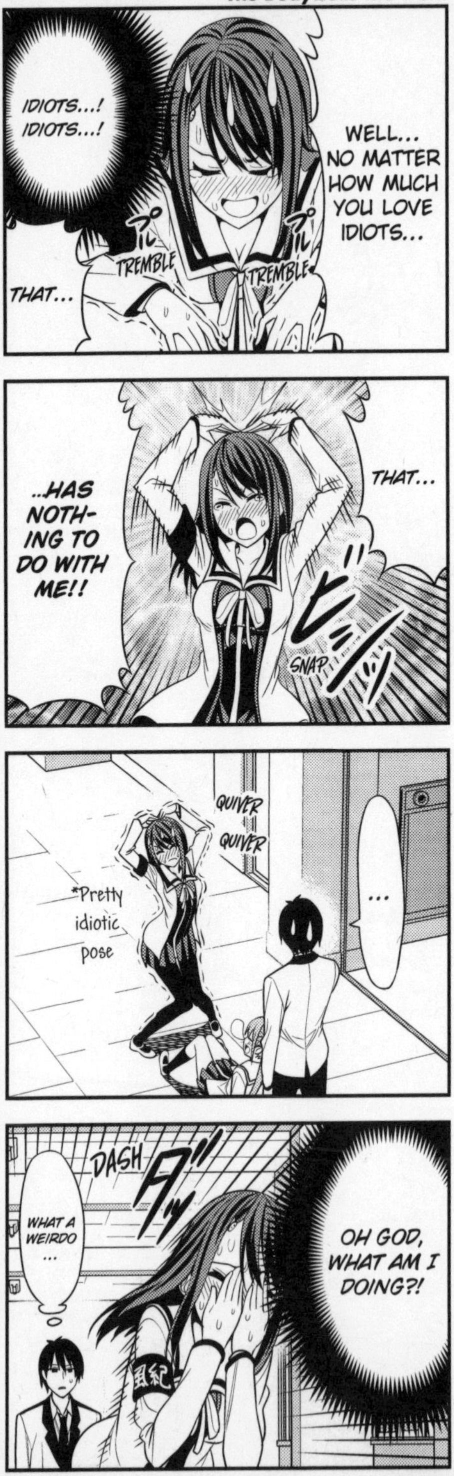
WELL... NO MATTER HOW MUCH YOU LOVE IDIOTS...
TREMBLE
TREMBLE
IDIOTS...! IDIOTS...!
THAT...
THAT...
...HAS NOTHING TO DO WITH ME!!
SNAP
QUIVER QUIVER
...
*Pretty idiotic pose
DASH
OH GOD, WHAT AM I DOING?!
WHAT A WEIRDO ...

Get It Together

I'M... JUST SO CONFUSED!!
プル TREMBLE
プル TREMBLE
IF I JUST COOL OFF AND THINK CALMLY, THAT KIND OF GUY SHOULDN'T GET ME SO... SO...!
...IT'S TOO LATE! I LIKE HIM!!
AND SO BEGAN HER JOURNEY DOWN A THORNY PATH...

Name	**Head Monitor**
Sex	
Height	**165 cm / 5'4"**
Weight	**52 kg / 114 lbs**
Blood type	**B**
Birthday	**07/13**
Memo	Has become smitten with Akkun and begun to stray from the moral path, but she hasn't quite realized it yet.

G cup. |

FUUKI IINCHOU

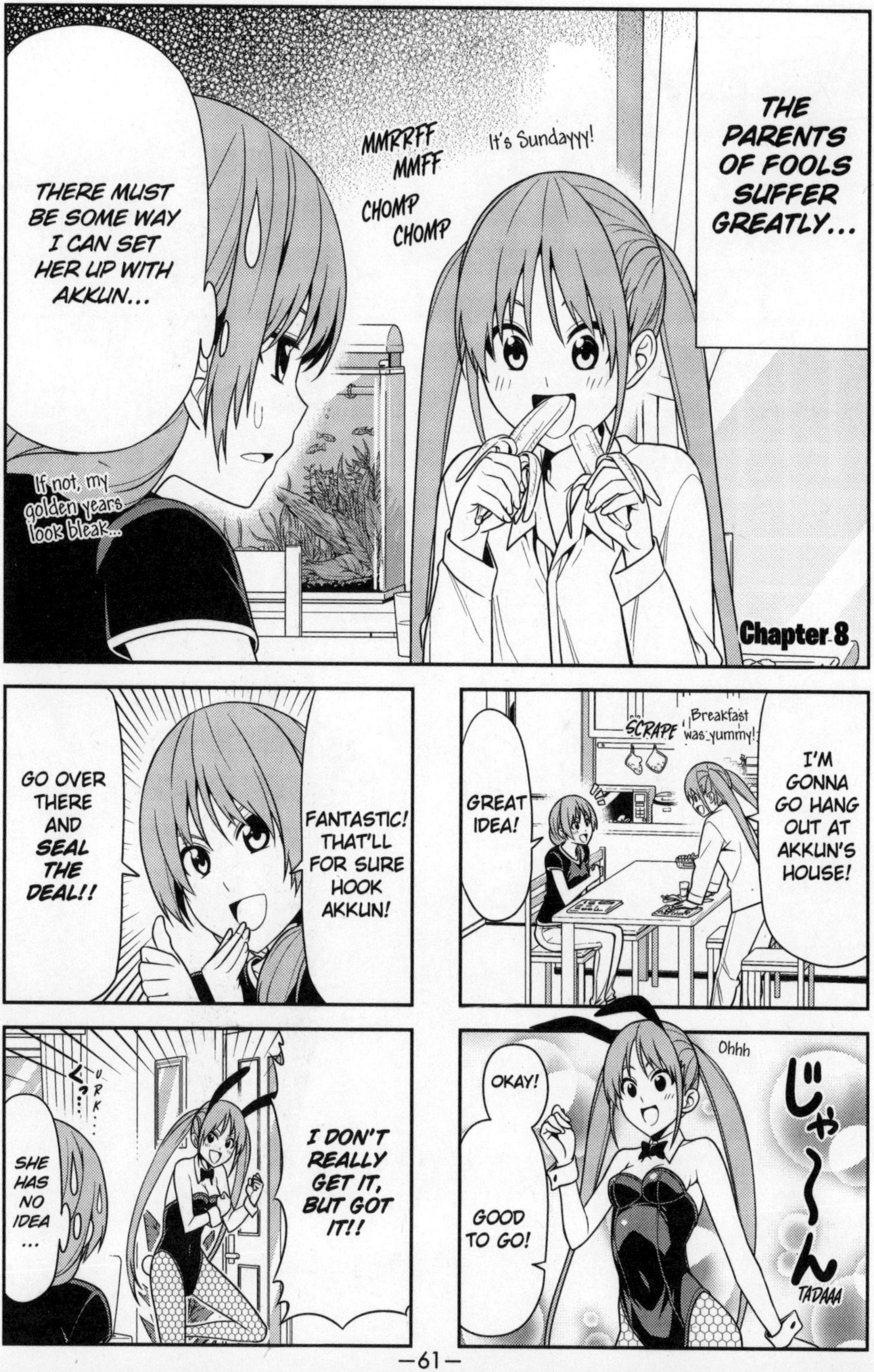
THE PARENTS OF FOOLS SUFFER GREATLY...
It's Sundayyy!
MMRRFF MMFF
CHOMP CHOMP
THERE MUST BE SOME WAY I CAN SET HER UP WITH AKKUN...
If not, my golden years look bleak...
Chapter 8
Breakfast was yummy!
SCRAPE
I'M GONNA GO HANG OUT AT AKKUN'S HOUSE!
GREAT IDEA!
FANTASTIC! THAT'LL FOR SURE HOOK AKKUN!
GO OVER THERE AND SEAL THE DEAL!!
Ohhh
じゃ〜ん
TADAAA
OKAY!
GOOD TO GO!
I DON'T REALLY GET IT, BUT GOT IT!!
URK...
SHE HAS NO IDEA...

A Happy Time

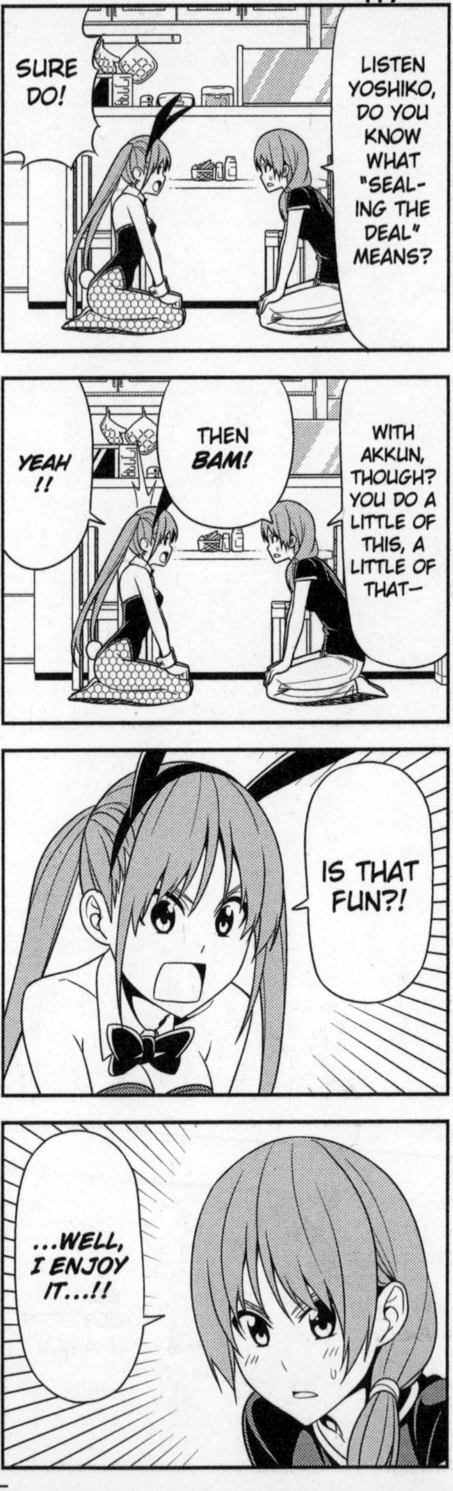
LISTEN YOSHIKO, DO YOU KNOW WHAT "SEAL-ING THE DEAL" MEANS?
SURE DO!
WITH AKKUN, THOUGH? YOU DO A LITTLE OF THIS, A LITTLE OF THAT—
THEN BAM!
YEAH !!
IS THAT FUN?!
...WELL, I ENJOY IT...!!

Use of Force

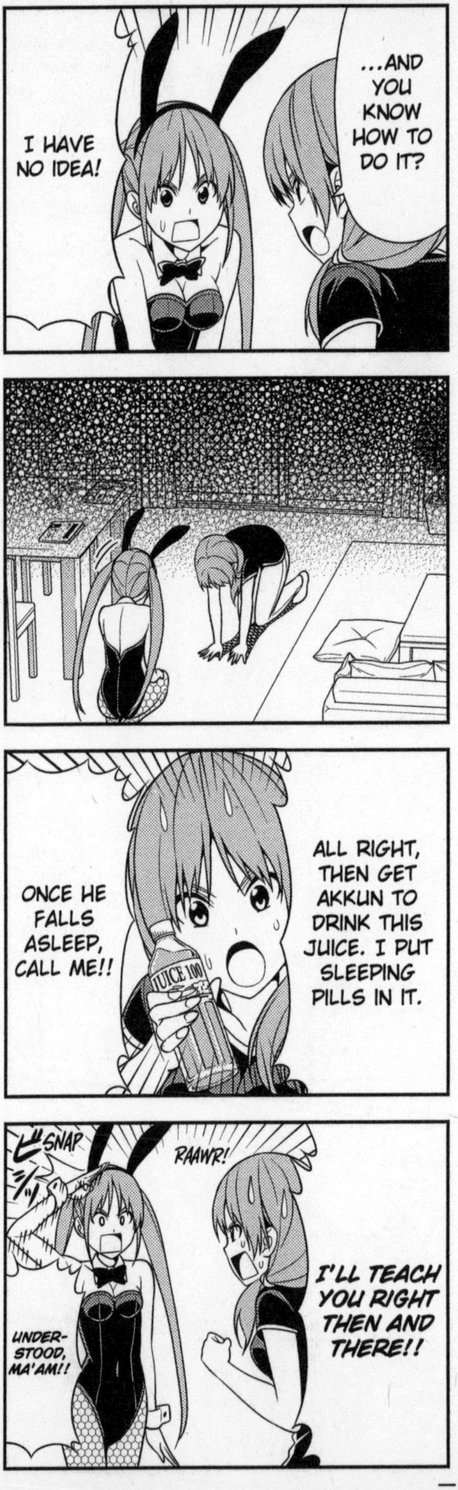
...AND YOU KNOW HOW TO DO IT?
I HAVE NO IDEA!
ALL RIGHT, THEN GET AKKUN TO DRINK THIS JUICE. I PUT SLEEPING PILLS IN IT.
JUICE 100
ONCE HE FALLS ASLEEP, CALL ME!!
RAAWR!
I'LL TEACH YOU RIGHT THEN AND THERE!!
SNAP
UNDER-STOOD, MA'AM!!

Yoshiko Repellant

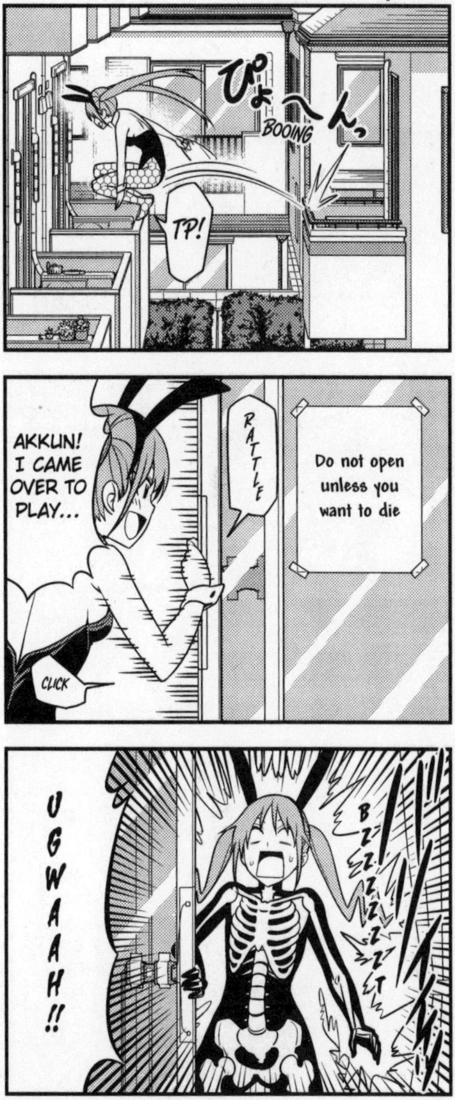
ぴょ〜ん
BOOING
TP!
Do not open unless you want to die
AKKUN! I CAME OVER TO PLAY...
RATTLE
CLICK
BZZZZZZZT
UGWAAH!!
HSST HSST
*Opening the window activates a taser
WHAT AN IDIOT...

Academic Ability: Zero

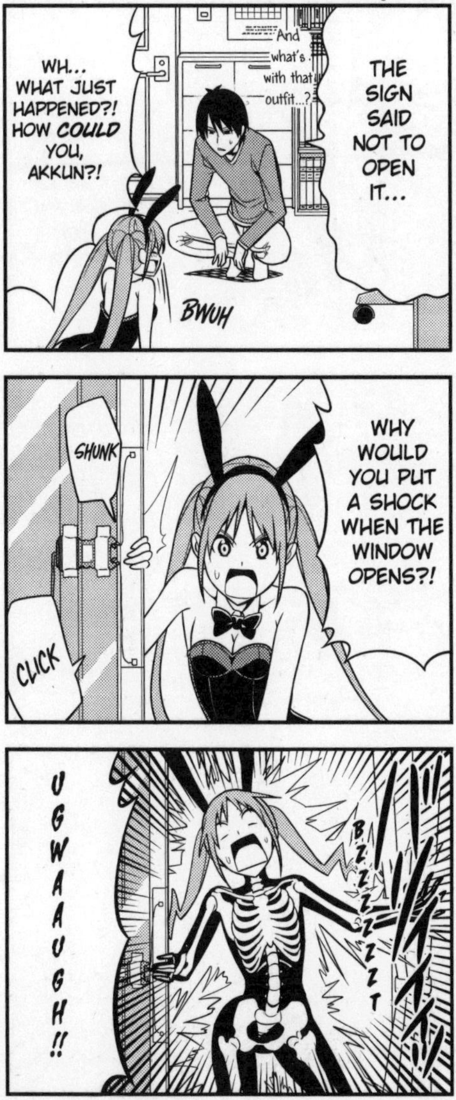
THE SIGN SAID NOT TO OPEN IT...
And what's with that outfit...?
WH... WHAT JUST HAPPENED?! HOW COULD YOU, AKKUN?!
BWUH
WHY WOULD YOU PUT A SHOCK WHEN THE WINDOW OPENS?!
SHUNK
CLICK
BZZZZZZZT
UGWAAAUGH!!
WELL...I GUESS IT IS KINDA FUN...
Getting shocked...
GRR
DAMMIT... THIS IDIOT ADAPTS WAY TOO FAST...
I have to think of something else...

Comprehension: Zero

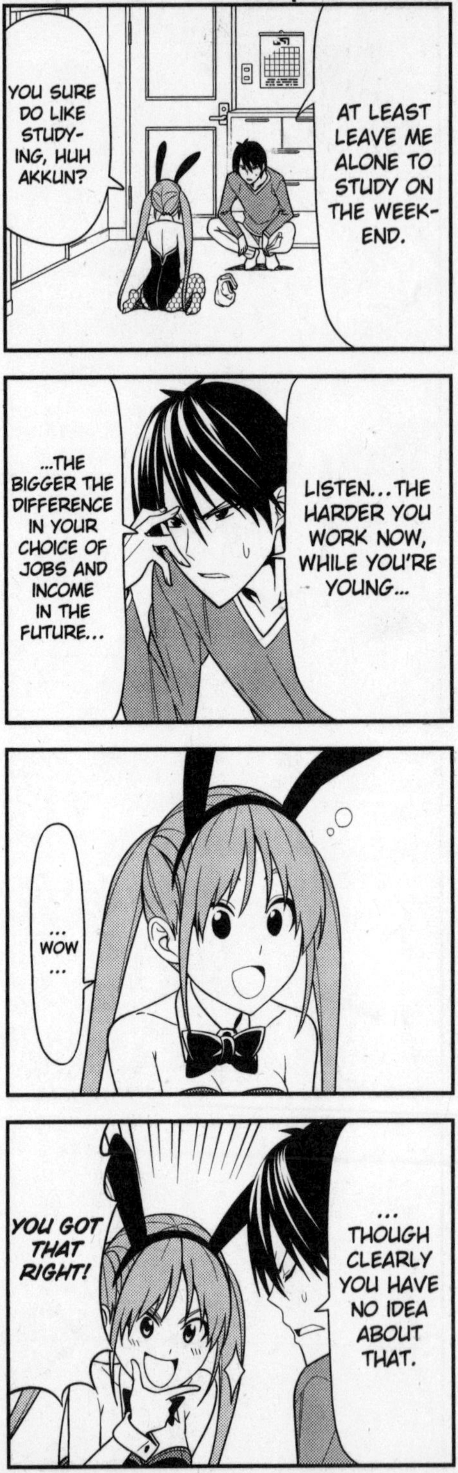
AT LEAST LEAVE ME ALONE TO STUDY ON THE WEEK-END.
YOU SURE DO LIKE STUDY-ING, HUH AKKUN?
LISTEN...THE HARDER YOU WORK NOW, WHILE YOU'RE YOUNG...
...THE BIGGER THE DIFFERENCE IN YOUR CHOICE OF JOBS AND INCOME IN THE FUTURE...
... WOW ...
... THOUGH CLEARLY YOU HAVE NO IDEA ABOUT THAT.
YOU GOT THAT RIGHT!

Retention: Zero

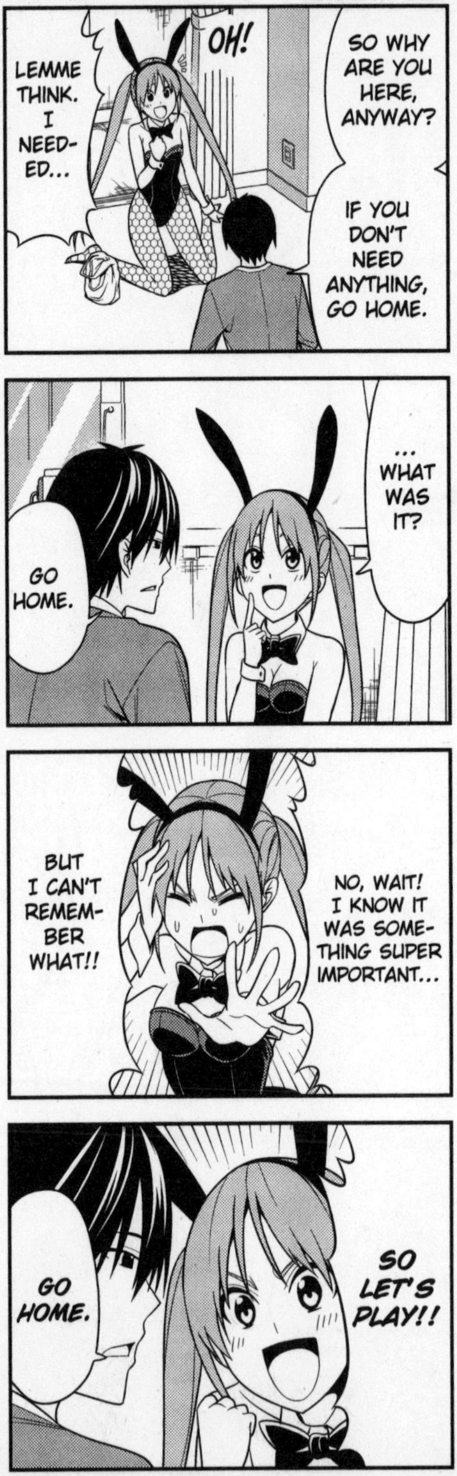
SO WHY ARE YOU HERE, ANYWAY?
IF YOU DON'T NEED ANYTHING, GO HOME.
OH!
LEMME THINK. I NEED-ED...
... WHAT WAS IT?
GO HOME.
NO, WAIT! I KNOW IT WAS SOME-THING SUPER IMPORTANT...
BUT I CAN'T REMEM-BER WHAT!!
SO LET'S PLAY!!
GO HOME.

Kindness

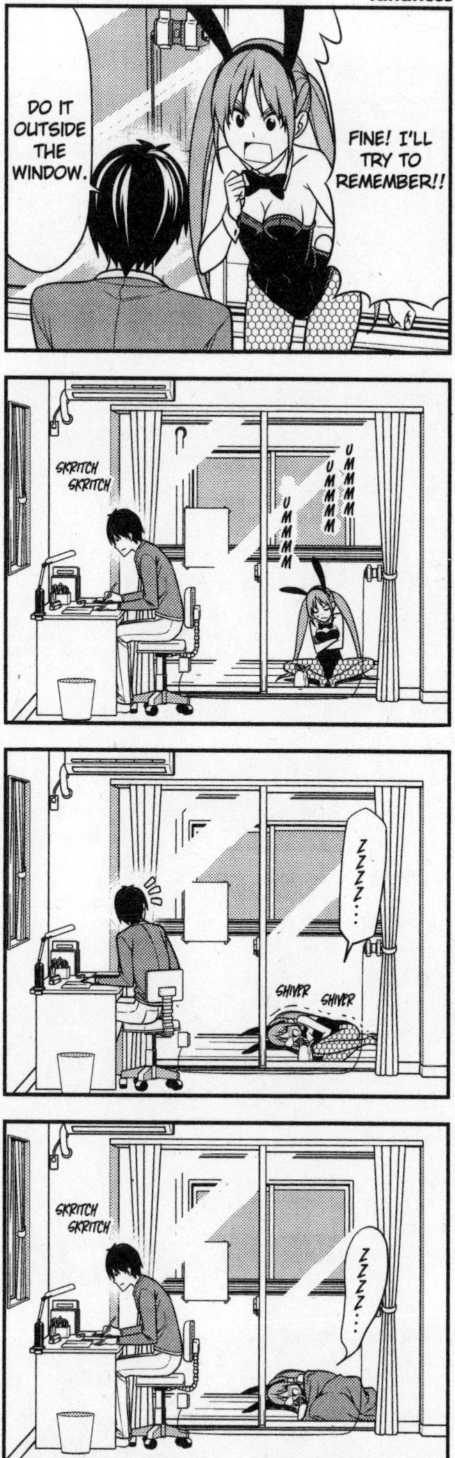
DO IT OUTSIDE THE WINDOW.
FINE! I'LL TRY TO REMEMBER!!
UMMMM
UMMMM
UMMMM
SKRITCH SKRITCH
ZZZZ…
SHIVER
SHIVER
ZZZZ…
SKRITCH SKRITCH

100% Suspicious

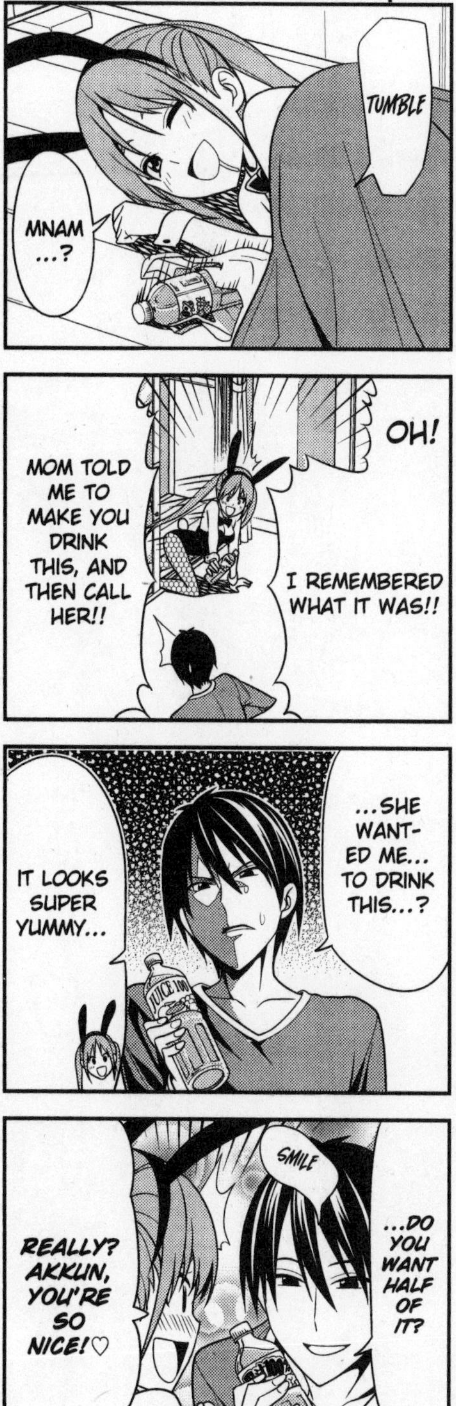
TUMBLE
MNAM …?
OH!
I REMEMBERED WHAT IT WAS!!
MOM TOLD ME TO MAKE YOU DRINK THIS, AND THEN CALL HER!!
…SHE WANT-ED ME… TO DRINK THIS…?
IT LOOKS SUPER YUMMY…
SMILE
…DO YOU WANT HALF OF IT?
REALLY? AKKUN, YOU'RE SO NICE!♡

From Suspicion to Certainty

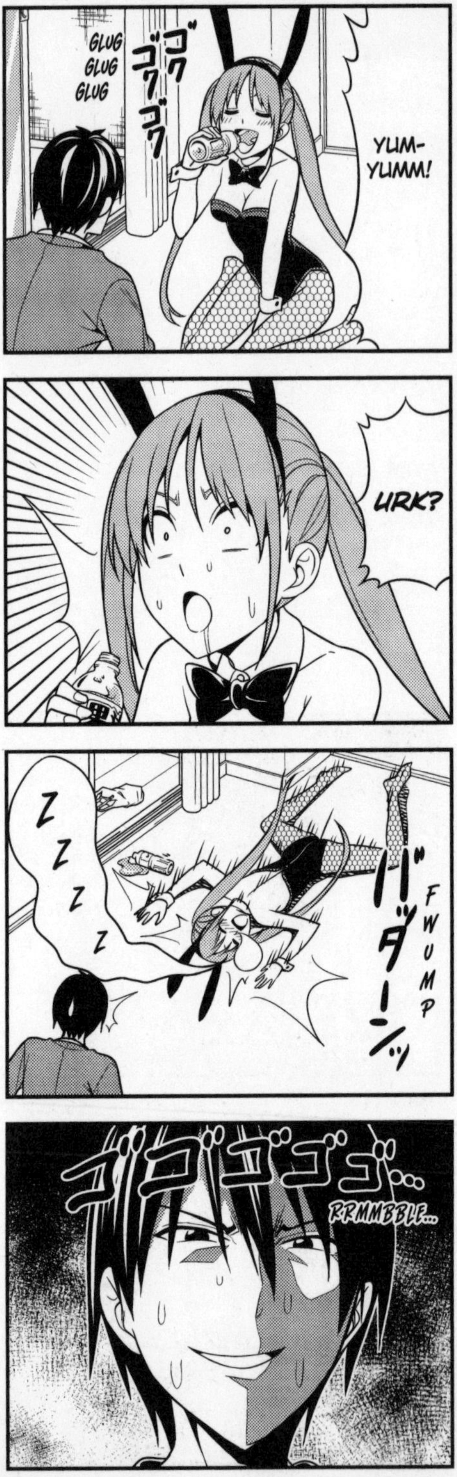
GLUG GLUG GLUG
ゴクゴクゴク
YUM-YUMM!
URK?
Z Z Z Z
バッターンッ
FWUMP
ゴゴゴゴゴ…
RRMMBBLE...

An Unhappy Moment

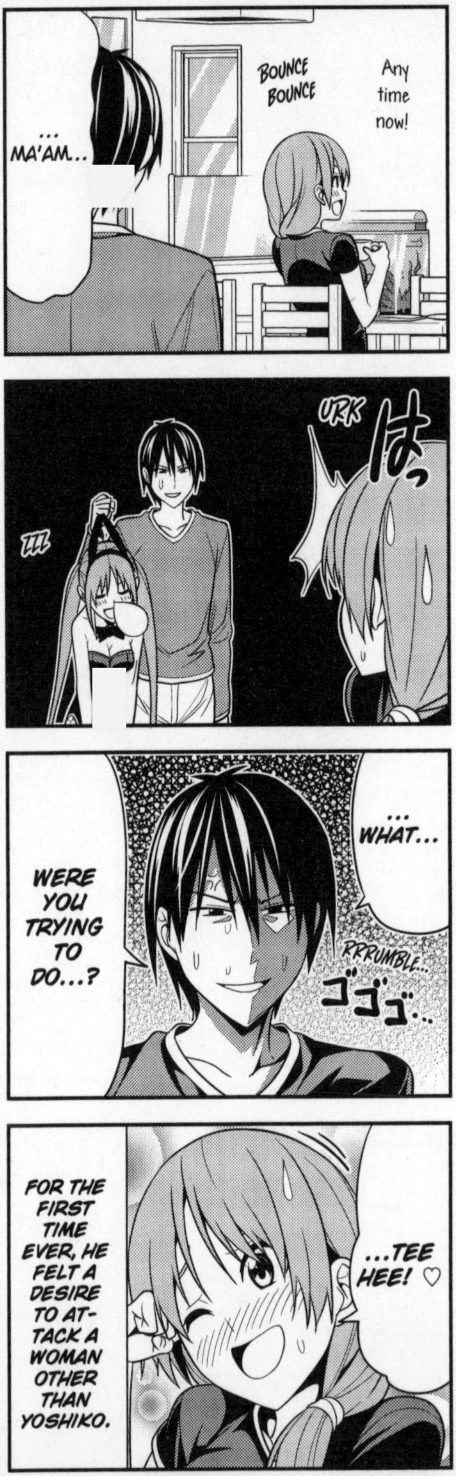
Any time now!
BOUNCE BOUNCE
... MA'AM...
URK
はっ
ZZZ
... WHAT...
WERE YOU TRYING TO DO...?
RRRUMBLE...
ゴゴゴ…
...TEE HEE! ♡
FOR THE FIRST TIME EVER, HE FELT A DESIRE TO ATTACK A WOMAN OTHER THAN YOSHIKO.

How Is This on Me?

WOULD YOU PLEASE STOP DOING THESE HORRIFYING THINGS...?
WELL, THEN JUST MARRY YO-SHIKO!!
WH-A-M
DON'T ASK THE IMPOSS-IBLE.

Name **Yoshie Hanabatake (Mom)**

Sex	
Height	**161 kg / 5'3"**
Weight	**49 kg / 108 lbs**
Blood type	**O**
Birthday	**01/09**

Memo Yoshiko's mother. While she does worry about Yoshiko, she's far more worried about her own golden years.

Though she's clearly put a lot of work into Yoshiko up to this point.

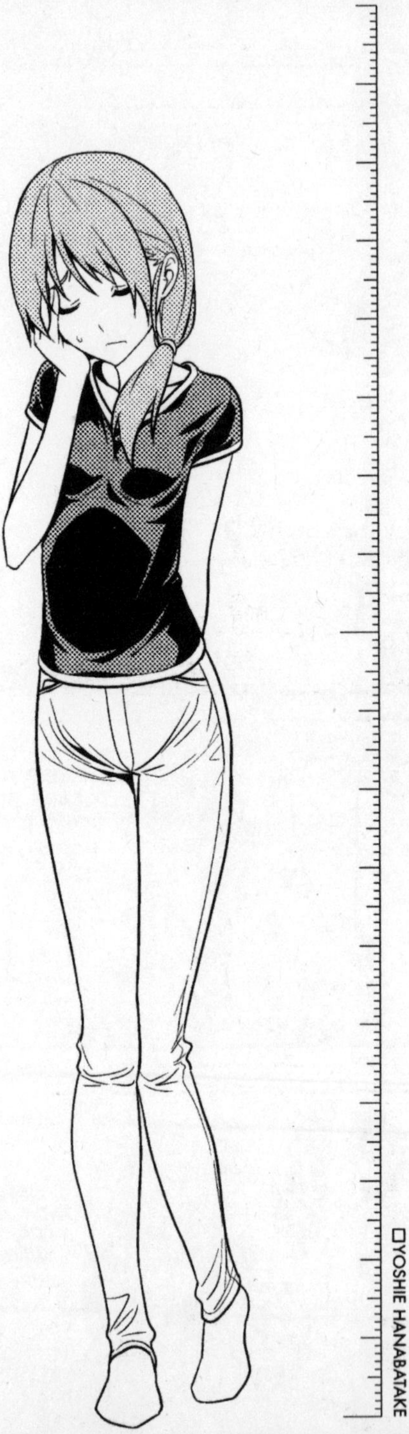
□YOSHIE HANABATAKE

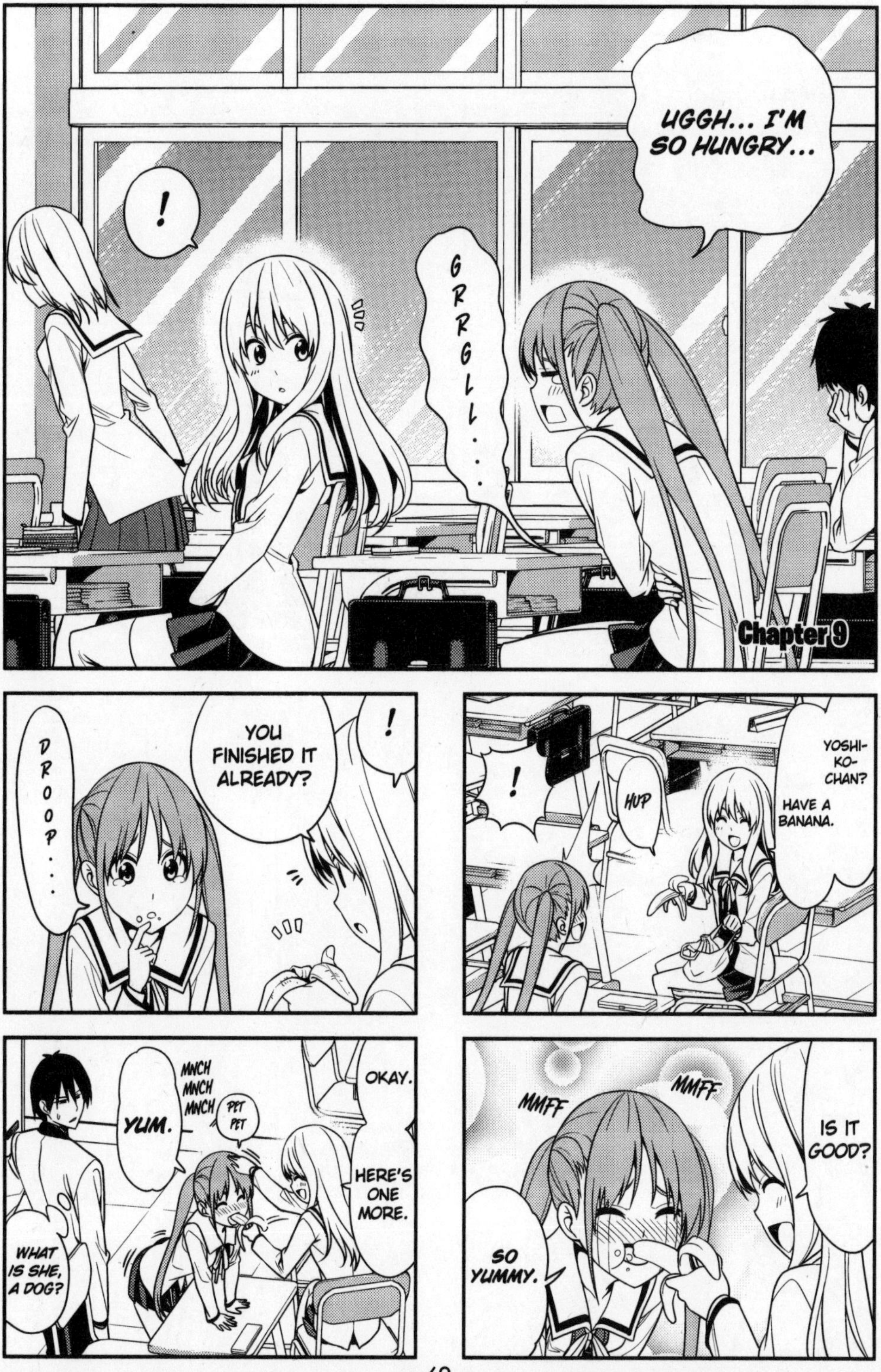
UGGH... I'M SO HUNGRY...
GRRGLL...
!
Chapter 9
YOSHI-KO-CHAN? HAVE A BANANA.
HUP
!
!
YOU FINISHED IT ALREADY?
DROOP...
MMFF
IS IT GOOD?
MMFF
SO YUMMY.
OKAY. HERE'S ONE MORE.
PET PET
MNCH MNCH MNCH
YUM.
WHAT IS SHE, A DOG?

Sayaka-chan's So Nice

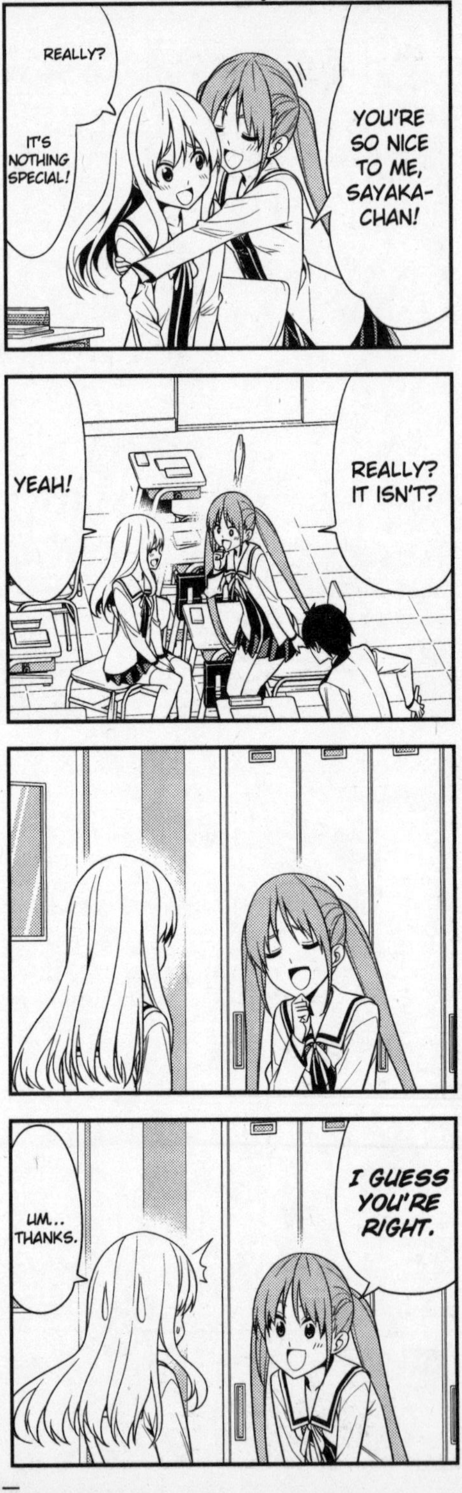
YOU'RE SO NICE TO ME, SAYAKA-CHAN!
REALLY?
IT'S NOTHING SPECIAL!
REALLY? IT ISN'T?
YEAH!
I GUESS YOU'RE RIGHT.
UM... THANKS.

What an Idiot Knows

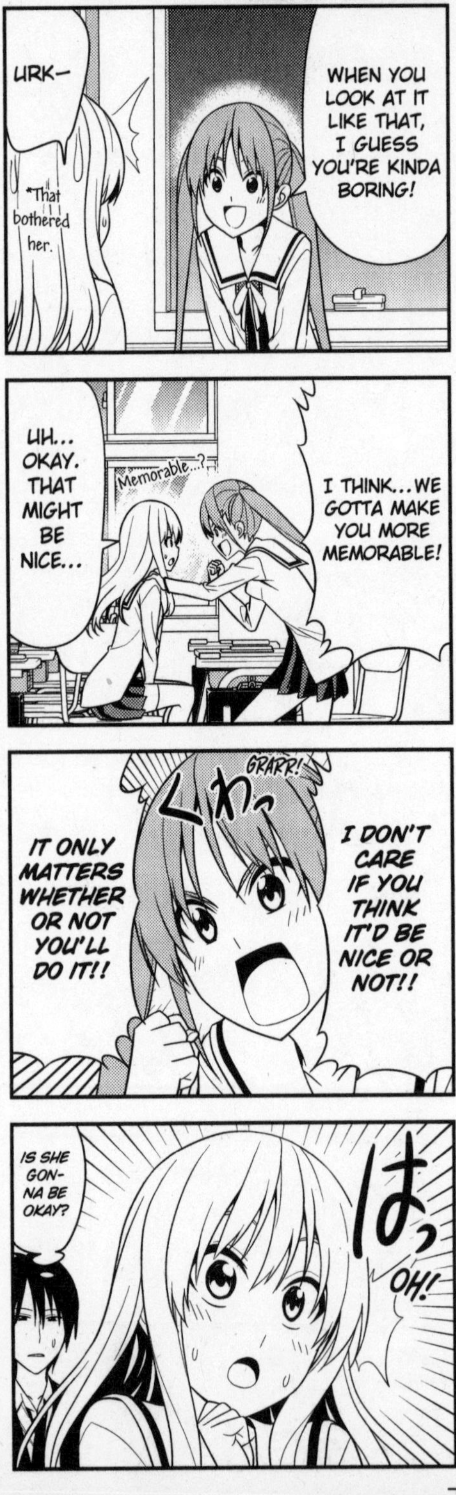
WHEN YOU LOOK AT IT LIKE THAT, I GUESS YOU'RE KINDA BORING!
URK—
*That bothered her.
I THINK...WE GOTTA MAKE YOU MORE MEMORABLE!
Memorable...?
UH... OKAY. THAT MIGHT BE NICE...
GRARR!
くわっ
I DON'T CARE IF YOU THINK IT'D BE NICE OR NOT!!
IT ONLY MATTERS WHETHER OR NOT YOU'LL DO IT!!
はっ
OH!
IS SHE GON-NA BE OKAY?

You Can't Just Brush This off That Easily

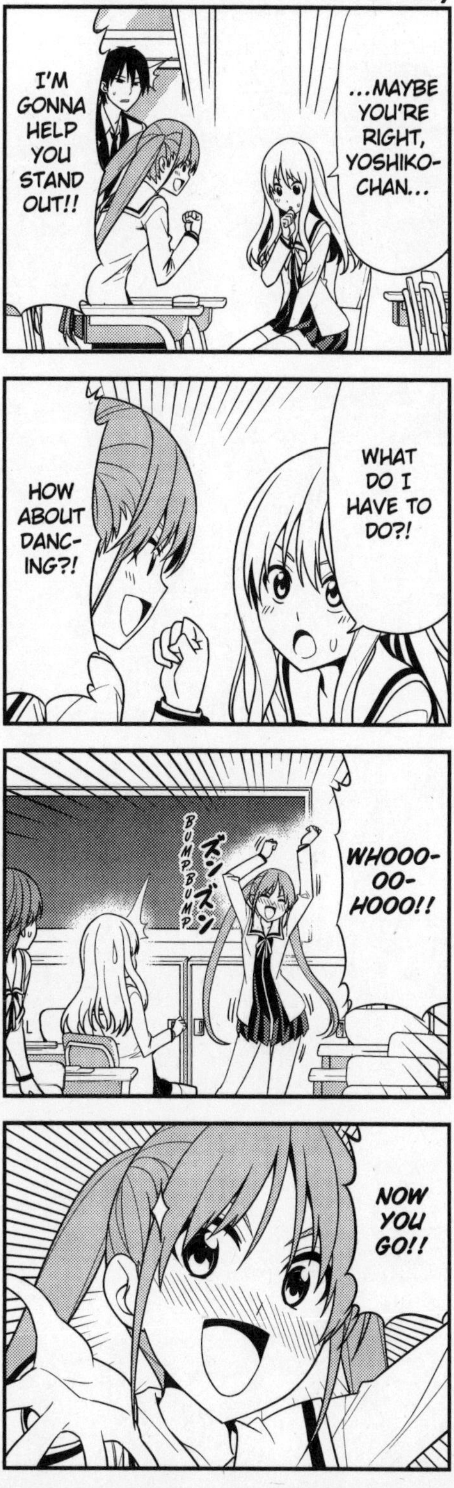
...MAYBE YOU'RE RIGHT, YOSHIKO-CHAN...
I'M GONNA HELP YOU STAND OUT!!
WHAT DO I HAVE TO DO?!
HOW ABOUT DANCING?!
WHOOOO-OO-HOOO!!
ズンズン
BUMP BUMP
NOW YOU GO!!

Humiliation

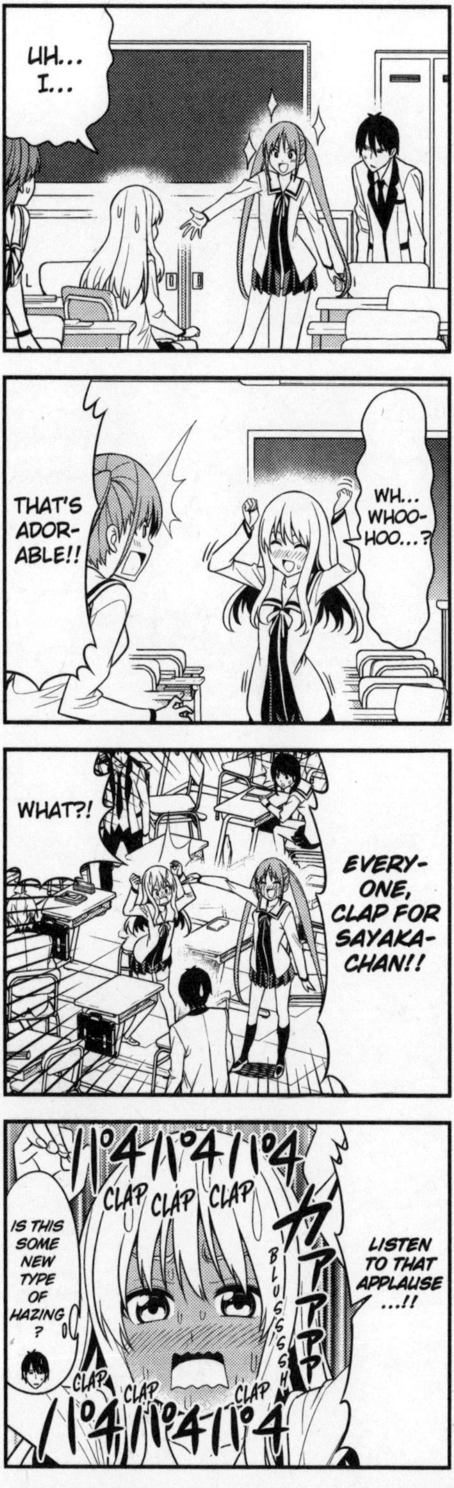
UH... I...
WH... WHOO-HOO...?
THAT'S ADORABLE!!
EVERY-ONE, CLAP FOR SAYAKA-CHAN!!
WHAT?!
パチパチパチ
CLAP CLAP CLAP
LISTEN TO THAT APPLAUSE...!!
カァァァァ
BLUSSSSH
IS THIS SOME NEW TYPE OF HAZING?
CLAP CLAP CLAP
パチパチパチ

The Classics

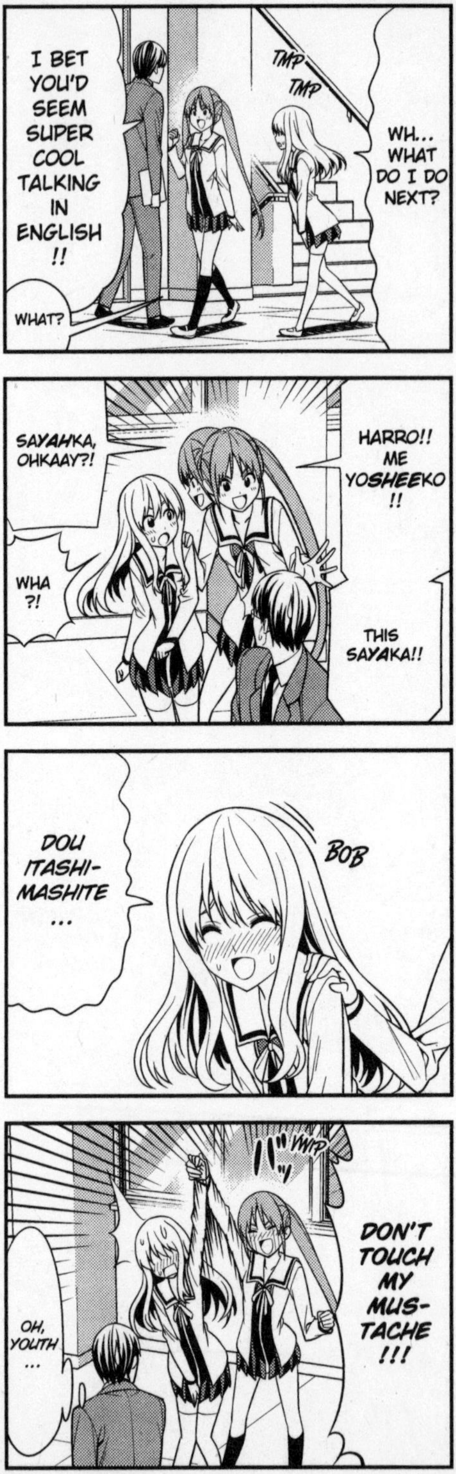
WH... WHAT DO I DO NEXT?
TMP TMP
I BET YOU'D SEEM SUPER COOL TALKING IN ENGLISH!!
WHAT?
HARRO!! ME YOSHEEKO!!
THIS SAYAKA!!
SAYAHKA, OHKAAY?!
WHA?!
BOB
DOU ITASHI-MASHITE...
DON'T TOUCH MY MUS-TACHE!!!
バッ WHIP
OH, YOUTH...

Running

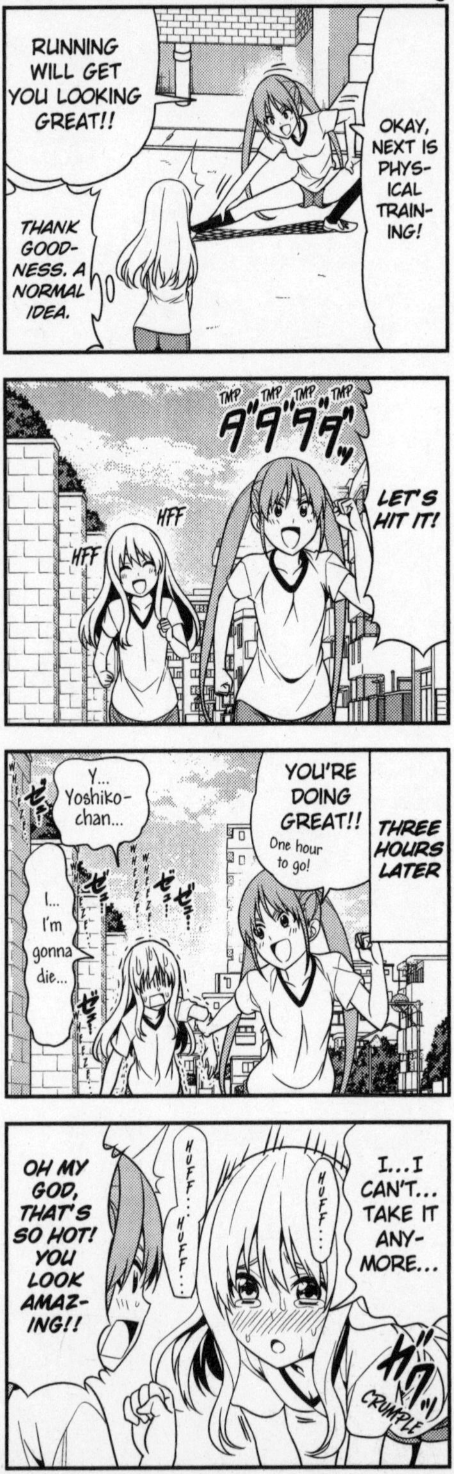
OKAY, NEXT IS PHYS-ICAL TRAIN-ING!
RUNNING WILL GET YOU LOOKING GREAT!!
THANK GOOD-NESS. A NORMAL IDEA.
LET'S HIT IT!
TMP TMP TMP TMP
ダダダダッ
HFF HFF
THREE HOURS LATER
YOU'RE DOING GREAT!!
One hour to go!
Y... Yoshiko-chan...
I... I'm gonna die...
WHEEZE
I...I CAN'T... TAKE IT ANY-MORE...
HUFF... HUFF...
HUFF...
OH MY GOD, THAT'S SO HOT! YOU LOOK AMAZ-ING!!
ガクッ CRUMPLE

Secret Weapon

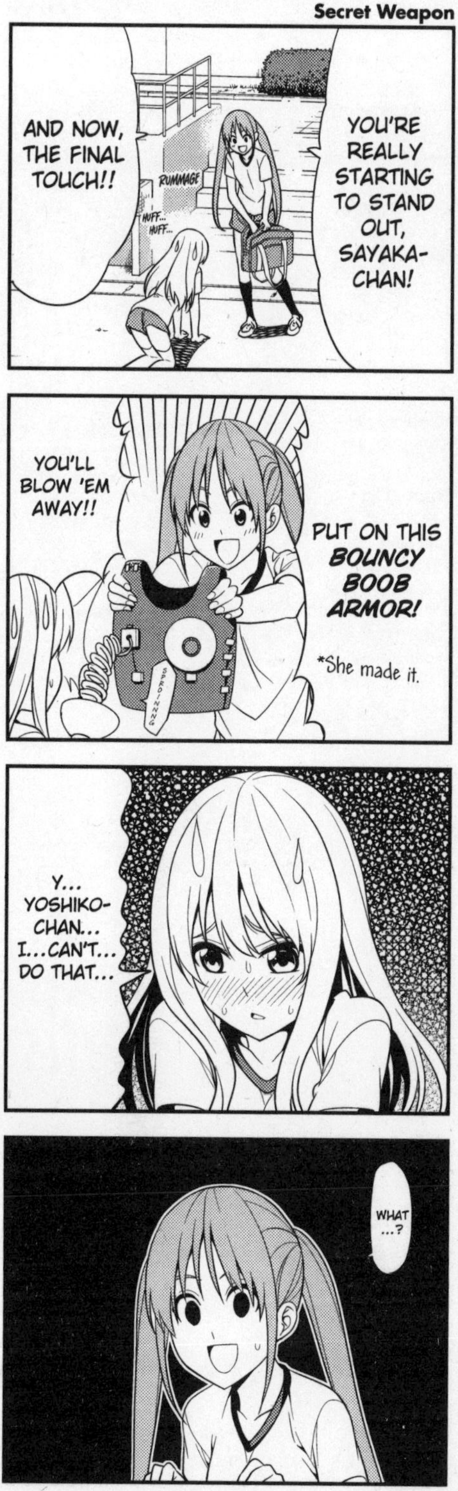
YOU'RE REALLY STARTING TO STAND OUT, SAYAKA-CHAN!
RUMMAGE
AND NOW, THE FINAL TOUCH!!
HUFF... HUFF...
PUT ON THIS BOUNCY BOOB ARMOR!
YOU'LL BLOW 'EM AWAY!!
SPROINNNG
*She made it.
Y... YOSHIKO-CHAN... I...CAN'T... DO THAT...
WHAT ...?

Friendship

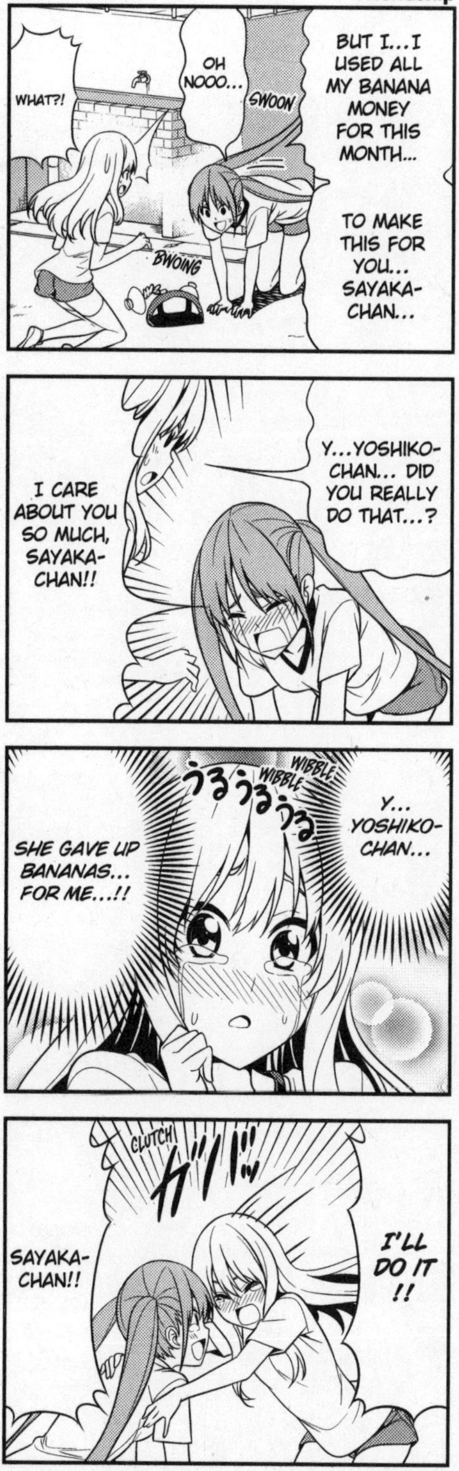
BUT I...I USED ALL MY BANANA MONEY FOR THIS MONTH...
TO MAKE THIS FOR YOU... SAYAKA-CHAN...
SWOON
OH NOOO...
WHAT?!
BWOING
Y...YOSHIKO-CHAN... DID YOU REALLY DO THAT...?
I CARE ABOUT YOU SO MUCH, SAYAKA-CHAN!!
Y... YOSHIKO-CHAN...
WIBBLE WIBBLE
うるうるうる
SHE GAVE UP BANANAS... FOR ME...!!
I'LL DO IT !!
ガバッ
CLUTCH
SAYAKA-CHAN!!

Public Launch

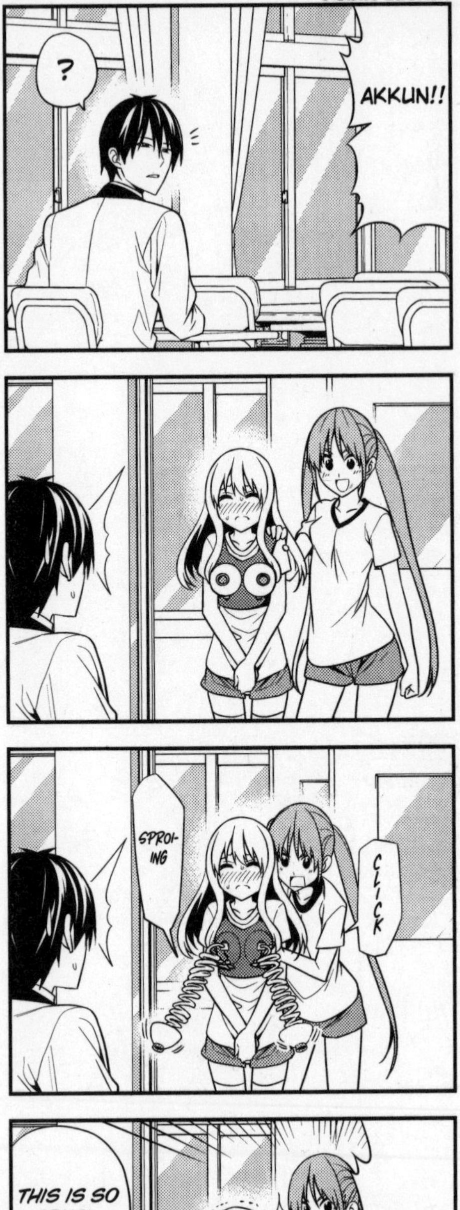
AKKUN!!
?
CLICK
SPROI-ING
HOW 'BOUT THAT?!
THIS IS SO CRUEL.
BWOIING

Crash

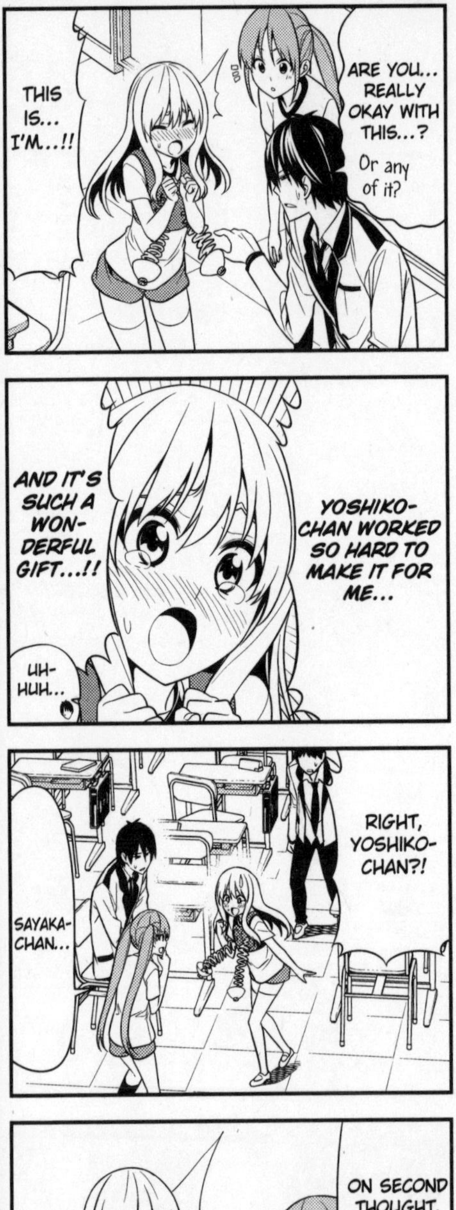
ARE YOU... REALLY OKAY WITH THIS...?
Or any of it?
THIS IS... I'M...!!
YOSHIKO-CHAN WORKED SO HARD TO MAKE IT FOR ME...
AND IT'S SUCH A WON-DERFUL GIFT...!!
UH-HUH...
RIGHT, YOSHIKO-CHAN?!
SAYAKA-CHAN...
ON SECOND THOUGHT, IT LOOKS A LITTLE WEIRD.
BWOIIING

You're a Good Person, Sayaka-chan

...WELL... IN ANY EVENT...

TH... THANK YOU...

YOU'RE DEFINITELY A GOOD PERSON...

Aho-Girl

\\'ahô͵gərl\\ *Japanese , noun.*
A clueless girl.

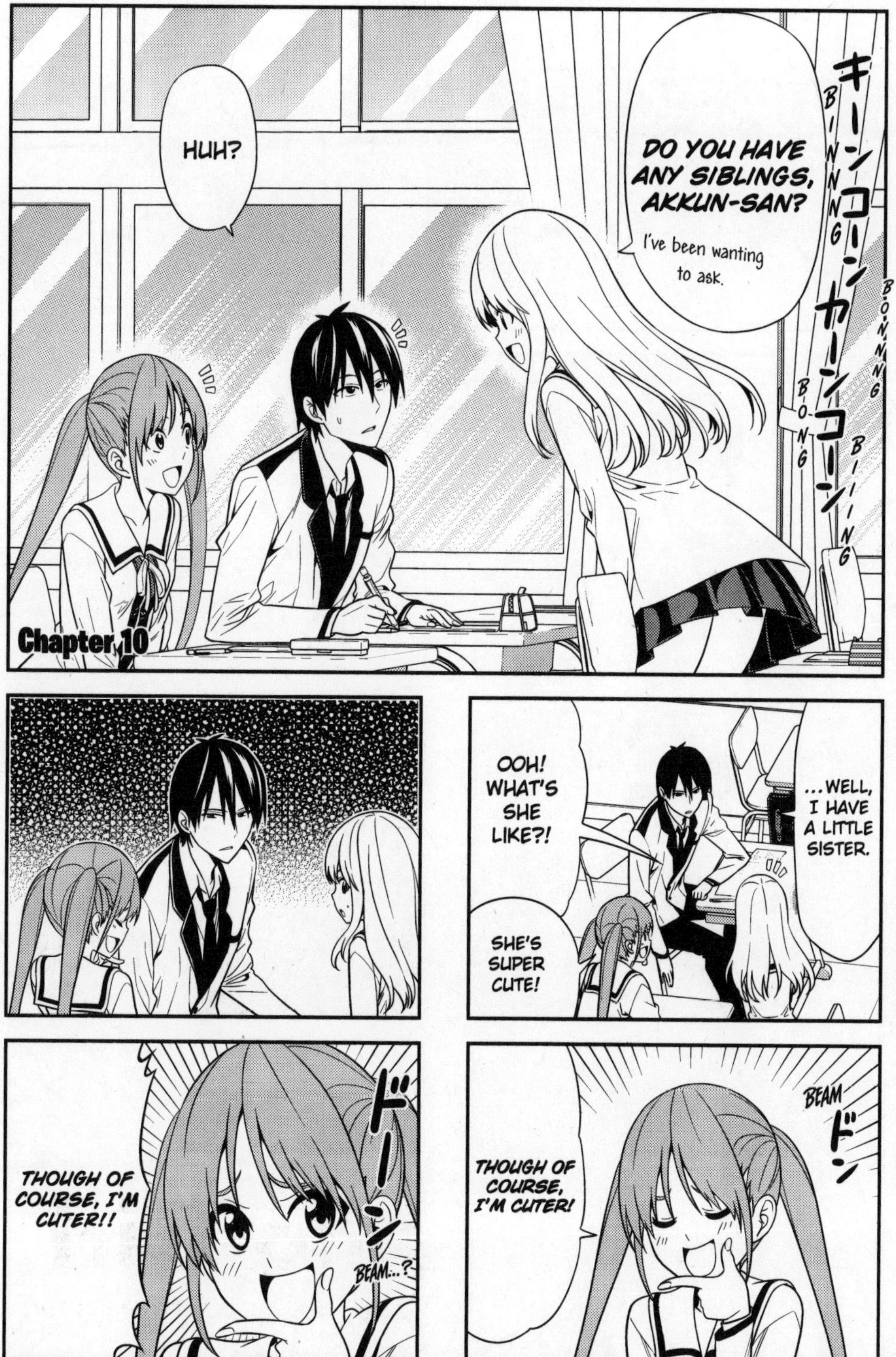
キーンコーンカーンコーン
BINNG
BONNNG
BONG
BIIING
DO YOU HAVE ANY SIBLINGS, AKKUN-SAN?
I've been wanting to ask.
HUH?
Chapter 10
...WELL, I HAVE A LITTLE SISTER.
OOH! WHAT'S SHE LIKE?!
SHE'S SUPER CUTE!
BEAM
ドーン
THOUGH OF COURSE, I'M CUTER!
ドーーン
BEAM...?
THOUGH OF COURSE, I'M CUTER!!

Puns

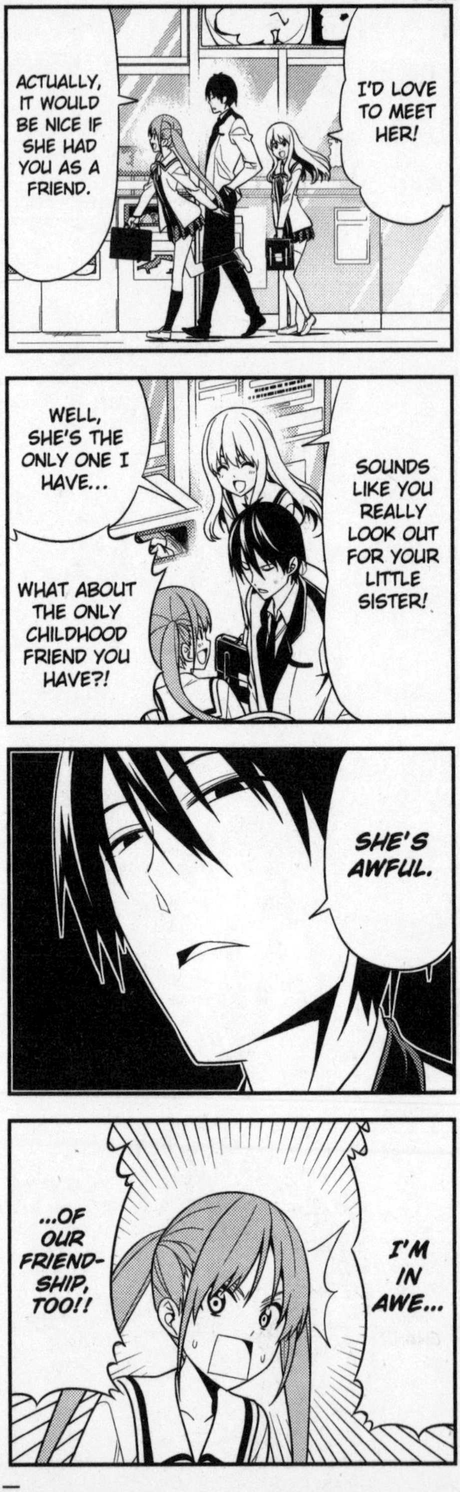
I'D LOVE TO MEET HER!
ACTUALLY, IT WOULD BE NICE IF SHE HAD YOU AS A FRIEND.
SOUNDS LIKE YOU REALLY LOOK OUT FOR YOUR LITTLE SISTER!
WELL, SHE'S THE ONLY ONE I HAVE...
WHAT ABOUT THE ONLY CHILDHOOD FRIEND YOU HAVE?!
SHE'S AWFUL.
I'M IN AWE...
...OF OUR FRIEND-SHIP, TOO!!

Ruri-chan Makes Her Debut!

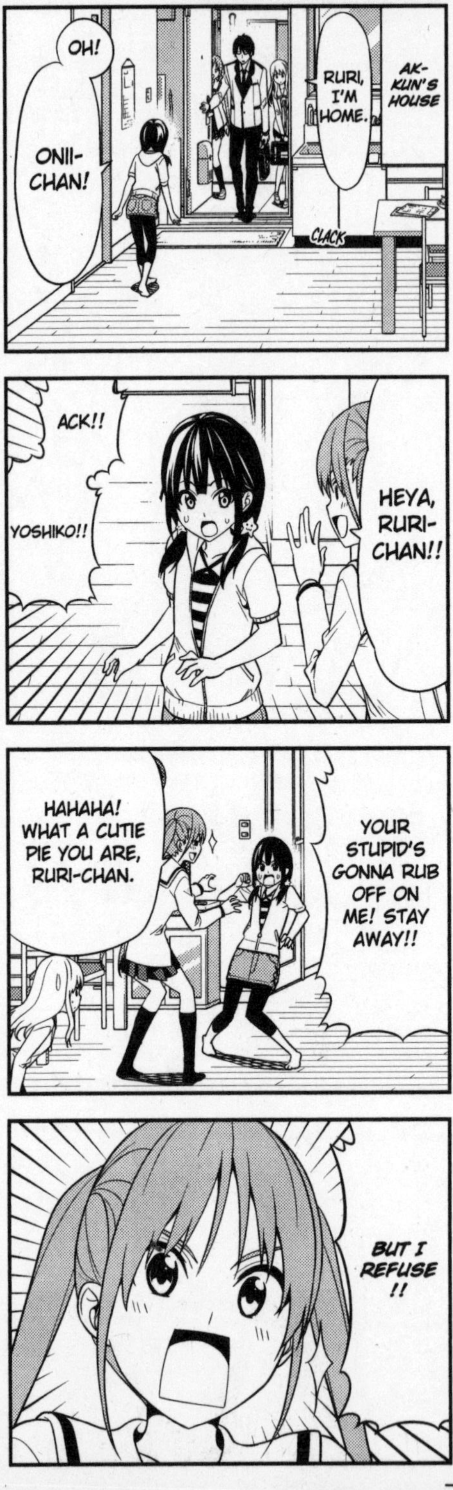
AK-KUN'S HOUSE
RURI, I'M HOME.
CLACK
OH!
ONII-CHAN!
HEYA, RURI-CHAN!!
ACK!!
YOSHIKO!!
YOUR STUPID'S GONNA RUB OFF ON ME! STAY AWAY!!
HAHAHA! WHAT A CUTIE PIE YOU ARE, RURI-CHAN.
BUT I REFUSE !!

The Kindness of an Older Brother

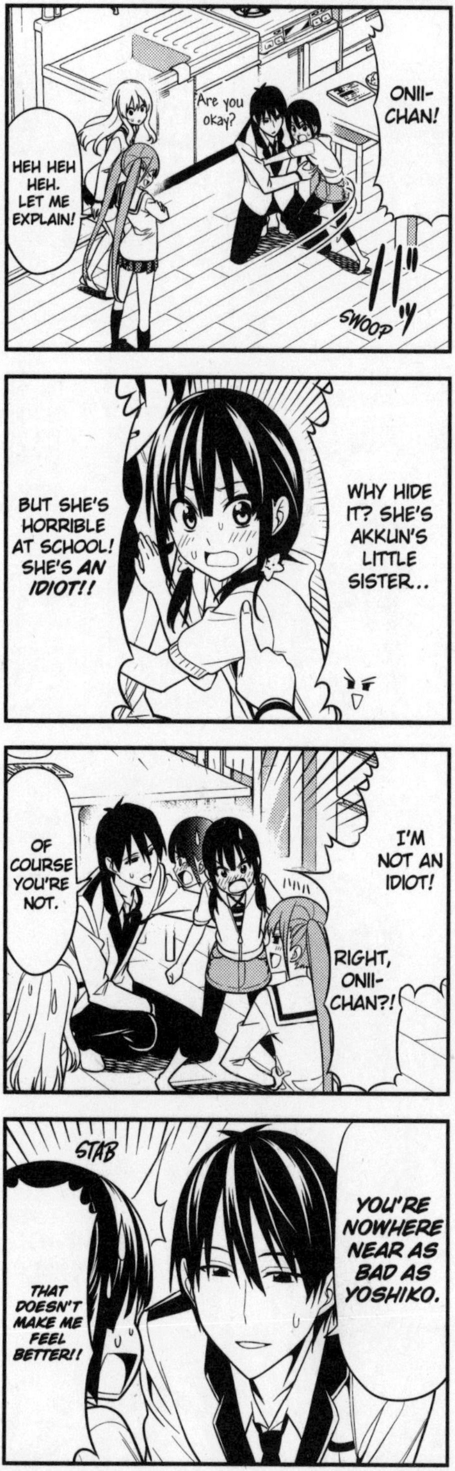
ONII-CHAN!
Are you okay?
HEH HEH HEH. LET ME EXPLAIN!
SWOOP
WHY HIDE IT? SHE'S AKKUN'S LITTLE SISTER...
BUT SHE'S HORRIBLE AT SCHOOL! SHE'S *AN IDIOT!!*
I'M NOT AN IDIOT!
RIGHT, ONII-CHAN?!
OF COURSE YOU'RE NOT.
STAB
YOU'RE NOWHERE NEAR AS BAD AS YOSHIKO.
THAT DOESN'T MAKE ME FEEL BETTER!!

He's Honest

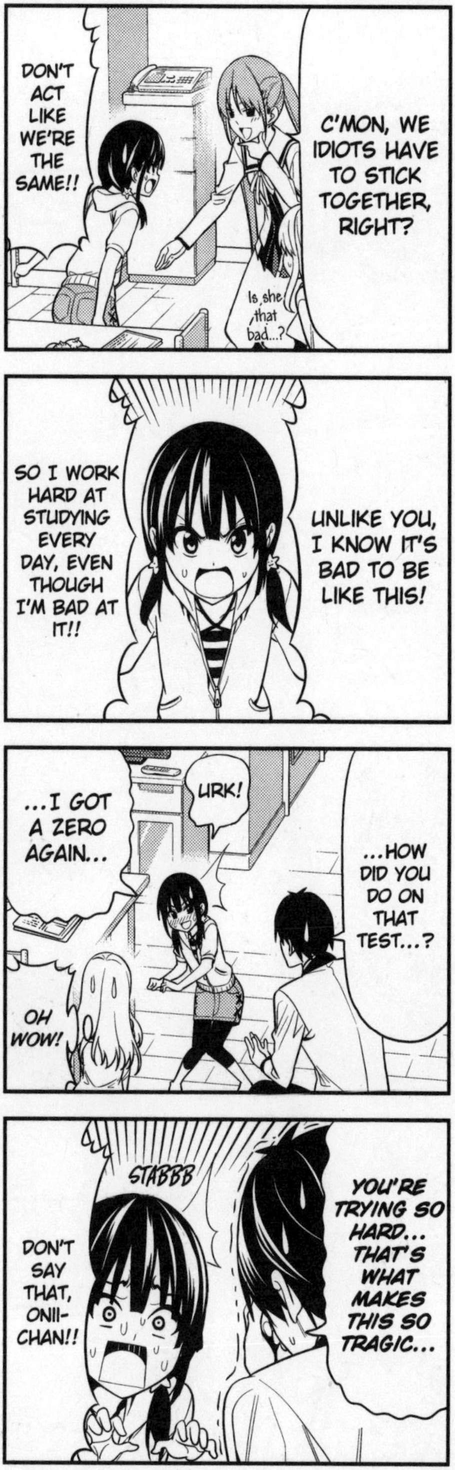
C'MON, WE IDIOTS HAVE TO STICK TOGETHER, RIGHT?
DON'T ACT LIKE WE'RE THE SAME!!
Is she that bad...?
UNLIKE YOU, I KNOW IT'S BAD TO BE LIKE THIS!
SO I WORK HARD AT STUDYING EVERY DAY, EVEN THOUGH I'M BAD AT IT!!
...HOW DID YOU DO ON THAT TEST...?
URK!
...I GOT A ZERO AGAIN...
OH WOW!
YOU'RE TRYING SO HARD... THAT'S WHAT MAKES THIS SO TRAGIC...
STABBB
DON'T SAY THAT, ONII-CHAN!!

The Argument Is Stupid, Too

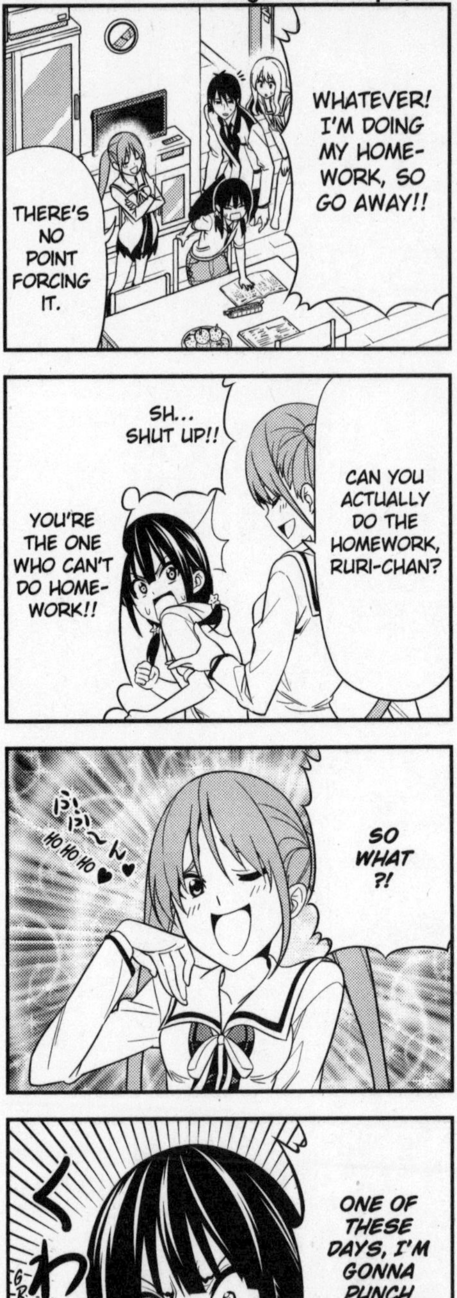
WHATEVER! I'M DOING MY HOME-WORK, SO GO AWAY!!
THERE'S NO POINT FORCING IT.
CAN YOU ACTUALLY DO THE HOMEWORK, RURI-CHAN?
SH... SHUT UP!!
YOU'RE THE ONE WHO CAN'T DO HOME-WORK!!
SO WHAT?!
ふふ～ん♥
HO HO HO♥
ONE OF THESE DAYS, I'M GONNA PUNCH YOU IN THE MOUTH!!
くわっ
GROWRR!

Psychological Attack

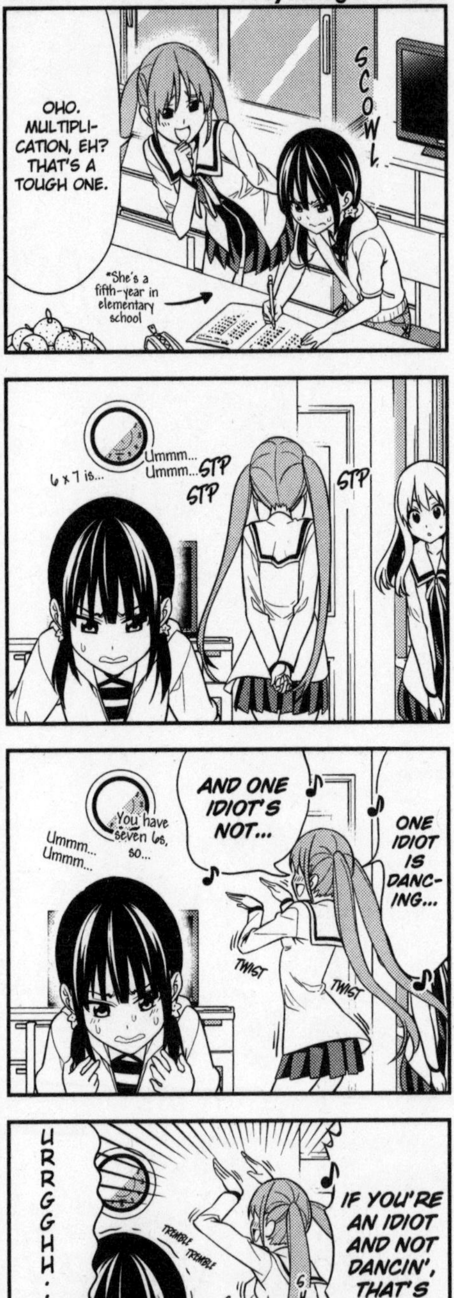
SCOWL
OHO. MULTIPLI-CATION, EH? THAT'S A TOUGH ONE.
*She's a fifth-year in elementary school
STP
STP STP
Ummm... Ummm...
6 x 7 is...
ONE IDIOT IS DANC-ING...
AND ONE IDIOT'S NOT...
You have seven 6s, so...
Ummm... Ummm...
TWIST
TWIST
IF YOU'RE AN IDIOT AND NOT DANCIN', THAT'S TOO!! BAD!!
SHAK
SHAK
TREMBLE TREMBLE
URRGGHH...

Now Recruiting

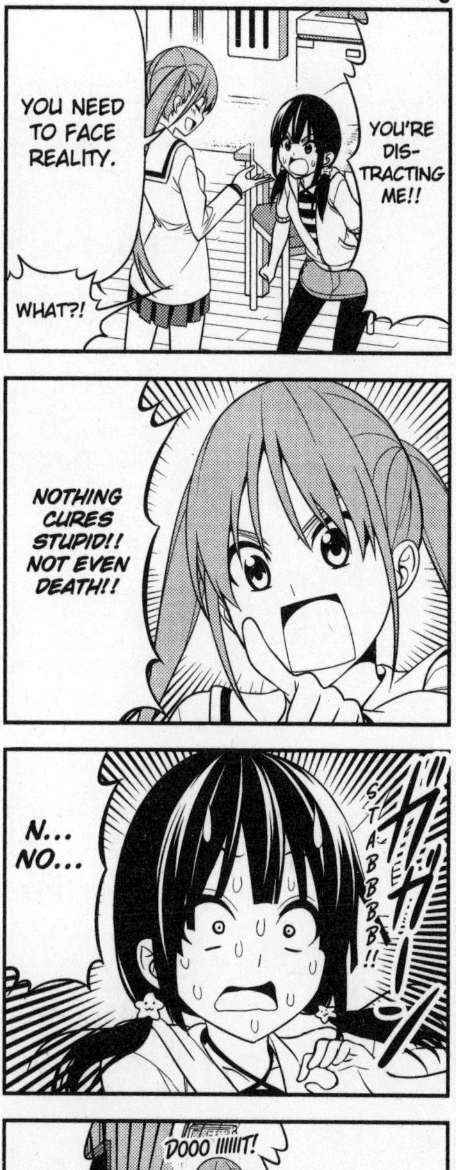
YOU'RE DIS-TRACTING ME!!
YOU NEED TO FACE REALITY.
WHAT?!
NOTHING CURES STUPID!! NOT EVEN DEATH!!
STABBBB!!
N... NO...
DOOO IIIIIIT!
JUST GIVE UP, AND ENJOY THE IDIOT LIFE WITH ME!!
N... NOOO!! STAY AWAY!!

Don't Be Nice!

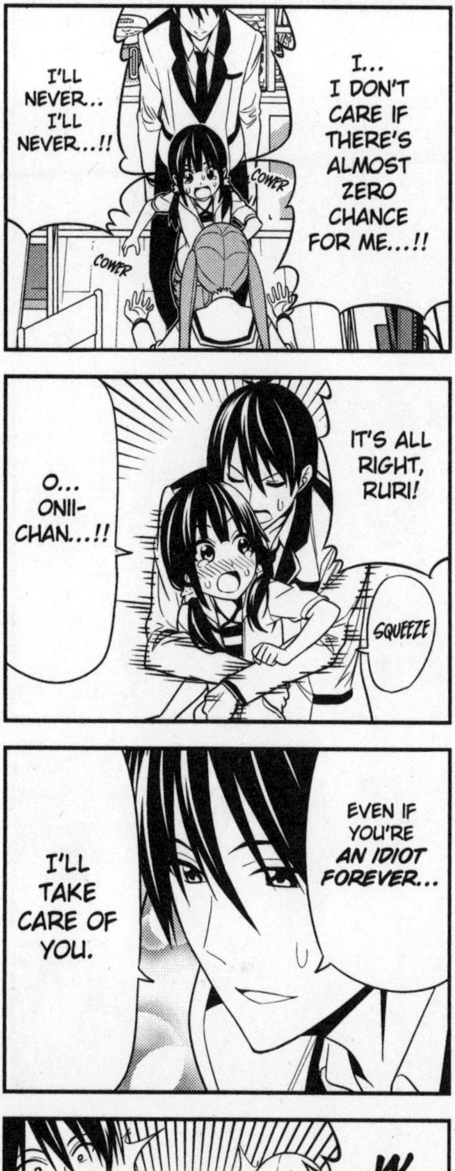
I... I DON'T CARE IF THERE'S ALMOST ZERO CHANCE FOR ME...!!
COWER
I'LL NEVER... I'LL NEVER...!!
COWER
IT'S ALL RIGHT, RURI!
SQUEEZE
O... ONII-CHAN...!!
EVEN IF YOU'RE AN IDIOT FOREVER...
I'LL TAKE CARE OF YOU.
WAAAAAH!!

Get Outta My Way!

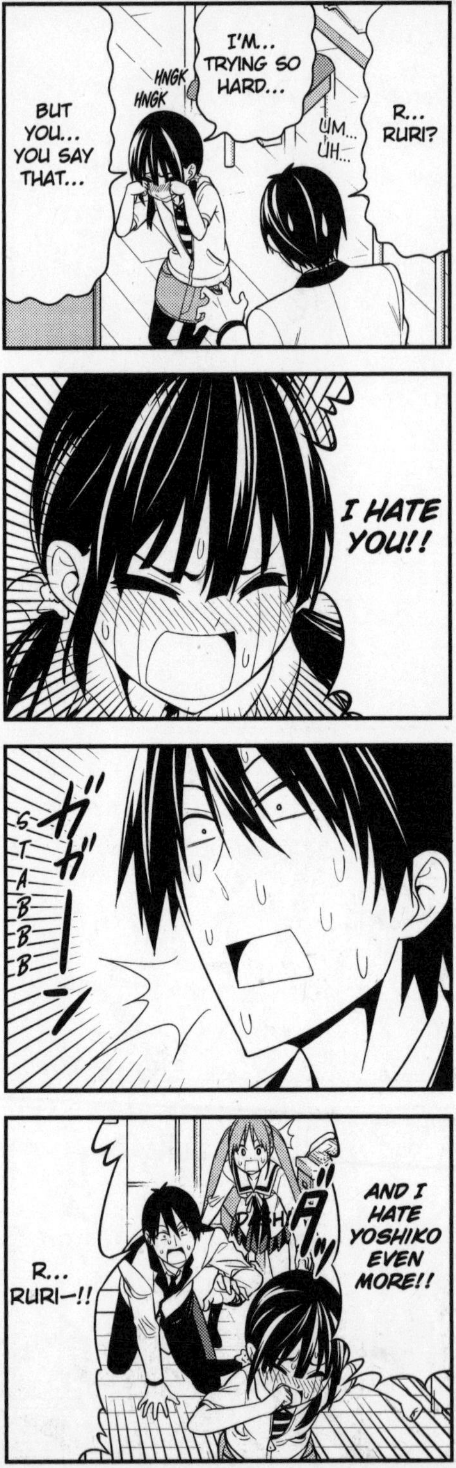
R... RURI?
UM... UH...
I'M... TRYING SO HARD...
HNGK HNGK
BUT YOU... YOU SAY THAT...
I HATE YOU!!
STABBB
AND I HATE YOSHIKO EVEN MORE!!
DASH
R... RURI—!!

Someone Who Understands

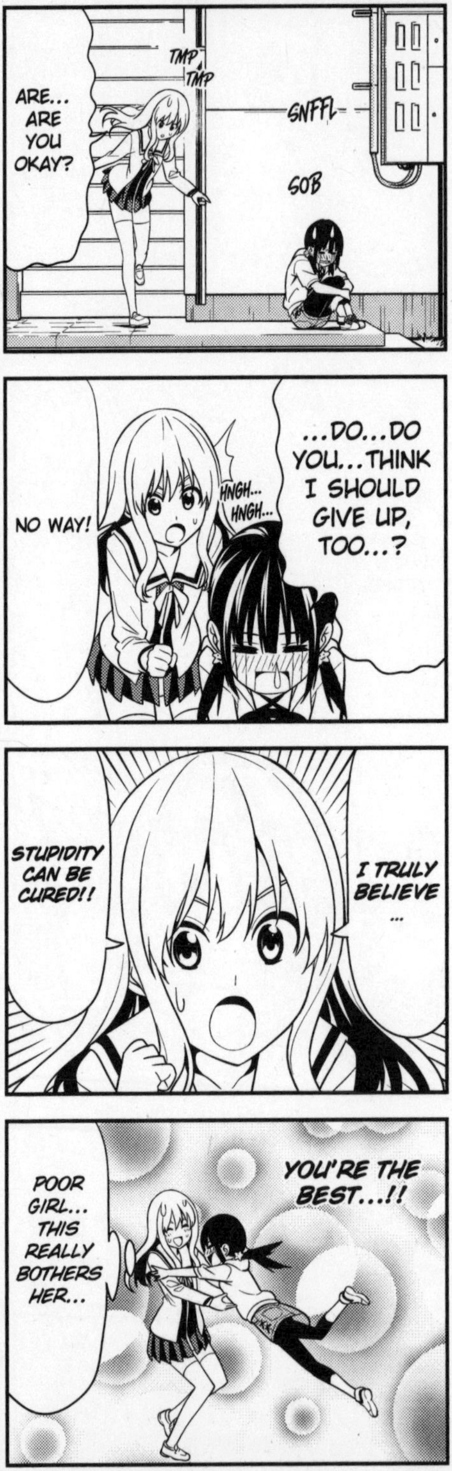
SNFFL
SOB
TMP TMP
ARE... ARE YOU OKAY?
...DO...DO YOU...THINK I SHOULD GIVE UP, TOO...?
HNGH... HNGH...
NO WAY!
I TRULY BELIEVE ...
STUPIDITY CAN BE CURED!!
YOU'RE THE BEST...!!
POOR GIRL... THIS REALLY BOTHERS HER...

No

R...
Ruri...
SWOOP
YOU HAVE ME, AKKUN!!
DUCK

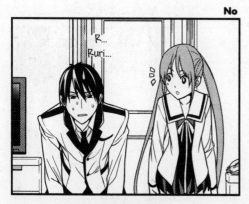

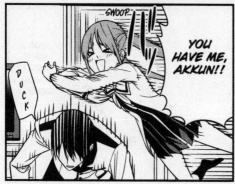

Name **Ruri Akutsu**

Sex	♀
Height	**138 cm / 4'6"**
Weight	**31 kg / 68 lbs**
Blood type	**A**
Birthday	**09/03**

Memo Her brother's outstanding, but she's a little unfortunate.

Perhaps the day will come when all her hard work pays off… She hates Yoshiko.

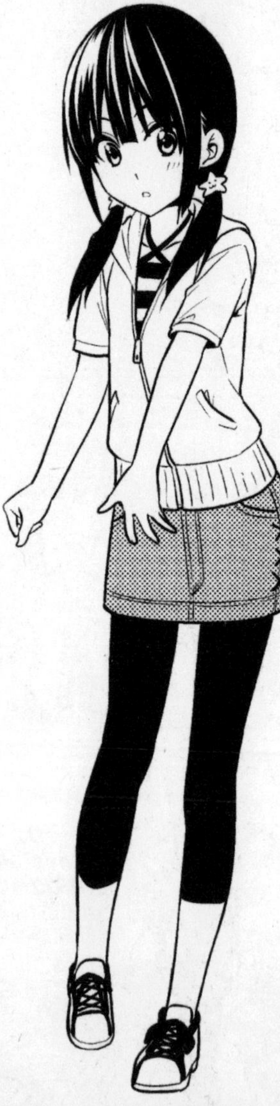

☐ RURI AKUTSU

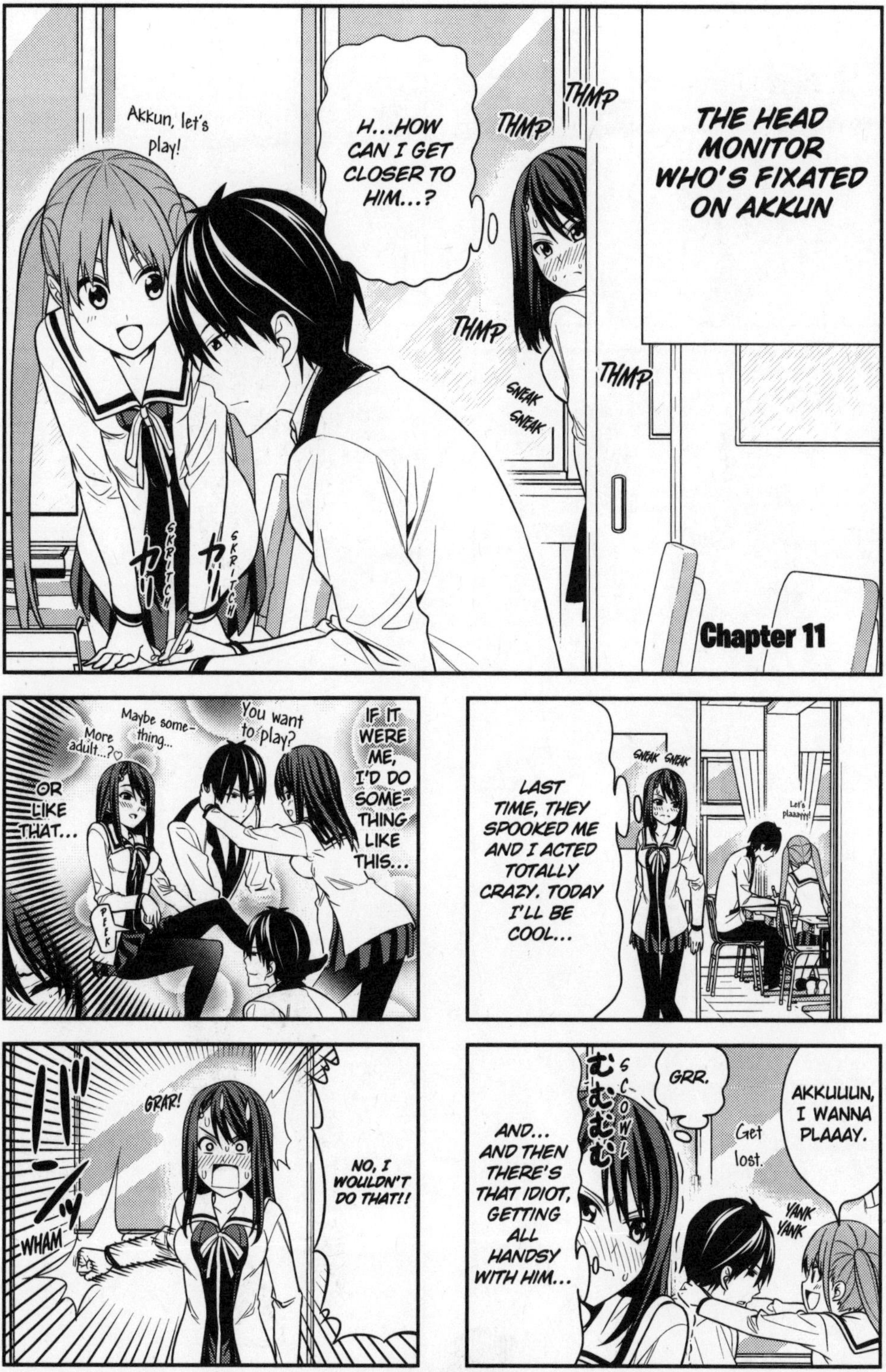
THE HEAD MONITOR WHO'S FIXATED ON AKKUN
Chapter 11
THMP
THMP
H...HOW CAN I GET CLOSER TO HIM...?
THMP
THMP
SNEAK SNEAK
Akkun, let's play!
SKRITCH
SKRITCH
LAST TIME, THEY SPOOKED ME AND I ACTED TOTALLY CRAZY. TODAY I'LL BE COOL...
SNEAK SNEAK
Let's plaaayyy!
IF IT WERE ME, I'D DO SOME-THING LIKE THIS...
You want to play?
Maybe some-thing...
More adult...?♡
OR LIKE THAT...
PEEK
AKKUUUN, I WANNA PLAAAY.
GRR.
むむむ
SCOWL
Get lost.
AND... AND THEN THERE'S THAT IDIOT, GETTING ALL HANDSY WITH HIM...
YANK YANK
NO, I WOULDN'T DO THAT!!
GRAR!
WHAM

The Head Monitor's Suffering

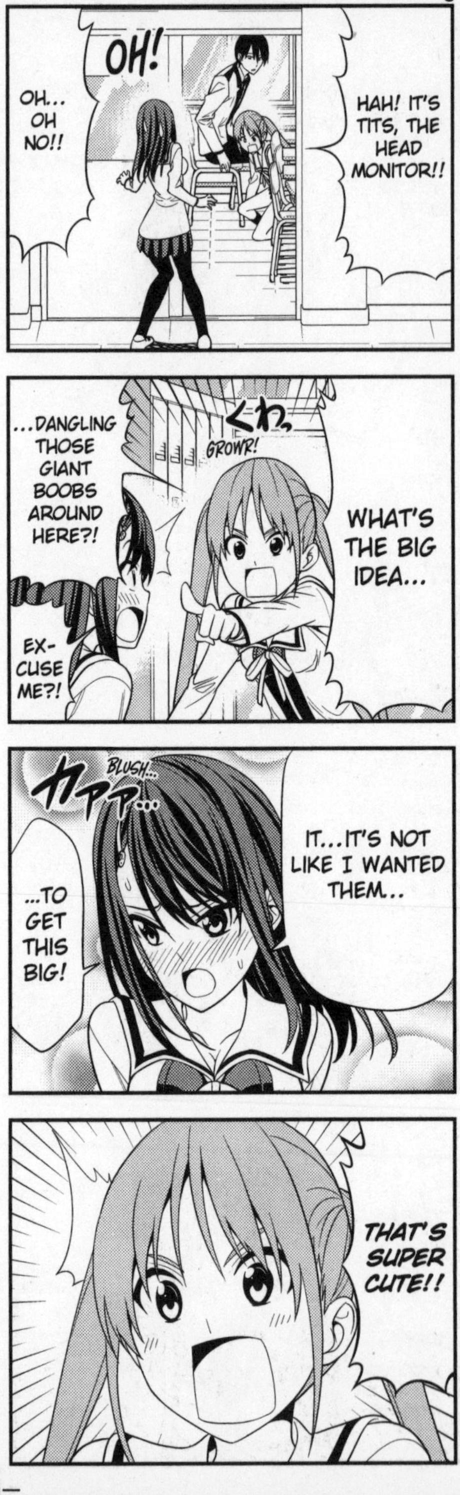
HAH! IT'S TITS, THE HEAD MONITOR!!
OH!
OH... OH NO!!
WHAT'S THE BIG IDEA...
くわっ
GROWR!
...DANGLING THOSE GIANT BOOBS AROUND HERE?!
EX-CUSE ME?!
IT...IT'S NOT LIKE I WANTED THEM...
カァァ...
BLUSH...
...TO GET THIS BIG!
THAT'S SUPER CUTE!!

Misunderstanding

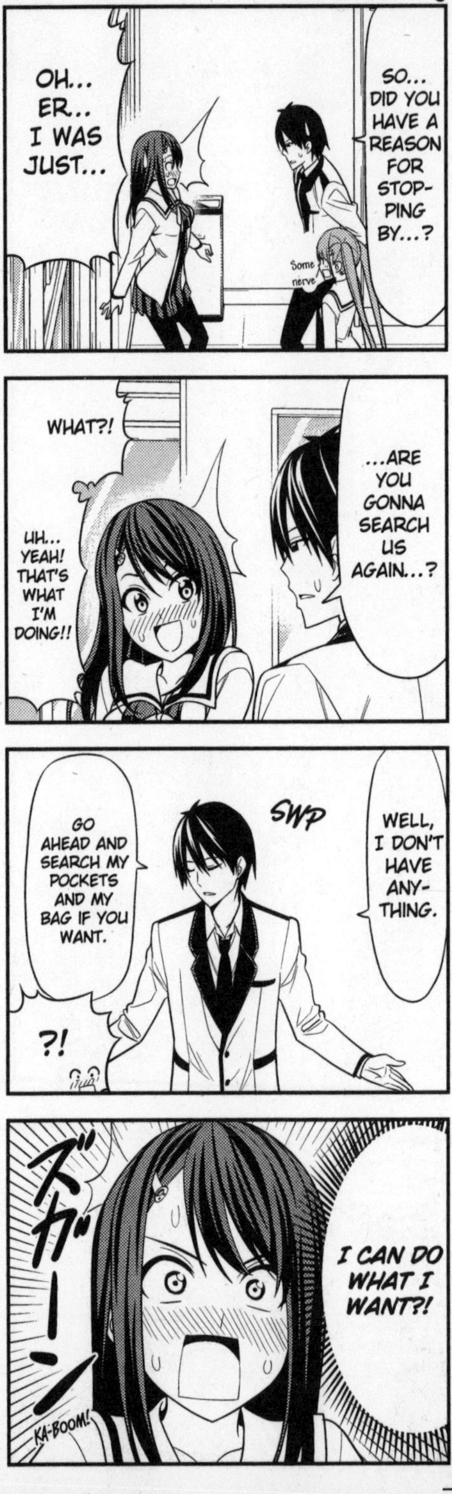
SO... DID YOU HAVE A REASON FOR STOP-PING BY...?
OH... ER... I WAS JUST...
Some nerve
...ARE YOU GONNA SEARCH US AGAIN...?
WHAT?!
UH... YEAH! THAT'S WHAT I'M DOING!!
WELL, I DON'T HAVE ANY-THING.
SWP
GO AHEAD AND SEARCH MY POCKETS AND MY BAG IF YOU WANT.
?!
I CAN DO WHAT I WANT?!
ズガーン
KA-BOOM!

Abuse of Power

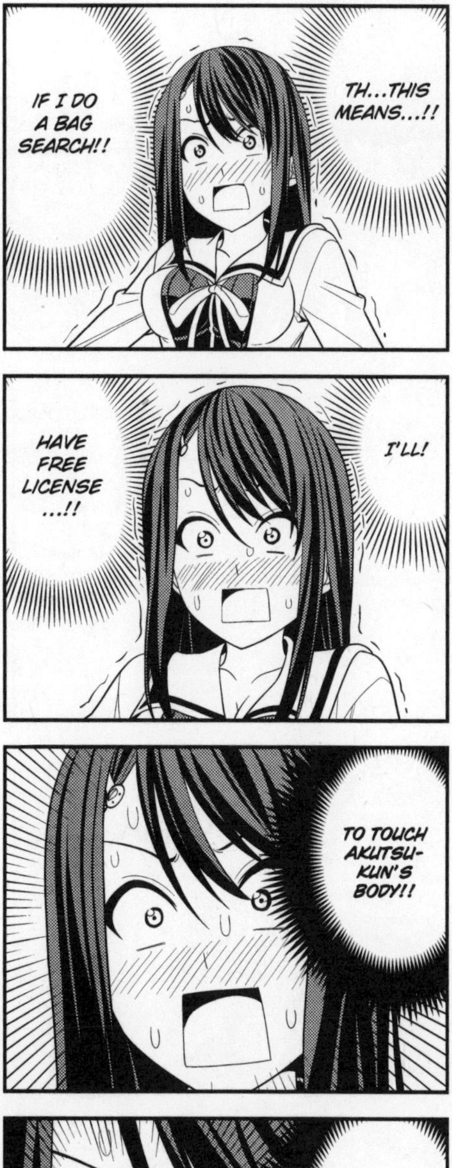
TH...THIS MEANS...!!
IF I DO A BAG SEARCH!!
I'LL!
HAVE FREE LICENSE ...!!
TO TOUCH AKUTSU-KUN'S BODY!!
LONG LIVE THE HEAD MONITOR!
くわっ
GLINT

Betrayed

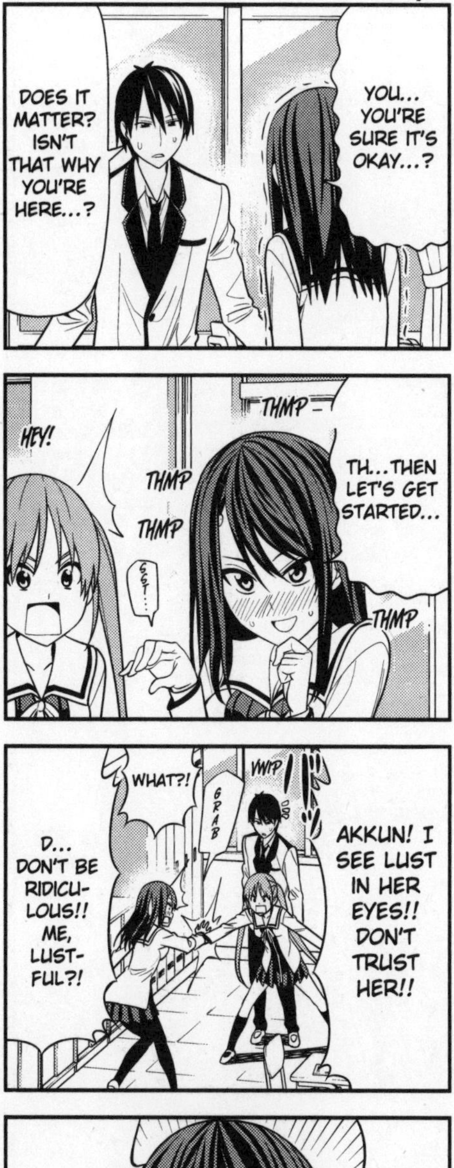
YOU... YOU'RE SURE IT'S OKAY...?
DOES IT MATTER? ISN'T THAT WHY YOU'RE HERE...?
THMP
TH...THEN LET'S GET STARTED...
HEY!
THMP
THMP
SST...
THMP
AKKUN! I SEE LUST IN HER EYES!! DON'T TRUST HER!!
VWIP
GRAB
WHAT?!
D... DON'T BE RIDICU-LOUS!! ME, LUST-FUL?!
I'M—
THE HEAD MONITOR!!
UMMM
YOU KNOW YOUR NOSE IS BLEED-ING...

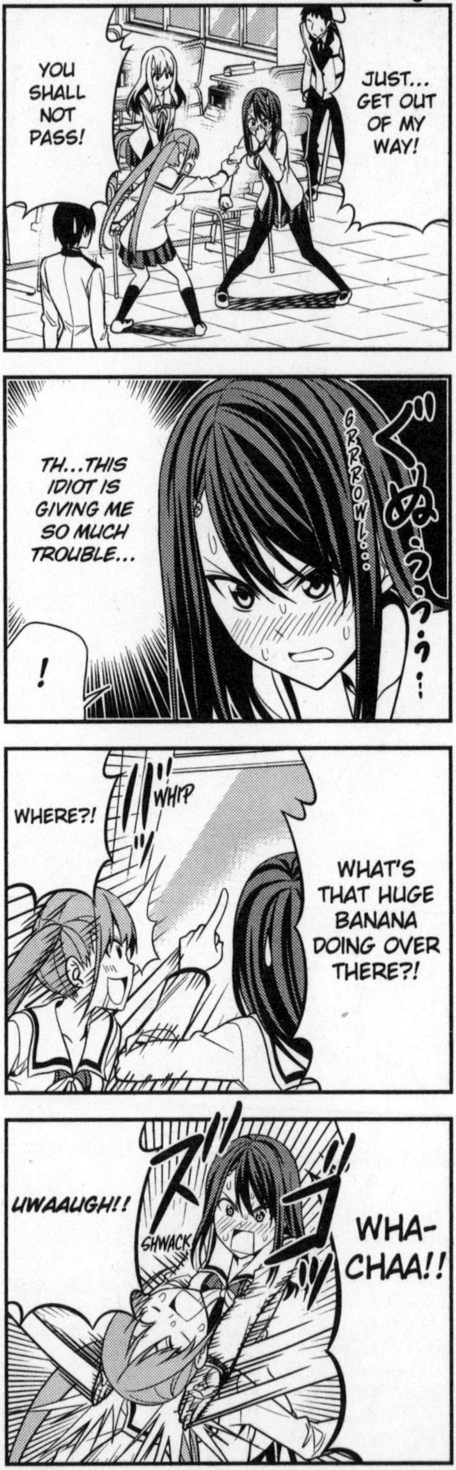
JUST... GET OUT OF MY WAY!
YOU SHALL NOT PASS!
GRRROWL...
TH...THIS IDIOT IS GIVING ME SO MUCH TROUBLE...
!
WHAT'S THAT HUGE BANANA DOING OVER THERE?!
WHIP
WHERE?!
WHA-CHAA!!
SHWACK
UWAAUGH!!

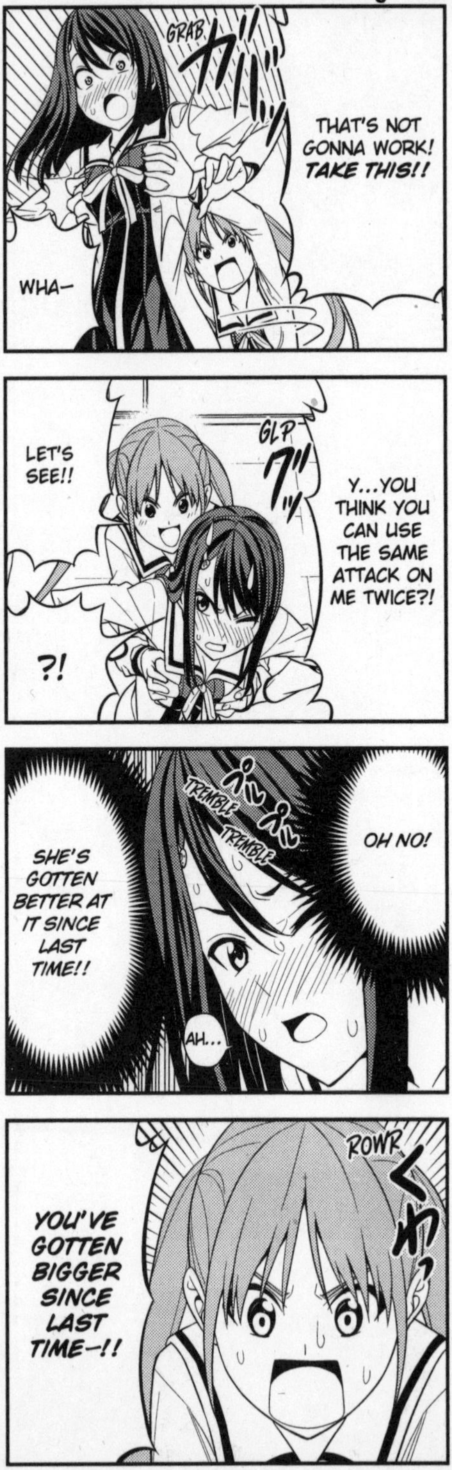
THAT'S NOT GONNA WORK! TAKE THIS!!
GRAB
WHA-
Y...YOU THINK YOU CAN USE THE SAME ATTACK ON ME TWICE?!
GLP
LET'S SEE!!
?!
OH NO!
TREMBLE
TREMBLE
SHE'S GOTTEN BETTER AT IT SINCE LAST TIME!!
AH...
ROWR
YOU'VE GOTTEN BIGGER SINCE LAST TIME-!!

Something about Her—She Refuses to Lose

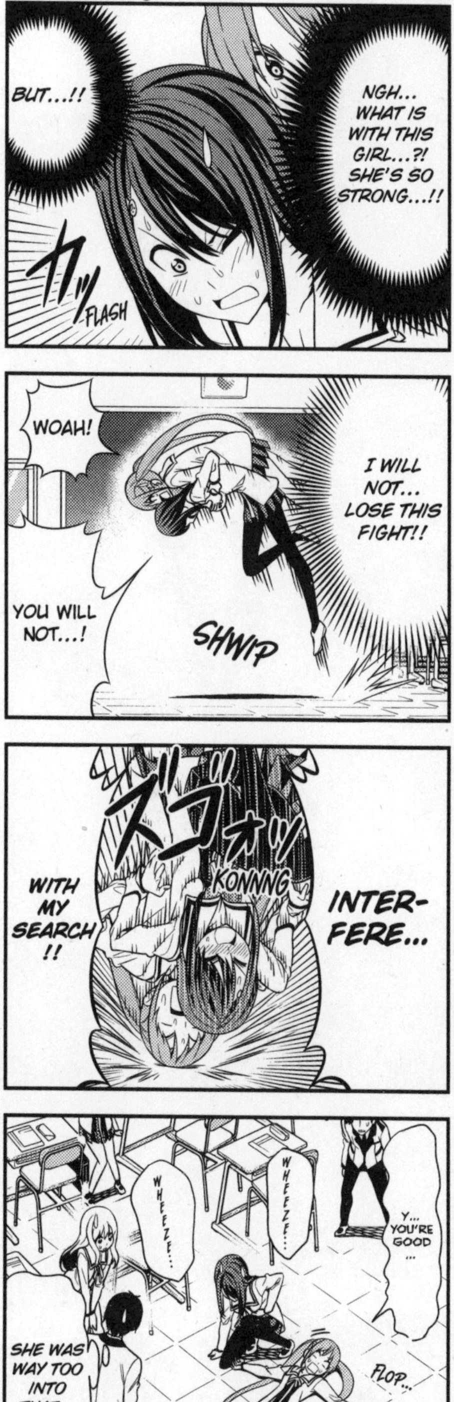
NGH... WHAT IS WITH THIS GIRL...?! SHE'S SO STRONG...!!
BUT...!!
FLASH
I WILL NOT... LOSE THIS FIGHT!!
WOAH!
YOU WILL NOT...!
SHWIP
INTER-FERE...
KONNNG
WITH MY SEARCH!!
Y... YOU'RE GOOD ...
WHEEZE...
WHEEZE...
FLOP...
SHE WAS WAY TOO INTO THAT...

The Obvious Result

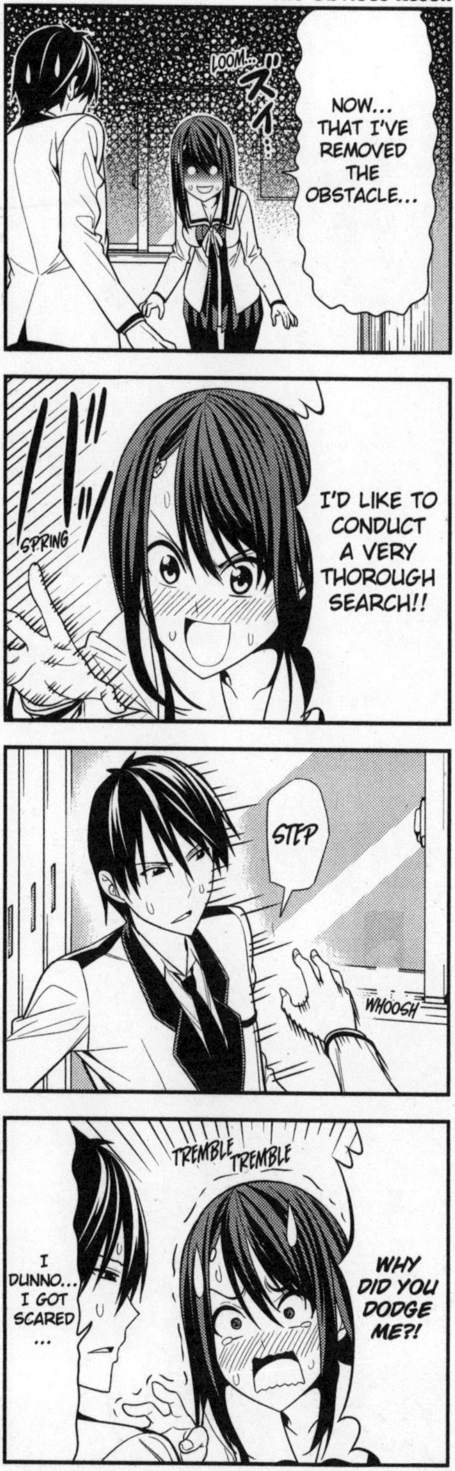
NOW... THAT I'VE REMOVED THE OBSTACLE...
LOOM...
I'D LIKE TO CONDUCT A VERY THOROUGH SEARCH!!
SPRING
STEP
WHOOSH
TREMBLE TREMBLE
WHY DID YOU DODGE ME?!
I DUNNO... I GOT SCARED ...

Just Desserts

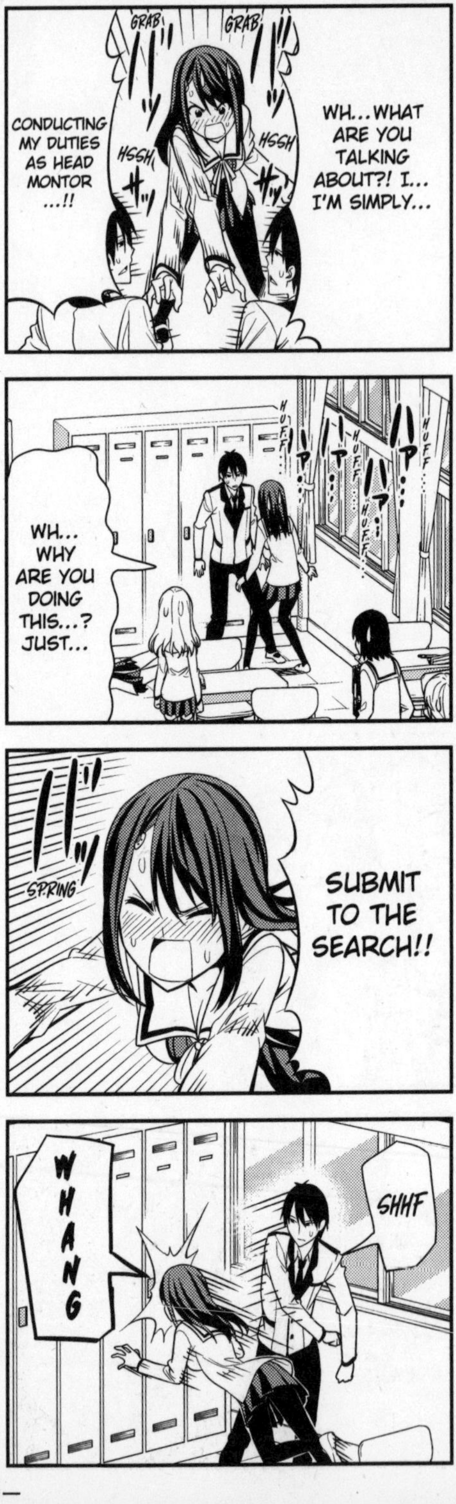
GRAB
GRAB
WH...WHAT ARE YOU TALKING ABOUT?! I... I'M SIMPLY...
HSSH
HSSH
CONDUCTING MY DUTIES AS HEAD MONTOR ...!!
HUFF...
HUFF...
HUFF...
HUFF...
WH... WHY ARE YOU DOING THIS...? JUST...
SUBMIT TO THE SEARCH!!
SPRING
SHHF
WHANG

Satisfied

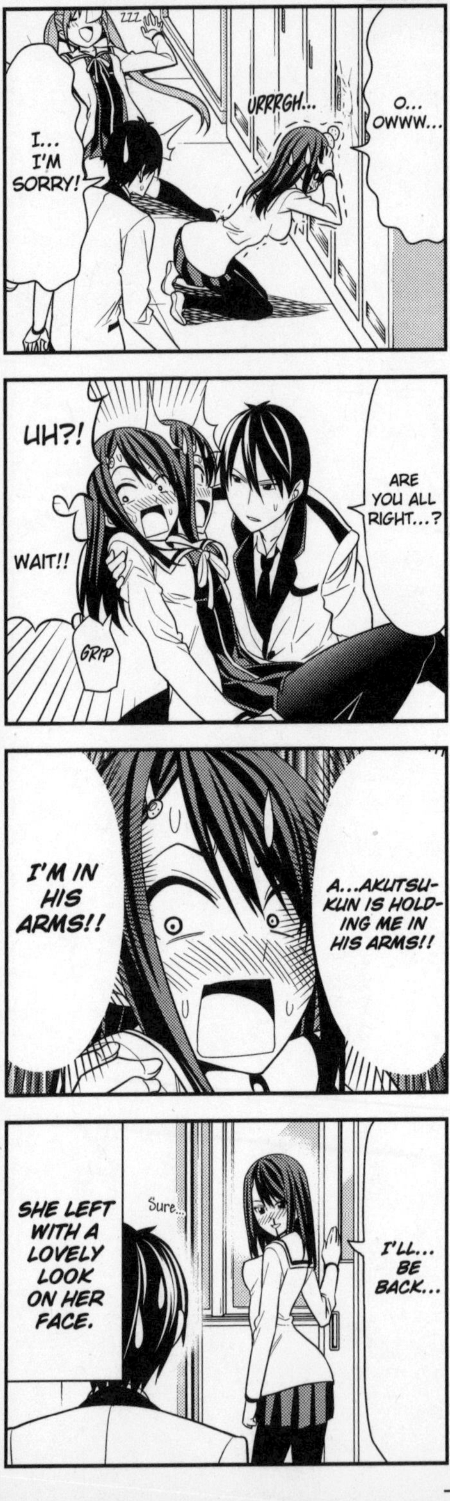
O... OWWW...
URRRGH...
ZZZ
I... I'M SORRY!
ARE YOU ALL RIGHT...?
UH?!
WAIT!!
GRIP
A...AKUTSU-KUN IS HOLDING ME IN HIS ARMS!!
I'M IN HIS ARMS!!
I'LL... BE BACK...
Sure...
SHE LEFT WITH A LOVELY LOOK ON HER FACE.

Not Sure It's So Obvious

THMP
THMP
THMP

...I THINK
THE DISTANCE
BETWEEN US
IS CLOSING
NICELY...

IT WASN'T
UNTIL SOME
TIME LATER
THAT SHE
REALIZED
SHE HASN'T
EVEN TOLD
HIM HER
NAME...

(Sturm und)

Aho-Girl

\ˈahô͵gərl\ *Japanese , noun.*
A clueless girl.

YOSHIKO... TODAY I'M FORCING YOU TO STUDY, UNDERSTAND?

!

LET'S PLAY HIDE AND SEEK!

OKAY!

CHATTER

CHATTER

CHATTER

KOIZUMI PAR

Chapter 12

I'M YOSHIKO!!

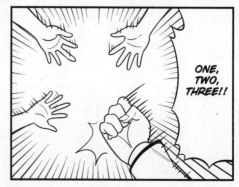

ONE, TWO, THREE!!

THAT'S NOT AN ANSWER!!

WHO ARE YOU?!

I guess I'm it...

A Pointless Skill

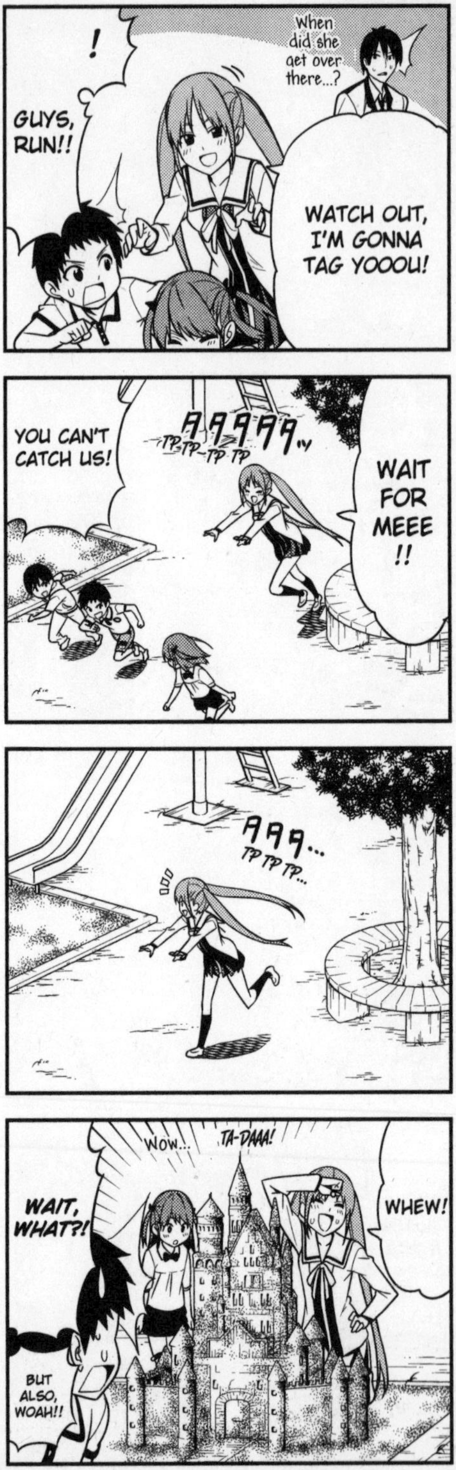

When did she get over there...?
WATCH OUT, I'M GONNA TAG YOOOU!
!
GUYS, RUN!!
WAIT FOR MEEE!!
TP TP TP TP
YOU CAN'T CATCH US!
TP TP TP...
WHEW!
TA-DAAA!
Wow...
WAIT, WHAT?!
BUT ALSO, WOAH!!

The Girl Who Brings the Storm

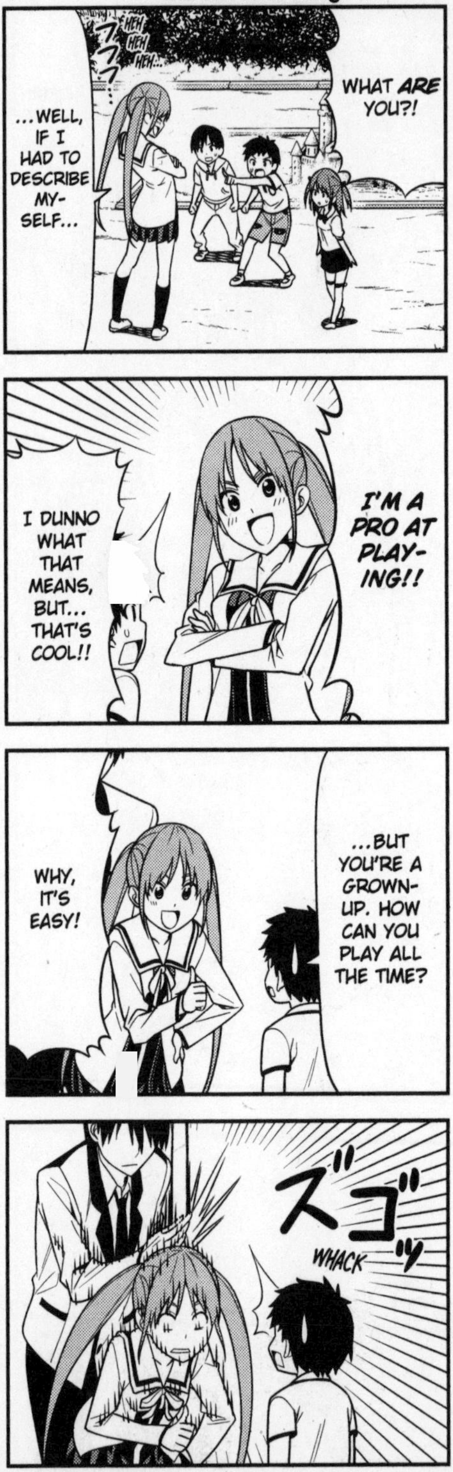

WHAT *ARE* YOU?!
HEH HEH HEH...
...WELL, IF I HAD TO DESCRIBE MY-SELF...
I'M A PRO AT PLAYING!!
I DUNNO WHAT THAT MEANS, BUT... THAT'S COOL!!
...BUT YOU'RE A GROWN-UP. HOW CAN YOU PLAY ALL THE TIME?
WHY, IT'S EASY!
WHACK

Use What You Have

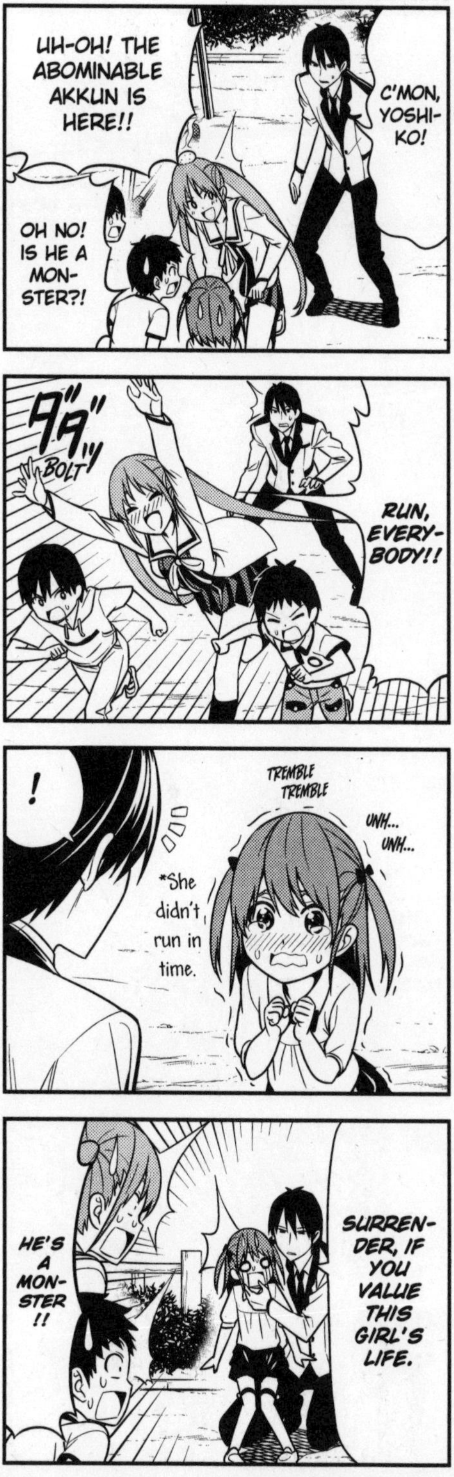
C'MON, YOSHIKO!
UH-OH! THE ABOMINABLE AKKUN IS HERE!!
OH NO! IS HE A MONSTER?!
RUN, EVERYBODY!!
BOLT
UNH... UNH...
TREMBLE TREMBLE
*She didn't run in time.
!
SURRENDER, IF YOU VALUE THIS GIRL'S LIFE.
HE'S A MONSTER!!

Why Are You Doing That?

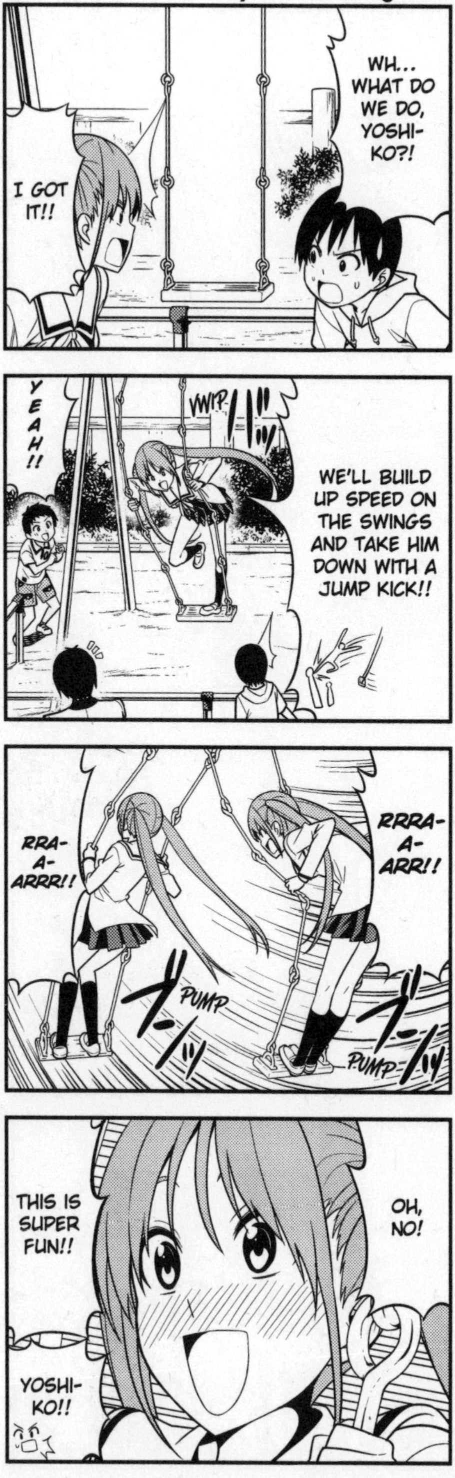
WH... WHAT DO WE DO, YOSHIKO?!
I GOT IT!!
WE'LL BUILD UP SPEED ON THE SWINGS AND TAKE HIM DOWN WITH A JUMP KICK!!
VWIP
YEAH!!
RRRA-A-ARR!!
RRA-A-ARRR!!
PUMP
PUMP
OH, NO!
THIS IS SUPER FUN!!
YOSHIKO!!

For All to See

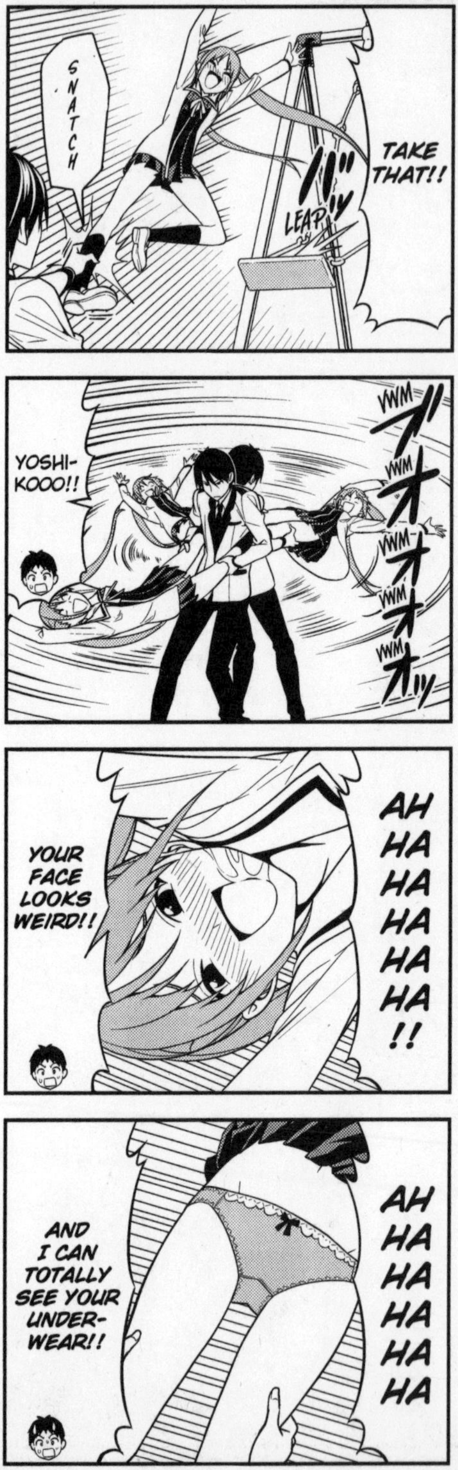
TAKE THAT!!
LEAP
SNATCH
YOSHI-KOOO!!
VWM VWM VWM VWM VWM
AH HA HA HA HA HA HA!!
YOUR FACE LOOKS WEIRD!!
AH HA HA HA HA HA HA
AND I CAN TOTALLY SEE YOUR UNDER-WEAR!!

Wide Open

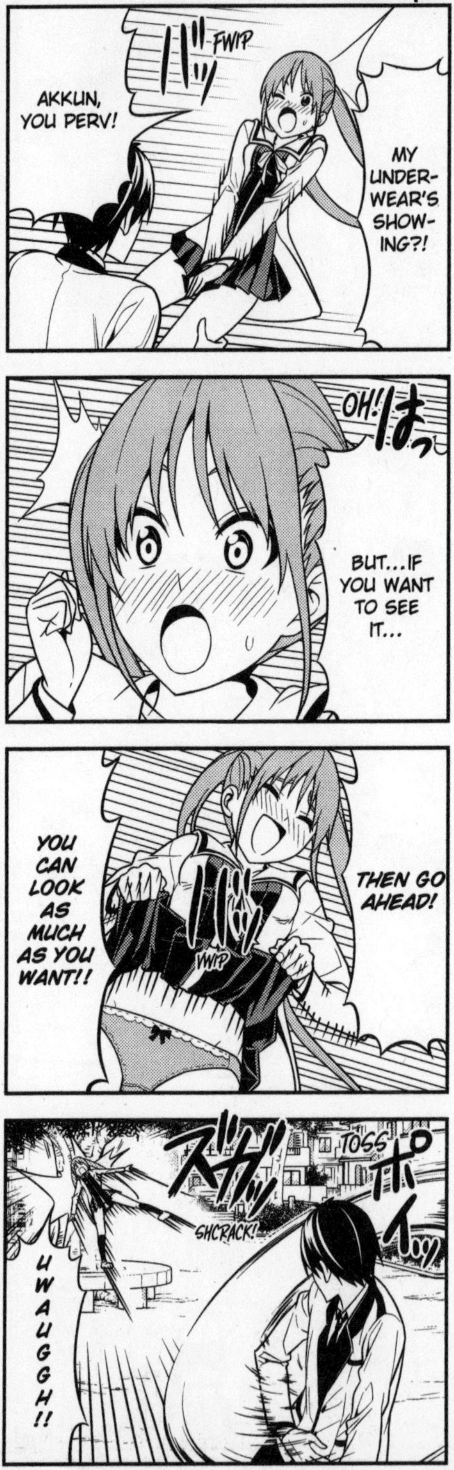
MY UNDER-WEAR'S SHOWING?!
FWIP
AKKUN, YOU PERV!
OH!
BUT...IF YOU WANT TO SEE IT...
THEN GO AHEAD!
VWIP
YOU CAN LOOK AS MUCH AS YOU WANT!!
TOSS
SHCRACK!
UWAUGGH!!

Friendship

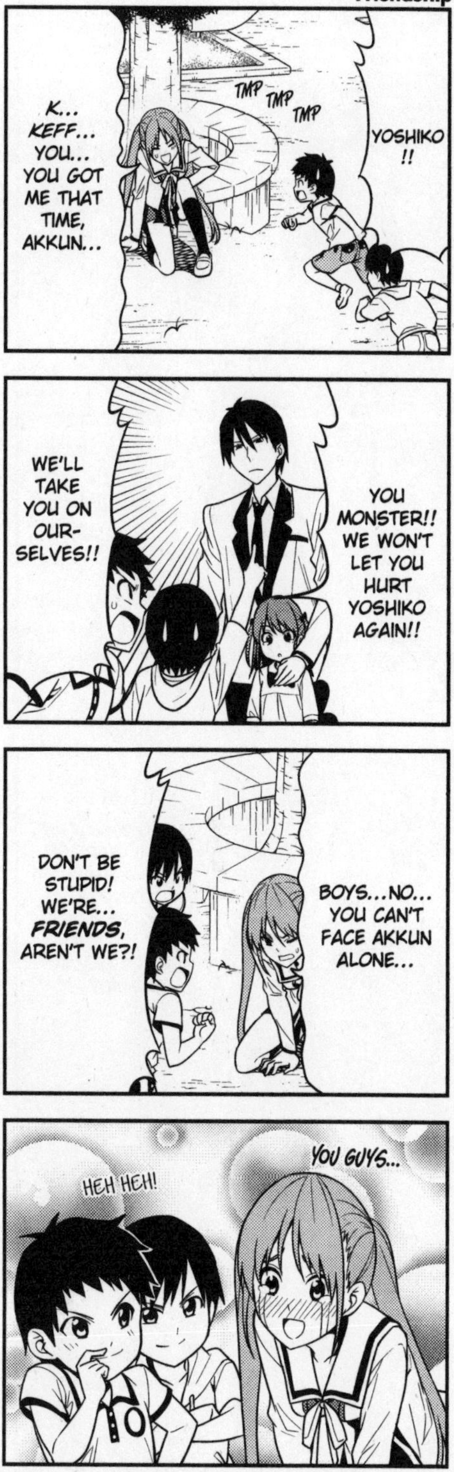
YOSHIKO !!
TMP TMP TMP
K... KEFF... YOU... YOU GOT ME THAT TIME, AKKUN...
YOU MONSTER!! WE WON'T LET YOU HURT YOSHIKO AGAIN!!
WE'LL TAKE YOU ON OUR-SELVES!!
BOYS...NO... YOU CAN'T FACE AKKUN ALONE...
DON'T BE STUPID! WE'RE... FRIENDS, AREN'T WE?!
YOU GUYS...
HEH HEH!

Truth

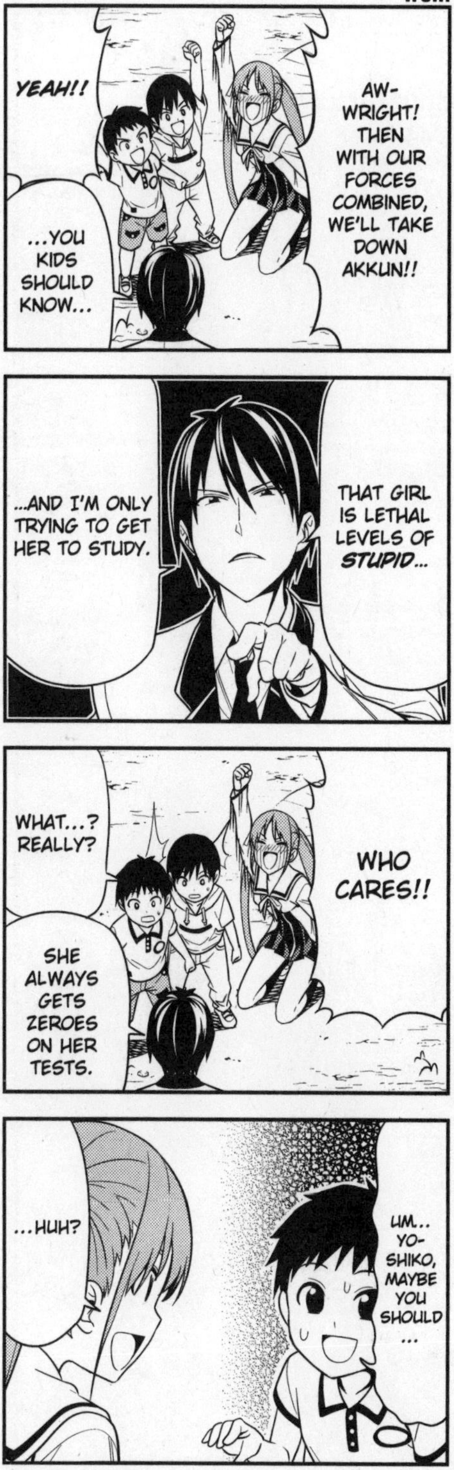
AW-WRIGHT! THEN WITH OUR FORCES COMBINED, WE'LL TAKE DOWN AKKUN!!
YEAH!!
...YOU KIDS SHOULD KNOW...
THAT GIRL IS LETHAL LEVELS OF STUPID...
...AND I'M ONLY TRYING TO GET HER TO STUDY.
WHO CARES!!
WHAT...? REALLY?
SHE ALWAYS GETS ZEROES ON HER TESTS.
UM... YO-SHIKO, MAYBE YOU SHOULD ...
...HUH?

Back Away

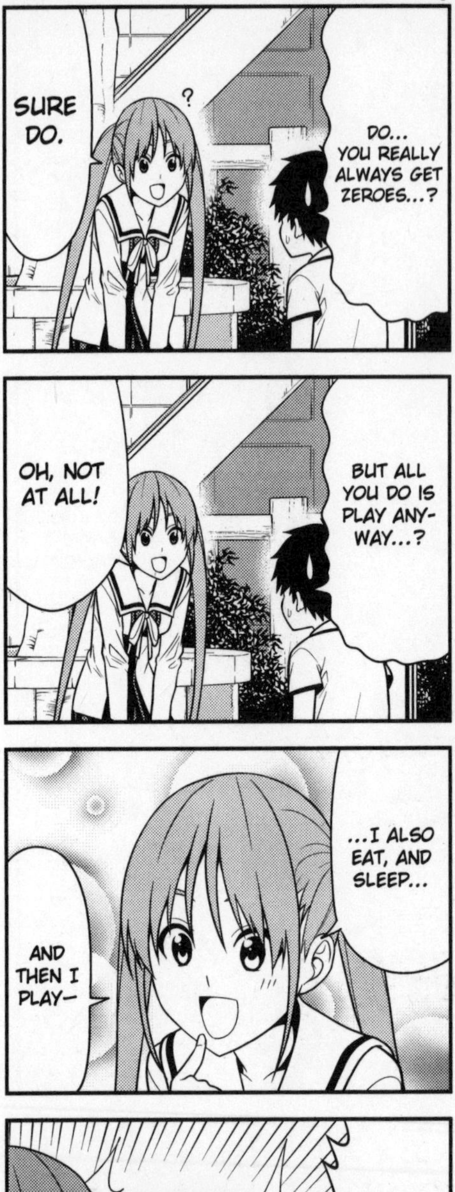
DO... YOU REALLY ALWAYS GET ZEROES...?
?
SURE DO.
BUT ALL YOU DO IS PLAY ANYWAY...?
OH, NOT AT ALL!
...I ALSO EAT, AND SLEEP...
AND THEN I PLAY—
WHAT A TERRIBLE GROWN-UP!!

Farewell, Friend

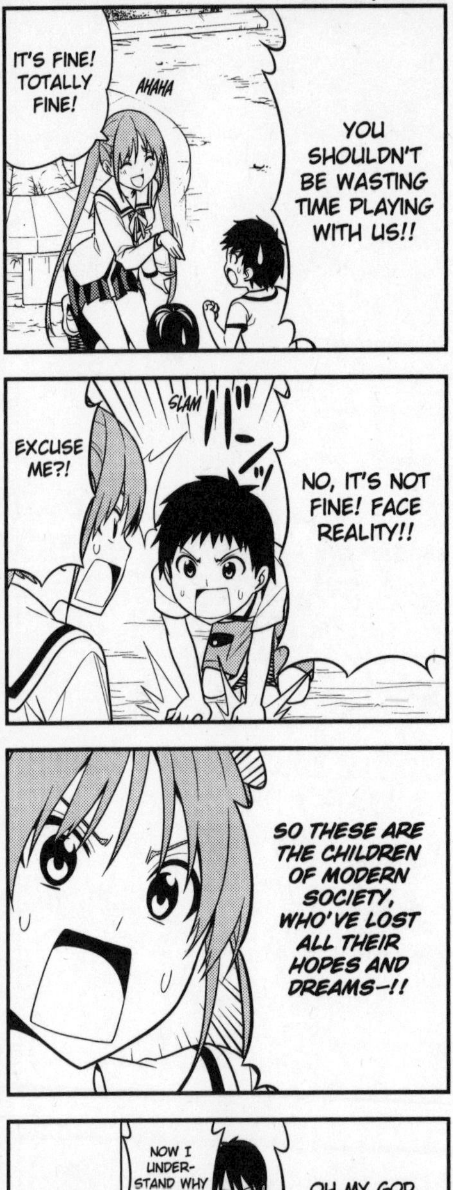
YOU SHOULDN'T BE WASTING TIME PLAYING WITH US!!
AHAHA
IT'S FINE! TOTALLY FINE!
NO, IT'S NOT FINE! FACE REALITY!!
SLAM
EXCUSE ME?!
SO THESE ARE THE CHILDREN OF MODERN SOCIETY, WHO'VE LOST ALL THEIR HOPES AND DREAMS—!!
Yoshiko is such an idiot!!
OH MY GOD, PLEASE, MAN! HIT HER OR DO WHATEVER, BUT MAKE HER STUDY!!
NOW I UNDERSTAND WHY YOU WERE HITTING HER!!
THE CHILDREN WERE MORE RESPONSIBLE THAN HER.

Providing a Bad Example

We'll play some other time!
DRAG DRAG
ズルズル
Yeah, okay...
THAT'S THE TYPE OF ADULT THAT'S RUINING THIS COUNTRY...
IT'S... GONNA BE ON US TO FIX THIS...
THE CHILDREN'S SENSE OF SELF-RELIANCE WAS INTENSIFIED.

(Shoo-ba-dooby Touch)

Aho-Girl

\'ahô,gərl\ *Japanese , noun.*

A clueless girl.

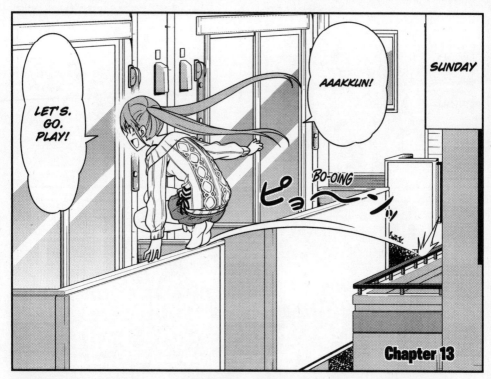

SUNDAY
AAAKKUN!
BO-OING
LET'S. GO. PLAY!
Chapter 13
C'MON, LET'S GO PLAY!
HURRY UP! LET'S PLAY!
*6 AM
...
GOOD MORNING...
...KISSSS!♡
YOUR DEAREST YOSHIKO HAS COME TO PLAY! ♡
RATTLE
WOULD YOU SHUT UP?!
FLUTTFR...
YAWN...
FLUTTFR...

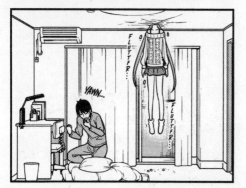

She'd Make a Good Manga Artist

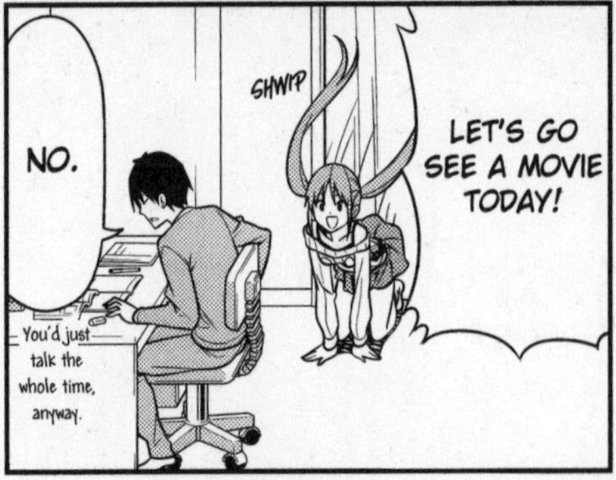
LET'S GO SEE A MOVIE TODAY!
SHWIP
NO.
You'd just talk the whole time, anyway.

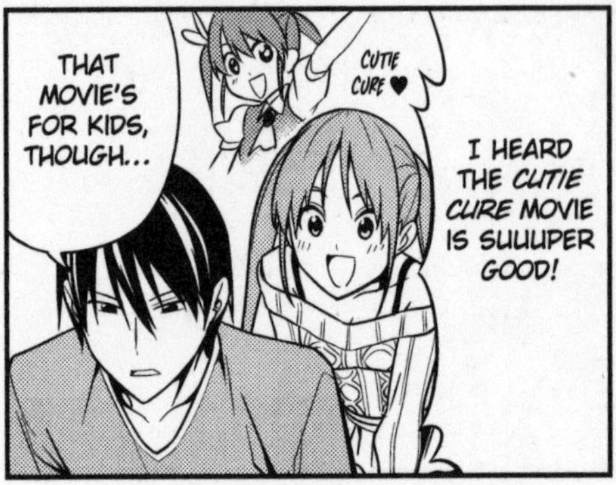
I HEARD THE CUTIE CURE MOVIE IS SUUUPER GOOD!
CUTIE CURE ♥
THAT MOVIE'S FOR KIDS, THOUGH...

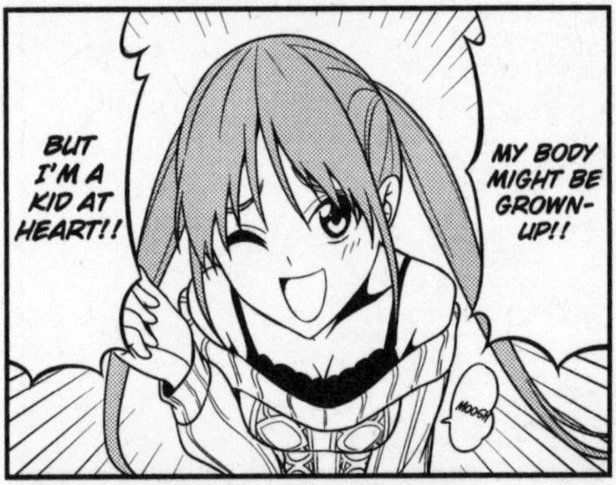
MY BODY MIGHT BE GROWN-UP!!
BUT I'M A KID AT HEART!!
MOOSH

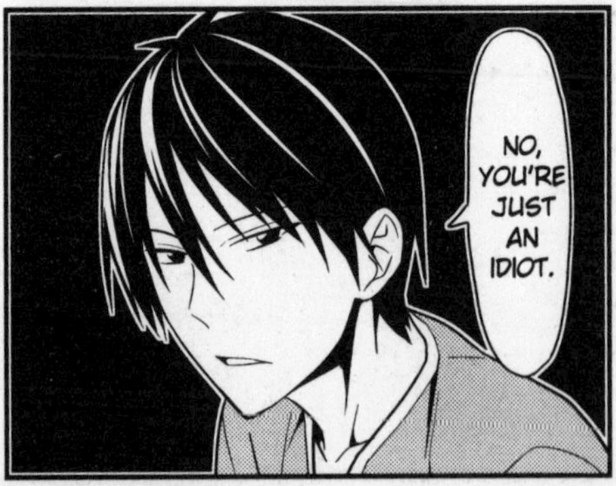
NO, YOU'RE JUST AN IDIOT.

She's Gonna Cry

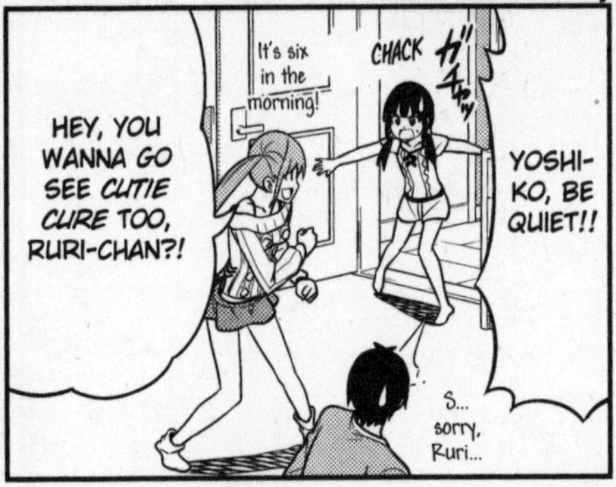
YOSHIKO, BE QUIET!!
CHACK
It's six in the morning!
HEY, YOU WANNA GO SEE CUTIE CURE TOO, RURI-CHAN?!
S... sorry, Ruri...

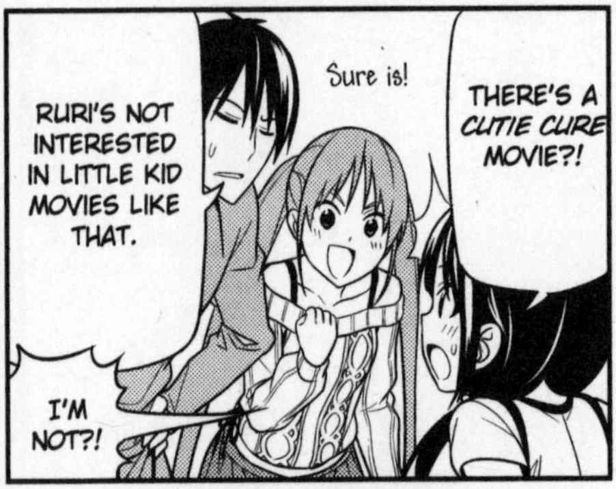
THERE'S A CUTIE CURE MOVIE?!
Sure is!
RURI'S NOT INTERESTED IN LITTLE KID MOVIES LIKE THAT.
I'M NOT?!

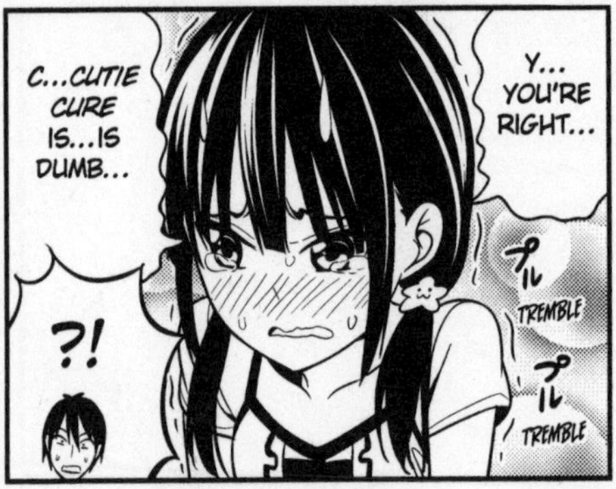
Y... YOU'RE RIGHT...
TREMBLE
TREMBLE
C...CUTIE CURE IS...IS DUMB...
?!

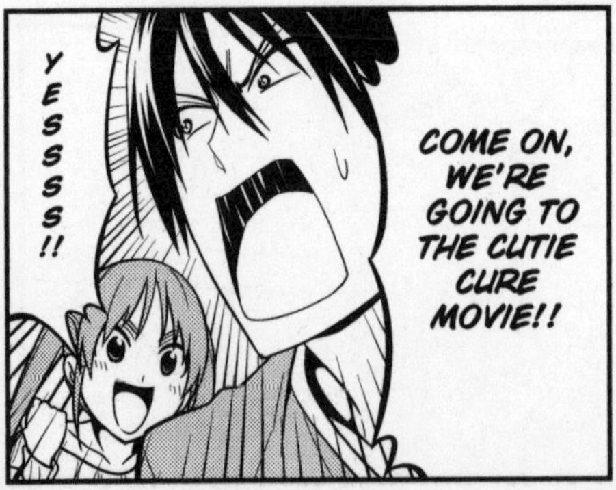
COME ON, WE'RE GOING TO THE CUTIE CURE MOVIE!!
YESSSS!!

That Reaction Is Unavoidable

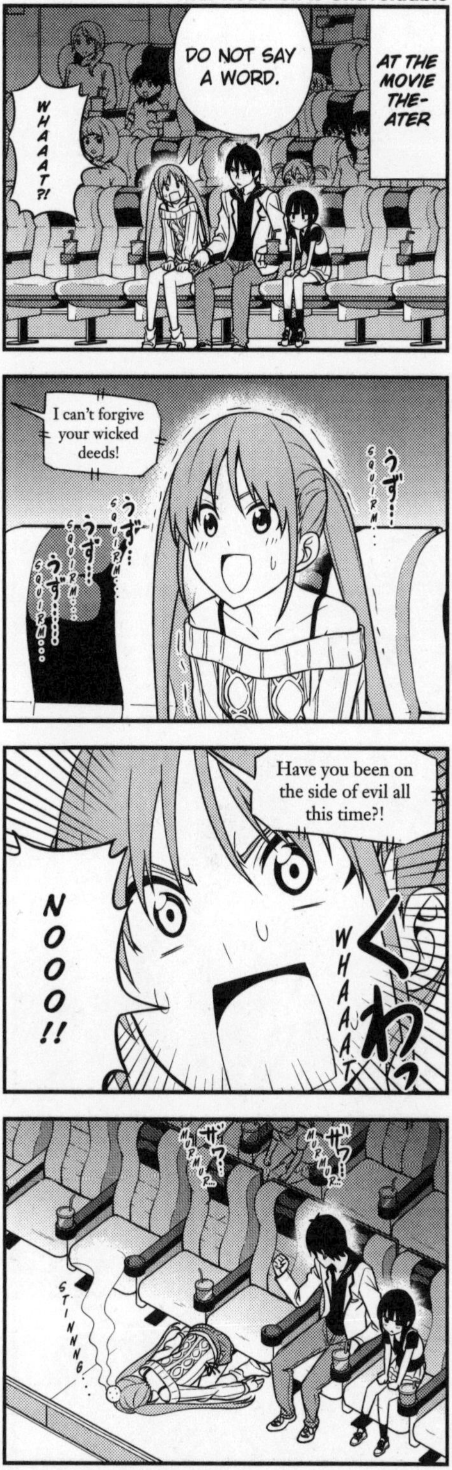
AT THE MOVIE THEATER
DO NOT SAY A WORD.
WHAAAAT?!
I can't forgive your wicked deeds!
うず… SQUIRM…
うず… SQUIRM…
うず… SQUIRM…
うず… SQUIRM…
Have you been on the side of evil all this time?!
くわっ WHAAAT
NOOOO!!
ザワ… MURMUR…
ザワ… MURMUR…
STINNNG…

She's Going to Do It Again

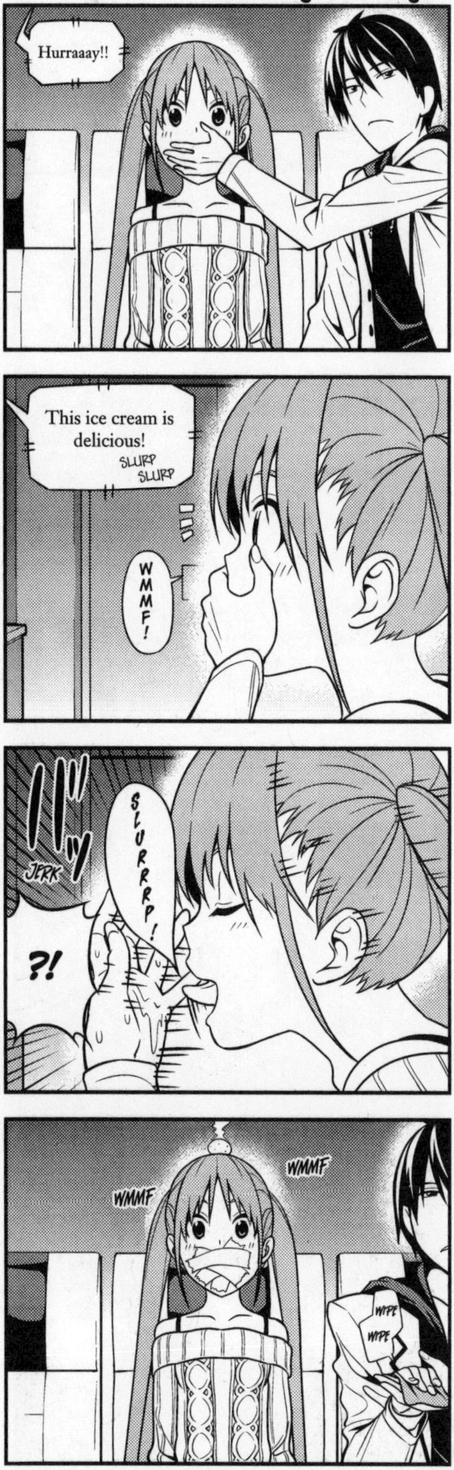
Hurraaay!!
This ice cream is delicious!
SLURP SLURP
WMMF!
SLURRRP!
JERK
?!
WMMF
WMMF
WIPE
WIPE

Bondage

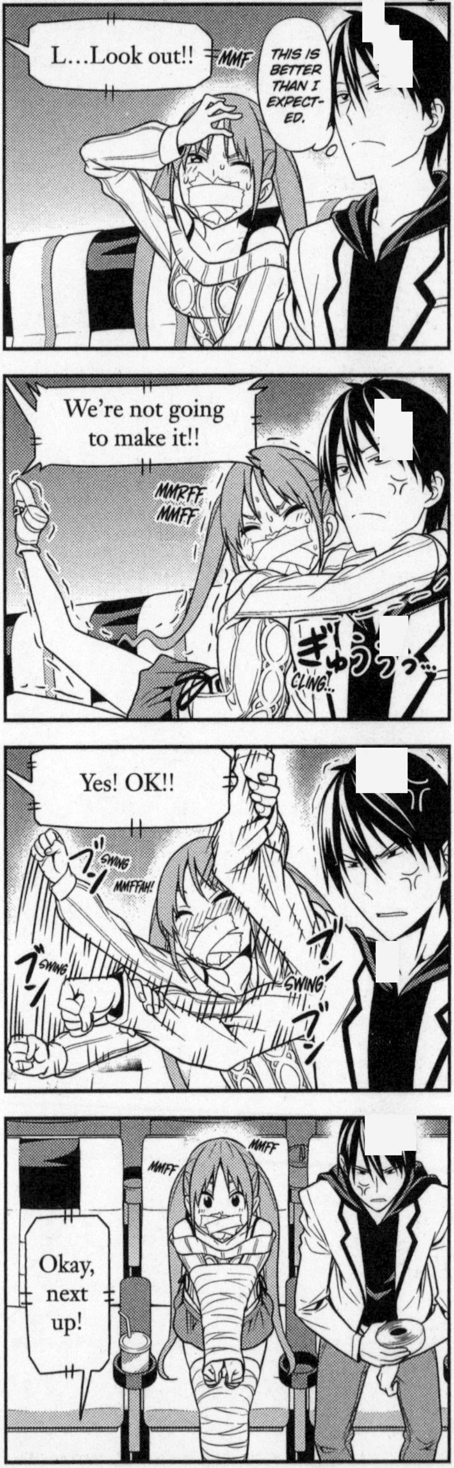
L…Look out!!
MMF
THIS IS BETTER THAN I EXPECTED.
We're not going to make it!!
MMRFF MMFF
ぎゅううっ…
CLING…
Yes! OK!!
ブン SWING
MMFFAH!
ブン SWING
ブン SWING
MMFF
MMFF
Okay, next up!

Limit Reached

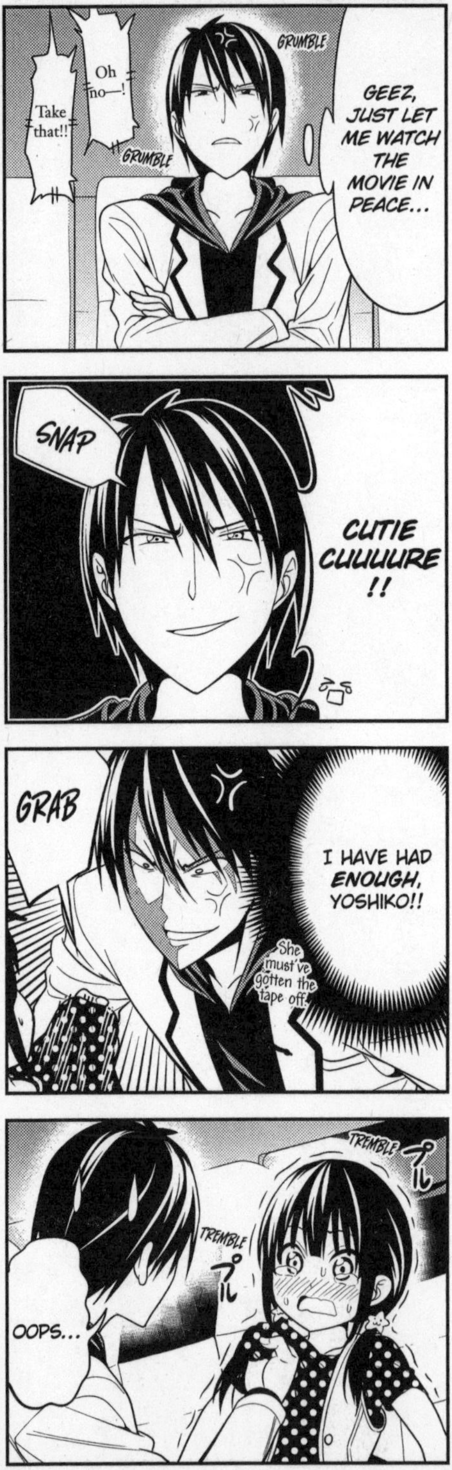
GEEZ, JUST LET ME WATCH THE MOVIE IN PEACE…
GRUMBLE
Oh no—!
Take that!!
GRUMBLE
SNAP
CUTIE CUUUURE!!
GRAB
I HAVE HAD ENOUGH, YOSHIKO!!
She must've gotten the tape off.
TREMBLE プル
TREMBLE プル
OOPS…

Lessons from Yoshiko

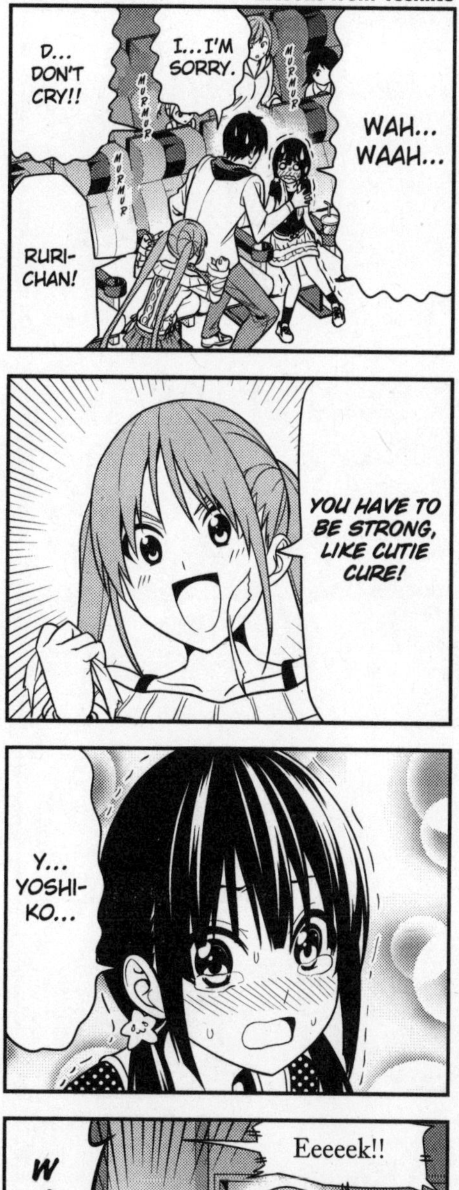
I...I'M SORRY.
MURMUR
MURMUR
MURMUR
MURMUR
WAH... WAAH...
D... DON'T CRY!!
RURI-CHAN!
YOU HAVE TO BE STRONG, LIKE CUTIE CURE!
Y... YOSHIKO...
Eeeeek!!
OH—
LOOKS LIKE CUTIE CURE'S GONNA LOSE.
WAAAAAH!!

Desperation

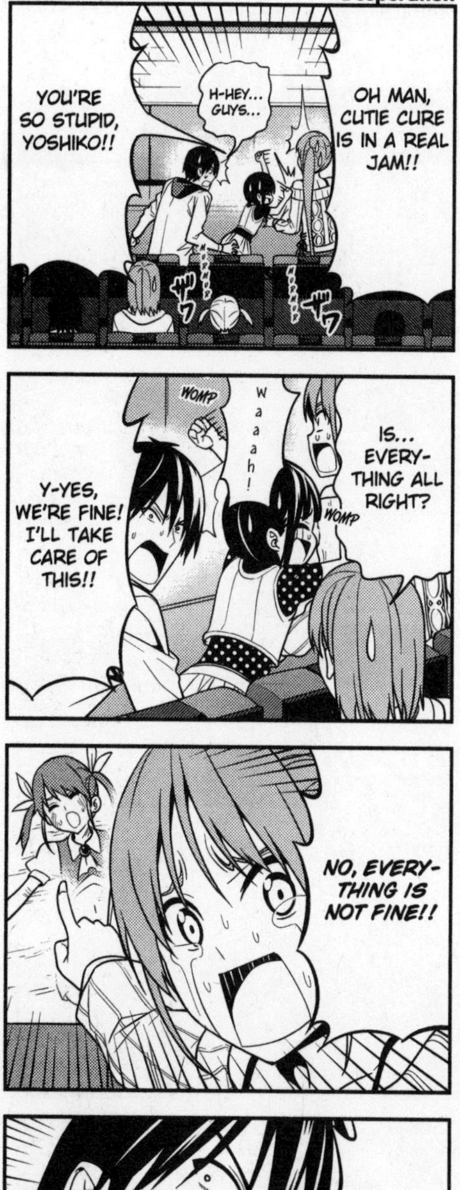
OH MAN, CUTIE CURE IS IN A REAL JAM!!
H-HEY... GUYS...
YOU'RE SO STUPID, YOSHIKO!!
MURMUR
MURMUR
ザワ
ザワ
IS... EVERYTHING ALL RIGHT?
WOMP
Waaah!
WOMP
Y-YES, WE'RE FINE! I'LL TAKE CARE OF THIS!!
NO, EVERY-THING IS NOT FINE!!
SHUT UP!!

Drastic Measures

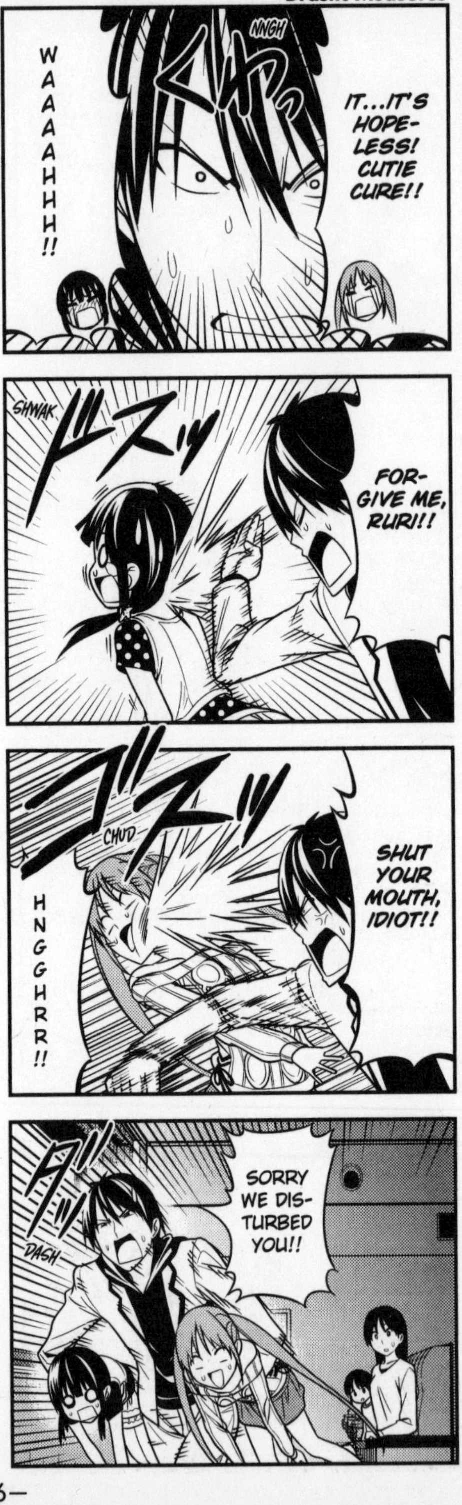
IT...IT'S HOPELESS! CUTIE CURE!!
NNGH
WAAAAAHHHH!!
FORGIVE ME, RURI!!
SHWAK
SHUT YOUR MOUTH, IDIOT!!
CHUD
HNGGHRR!!
SORRY WE DISTURBED YOU!!
DASH

It Took Akkun Five Seconds

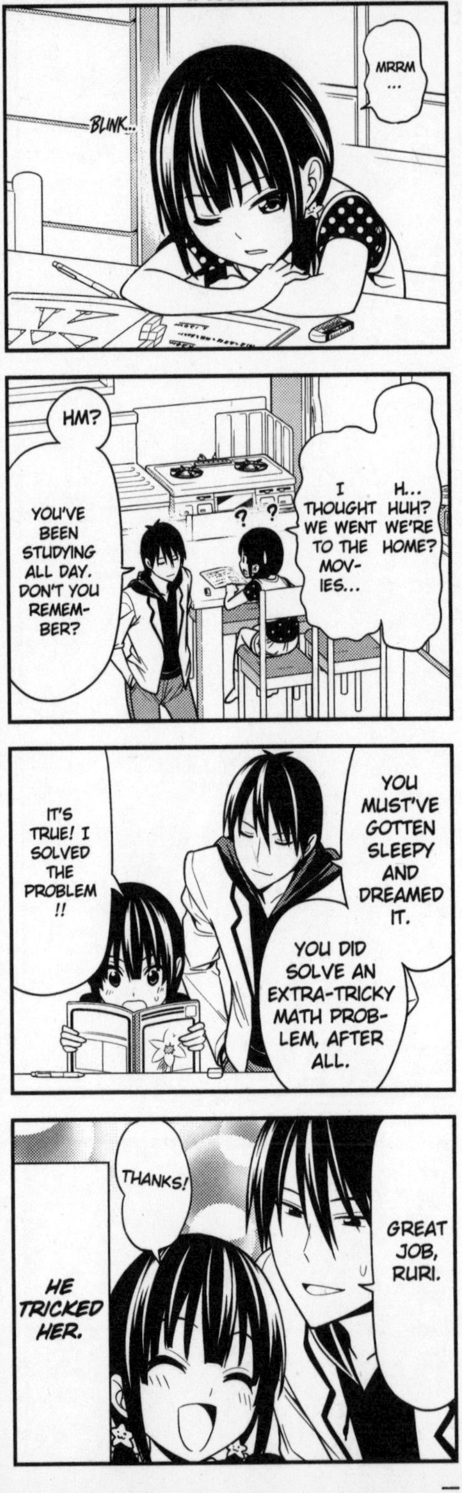
MRRM ...
BLINK...
H... HUH? WE'RE HOME?
I THOUGHT WE WENT TO THE MOVIES...
HM?
YOU'VE BEEN STUDYING ALL DAY. DON'T YOU REMEMBER?
YOU MUST'VE GOTTEN SLEEPY AND DREAMED IT.
YOU DID SOLVE AN EXTRA-TRICKY MATH PROBLEM, AFTER ALL.
IT'S TRUE! I SOLVED THE PROBLEM!!
GREAT JOB, RURI.
THANKS!
HE TRICKED HER.

He Made Sure She Got Home

MEAN-WHILE
OH!
はっ
WHA?!
WE WERE AT THE MOVIES, AND NOW I'M HOME?!
HUP!
ガバッ
I MUST HAVE FINALLY DISCOVERED HOW TO TELEPORT!!

(Humanity is but a thinking)

Aho-Girl

\\'ahô͵gərl\\ *Japanese , noun.*
A clueless girl.

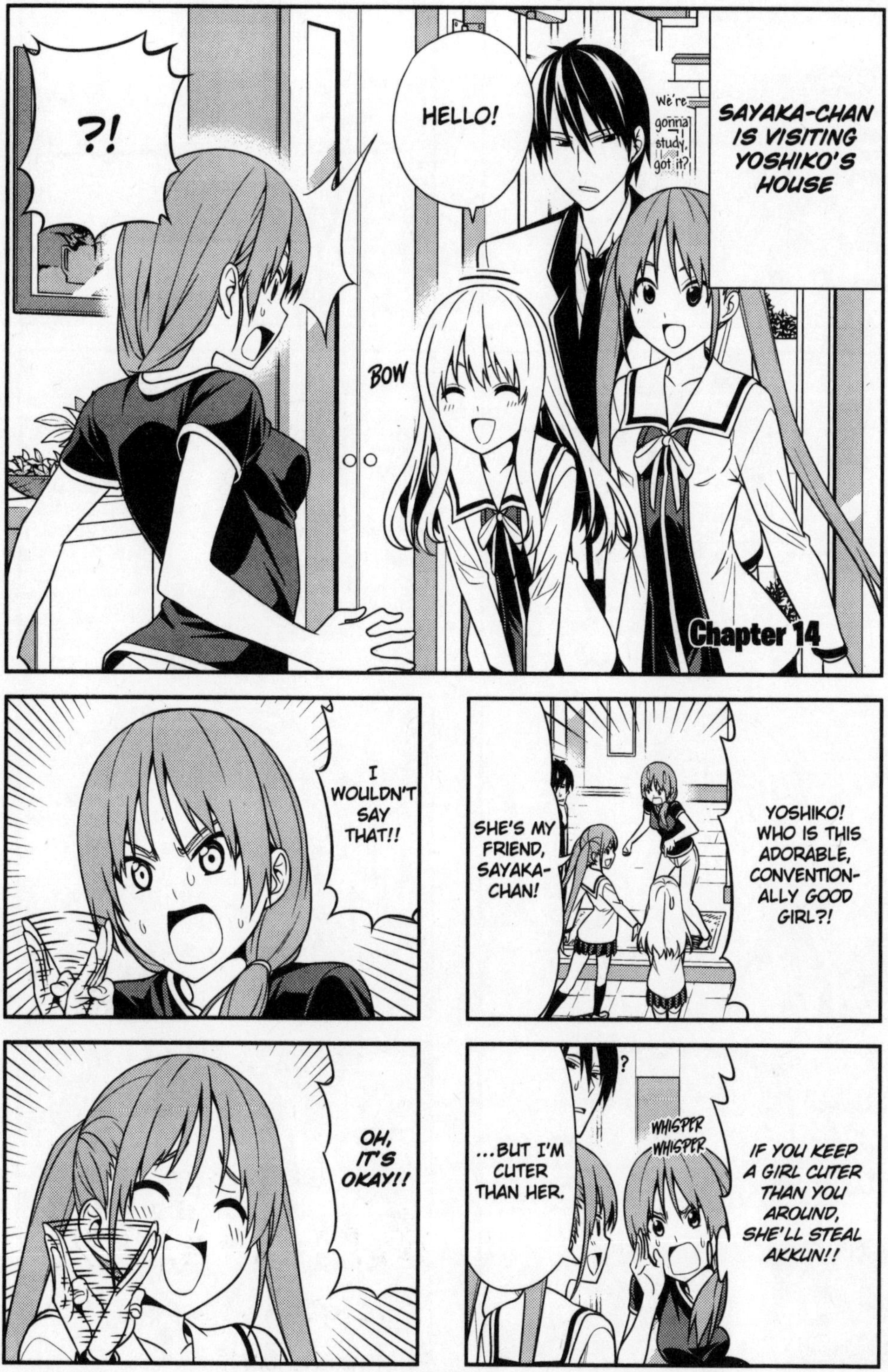
SAYAKA-CHAN IS VISITING YOSHIKO'S HOUSE
We're gonna study, got it?
HELLO!
BOW
?!
Chapter 14
YOSHIKO! WHO IS THIS ADORABLE, CONVENTION-ALLY GOOD GIRL?!
SHE'S MY FRIEND, SAYAKA-CHAN!
I WOULDN'T SAY THAT!!
IF YOU KEEP A GIRL CUTER THAN YOU AROUND, SHE'LL STEAL AKKUN!!
WHISPER WHISPER
?
...BUT I'M CUTER THAN HER.
OH, IT'S OKAY!!

20 Years Ago

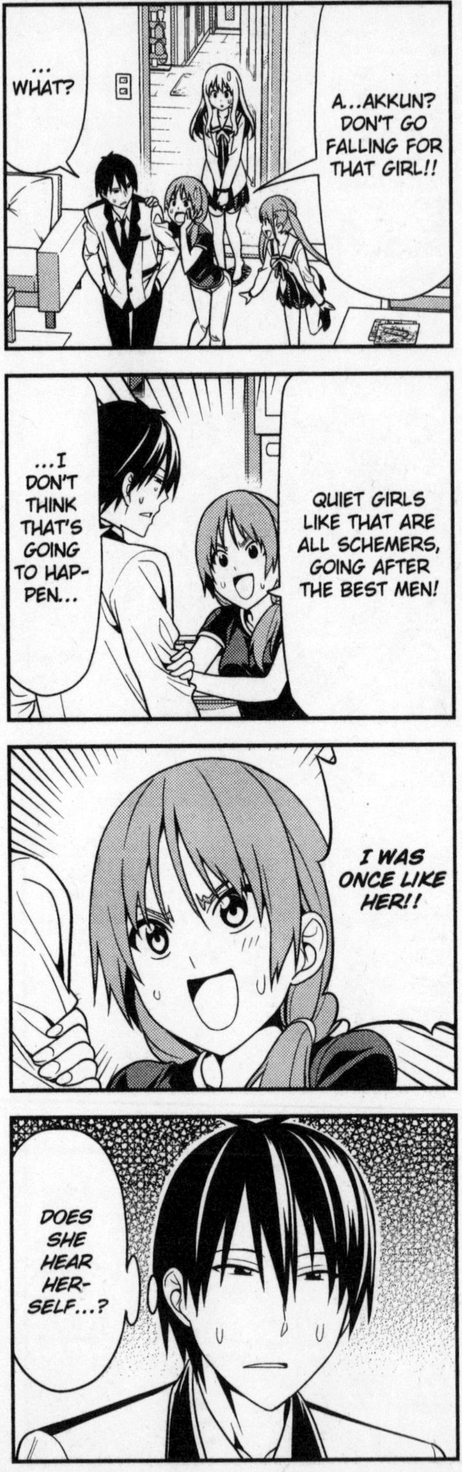
A...AKKUN? DON'T GO FALLING FOR THAT GIRL!!
...WHAT?
QUIET GIRLS LIKE THAT ARE ALL SCHEMERS, GOING AFTER THE BEST MEN!
...I DON'T THINK THAT'S GOING TO HAP-PEN...
I WAS ONCE LIKE HER!!
DOES SHE HEAR HER-SELF...?

She's Spilling Everything

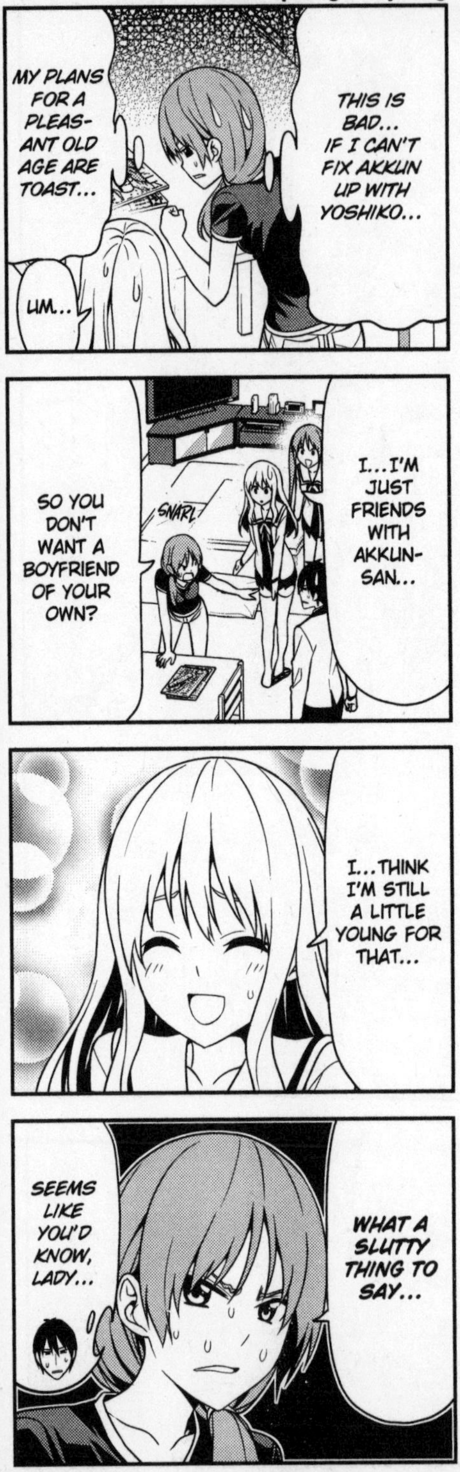
THIS IS BAD... IF I CAN'T FIX AKKUN UP WITH YOSHIKO...
MY PLANS FOR A PLEAS-ANT OLD AGE ARE TOAST...
UM...
I...I'M JUST FRIENDS WITH AKKUN-SAN...
SNARL
SO YOU DON'T WANT A BOYFRIEND OF YOUR OWN?
I...THINK I'M STILL A LITTLE YOUNG FOR THAT...
WHAT A SLUTTY THING TO SAY...
SEEMS LIKE YOU'D KNOW, LADY...

It's Totally Obvious

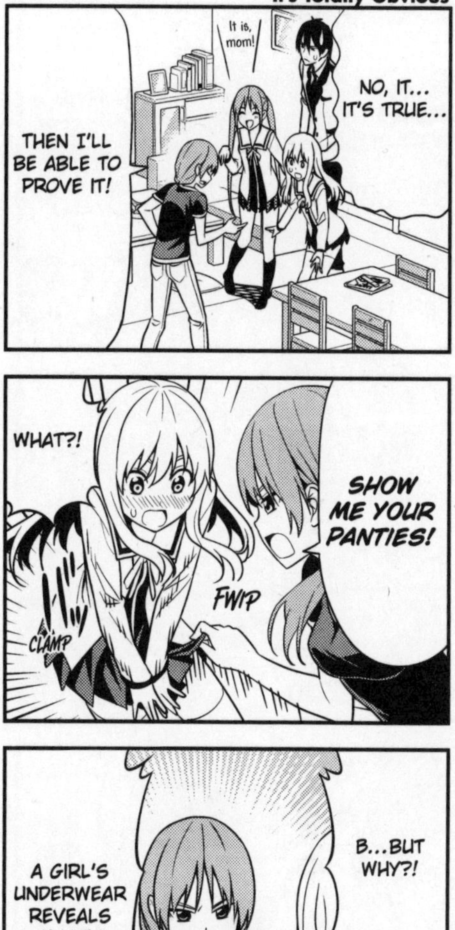
NO, IT... IT'S TRUE...
It is, mom!
THEN I'LL BE ABLE TO PROVE IT!
SHOW ME YOUR PANTIES!
FWIP
WHAT?!
CLAMP
B...BUT WHY?!
A GIRL'S UNDERWEAR REVEALS WHAT'S HIDDEN IN HER HEART.
WHAT DO YOU SEE IN MINE...?
FWIP
STUPIDITY, OBVIOUSLY.

Aho-Girl Mystery Something

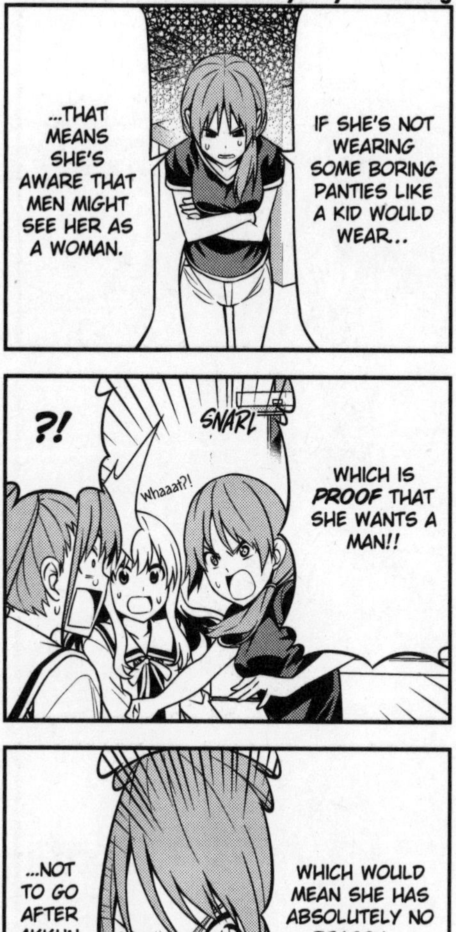
IF SHE'S NOT WEARING SOME BORING PANTIES LIKE A KID WOULD WEAR...
...THAT MEANS SHE'S AWARE THAT MEN MIGHT SEE HER AS A WOMAN.
WHICH IS *PROOF* THAT SHE WANTS A MAN!!
SNARL
Whaaat?!
?!
WHICH WOULD MEAN SHE HAS ABSOLUTELY NO REASON...
...NOT TO GO AFTER AKKUN SOME-DAY!!
SHE...
...SHE WHAT?!

Obviously

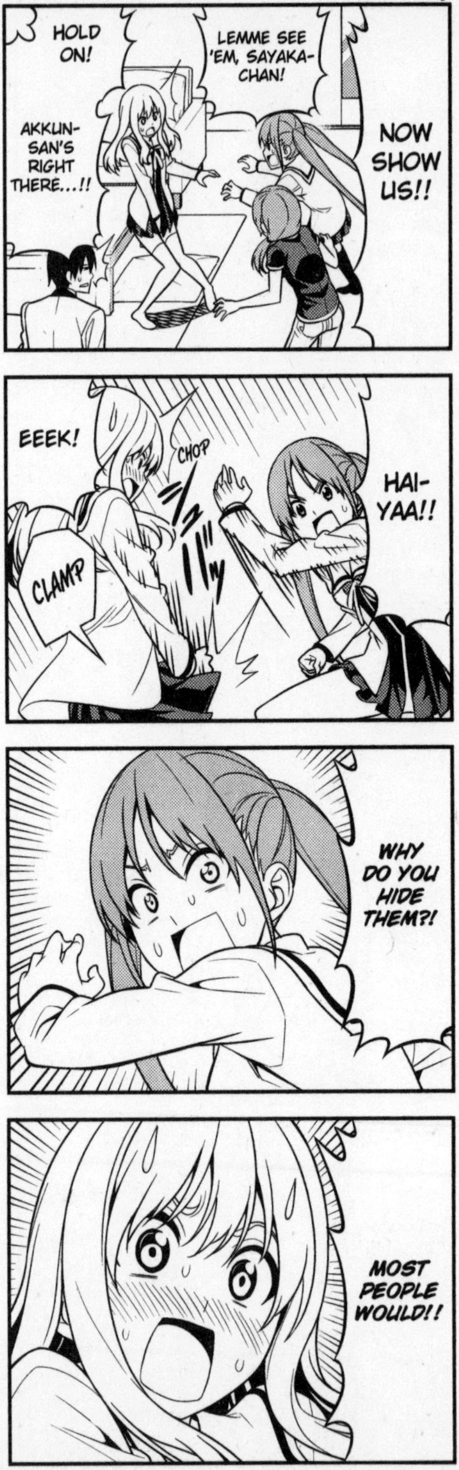
LEMME SEE 'EM, SAYAKA-CHAN!
NOW SHOW US!!
HOLD ON!
AKKUN-SAN'S RIGHT THERE...!!
HAI-YAA!!
CHOP
EEEK!
CLAMP
WHY DO YOU HIDE THEM?!
MOST PEOPLE WOULD!!

Nineteen Years Ago

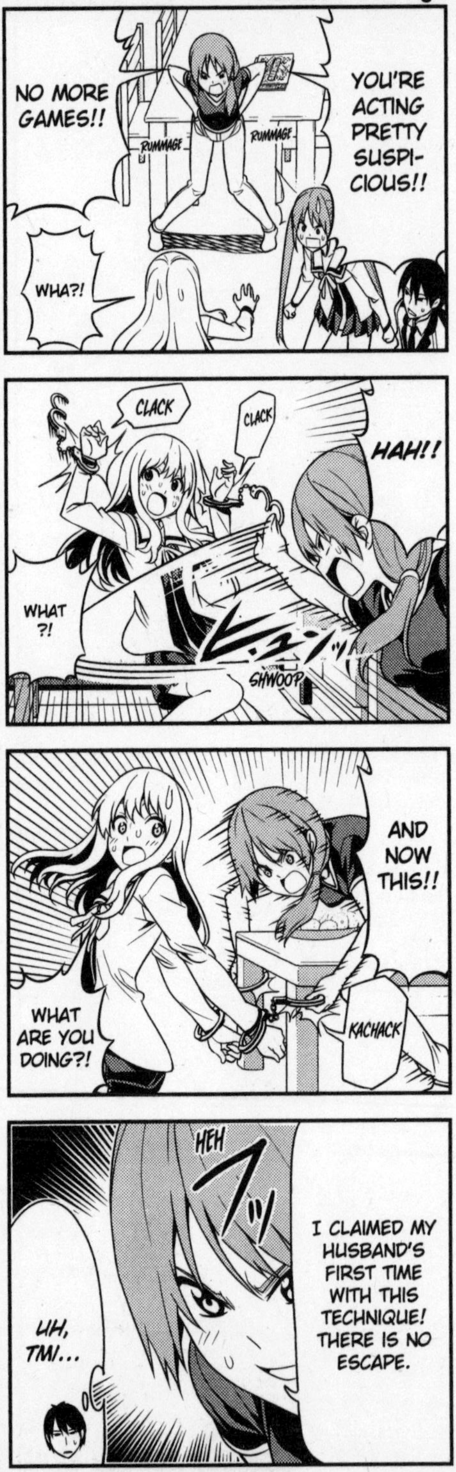
YOU'RE ACTING PRETTY SUSPI-CIOUS!!
RUMMAGE
RUMMAGE
NO MORE GAMES!!
WHA?!
HAH!!
CLACK
CLACK
WHAT ?!
SHWOOP
AND NOW THIS!!
KACHACK
WHAT ARE YOU DOING?!
I CLAIMED MY HUSBAND'S FIRST TIME WITH THIS TECHNIQUE! THERE IS NO ESCAPE.
HEH
UH, TMI...

Nice One, Akkun

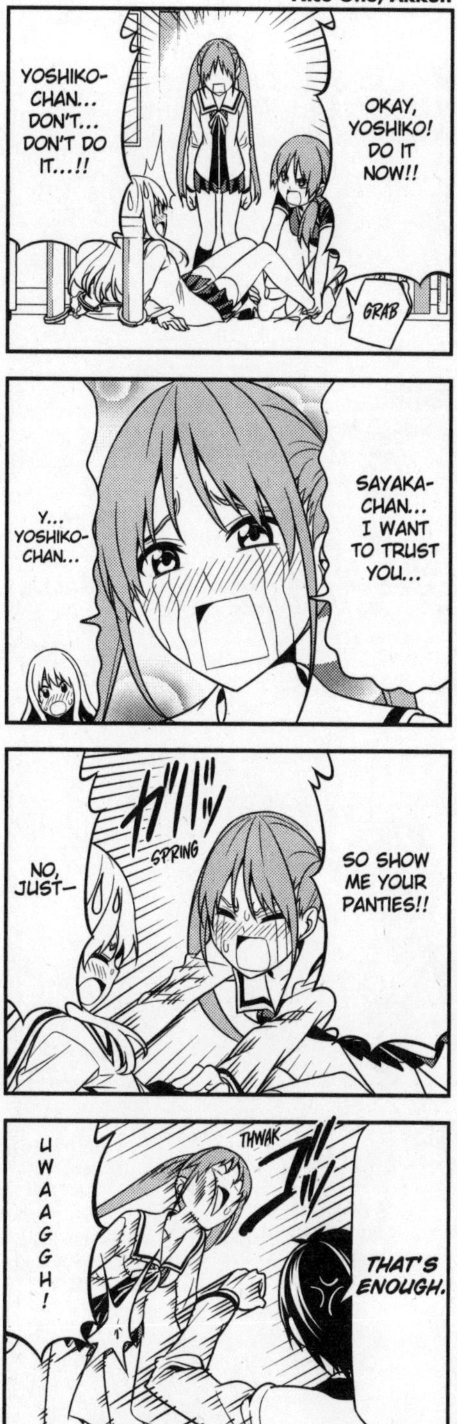
OKAY, YOSHIKO! DO IT NOW!!
YOSHIKO-CHAN... DON'T... DON'T DO IT...!!
GRAB
SAYAKA-CHAN... I WANT TO TRUST YOU...
Y... YOSHIKO-CHAN...
SO SHOW ME YOUR PANTIES!!
ガバッ
SPRING
NO, JUST—
THWAK
THAT'S ENOUGH.
UWAAGGH!

Pacifism

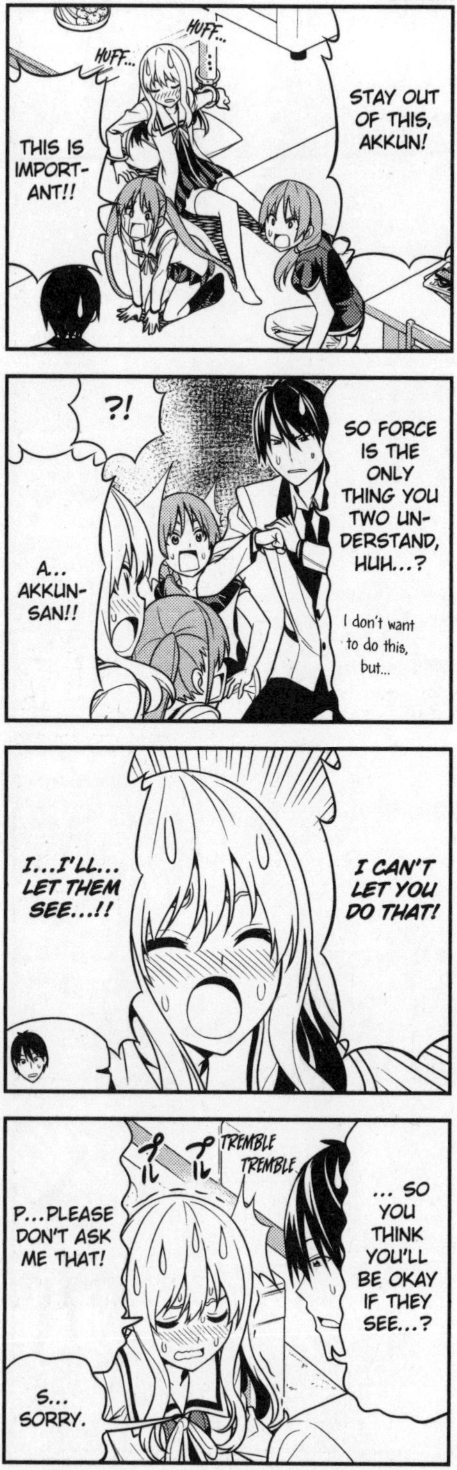
STAY OUT OF THIS, AKKUN!
HUFF...
HUFF...
THIS IS IMPORTANT!!
SO FORCE IS THE ONLY THING YOU TWO UNDERSTAND, HUH...?
I don't want to do this, but...
?!
A... AKKUN-SAN!!
I CAN'T LET YOU DO THAT!
I...I'LL... LET THEM SEE...!!
... SO YOU THINK YOU'LL BE OKAY IF THEY SEE...?
プル プル
TREMBLE TREMBLE
P...PLEASE DON'T ASK ME THAT!
S... SORRY.

I Never Expected—

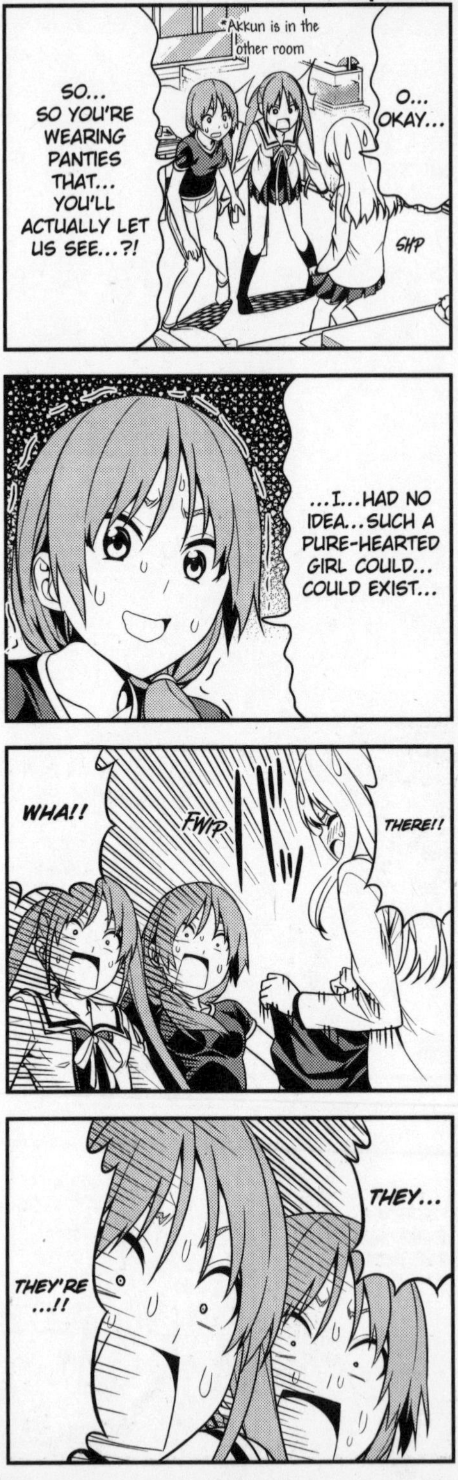

*Akkun is in the other room
SO... SO YOU'RE WEARING PANTIES THAT... YOU'LL ACTUALLY LET US SEE...?!
O... OKAY...
SHP
...I...HAD NO IDEA...SUCH A PURE-HEARTED GIRL COULD... COULD EXIST...
THERE!!
FWIP
WHA!!
THEY...
THEY'RE ...!!

A Peaceful Resolution

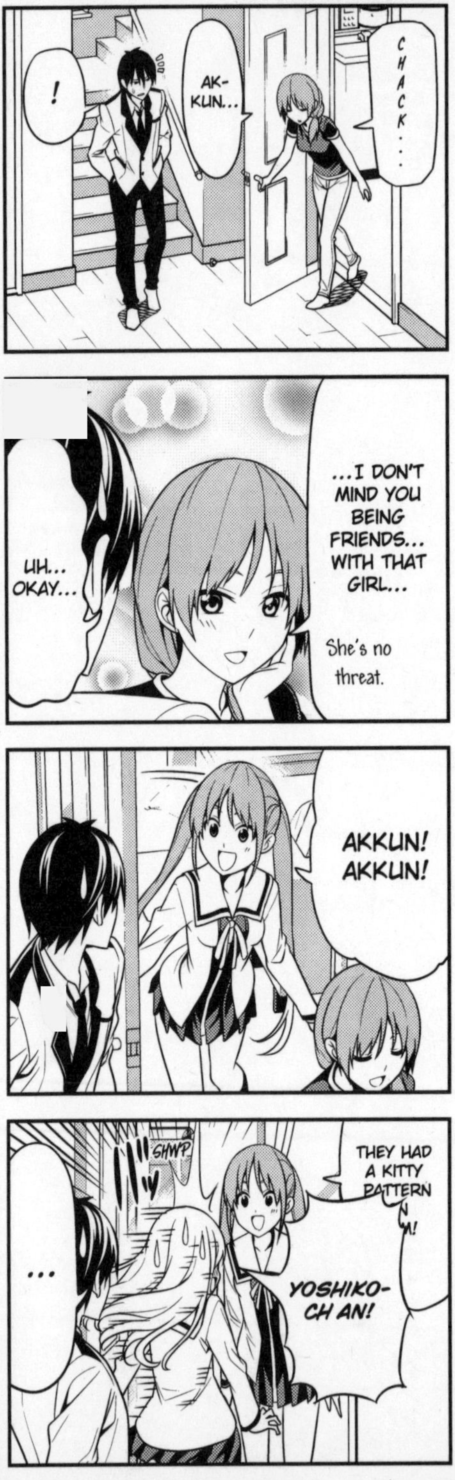

CHACK...
AK-KUN...
!
...I DON'T MIND YOU BEING FRIENDS... WITH THAT GIRL...
She's no threat.
UH... OKAY...
AKKUN! AKKUN!
THEY HAD A KITTY PATTERNNNA!
SHWP
YOSHIKO-CHAN!
...

The Training Continues

SIIIGH...
ぶぅ〜…
OKAY! LET'S GO PLAY!
YOU MEAN GO STUDY, RIGHT?!
バッ
SPRING
SHE'S GETTING STRONGER, IT SEEMS...
Keep it up, girl...

(Boogie Woogie Choo Choo)

Aho-Girl

\'ahô,gərl\ *Japanese , noun*.

A clueless girl.

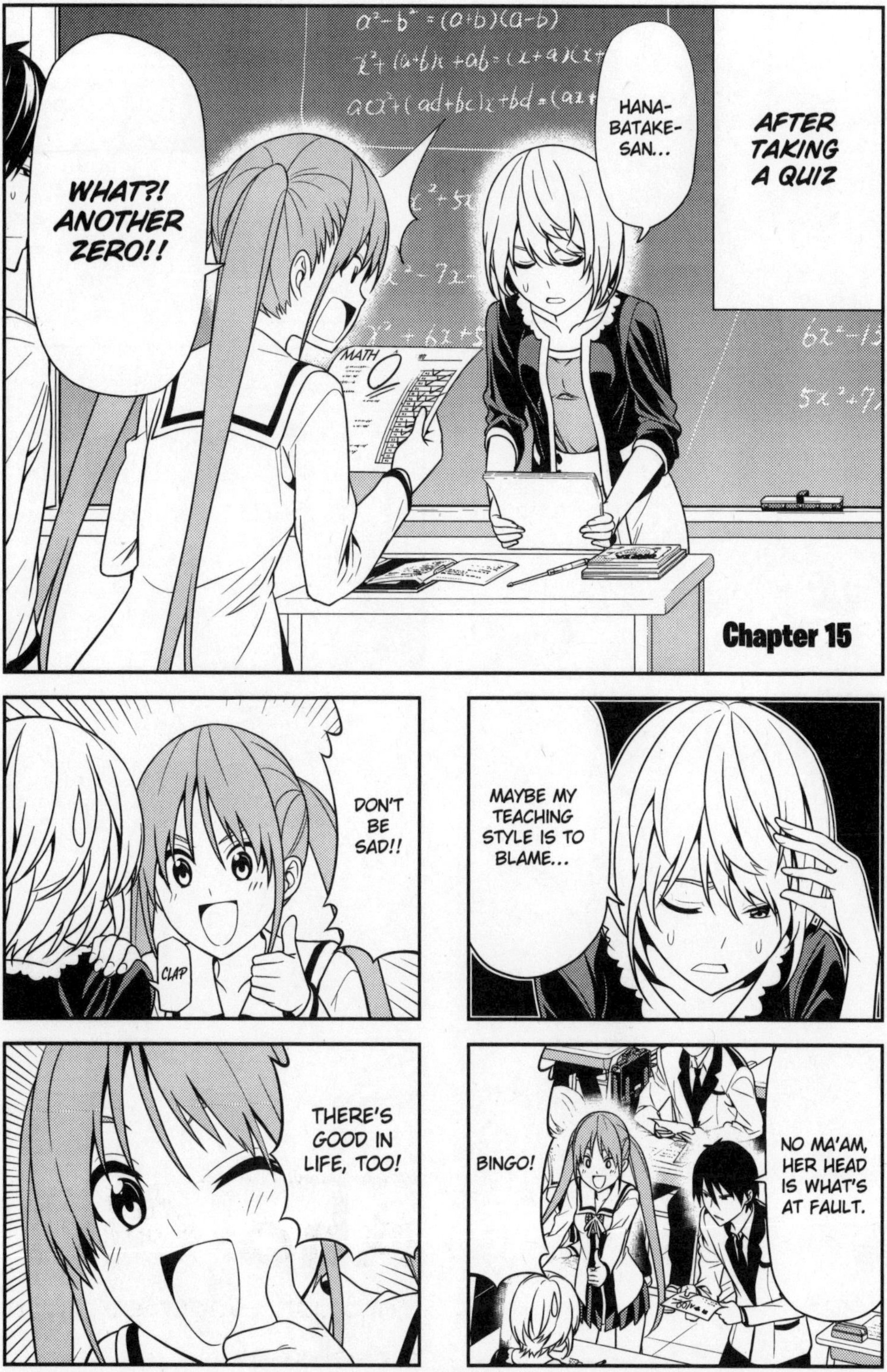
AFTER TAKING A QUIZ
HANA-BATAKE-SAN...
WHAT?! ANOTHER ZERO!!
MATH
Chapter 15
MAYBE MY TEACHING STYLE IS TO BLAME...
DON'T BE SAD!!
CLAP
NO MA'AM, HER HEAD IS WHAT'S AT FAULT.
BINGO!
THERE'S GOOD IN LIFE, TOO!

Yoshiko, She's Being Serious!

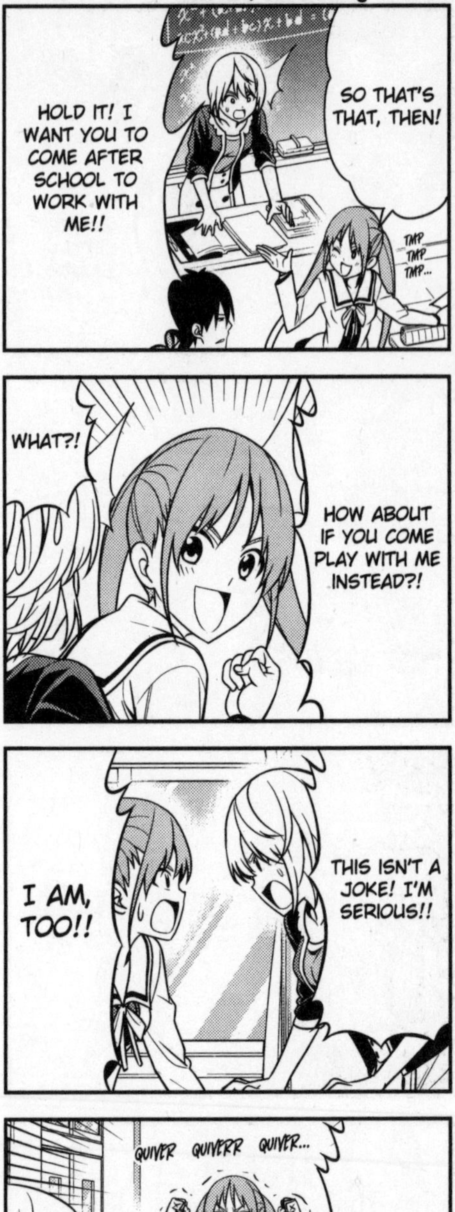
SO THAT'S THAT, THEN!
HOLD IT! I WANT YOU TO COME AFTER SCHOOL TO WORK WITH ME!!
TMP TMP TMP...
WHAT?!
HOW ABOUT IF YOU COME PLAY WITH ME INSTEAD?!
THIS ISN'T A JOKE! I'M SERIOUS!!
I AM, TOO!!
QUIVER QUIVERR QUIVER...
LET'S GO PLAY!!

Upper Hand

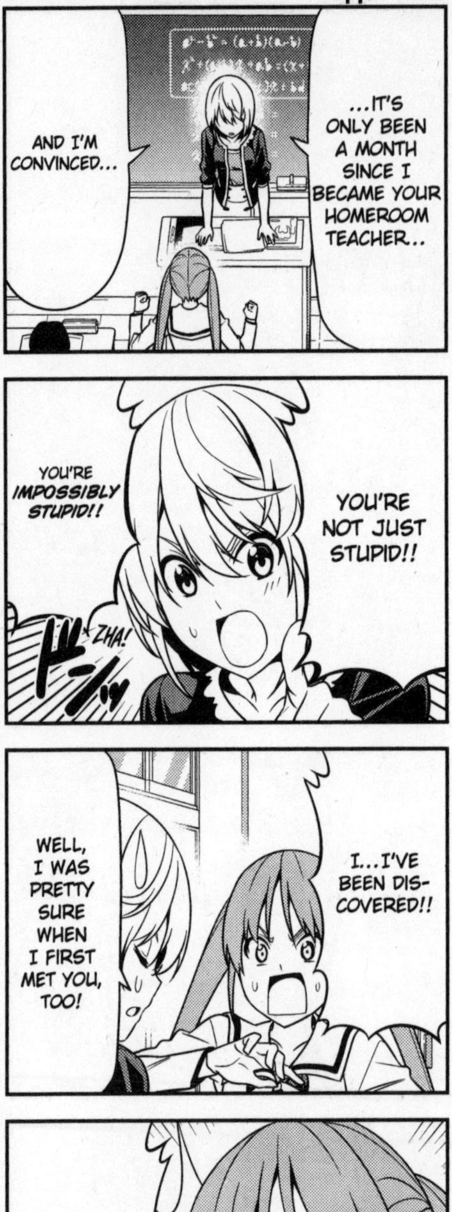
...IT'S ONLY BEEN A MONTH SINCE I BECAME YOUR HOMEROOM TEACHER...
AND I'M CONVINCED...
YOU'RE NOT JUST STUPID!!
YOU'RE *IMPOSSIBLY* STUPID!!
ZHA!
I...I'VE BEEN DIS-COVERED!!
WELL, I WAS PRETTY SURE WHEN I FIRST MET YOU, TOO!
IM... IMPRESSIVE!!

Hold on, That Sounds Like You, Sensei...

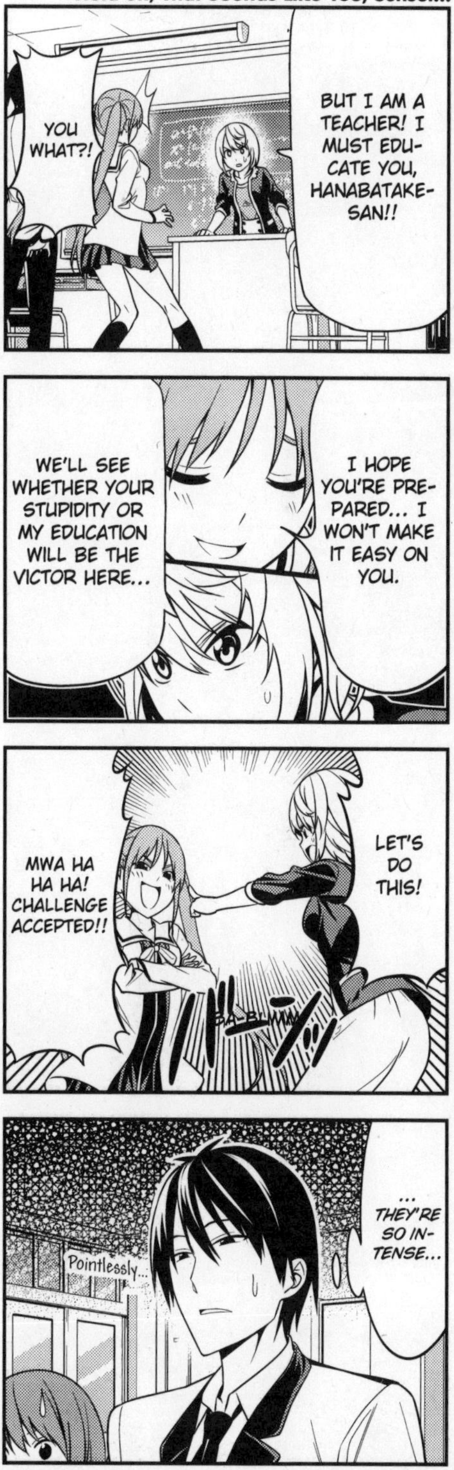
BUT I AM A TEACHER! I MUST EDUCATE YOU, HANABATAKE-SAN!!
YOU WHAT?!
I HOPE YOU'RE PREPARED... I WON'T MAKE IT EASY ON YOU.
WE'LL SEE WHETHER YOUR STUPIDITY OR MY EDUCATION WILL BE THE VICTOR HERE...
LET'S DO THIS!
MWA HA HA HA! CHALLENGE ACCEPTED!!
...THEY'RE SO INTENSE...
Pointlessly...

No Holds Barred

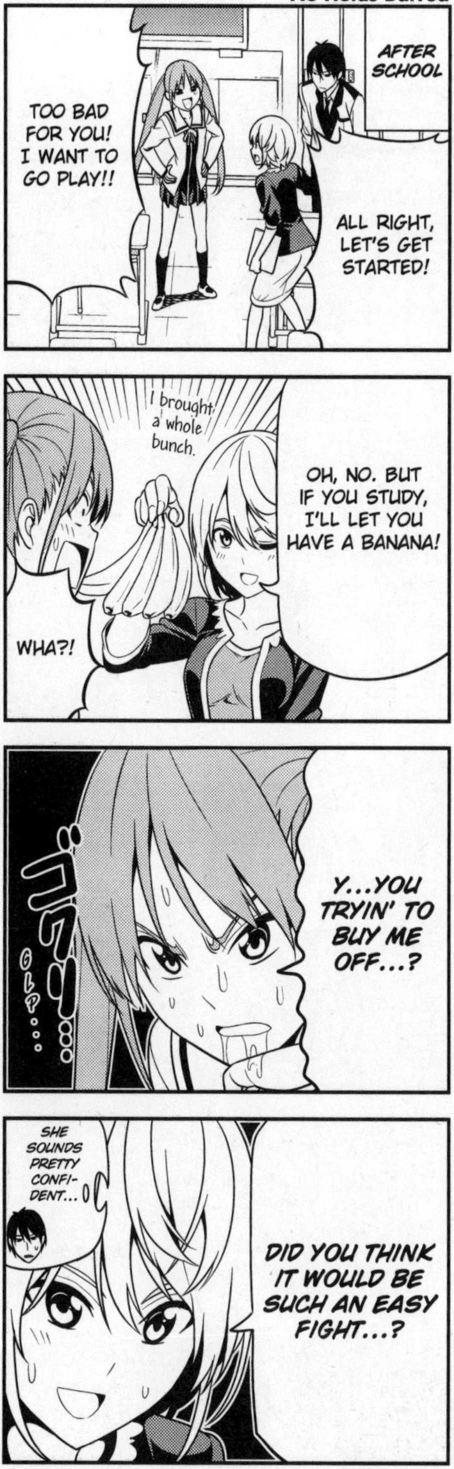
AFTER SCHOOL
ALL RIGHT, LET'S GET STARTED!
TOO BAD FOR YOU! I WANT TO GO PLAY!!
OH, NO. BUT IF YOU STUDY, I'LL LET YOU HAVE A BANANA!
I brought a whole bunch.
WHA?!
Y...YOU TRYIN' TO BUY ME OFF...?
ゴクリ…
GLP...
DID YOU THINK IT WOULD BE SUCH AN EASY FIGHT...?
SHE SOUNDS PRETTY CONFIDENT...

The Very First Blow

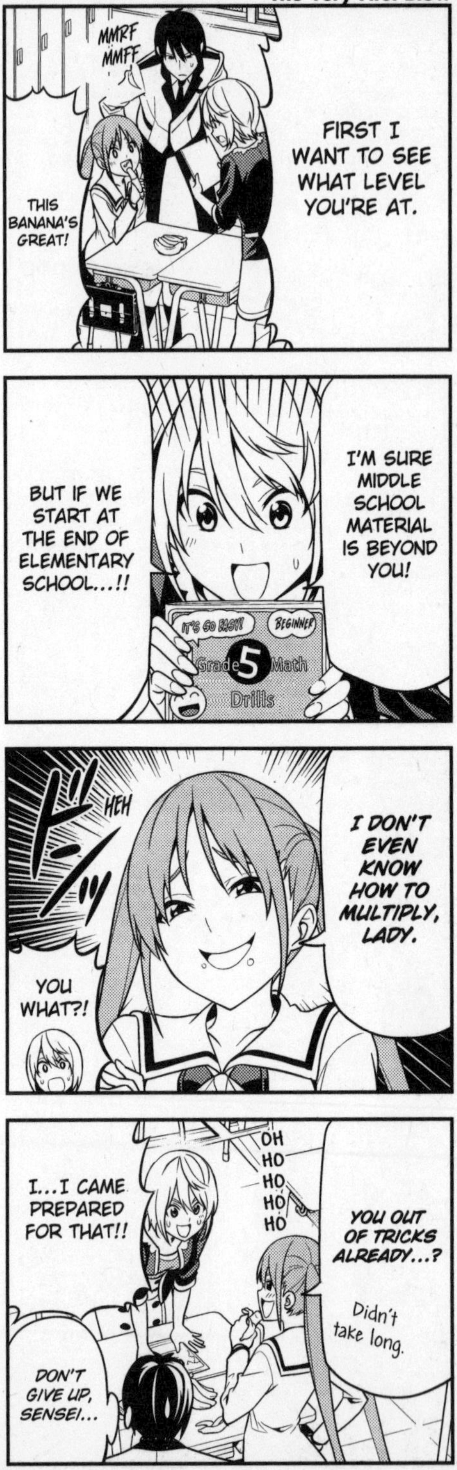
FIRST I WANT TO SEE WHAT LEVEL YOU'RE AT.
MMRF MMFF
THIS BANANA'S GREAT!
I'M SURE MIDDLE SCHOOL MATERIAL IS BEYOND YOU!
BUT IF WE START AT THE END OF ELEMENTARY SCHOOL...!!
IT'S SO EASY!
BEGINNER
Grade 5 Math
Drills
I DON'T EVEN KNOW HOW TO MULTIPLY, LADY.
HEH
YOU WHAT?!
YOU OUT OF TRICKS ALREADY...?
Didn't take long.
OH HO HO HO HO HO
I...I CAME PREPARED FOR THAT!!
DON'T GIVE UP, SENSEI...

Something That's Easy to Get

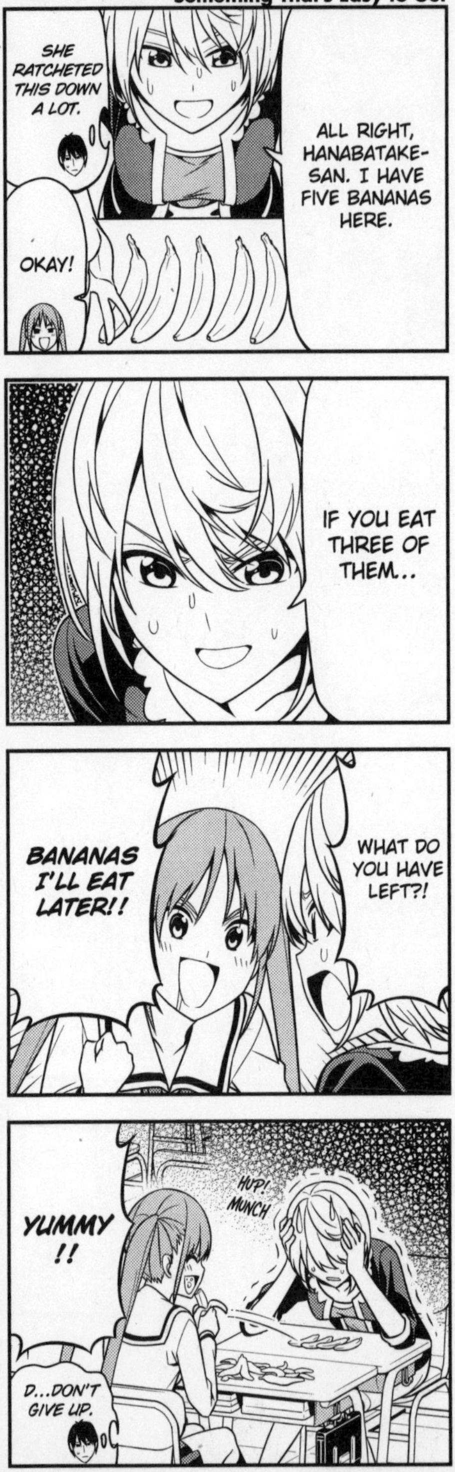
ALL RIGHT, HANABATAKE-SAN. I HAVE FIVE BANANAS HERE.
SHE RATCHETED THIS DOWN A LOT.
OKAY!
IF YOU EAT THREE OF THEM...
WHAT DO YOU HAVE LEFT?!
BANANAS I'LL EAT LATER!!
HUP! MUNCH
YUMMY!!
D...DON'T GIVE UP.

Spark of Hope

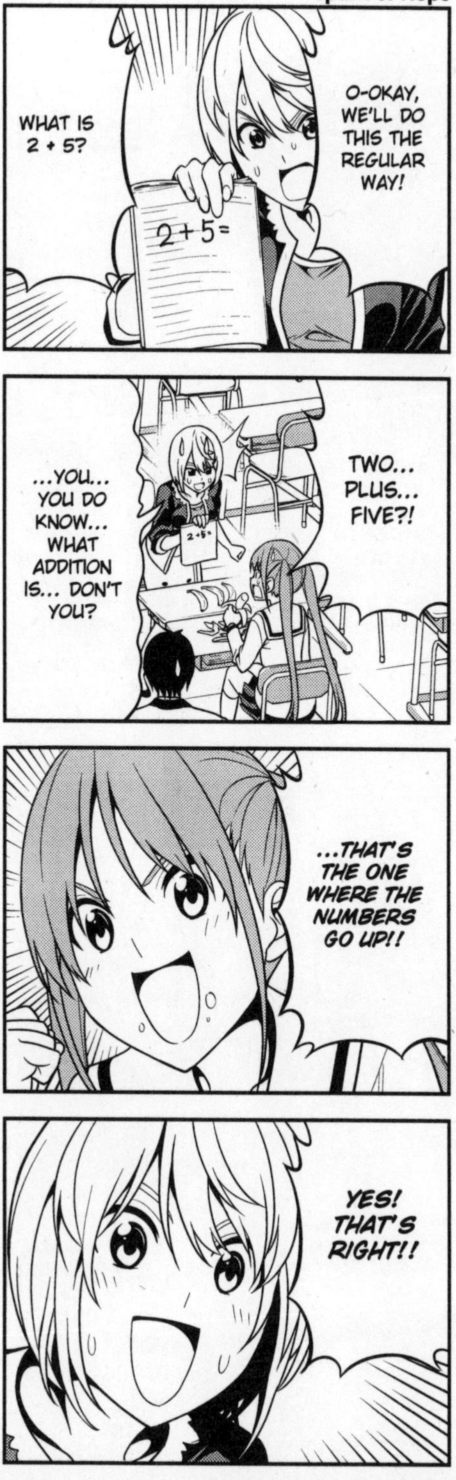
O-OKAY, WE'LL DO THIS THE REGULAR WAY!
WHAT IS 2 + 5?
2 + 5 =
TWO... PLUS... FIVE?!
...YOU... YOU DO KNOW... WHAT ADDITION IS... DON'T YOU?
...THAT'S THE ONE WHERE THE NUMBERS GO UP!!
YES! THAT'S RIGHT!!

Rumination

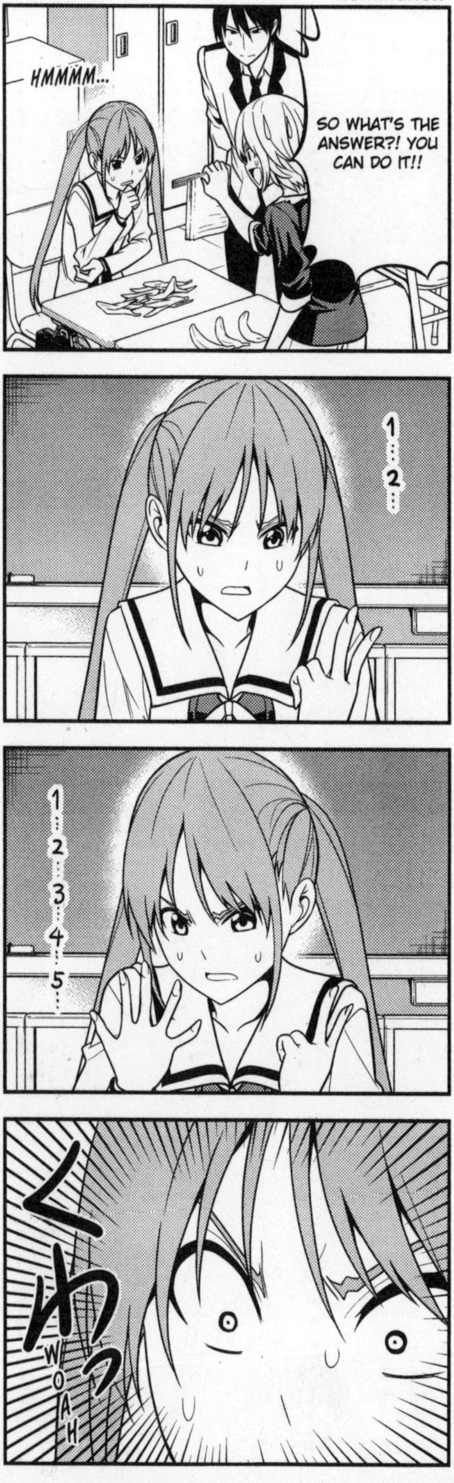
SO WHAT'S THE ANSWER?! YOU CAN DO IT!!
HMMMM...
1... 2...
1... 2... 3... 4... 5...
くわっ
WOAH

Joy

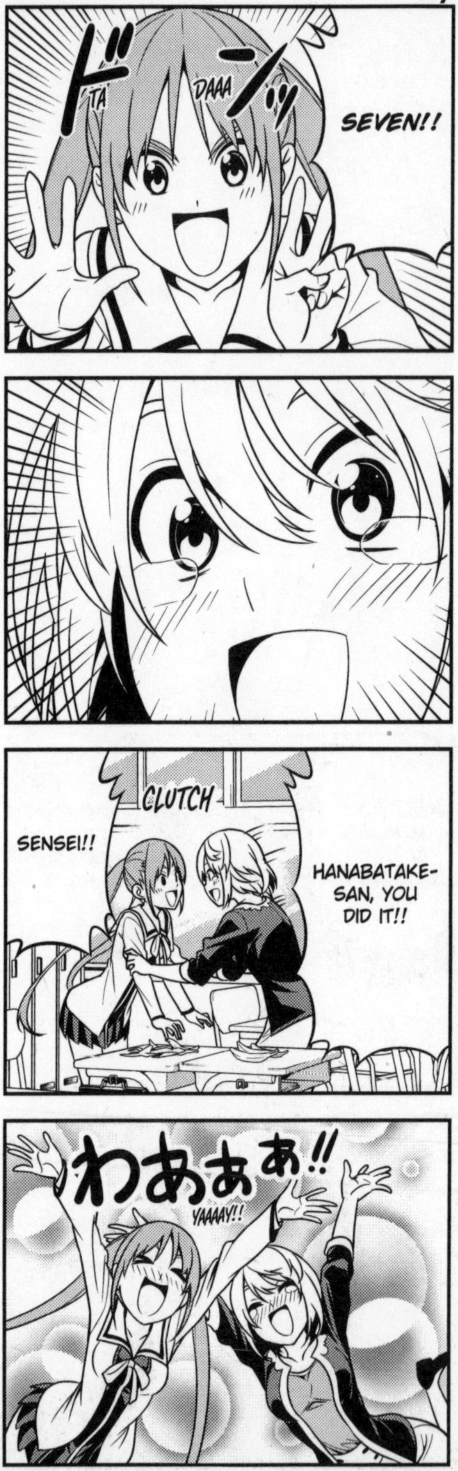
ドーンッ
TA DAAA
SEVEN!!
CLUTCH
HANABATAKE-SAN, YOU DID IT!!
SENSEI!!
わあぁぁあ!!
YAAAAY!!

Loop

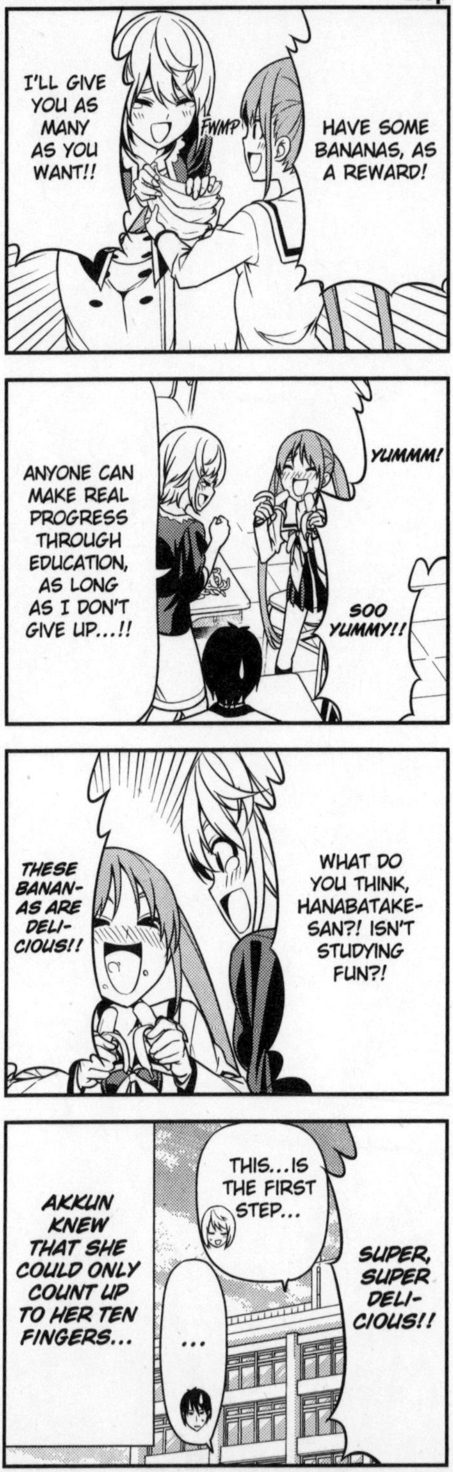
HAVE SOME BANANAS, AS A REWARD!
FWMP
I'LL GIVE YOU AS MANY AS YOU WANT!!
YUMMM!
SOO YUMMY!!
ANYONE CAN MAKE REAL PROGRESS THROUGH EDUCATION, AS LONG AS I DON'T GIVE UP...!!
WHAT DO YOU THINK, HANABATAKE-SAN?! ISN'T STUDYING FUN?!
THESE BANAN-AS ARE DELI-CIOUS!!
THIS...IS THE FIRST STEP...
SUPER, SUPER DELI-CIOUS!!
...
AKKUN KNEW THAT SHE COULD ONLY COUNT UP TO HER TEN FINGERS...

Still, Perhaps This Teacher...

IT'S TOUGH TO TEACH HER HOW TO STUDY.
BUT I HOPE YOU WON'T GIVE UP, SENSEI...!!
PLEASE... DO THE IMPOSSIBLE ...!!
THESE ARE HIS SINCERE FEEL-INGS.

(Stop! Put your guns down and raise your hands! We are)

Aho-Girl

\'ahô,gərl\ *Japanese , noun .*

A clueless girl.

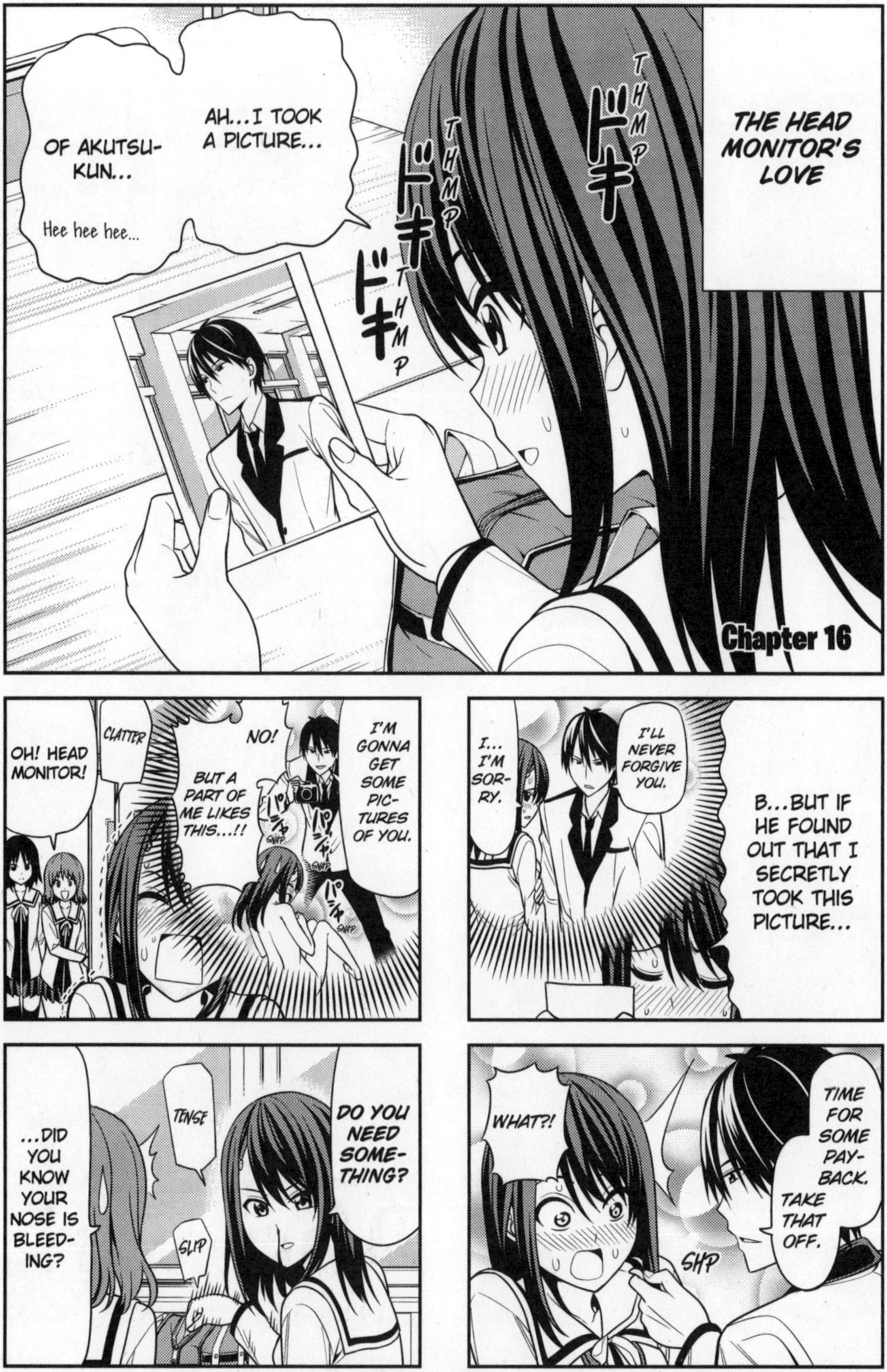
THE HEAD MONITOR'S LOVE
ドキ THMP
ドキ THMP
ドキ THMP
AH...I TOOK A PICTURE...
OF AKUTSU-KUN...
Hee hee hee...
Chapter 16
B...BUT IF HE FOUND OUT THAT I SECRETLY TOOK THIS PICTURE...
I'LL NEVER FORGIVE YOU.
I... I'M SORRY.
I'M GONNA GET SOME PICTURES OF YOU.
NO!
BUT A PART OF ME LIKES THIS...!!
SNAP
SNAP
SNAP
CLATTER
OH! HEAD MONITOR!
TIME FOR SOME PAYBACK. TAKE THAT OFF.
WHAT?!
SHP
DO YOU NEED SOMETHING?
TENSE
SLIP
...DID YOU KNOW YOUR NOSE IS BLEEDING?

Well, Of Course

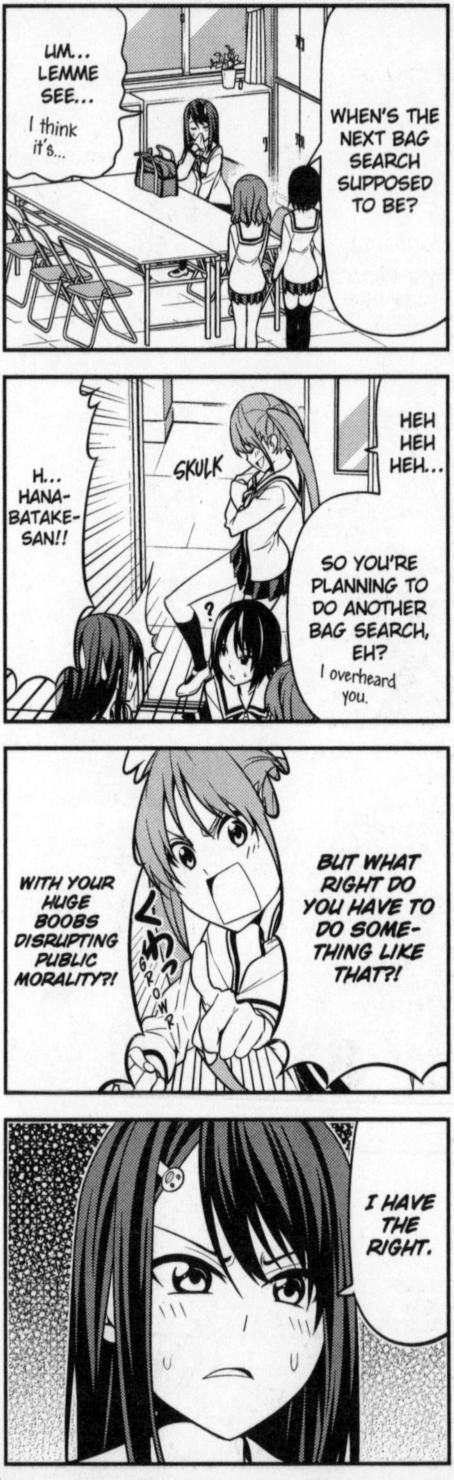
WHEN'S THE NEXT BAG SEARCH SUPPOSED TO BE?
UM... LEMME SEE...
I think it's...
HEH HEH HEH...
SO YOU'RE PLANNING TO DO ANOTHER BAG SEARCH, EH?
I overheard you.
SKULK
H... HANA-BATAKE-SAN!!
?
BUT WHAT RIGHT DO YOU HAVE TO DO SOME-THING LIKE THAT?!
GROWR
WITH YOUR HUGE BOOBS DISRUPTING PUBLIC MORALITY?!
I HAVE THE RIGHT.

There It Is!

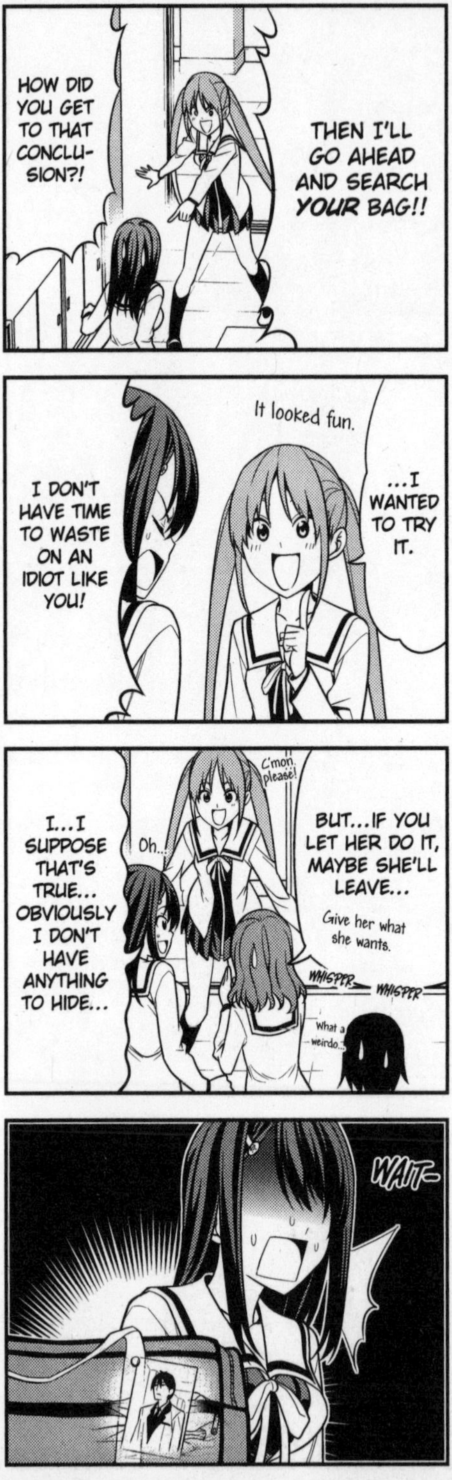
THEN I'LL GO AHEAD AND SEARCH *YOUR* BAG!!
HOW DID YOU GET TO THAT CONCLU-SION?!
...I WANTED TO TRY IT.
It looked fun.
I DON'T HAVE TIME TO WASTE ON AN IDIOT LIKE YOU!
C'mon please!
BUT...IF YOU LET HER DO IT, MAYBE SHE'LL LEAVE...
Give her what she wants.
WHISPER WHISPER
What a weirdo...
Oh...
I...I SUPPOSE THAT'S TRUE... OBVIOUSLY I DON'T HAVE ANYTHING TO HIDE...
WAIT-

A Victorious Smile

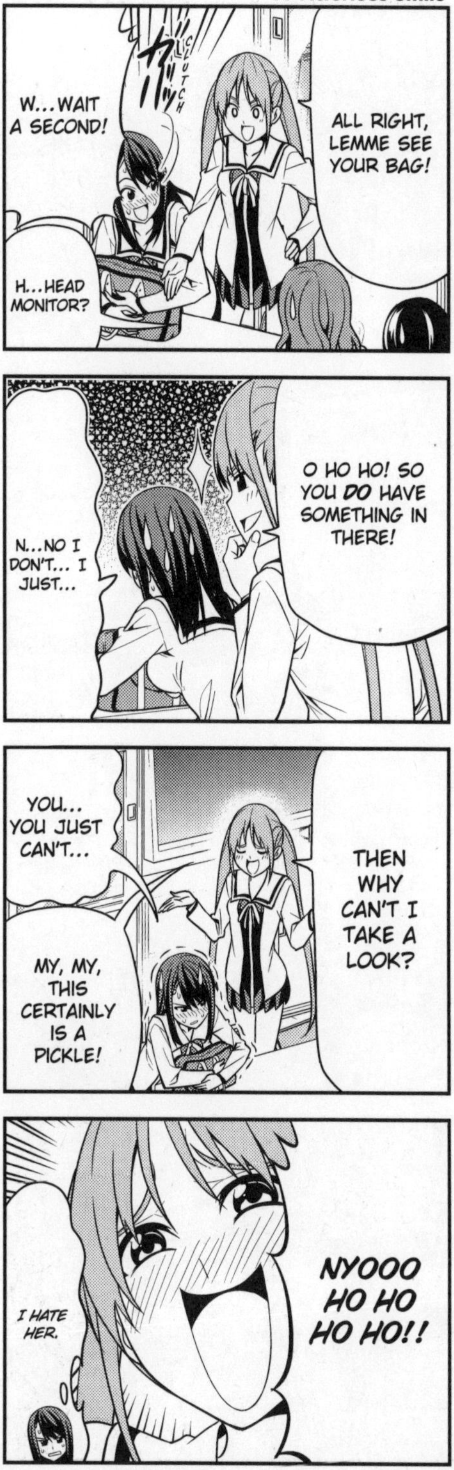
ALL RIGHT, LEMME SEE YOUR BAG!
CLUTCH
W...WAIT A SECOND!
H...HEAD MONITOR?
O HO HO! SO YOU **DO** HAVE SOMETHING IN THERE!
N...NO I DON'T... I JUST...
THEN WHY CAN'T I TAKE A LOOK?
YOU... YOU JUST CAN'T...
MY, MY, THIS CERTAINLY IS A PICKLE!
NYOOO HO HO HO HO!!
I HATE HER.

Danger Approaches

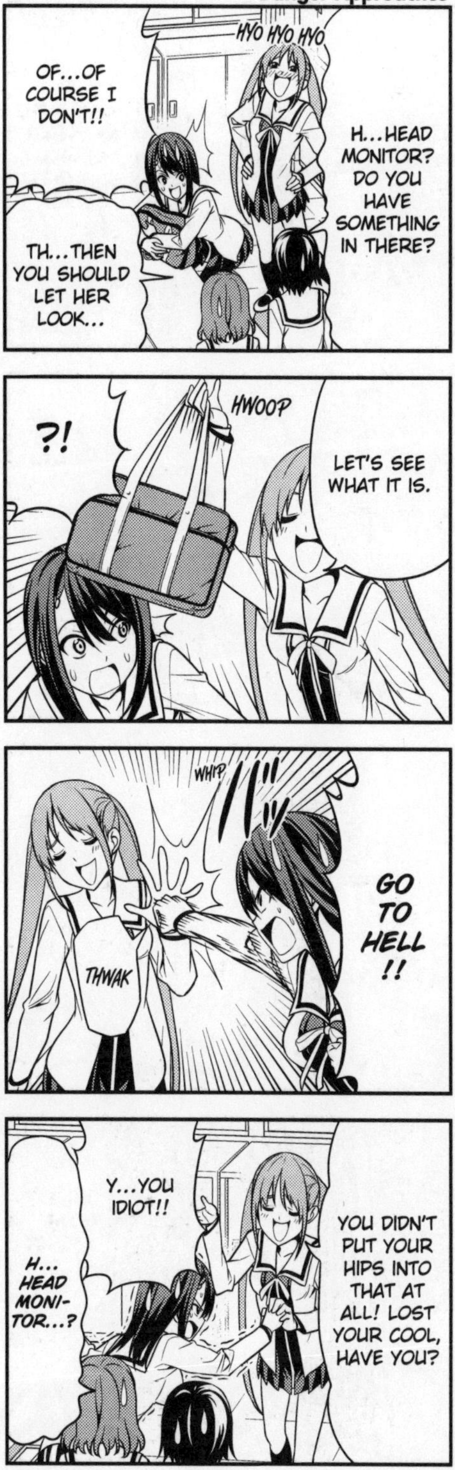
H...HEAD MONITOR? DO YOU HAVE SOMETHING IN THERE?
HYO HYO HYO
OF...OF COURSE I DON'T!!
TH...THEN YOU SHOULD LET HER LOOK...
LET'S SEE WHAT IT IS.
HWOOP
?!
GO TO HELL!!
WHIP
THWAK
YOU DIDN'T PUT YOUR HIPS INTO THAT AT ALL! LOST YOUR COOL, HAVE YOU?
Y...YOU IDIOT!!
H... HEAD MONI-TOR...?

Because It's Suspicious

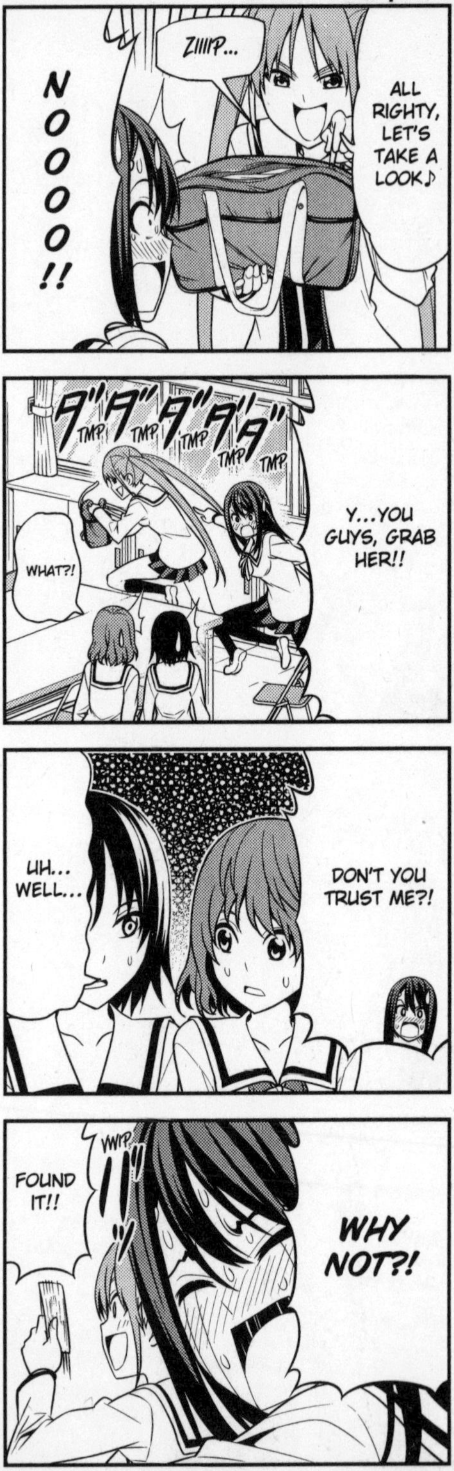
ZIIIP...
ALL RIGHTY, LET'S TAKE A LOOK♪
NOOOOO!!
ダダダダダ
TMP TMP TMP TMP TMP
Y...YOU GUYS, GRAB HER!!
WHAT?!
DON'T YOU TRUST ME?!
UH... WELL...
WHY NOT?!
VWIP
FOUND IT!!

Decisive Moral Leadership

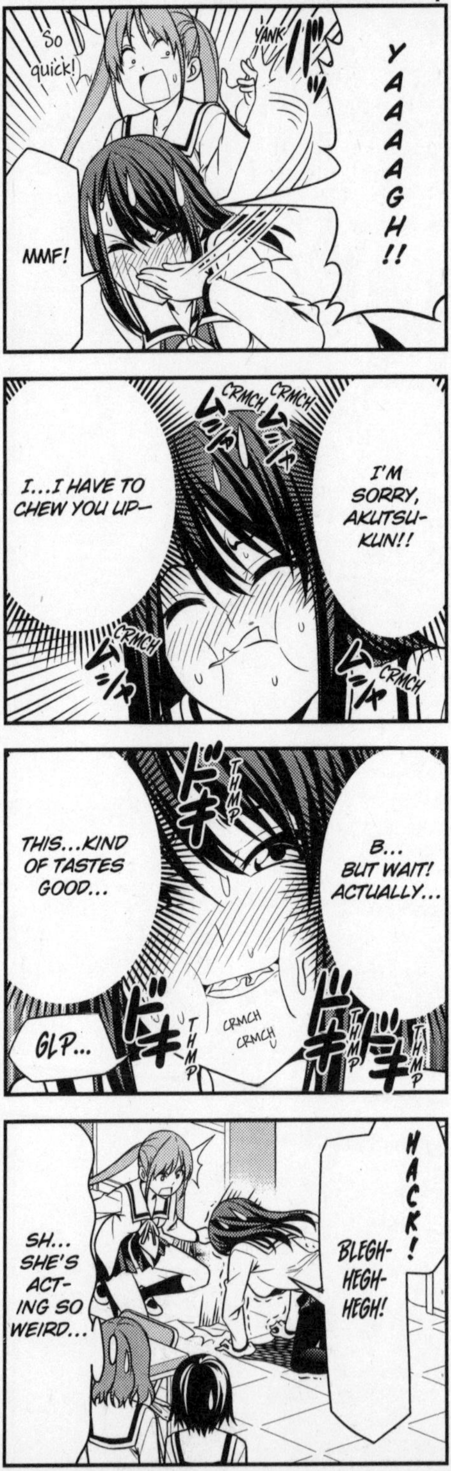
YAAAAAGH!!
バッ
YANK
So quick!
MMF!
I'M SORRY, AKUTSU-KUN!!
ムシャムシャ
CRMCH CRMCH
I...I HAVE TO CHEW YOU UP—
ムシャムシャ
CRMCH CRMCH
B... BUT WAIT! ACTUALLY...
ドキドキドキ
THMP THMP THMP THMP
THIS...KIND OF TASTES GOOD...
CRMCH CRMCH
GLP...
HACK!
BLEGH-HEGH-HEGH!
SH... SHE'S ACT-ING SO WEIRD...

Preposterous

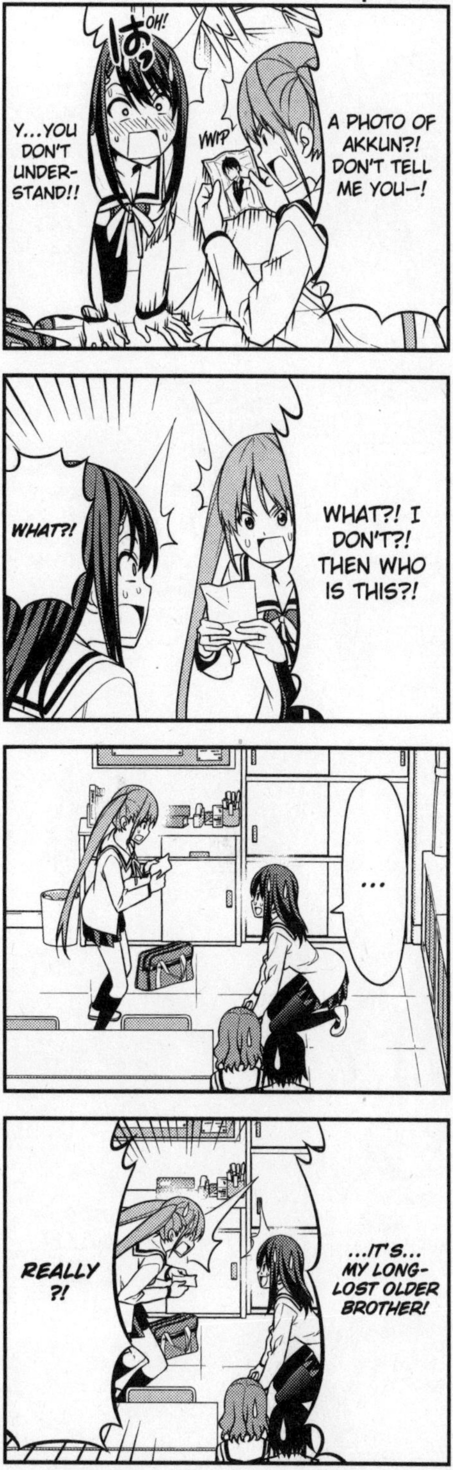
OH!
A PHOTO OF AKKUN?! DON'T TELL ME YOU—!
VWIP
Y...YOU DON'T UNDERSTAND!!
WHAT?! I DON'T?! THEN WHO IS THIS?!
WHAT?!
...
...IT'S... MY LONG-LOST OLDER BROTHER!
REALLY?!

Like a Rolling Stone

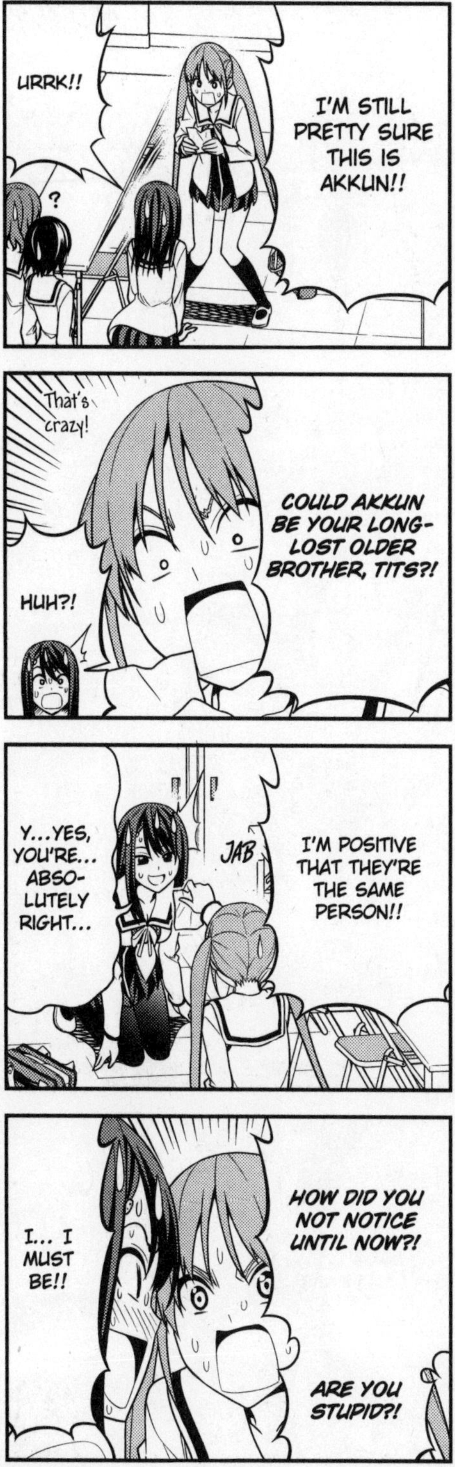
I'M STILL PRETTY SURE THIS IS AKKUN!!
URRK!!
?
COULD AKKUN BE YOUR LONG-LOST OLDER BROTHER, TITS?!
That's crazy!
HUH?!
I'M POSITIVE THAT THEY'RE THE SAME PERSON!!
JAB
Y...YES, YOU'RE... ABSOLUTELY RIGHT...
HOW DID YOU NOT NOTICE UNTIL NOW?!
ARE YOU STUPID?!
I... I MUST BE!!

Emotional

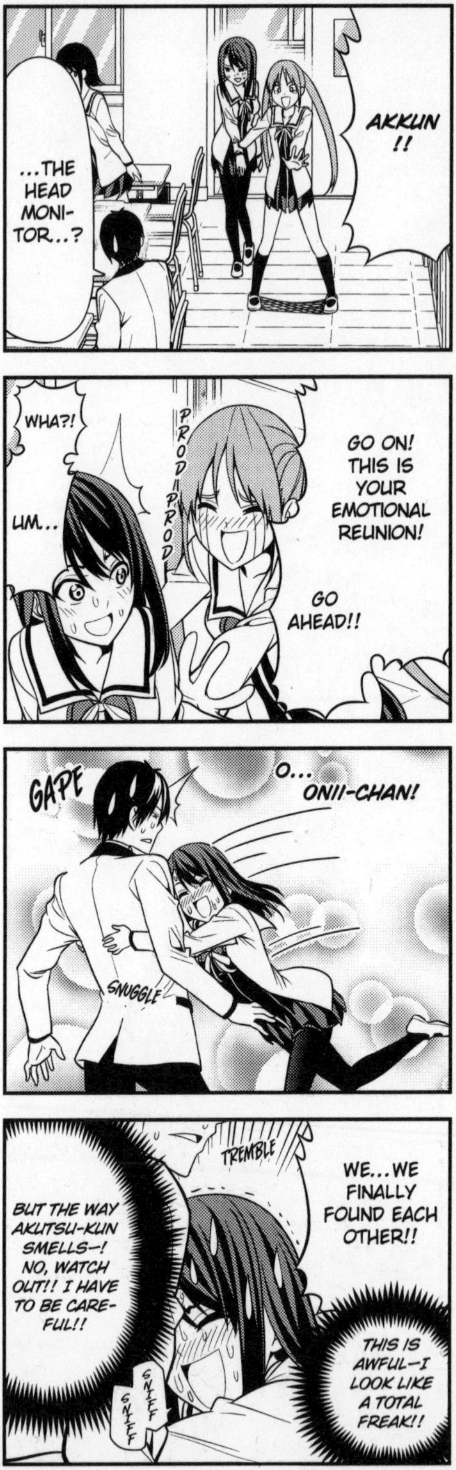
AKKUN !!
...THE HEAD MONI-TOR...?
GO ON! THIS IS YOUR EMOTIONAL REUNION!
GO AHEAD!!
PROD PROD PROD
WHA?!
UM...
O... ONII-CHAN!
GAPE
SNUGGLE
WE...WE FINALLY FOUND EACH OTHER!!
TREMBLE
THIS IS AWFUL—I LOOK LIKE A TOTAL FREAK!!
BUT THE WAY AKUTSU-KUN SMELLS—! NO, WATCH OUT!! I HAVE TO BE CARE-FUL!!
SNIFF SNIFF

She's a Good Person

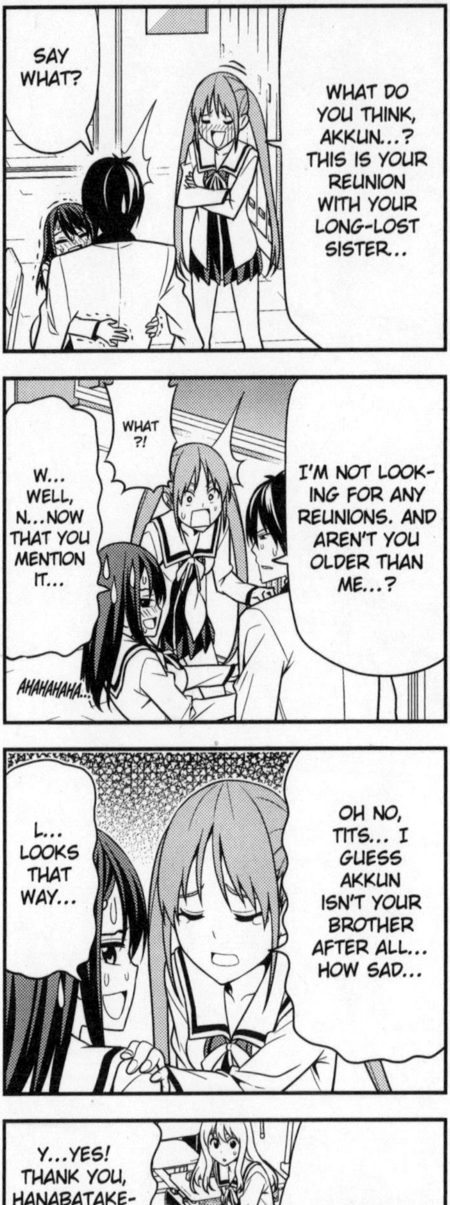
WHAT DO YOU THINK, AKKUN...? THIS IS YOUR REUNION WITH YOUR LONG-LOST SISTER...
SAY WHAT?
I'M NOT LOOK-ING FOR ANY REUNIONS. AND AREN'T YOU OLDER THAN ME...?
WHAT ?!
W... WELL, N...NOW THAT YOU MENTION IT...
AHAHAHAHA...
OH NO, TITS... I GUESS AKKUN ISN'T YOUR BROTHER AFTER ALL... HOW SAD...
L... LOOKS THAT WAY...
BUT DON'T GIVE UP! YOU'LL FIND HIM SOME DAY!
Y...YES! THANK YOU, HANABATAKE-SAN!
SUCH A WEIRDO...

But It's Cute, Too

HUFF...
HUFF...
TH...THAT WAS SO CLOSE...
IF AKUTSU-KUN FOUND OUT I'D SECRETLY TAKEN A PICTURE OF HIM, HE'D THINK I'M STRANGE...
WHEW...
IT WAS NOT UNTIL MUCH LATER THAT SHE WOULD REALIZE IT WAS FAR TOO LATE FOR THAT...

(Got My Eye On)

Aho-Girl

\\'ahô͵gərl\\ *Japanese , noun.*
A clueless girl.

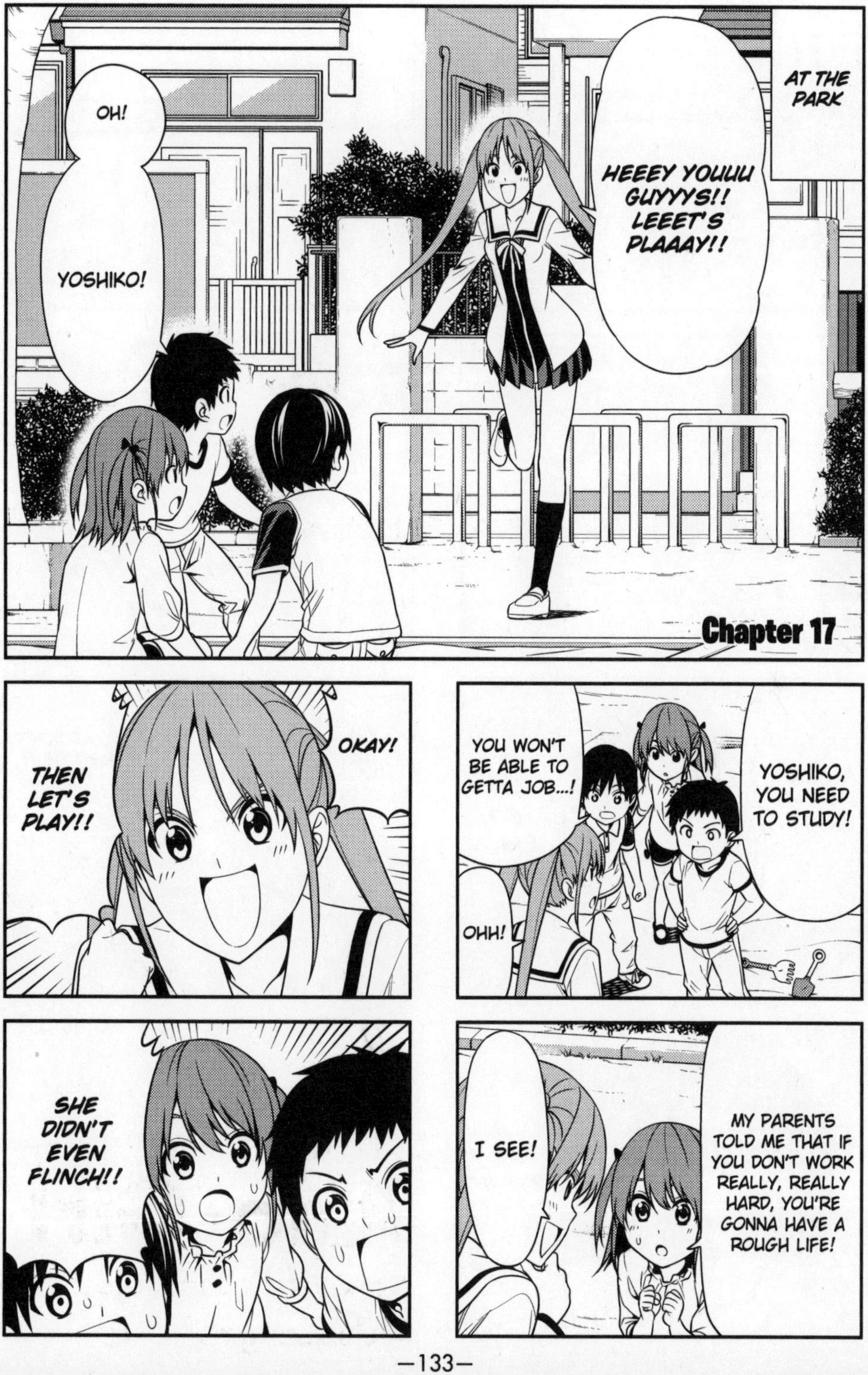
AT THE PARK
HEEEY YOUUU GUYYYS!! LEEET'S PLAAAY!!
OH! YOSHIKO!
Chapter 17
YOSHIKO, YOU NEED TO STUDY!
YOU WON'T BE ABLE TO GETTA JOB...!
OHH!
OKAY!
THEN LET'S PLAY!!
MY PARENTS TOLD ME THAT IF YOU DON'T WORK REALLY, REALLY HARD, YOU'RE GONNA HAVE A ROUGH LIFE!
I SEE!
SHE DIDN'T EVEN FLINCH!!

An Intruder Enters the Scene

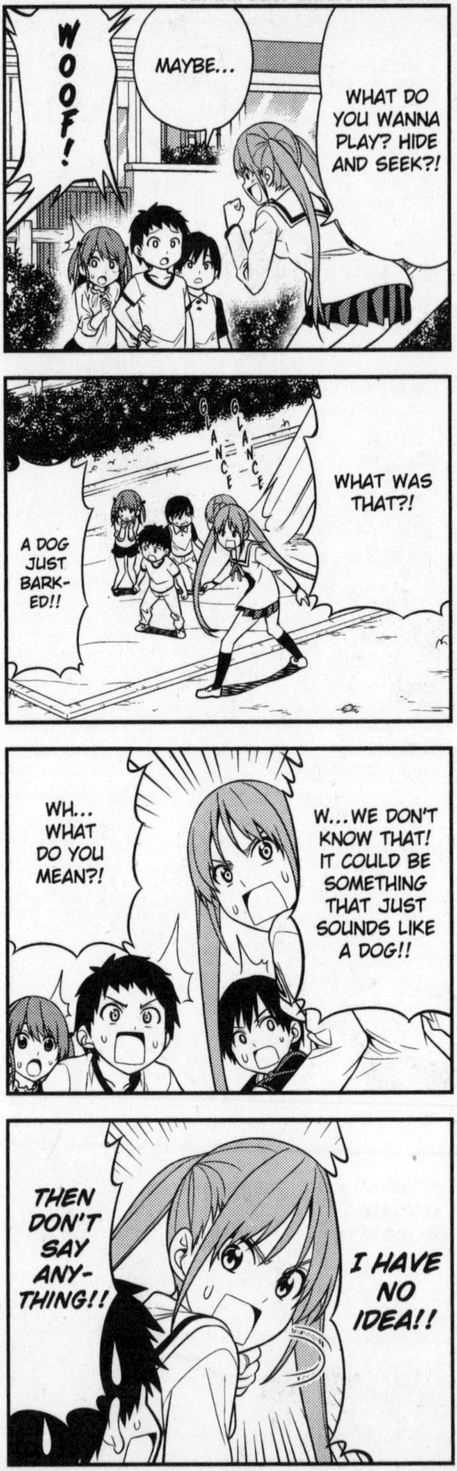
WHAT DO YOU WANNA PLAY? HIDE AND SEEK?!
MAYBE...
WOOF!
WHAT WAS THAT?!
GLANCE GLANCE
A DOG JUST BARKED!!
W...WE DON'T KNOW THAT! IT COULD BE SOMETHING THAT JUST SOUNDS LIKE A DOG!!
WH... WHAT DO YOU MEAN?!
I HAVE NO IDEA!!
THEN DON'T SAY ANYTHING!!

It Wasn't a Person

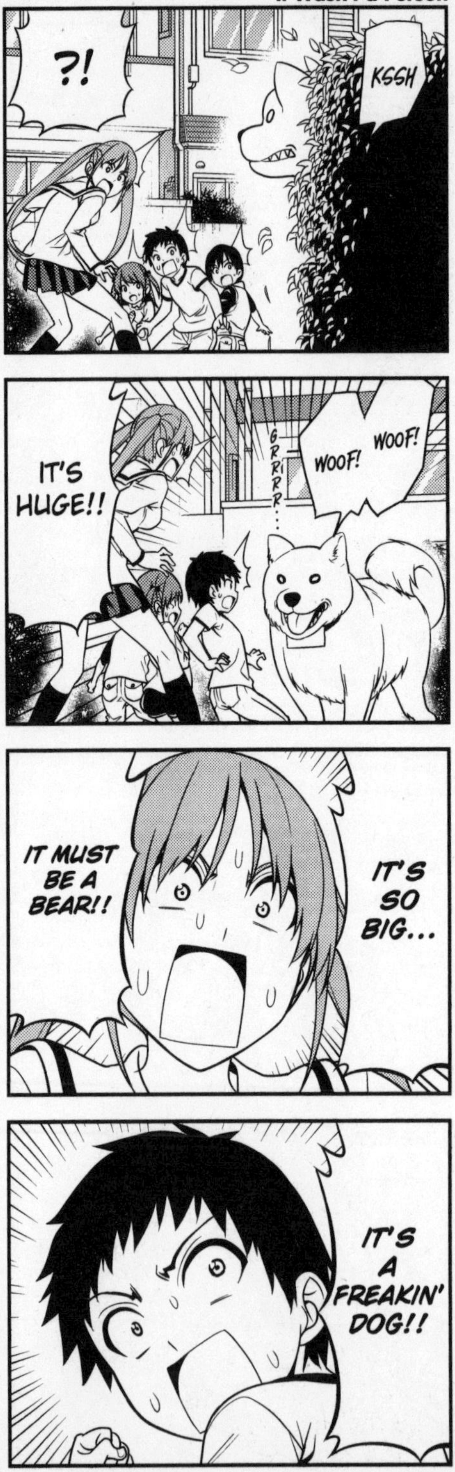
KSSH
?!
WOOF!
WOOF!
GRRRR...
IT'S HUGE!!
IT'S SO BIG...
IT MUST BE A BEAR!!
IT'S A FREAKIN' DOG!!

She Lost Sight Of The Mission

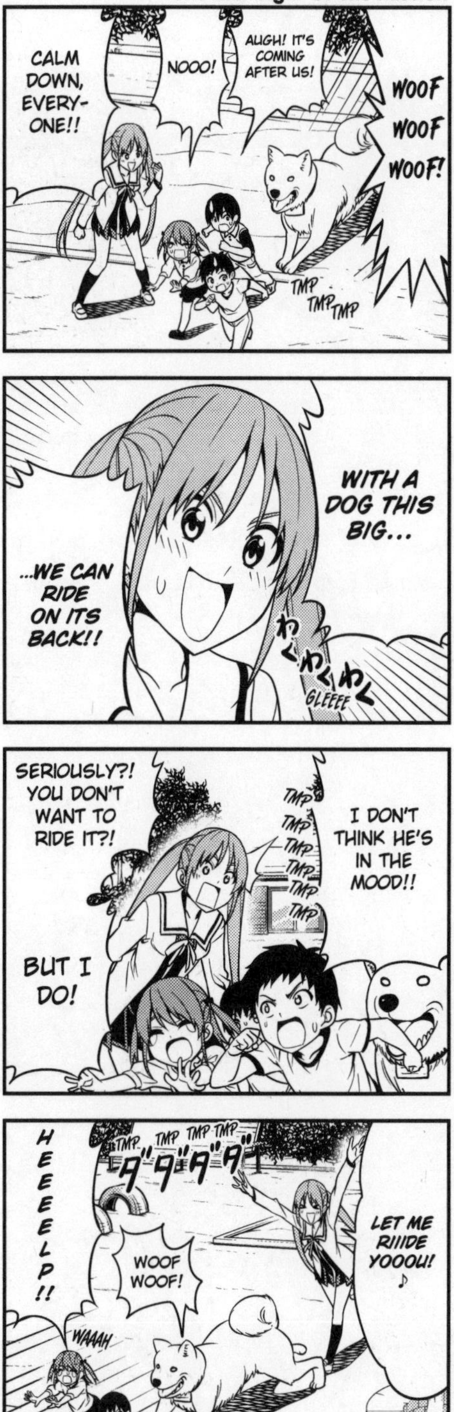
WOOF WOOF WOOF!
AUGH! IT'S COMING AFTER US!
NOOO!
CALM DOWN, EVERY-ONE!!
TMP TMP TMP
WITH A DOG THIS BIG...
...WE CAN RIDE ON ITS BACK!!
わくわくわく
GLEEEE
I DON'T THINK HE'S IN THE MOOD!!
TMP TMP TMP TMP TMP TMP
SERIOUSLY?! YOU DON'T WANT TO RIDE IT?!
BUT I DO!
LET ME RIIIDE YOOOU! ♪
TMP TMP TMP TMP
ダダダダ
HEEEEELP!!
WOOF WOOF!
WAAAH

He's Just Playing

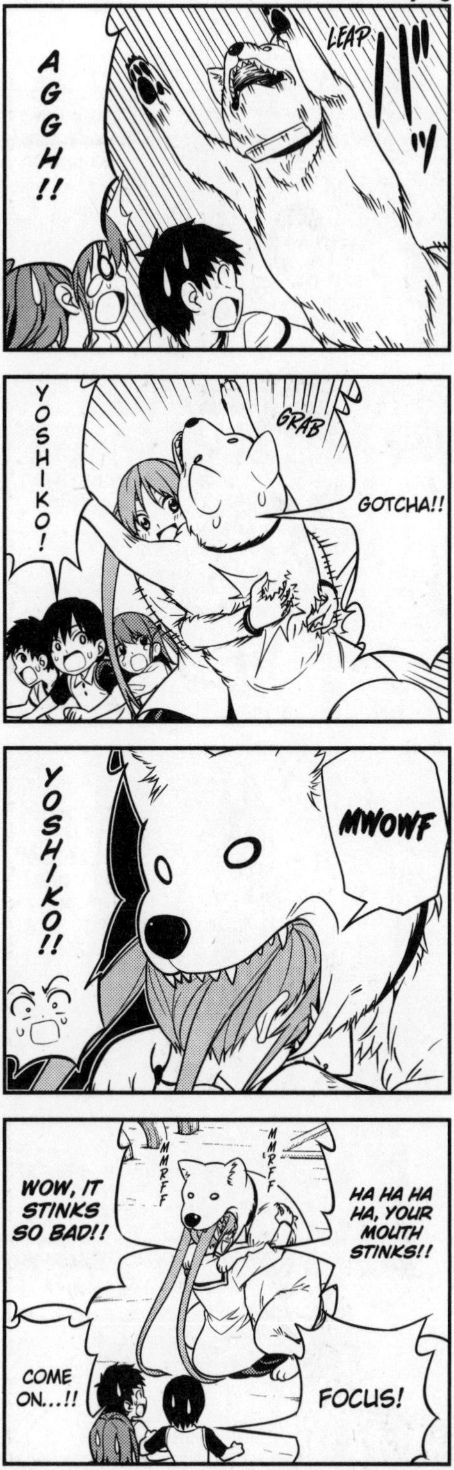
バッ
LEAP
AGGGH!!
GOTCHA!!
GRAB
YOSHIKO!
MWOWF
YOSHIKO!!
HA HA HA HA, YOUR MOUTH STINKS!!
MMRFF
MMRFF
WOW, IT STINKS SO BAD!!
FOCUS!
COME ON...!!

Like She's a Slime Knight

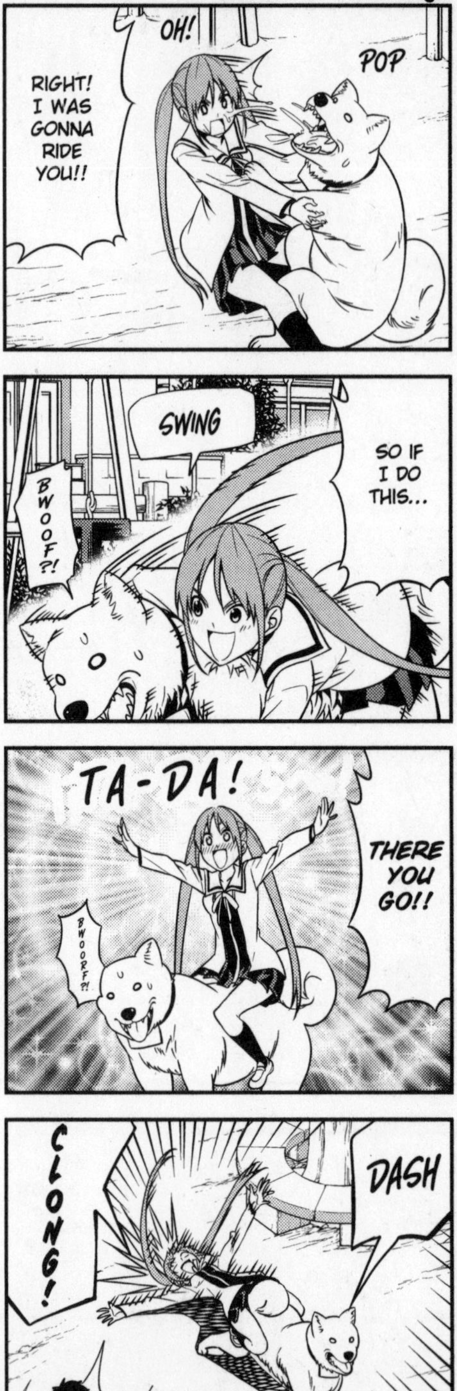
OH!
POP
RIGHT! I WAS GONNA RIDE YOU!!
SWING
SO IF I DO THIS...
BWOOF?!
TA-DA!
THERE YOU GO!!
BWOORF?!
DASH
CLONG!

Like She's Getting Turned into Butter

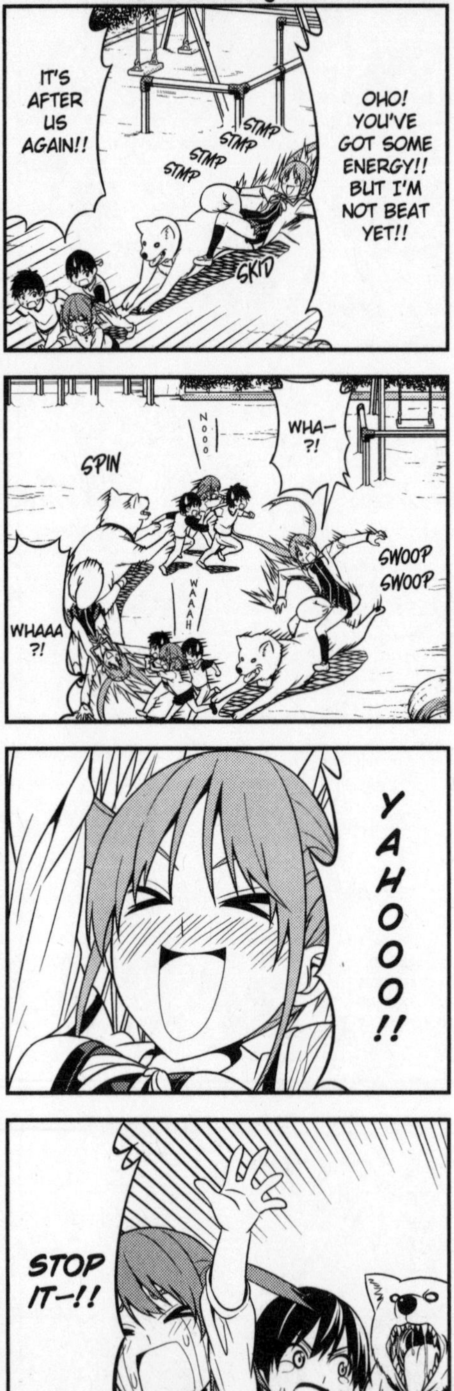
OHO! YOU'VE GOT SOME ENERGY!! BUT I'M NOT BEAT YET!!
STMP
STMP
STMP
STMP
SKID
IT'S AFTER US AGAIN!!
WHA-?!
NOOO—
SPIN
SWOOP SWOOP
WAAAH
WHAAA?!
YAHOOOO!!
STOP IT-!!

That's Not a Bad Idea

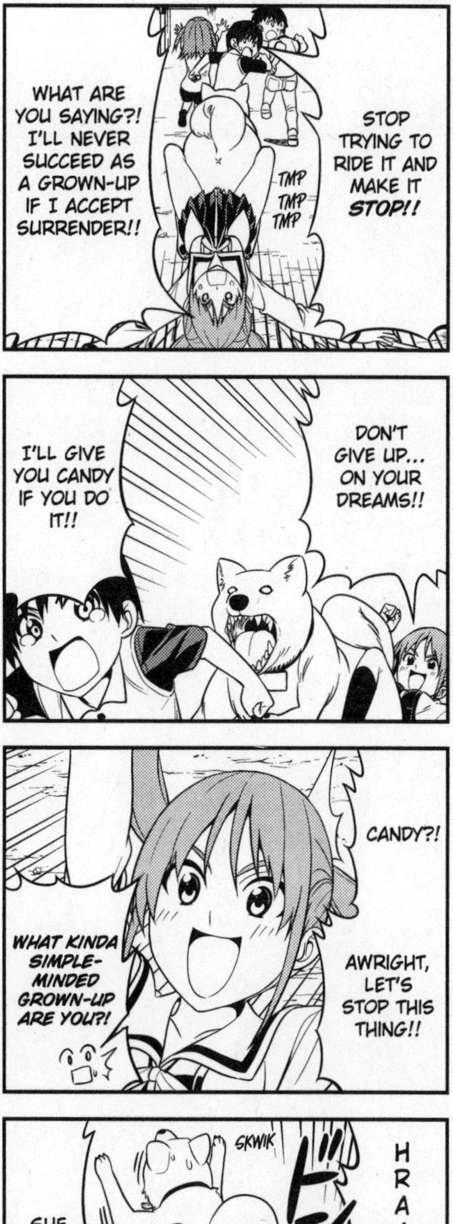
STOP TRYING TO RIDE IT AND MAKE IT STOP!!
TMP TMP TMP
WHAT ARE YOU SAYING?! I'LL NEVER SUCCEED AS A GROWN-UP IF I ACCEPT SURRENDER!!
DON'T GIVE UP... ON YOUR DREAMS!!
I'LL GIVE YOU CANDY IF YOU DO IT!!
CANDY?!
AWRIGHT, LET'S STOP THIS THING!!
WHAT KINDA SIMPLE-MINDED GROWN-UP ARE YOU?!
HRAAGH!!
SKWIK
THUNK
SHE STOPPED IT—!!

Yoshiko's Killer Special

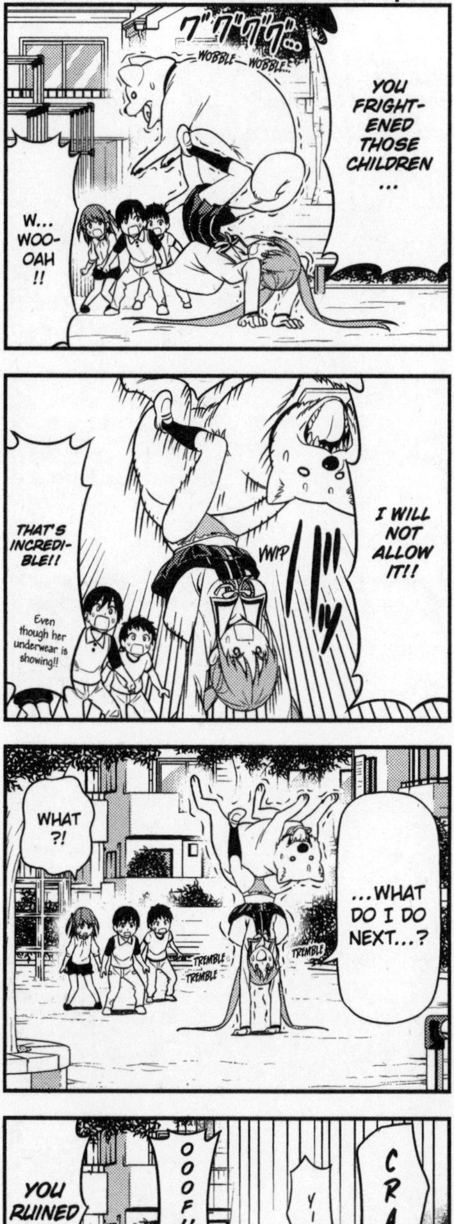
グググ…
WOBBLE—WOBBLE…
YOU FRIGHT-ENED THOSE CHILDREN …
W… WOO-OAH !!
I WILL NOT ALLOW IT!!
VWIP
THAT'S INCREDI-BLE!!
Even though her underwear is showing!!
...WHAT DO I DO NEXT...?
TREMBLE
TREMBLE TREMBLE
WHAT ?!
CRASH!
YIPE
OOOF!!
YOU RUINED IT!!

Proof of Surrender

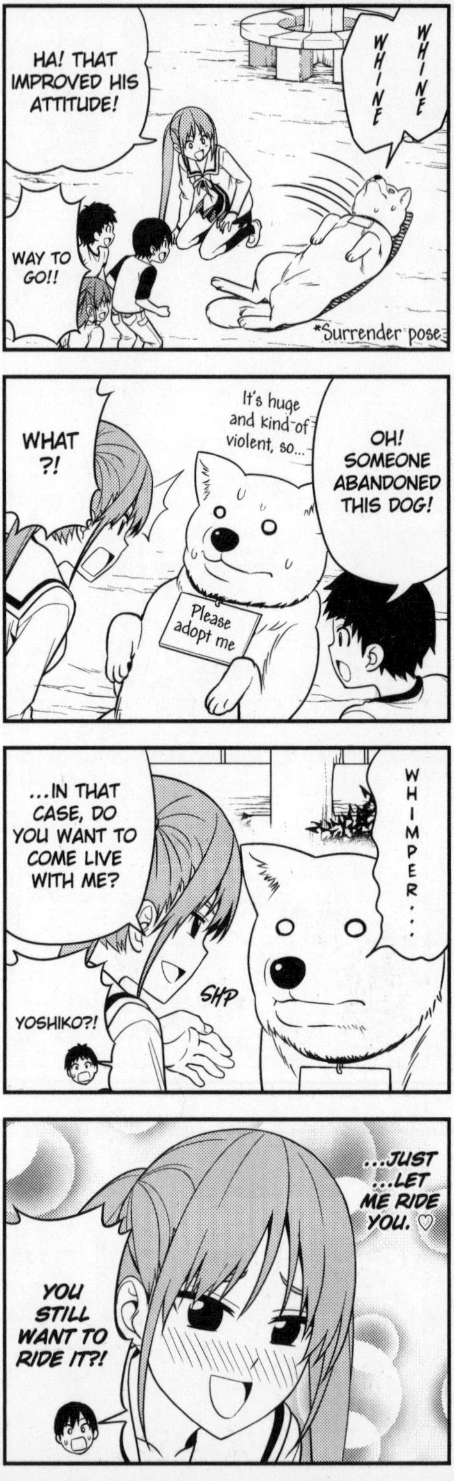

HA! THAT IMPROVED HIS ATTITUDE!
WHINE WHINE
WAY TO GO!!
*Surrender pose
OH! SOMEONE ABANDONED THIS DOG!
It's huge and kind of violent, so...
WHAT?!
Please adopt me
WHIMPER...
...IN THAT CASE, DO YOU WANT TO COME LIVE WITH ME?
SHP
YOSHIKO?!
...JUST ...LET ME RIDE YOU. ♡
YOU STILL WANT TO RIDE IT?!

Yoshiko's Mobility: Improved

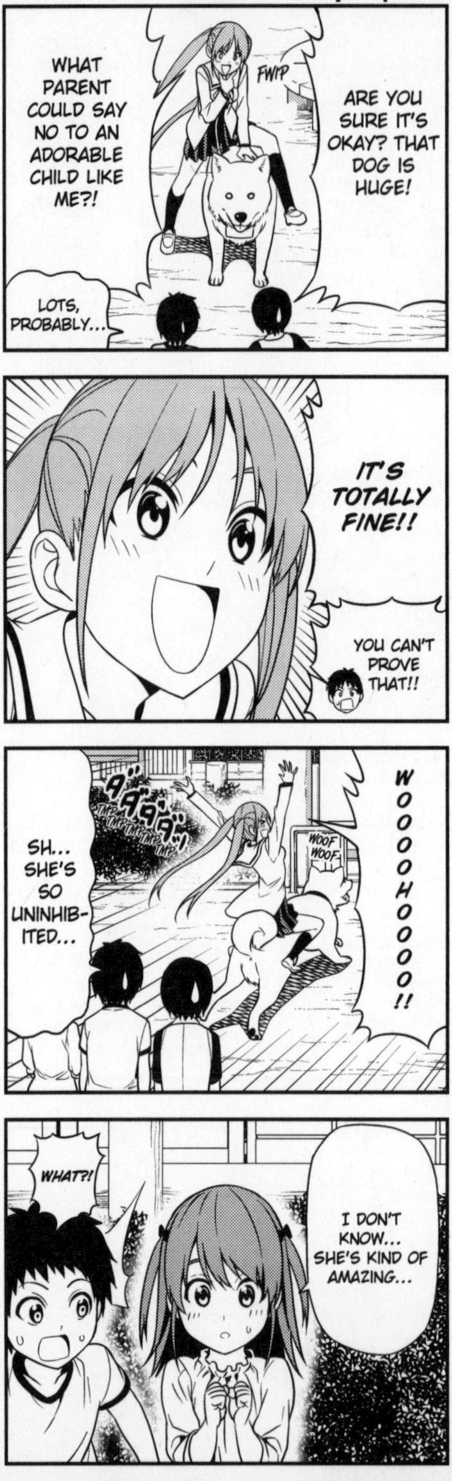

ARE YOU SURE IT'S OKAY? THAT DOG IS HUGE!
FWIP
WHAT PARENT COULD SAY NO TO AN ADORABLE CHILD LIKE ME?!
LOTS, PROBABLY...
IT'S TOTALLY FINE!!
YOU CAN'T PROVE THAT!!
WOOOOOHOOOOOO!!
WOOF WOOF
SH... SHE'S SO UNINHIBITED...
I DON'T KNOW... SHE'S KIND OF AMAZING...
WHAT?!

She'll Still Get Her Way

LET'S KEEP HIM, MOM!
NO.
YOU CAN RIDE HIM, Y'KNOW!
I SAID NO!!

(I get depressed sometimes, but I'm an)

Aho-Girl

\\'ahô,gərl\\ *Japanese , noun.*
A clueless girl.

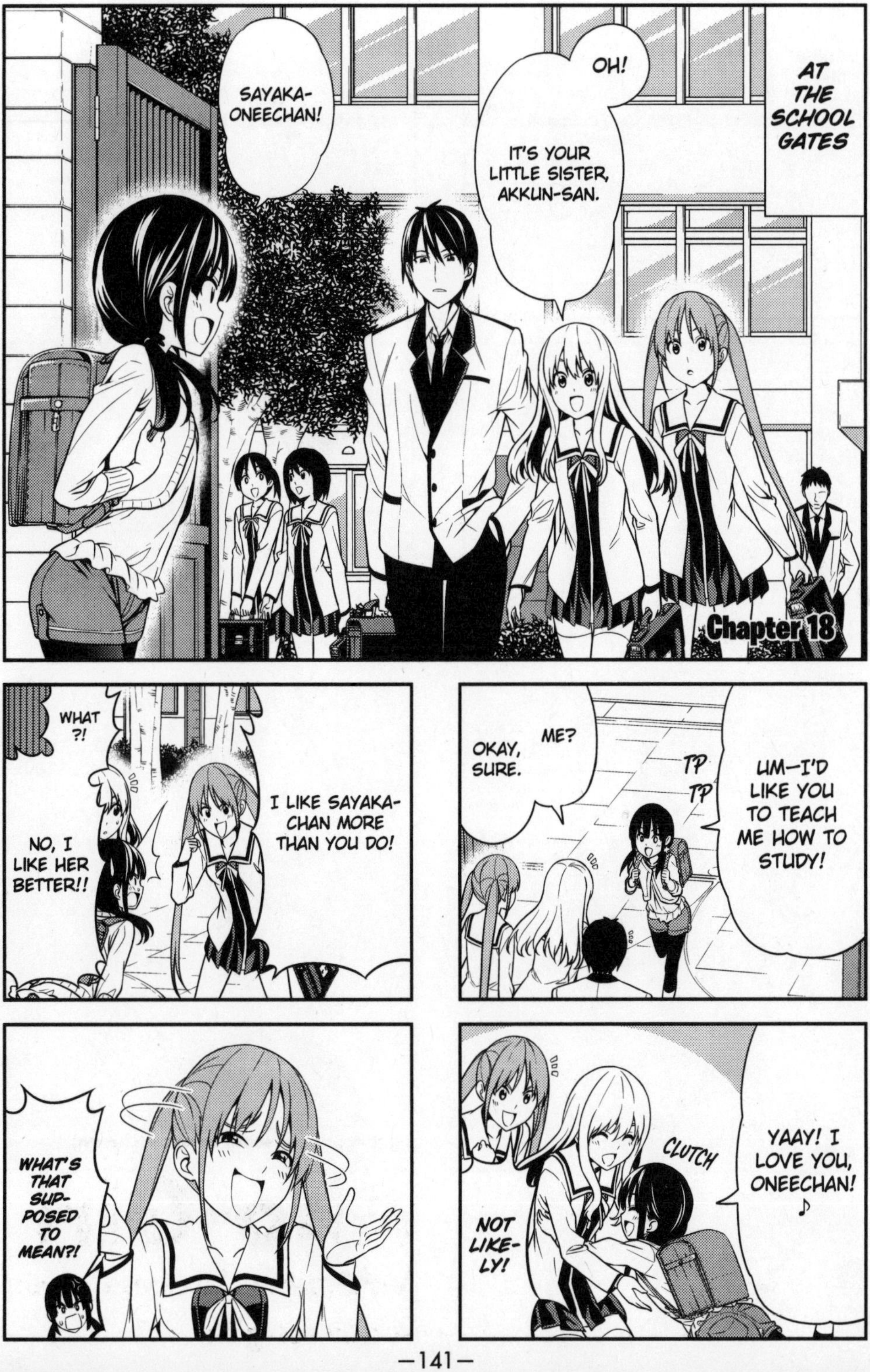

AT THE SCHOOL GATES
OH!
IT'S YOUR LITTLE SISTER, AKKUN-SAN.
SAYAKA-ONEECHAN!
Chapter 18
UM—I'D LIKE YOU TO TEACH ME HOW TO STUDY!
TP TP
ME?
OKAY, SURE.
I LIKE SAYAKA-CHAN MORE THAN YOU DO!
WHAT ?!
NO, I LIKE HER BETTER!!
YAAY! I LOVE YOU, ONEECHAN! ♪
CLUTCH
NOT LIKE-LY!
WHAT'S THAT SUP-POSED TO MEAN?!

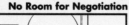

Shock

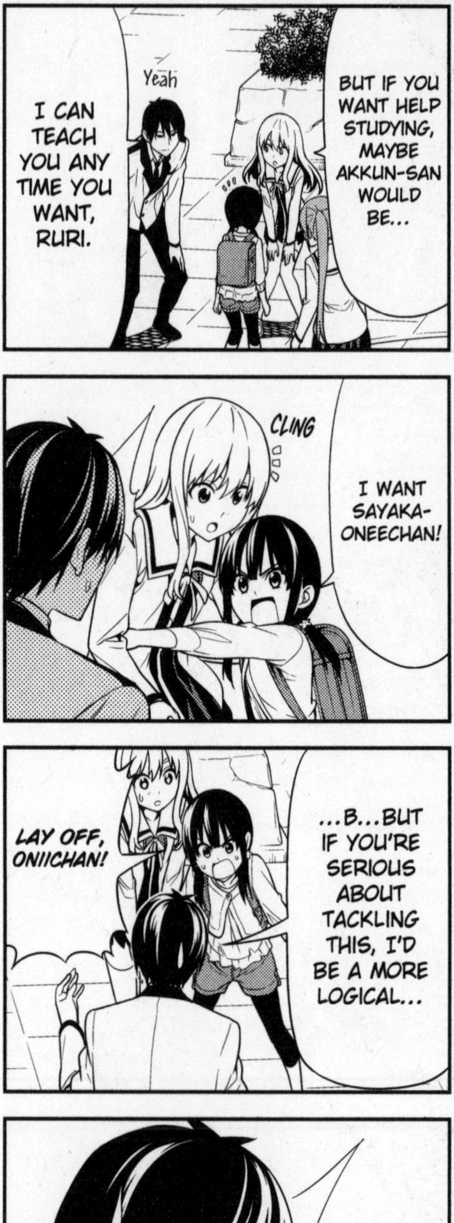
BUT IF YOU WANT HELP STUDYING, MAYBE AKKUN-SAN WOULD BE...
Yeah
I CAN TEACH YOU ANY TIME YOU WANT, RURI.
I WANT SAYAKA-ONEECHAN!
CLING
...B...BUT IF YOU'RE SERIOUS ABOUT TACKLING THIS, I'D BE A MORE LOGICAL...
LAY OFF, ONIICHAN!

No Room for Negotiation

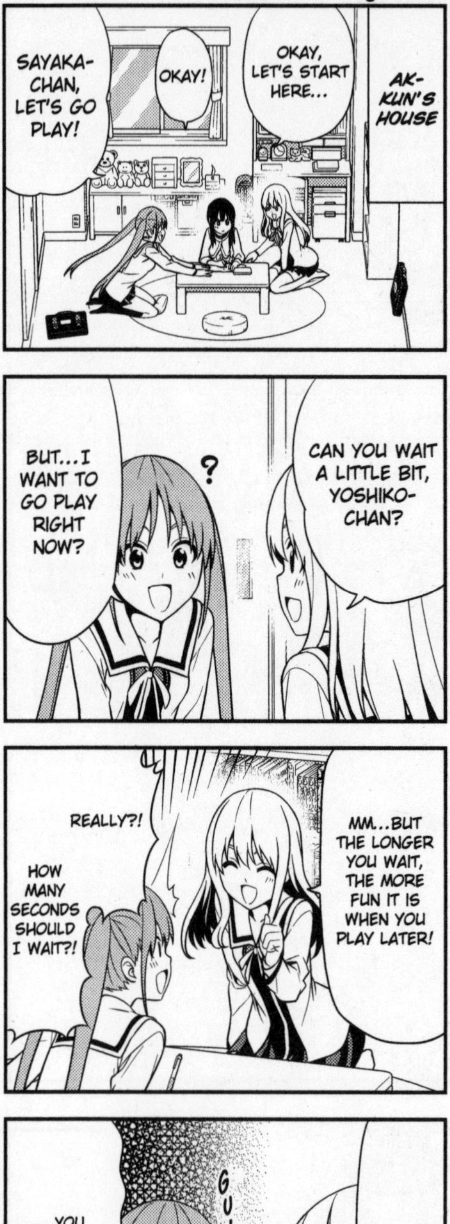
AK-KUN'S HOUSE
OKAY, LET'S START HERE...
OKAY!
SAYAKA-CHAN, LET'S GO PLAY!
CAN YOU WAIT A LITTLE BIT, YOSHIKO-CHAN?
?
BUT...I WANT TO GO PLAY RIGHT NOW?
MM...BUT THE LONGER YOU WAIT, THE MORE FUN IT IS WHEN YOU PLAY LATER!
REALLY?!
HOW MANY SECONDS SHOULD I WAIT?!
...ONE HOUR...?
GULP...
...YOU ASK THE IMPOSSIBLE...

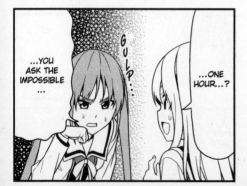

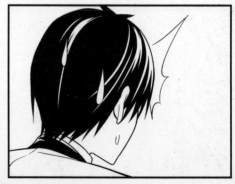

Withdrawal Symptoms

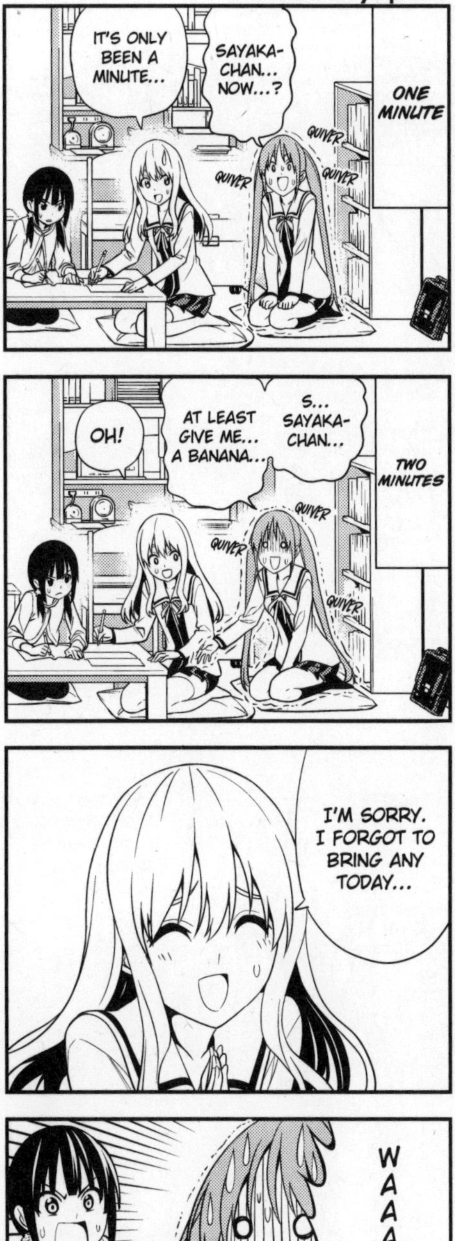
ONE MINUTE
SAYAKA-CHAN... NOW...?
IT'S ONLY BEEN A MINUTE...
QUIVER
QUIVER
QUIVER
TWO MINUTES
S... SAYAKA-CHAN...
AT LEAST GIVE ME... A BANANA...
OH!
QUIVER
QUIVER
QUIVER
I'M SORRY. I FORGOT TO BRING ANY TODAY...
WAAAUUGGGH!!
YOU'RE SO ANNOYING, YOSHIKO!!

Withdrawal Simpleton

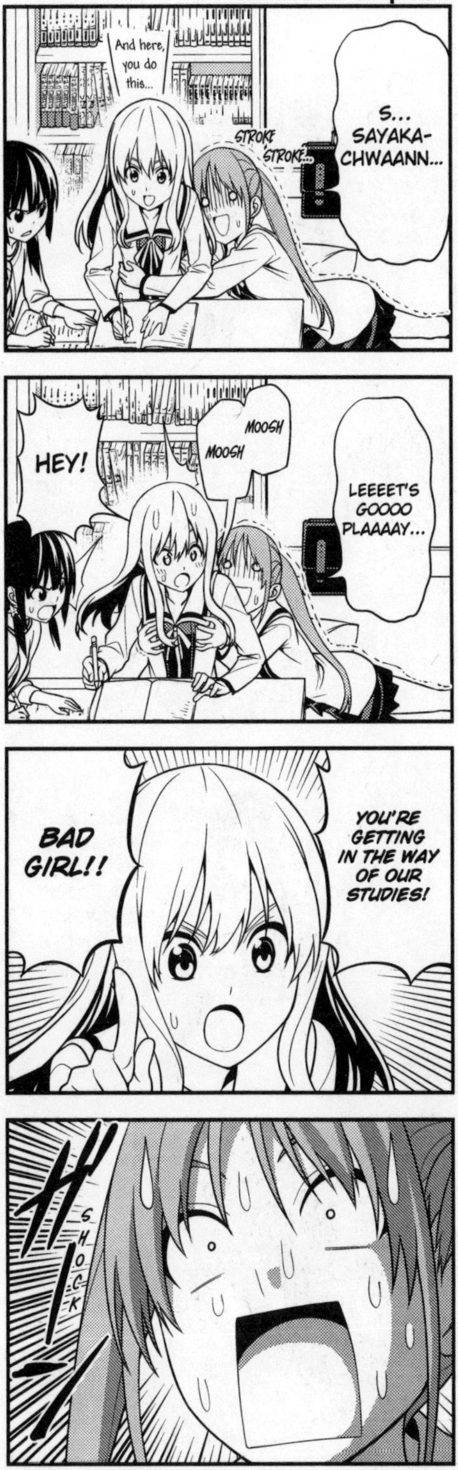
S... SAYAKA-CHWAANN...
STROKE
STROKE
And here, you do this...
LEEEET'S GOOOO PLAAAAY...
MOOSH
MOOSH
HEY!
YOU'RE GETTING IN THE WAY OF OUR STUDIES!
BAD GIRL!!
SHOCK

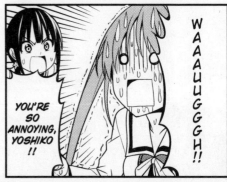

The Depths of Despair

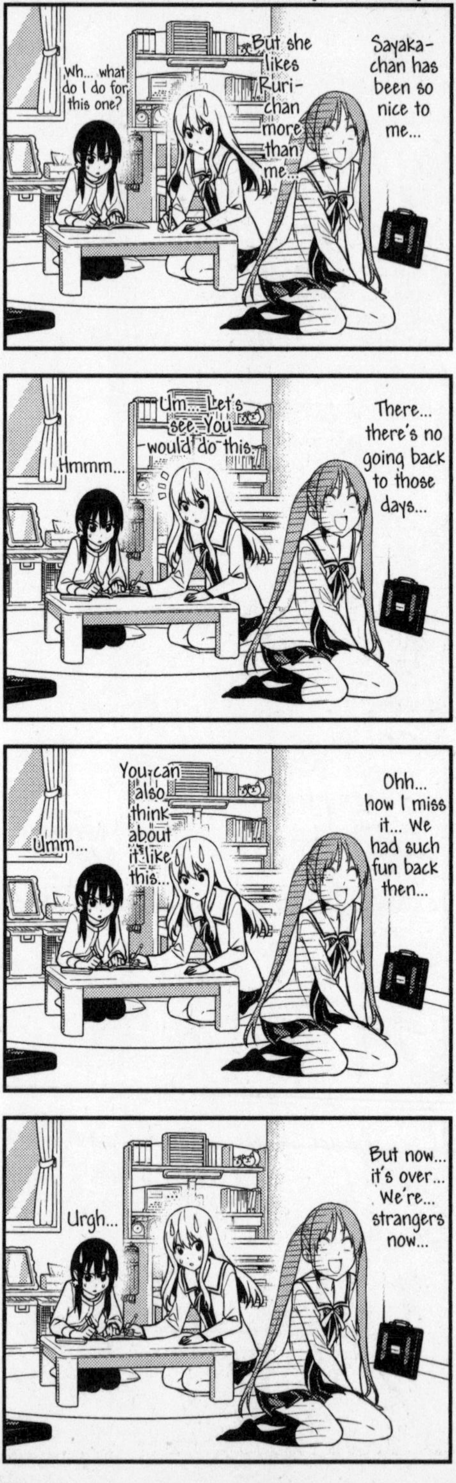
Sayaka-chan has been so nice to me...
But she likes Ruri-chan more than me...
Wh... what do I do for this one?
There... there's no going back to those days...
Um... Let's see. You would do this.
Hmmm...
Ohh... how I miss it... We had such fun back then...
You can also think about it like this...
Umm...
But now... it's over... We're... strangers now...
Urgh...

What Is This Conversation?

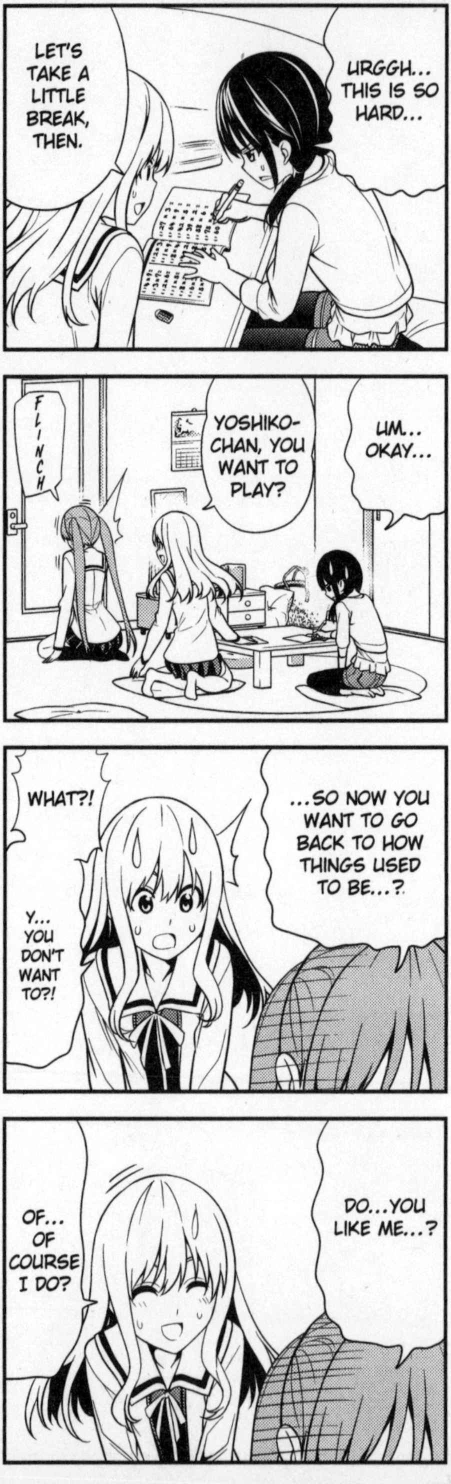
URGGH... THIS IS SO HARD...
LET'S TAKE A LITTLE BREAK, THEN.
UM... OKAY...
YOSHIKO-CHAN, YOU WANT TO PLAY?
FLINCH
...SO NOW YOU WANT TO GO BACK TO HOW THINGS USED TO BE...?
WHAT?!
Y... YOU DON'T WANT TO?!
DO...YOU LIKE ME...?
OF... OF COURSE I DO?

The Tables Have Turned

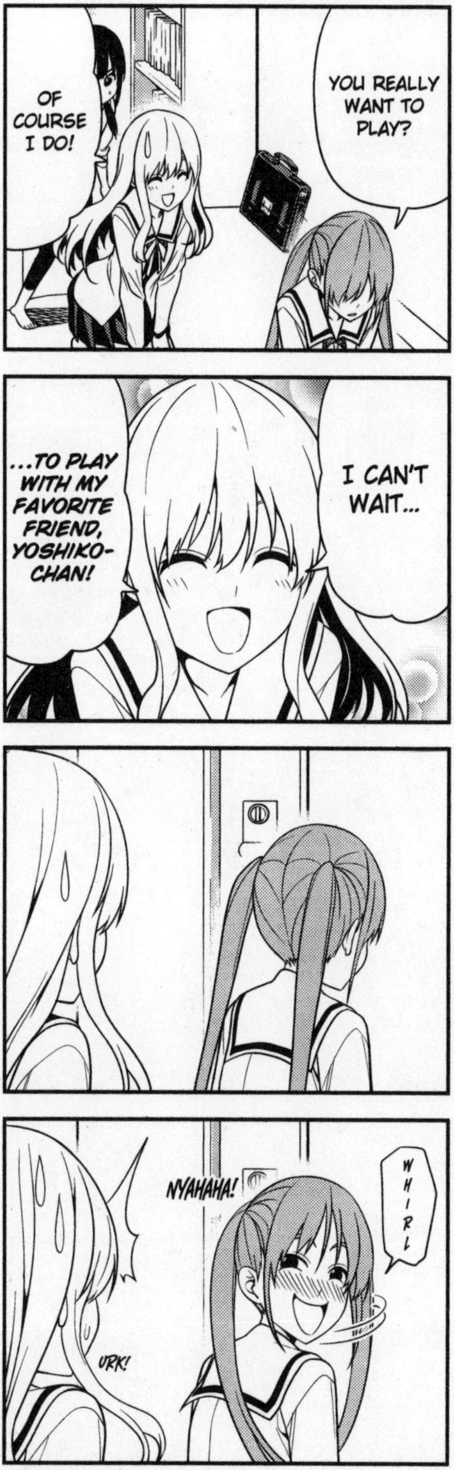
YOU REALLY WANT TO PLAY?
OF COURSE I DO!
I CAN'T WAIT...
...TO PLAY WITH MY FAVORITE FRIEND, YOSHIKO-CHAN!
WHIRL
NYAHAHA!
URK!

Better Make Sure

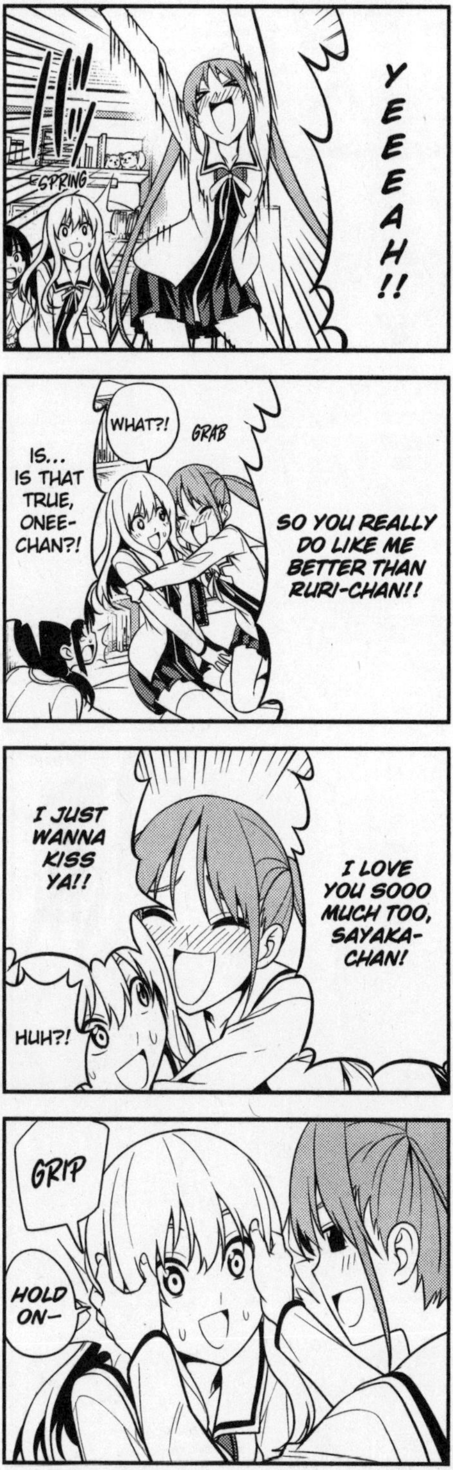
YEEEEAH!!
SPRING
SO YOU REALLY DO LIKE ME BETTER THAN RURI-CHAN!!
GRAB
WHAT?!
IS... IS THAT TRUE, ONEE-CHAN?!
I LOVE YOU SOOO MUCH TOO, SAYAKA-CHAN!
I JUST WANNA KISS YA!!
HUH?!
GRIP
HOLD ON—

Yoshiko the Wild Animal

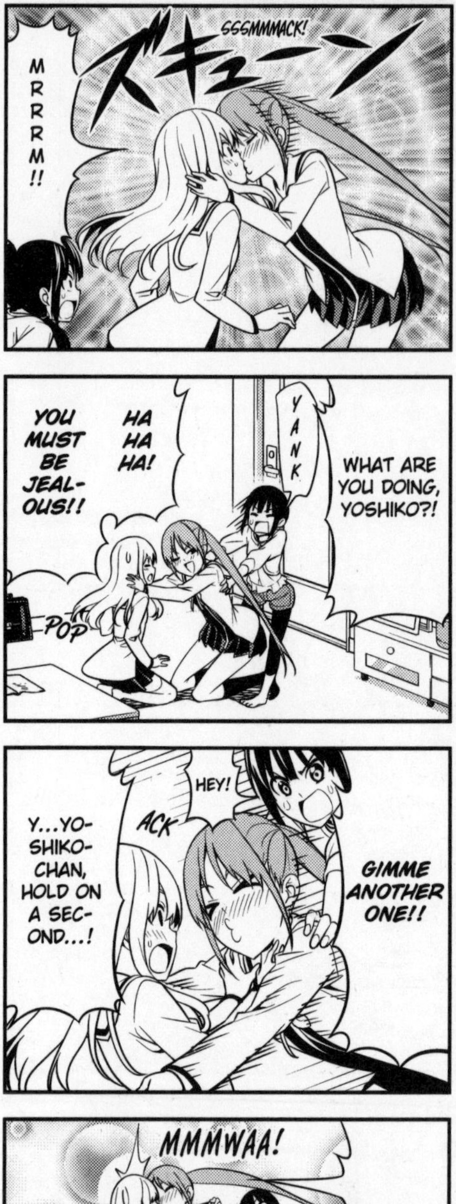
ズキューン
SSSMMMACK!
MRRRM!!
WHAT ARE YOU DOING, YOSHIKO?!
YANK
HA HA HA!
YOU MUST BE JEAL-OUS!!
POP
GIMME ANOTHER ONE!!
HEY!
ACK
Y...YO-SHIKO-CHAN, HOLD ON A SEC-OND...!
MMMWAA!
I CAN'T POSSIBLY WAIT!!
BOUND

Training

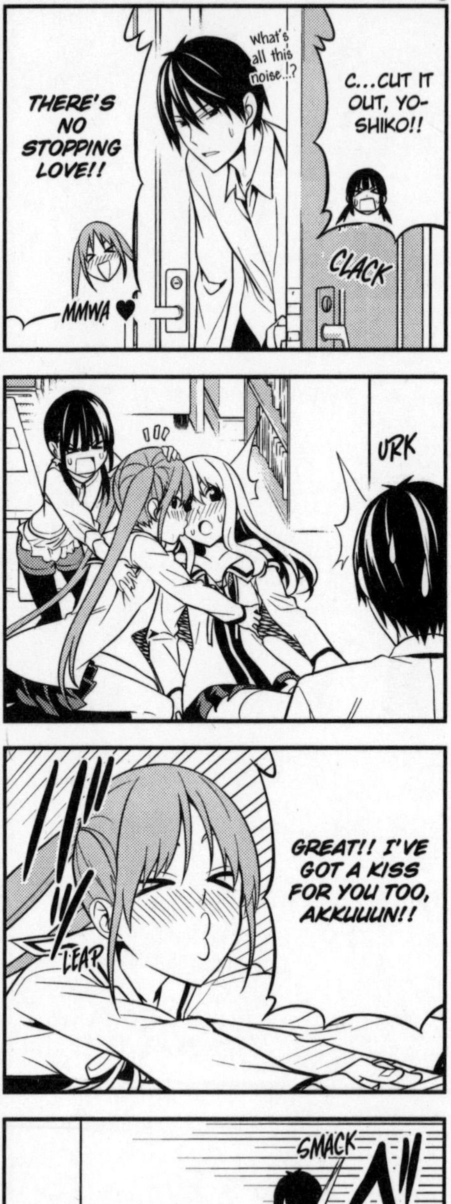
C...CUT IT OUT, YO-SHIKO!!
What's all this noise..!?
THERE'S NO STOPPING LOVE!!
CLACK
MMWA ♥
URK
GREAT!! I'VE GOT A KISS FOR YOU TOO, AKKUUUN!!
LEAP
SMACK
THEY DIDN'T GET MUCH STUDY DONE.

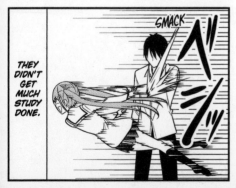

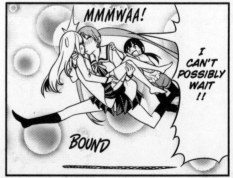

The Limits of Stupidity

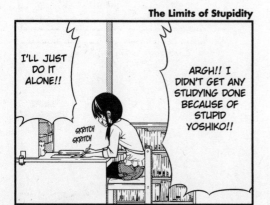

ARGH!! I DIDN'T GET ANY STUDYING DONE BECAUSE OF STUPID YOSHIKO!!
SKRITCH SKRITCH
I'LL JUST DO IT ALONE!!
BUT SHE DIDN'T GET ANY-THING DONE ALONE, EITHER.
I don't get it!
Ruri...

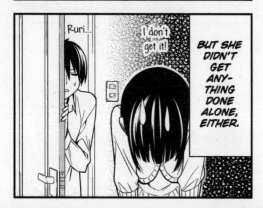

(Miracles, Magic, and)

Aho-Girl

\'ahô,gərl\ *Japanese , noun*.

A clueless girl.

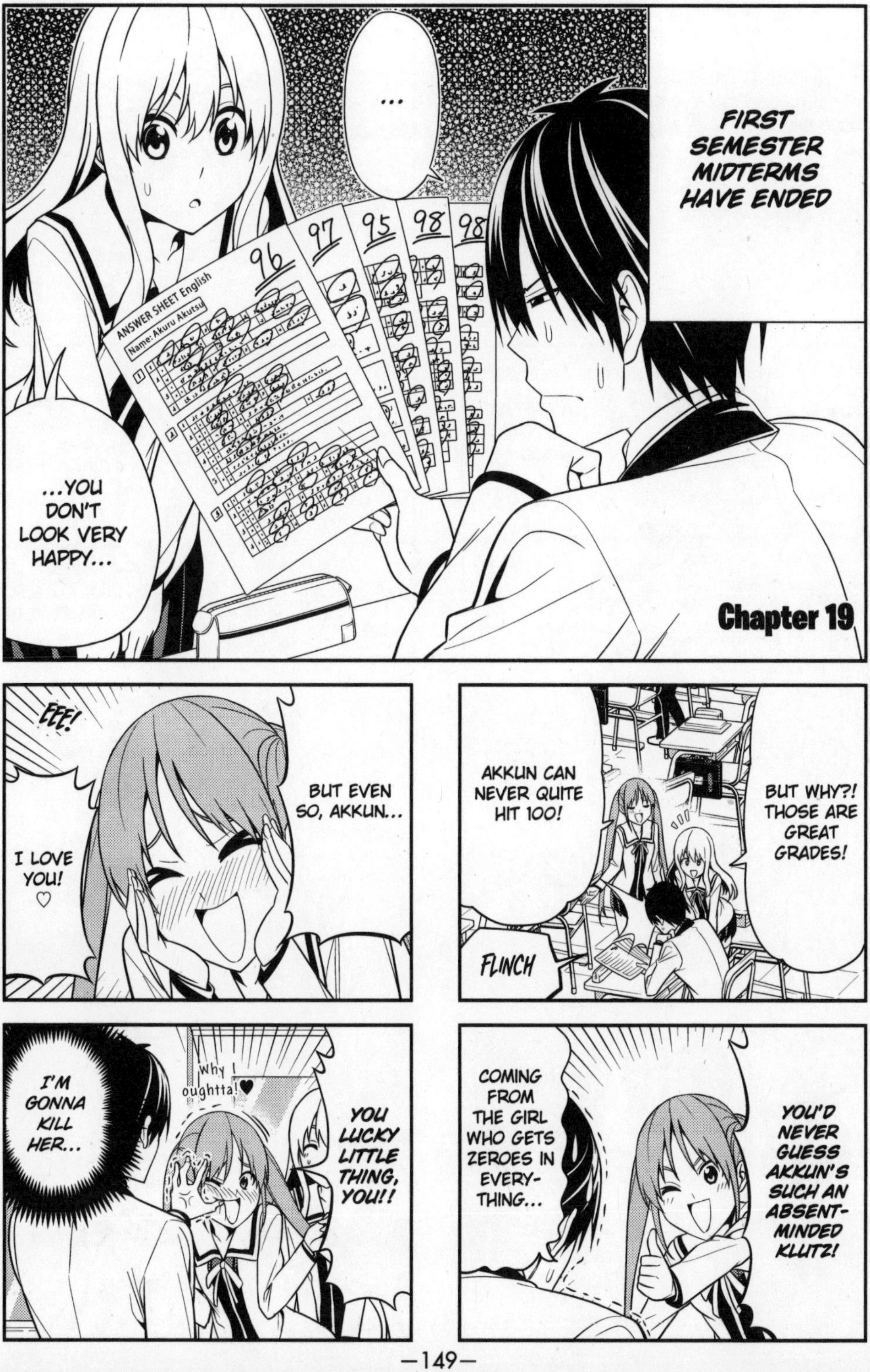
FIRST SEMESTER MIDTERMS HAVE ENDED
...
ANSWER SHEET English
Name: Akuru Akutsu
96
97
95
98
98
...YOU DON'T LOOK VERY HAPPY...
Chapter 19
BUT WHY?! THOSE ARE GREAT GRADES!
AKKUN CAN NEVER QUITE HIT 100!
FLINCH
EEE!
BUT EVEN SO, AKKUN...
I LOVE YOU! ♡
YOU'D NEVER GUESS AKKUN'S SUCH AN ABSENT-MINDED KLUTZ!
COMING FROM THE GIRL WHO GETS ZEROES IN EVERY-THING...
YOU LUCKY LITTLE THING, YOU!!
Why I oughtta! ♥
I'M GONNA KILL HER...

Yoshiko's Mom = Pervert

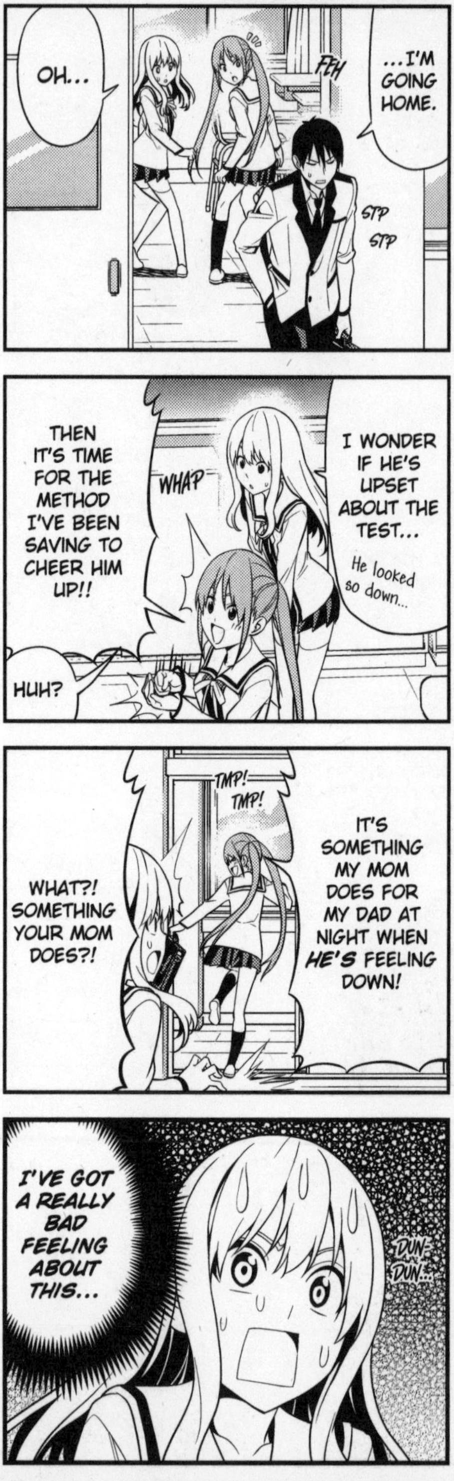
...I'M GOING HOME.
FEH
OH...
STP STP
I WONDER IF HE'S UPSET ABOUT THE TEST...
He looked so down...
THEN IT'S TIME FOR THE METHOD I'VE BEEN SAVING TO CHEER HIM UP!!
WHAP
HUH?
TMP! TMP!
IT'S SOMETHING MY MOM DOES FOR MY DAD AT NIGHT WHEN HE'S FEELING DOWN!
WHAT?! SOMETHING YOUR MOM DOES?!
DUN-DUN...
I'VE GOT A REALLY BAD FEELING ABOUT THIS...

?!

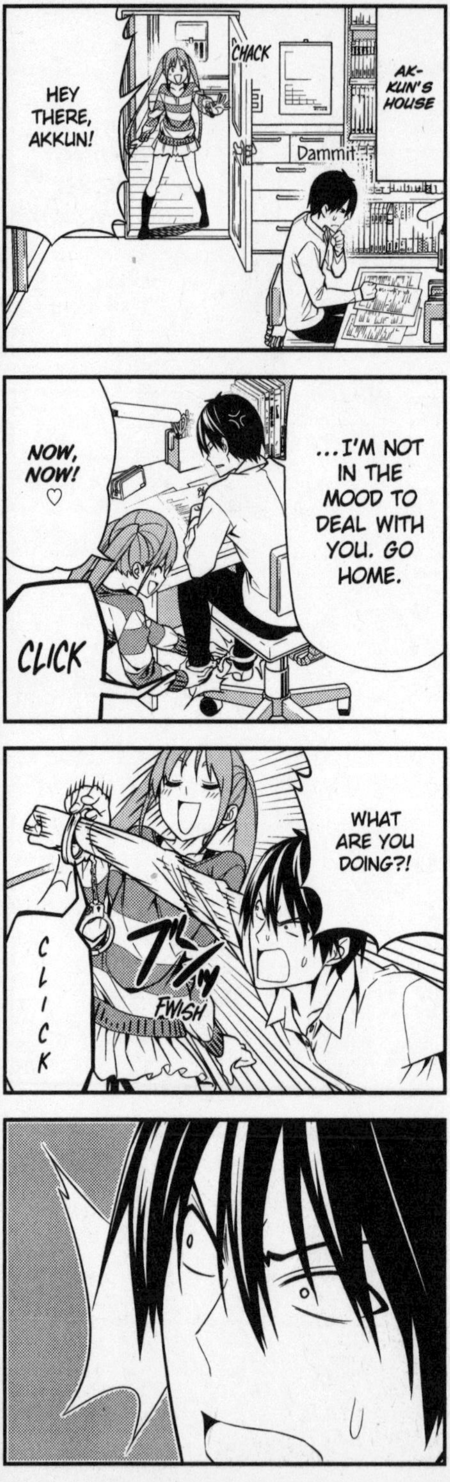
AK-KUN'S HOUSE
CHACK
Dammit...
HEY THERE, AKKUN!
...I'M NOT IN THE MOOD TO DEAL WITH YOU. GO HOME.
NOW, NOW! ♡
CLICK
WHAT ARE YOU DOING?!
FWISH
CLICK

Despair

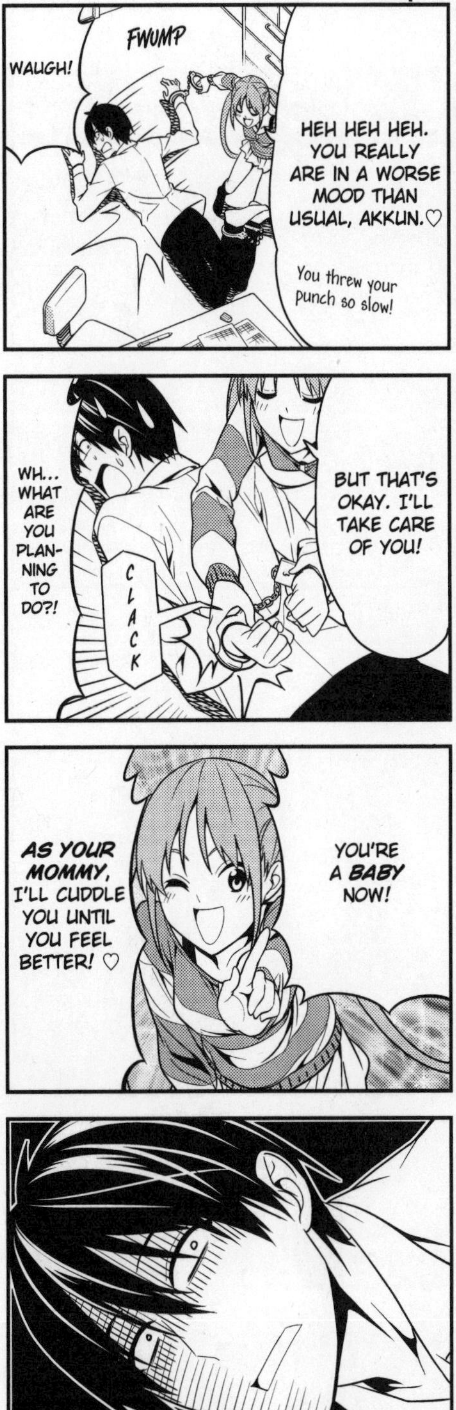
HEH HEH HEH. YOU REALLY ARE IN A WORSE MOOD THAN USUAL, AKKUN.♡
You threw your punch so slow!
FWUMP
WAUGH!
BUT THAT'S OKAY. I'LL TAKE CARE OF YOU!
CLACK
WH... WHAT ARE YOU PLANNING TO DO?!
YOU'RE A BABY NOW!
AS YOUR MOMMY, I'LL CUDDLE YOU UNTIL YOU FEEL BETTER! ♡

No Mercy

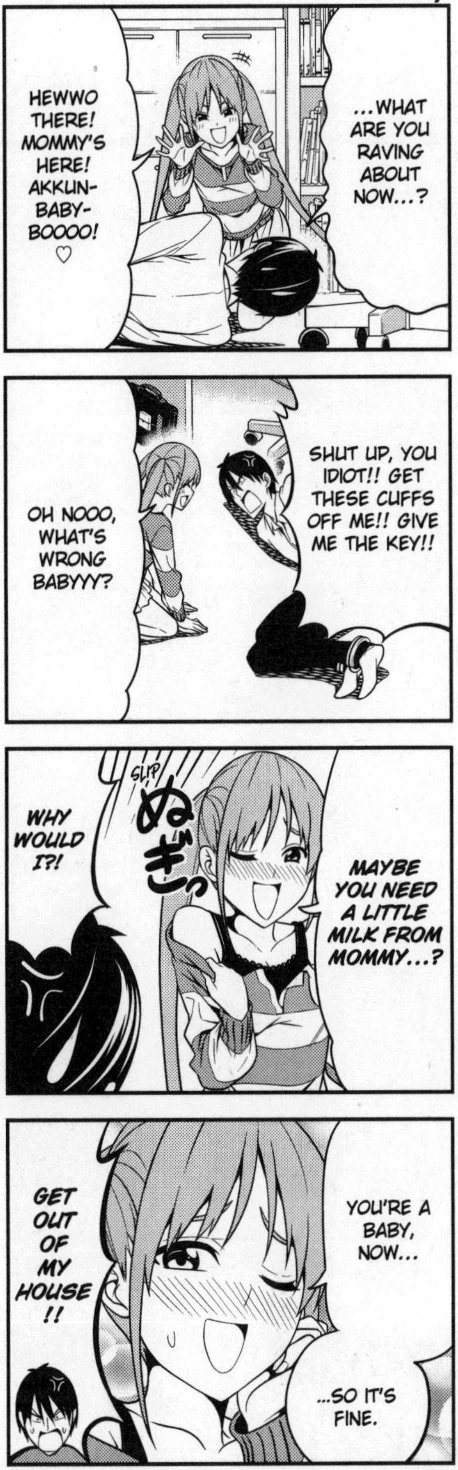
...WHAT ARE YOU RAVING ABOUT NOW...?
HEWWO THERE! MOMMY'S HERE! AKKUN-BABY-BOOOO! ♡
SHUT UP, YOU IDIOT!! GET THESE CUFFS OFF ME!! GIVE ME THE KEY!!
OH NOOO, WHAT'S WRONG BABYYY?
MAYBE YOU NEED A LITTLE MILK FROM MOMMY...?
SLIP
ぬぎっ
WHY WOULD I?!
YOU'RE A BABY, NOW...
...SO IT'S FINE.
GET OUT OF MY HOUSE!!

Helicopter Parent

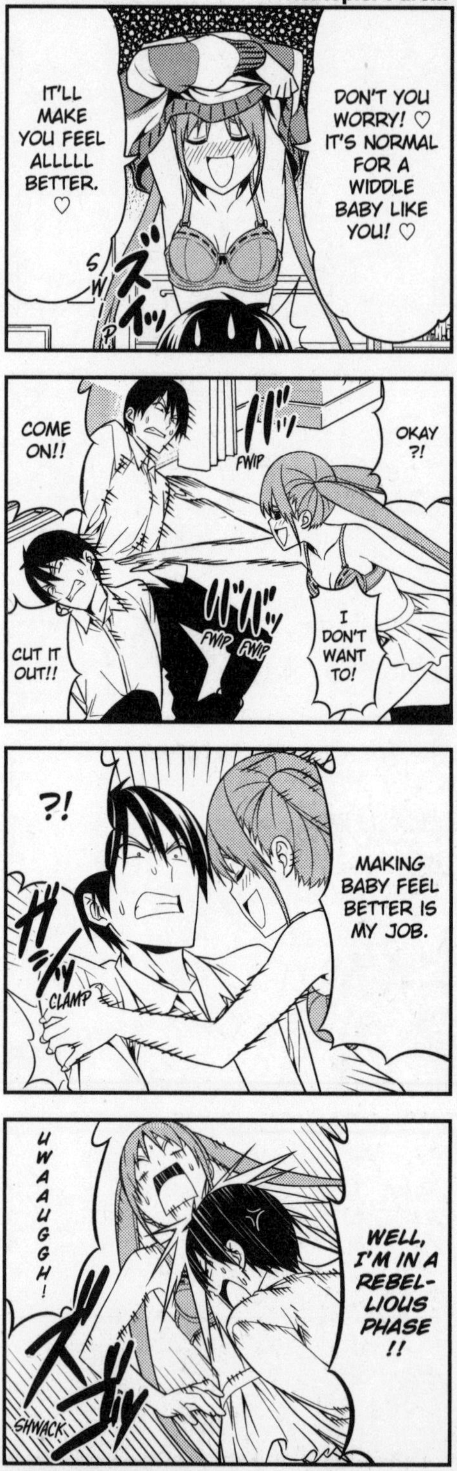
DON'T YOU WORRY! ♡ IT'S NORMAL FOR A WIDDLE BABY LIKE YOU! ♡
IT'LL MAKE YOU FEEL ALLLLL BETTER. ♡
ズイッ
SWIP
OKAY ?!
バッ
FWIP
COME ON!!
I DON'T WANT TO!
バババッ
FWIP FWIP
CUT IT OUT!!
MAKING BABY FEEL BETTER IS MY JOB.
?!
ガシッ
CLAMP
WELL, I'M IN A REBEL-LIOUS PHASE !!
UWAAAUGGH!
ズザッ
SHWACK

Think of Death

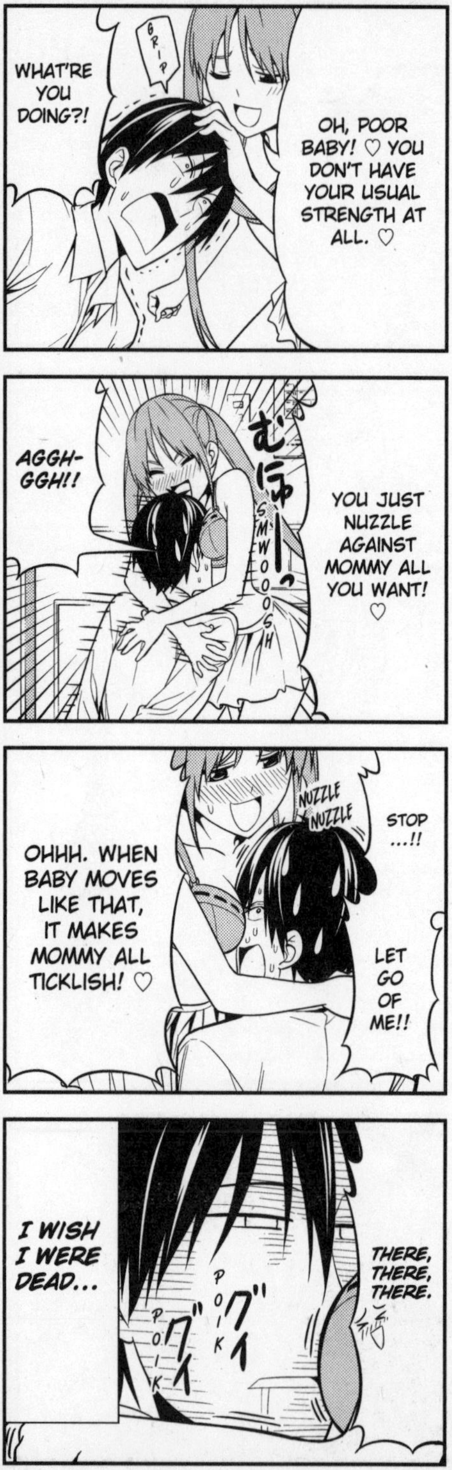
OH, POOR BABY! ♡ YOU DON'T HAVE YOUR USUAL STRENGTH AT ALL. ♡
GRIP
WHAT'RE YOU DOING?!
YOU JUST NUZZLE AGAINST MOMMY ALL YOU WANT! ♡
むふーっ
SMWOOOOSH
AGGH-GGH!!
STOP ...!!
LET GO OF ME!!
NUZZLE NUZZLE
OHHH. WHEN BABY MOVES LIKE THAT, IT MAKES MOMMY ALL TICKLISH! ♡
THERE, THERE, THERE.
グイグイ
POIK POIK
I WISH I WERE DEAD...

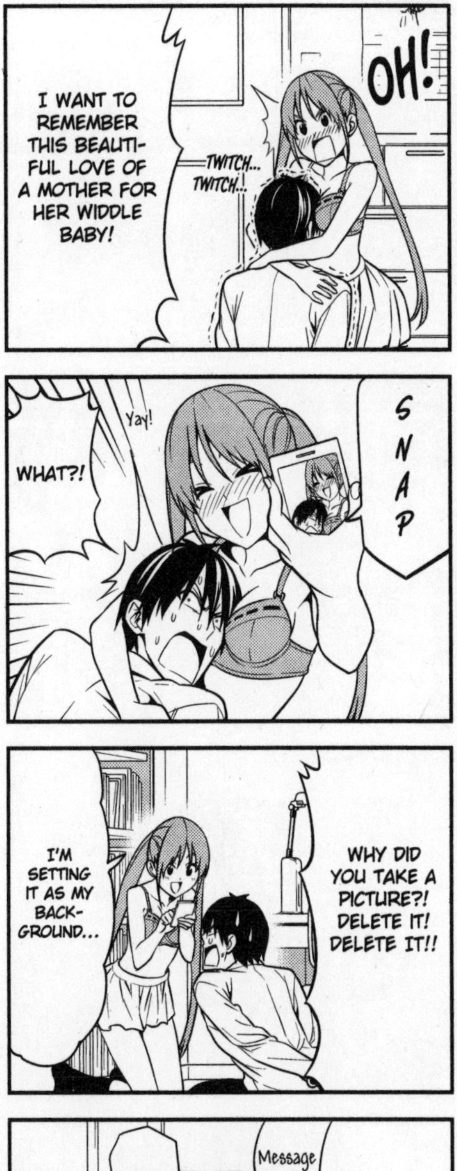
OH!
TWITCH... TWITCH...
I WANT TO REMEMBER THIS BEAUTIFUL LOVE OF A MOTHER FOR HER WIDDLE BABY!
SNAP
Yay!
WHAT?!
WHY DID YOU TAKE A PICTURE?! DELETE IT! DELETE IT!!
I'M SETTING IT AS MY BACKGROUND...
BING!
Message sent!
OH! I HAVE TO SHOW THIS TO SAYAKA-CHAN! ♡

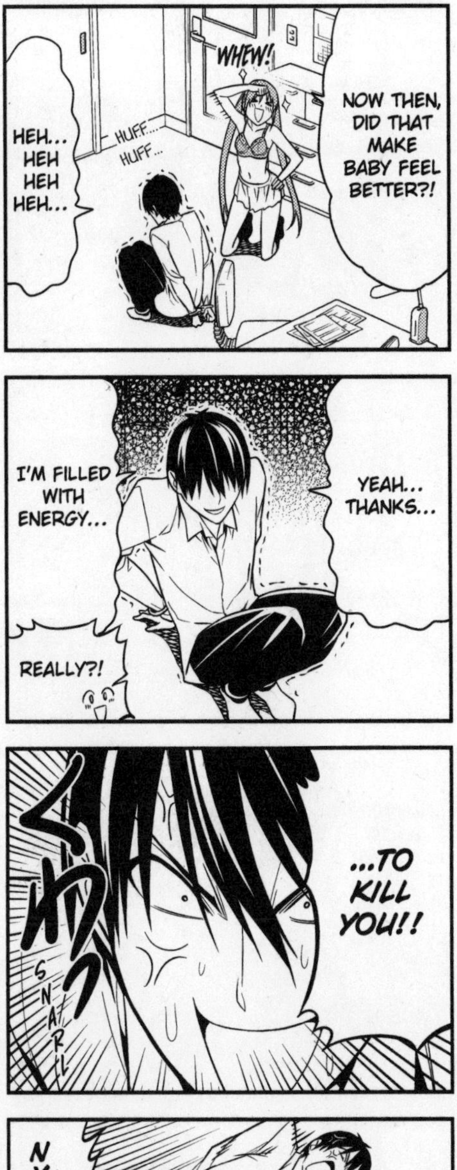
NOW THEN, DID THAT MAKE BABY FEEL BETTER?!
WHEW!
HUFF... HUFF...
HEH... HEH HEH HEH...
YEAH... THANKS...
I'M FILLED WITH ENERGY...
REALLY?!
...TO KILL YOU!!
SNARL
TAKE THAT!!
SHWAKK
NYAAAARGH!!

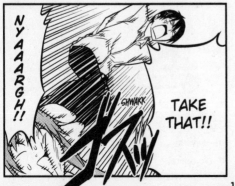

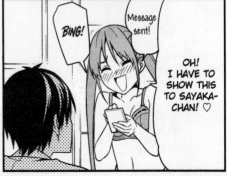

Happy Ending

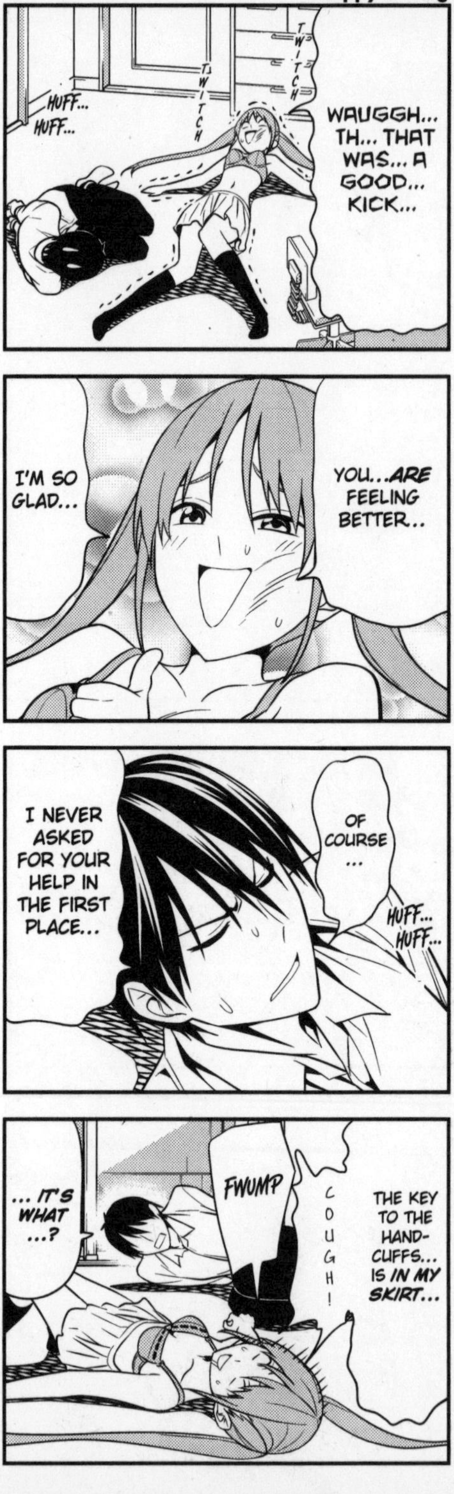
TWITCH
TWITCH
WAUGGH... TH... THAT WAS... A GOOD... KICK...
HUFF... HUFF...
TWITCH
YOU...*ARE* FEELING BETTER...
I'M SO GLAD...
OF COURSE...
HUFF... HUFF...
I NEVER ASKED FOR YOUR HELP IN THE FIRST PLACE...
THE KEY TO THE HAND-CUFFS... IS *IN MY SKIRT*...
COUGH!
FWUMP
...IT'S WHAT...?

Oniichan! Gross!

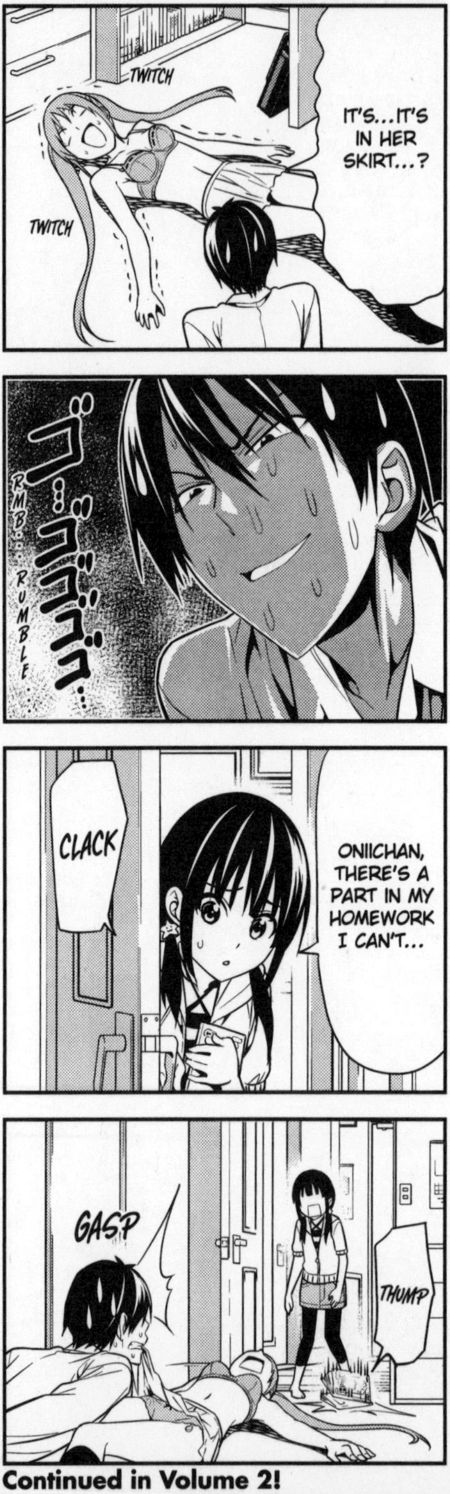
IT'S...IT'S IN HER SKIRT...?
TWITCH
TWITCH
ゴ…ゴゴゴゴ…
RMB... RUMBLE...
ONIICHAN, THERE'S A PART IN MY HOMEWORK I CAN'T...
CLACK
THUMP
GASP

Continued in Volume 2!

Time for Excuses

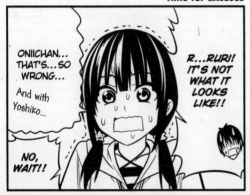

R...RURI! IT'S NOT WHAT IT LOOKS LIKE!!
ONIICHAN... THAT'S...SO WRONG...
And with Yoshiko...
NO, WAIT!!
LISTEN, THAT PICTURE YOU SAW—YOSHIKO FORCED ME TO...!!
B... BELIEVE ME, I GET IT.
Must've been awful.

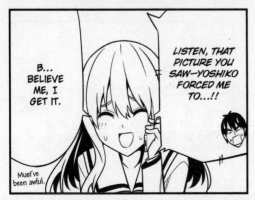

(She does the stuff we're too chicken to do! I want to be like her!)

Aho-Girl

\\'ahô͵gərl\\ *Japanese , noun.*
A clueless girl.

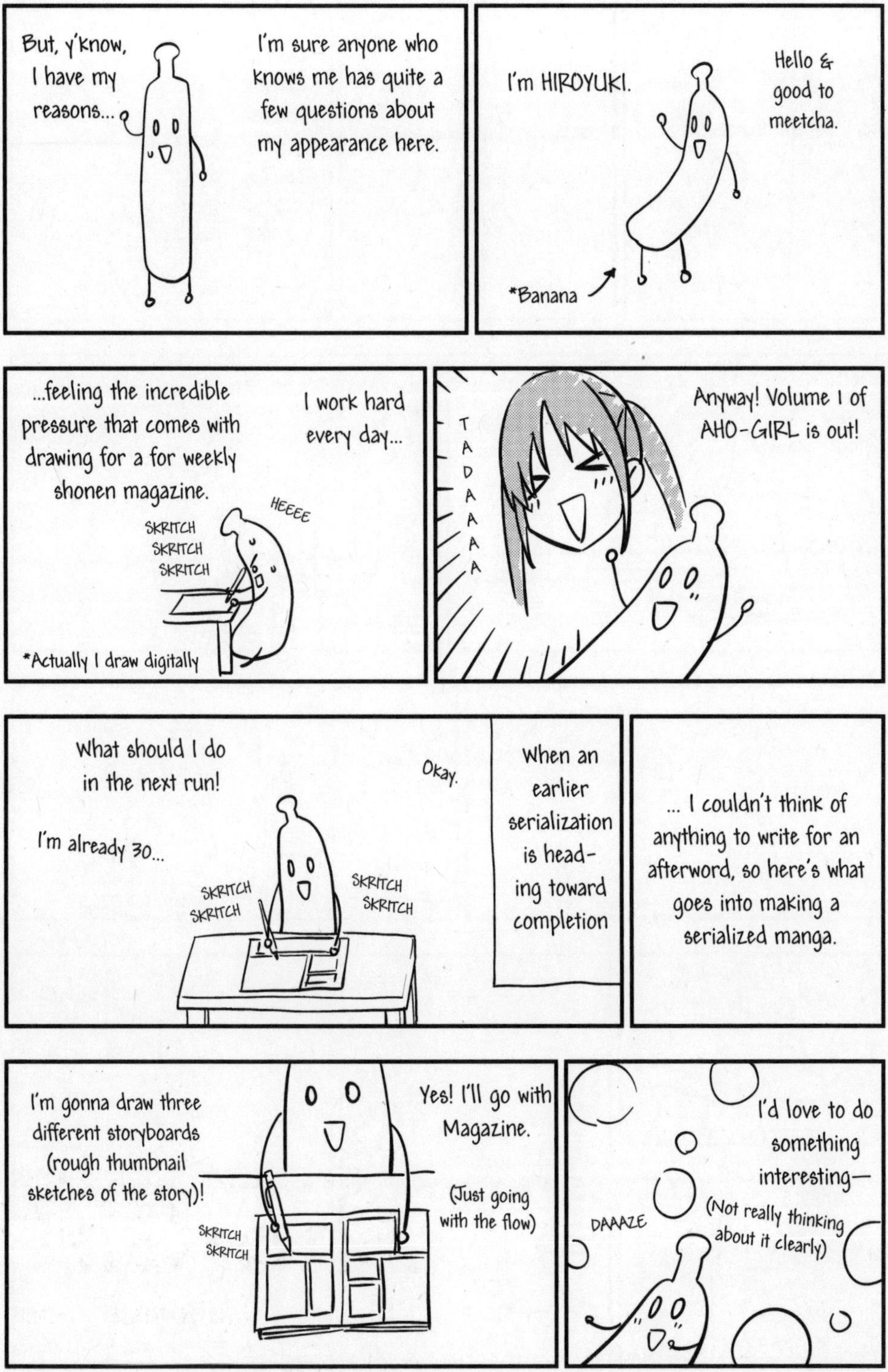
Hello & good to meetcha.
I'm HIROYUKI.
*Banana
I'm sure anyone who knows me has quite a few questions about my appearance here.
But, y'know, I have my reasons...
Anyway! Volume 1 of AHO-GIRL is out!
TADAAAAA
I work hard every day...
...feeling the incredible pressure that comes with drawing for a for weekly shonen magazine.
HEEEE
SKRITCH SKRITCH SKRITCH
*Actually I draw digitally
... I couldn't think of anything to write for an afterword, so here's what goes into making a serialized manga.
When an earlier serialization is head-ing toward completion
Okay.
What should I do in the next run!
I'm already 30...
SKRITCH SKRITCH
SKRITCH SKRITCH
I'd love to do something interesting—
(Not really thinking about it clearly)
DAAAZE
Yes! I'll go with Magazine.
(Just going with the flow)
I'm gonna draw three different storyboards (rough thumbnail sketches of the story)!
SKRITCH SKRITCH

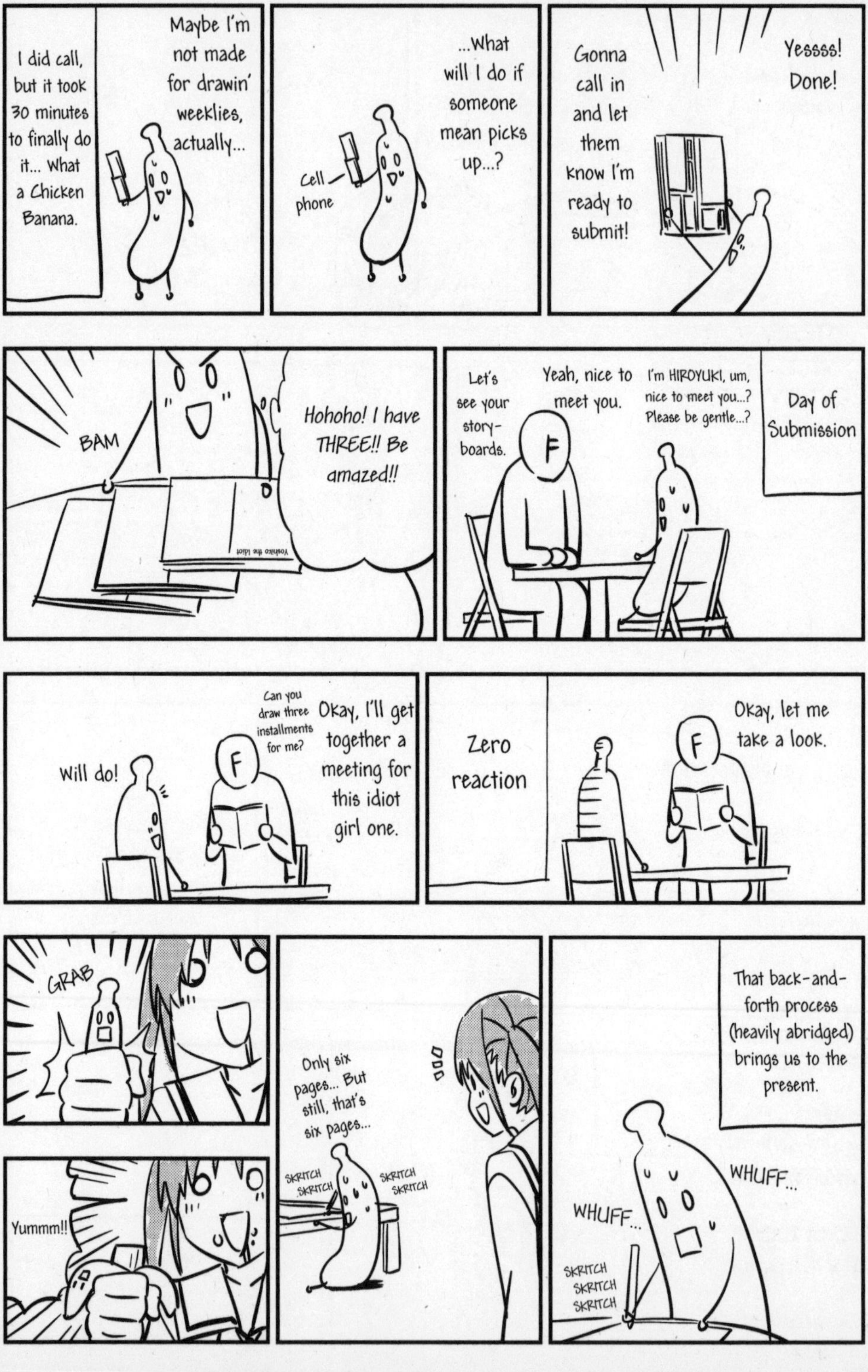
Yessss! Done!
Gonna call in and let them know I'm ready to submit!
...What will I do if someone mean picks up...?
Cell phone
Maybe I'm not made for drawin' weeklies, actually...
I did call, but it took 30 minutes to finally do it... What a Chicken Banana.
Day of Submission
I'm HIROYUKI, um, nice to meet you...? Please be gentle...?
Yeah, nice to meet you.
Let's see your storyboards.
Hohoho! I have THREE!! Be amazed!!
BAM
Yoshiko the idiot
Okay, let me take a look.
Zero reaction
Okay, I'll get together a meeting for this idiot girl one.
Can you draw three installments for me?
Will do!
That back-and-forth process (heavily abridged) brings us to the present.
WHUFF...
WHUFF...
SKRITCH SKRITCH SKRITCH
Only six pages... But still, that's six pages...
SKRITCH SKRITCH
SKRITCH SKRITCH
GRAB
Yummm!!

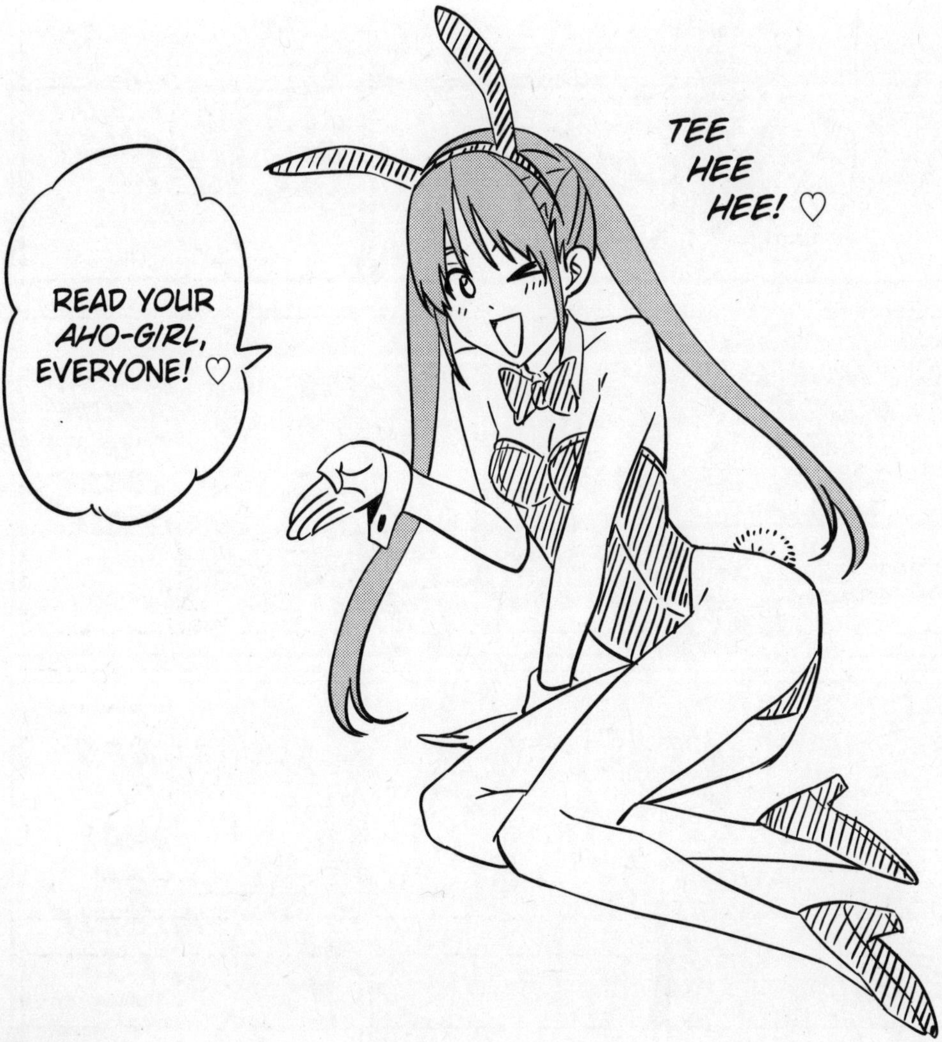
TEE HEE HEE! ♡
READ YOUR AHO-GIRL, EVERYONE! ♡

■ Author
HIROYUKI

■ Staff
Omae-san
Horikoshi-san

■ Main Editor
Fujikawa-sama

■ Comics Editor
Ito-sama

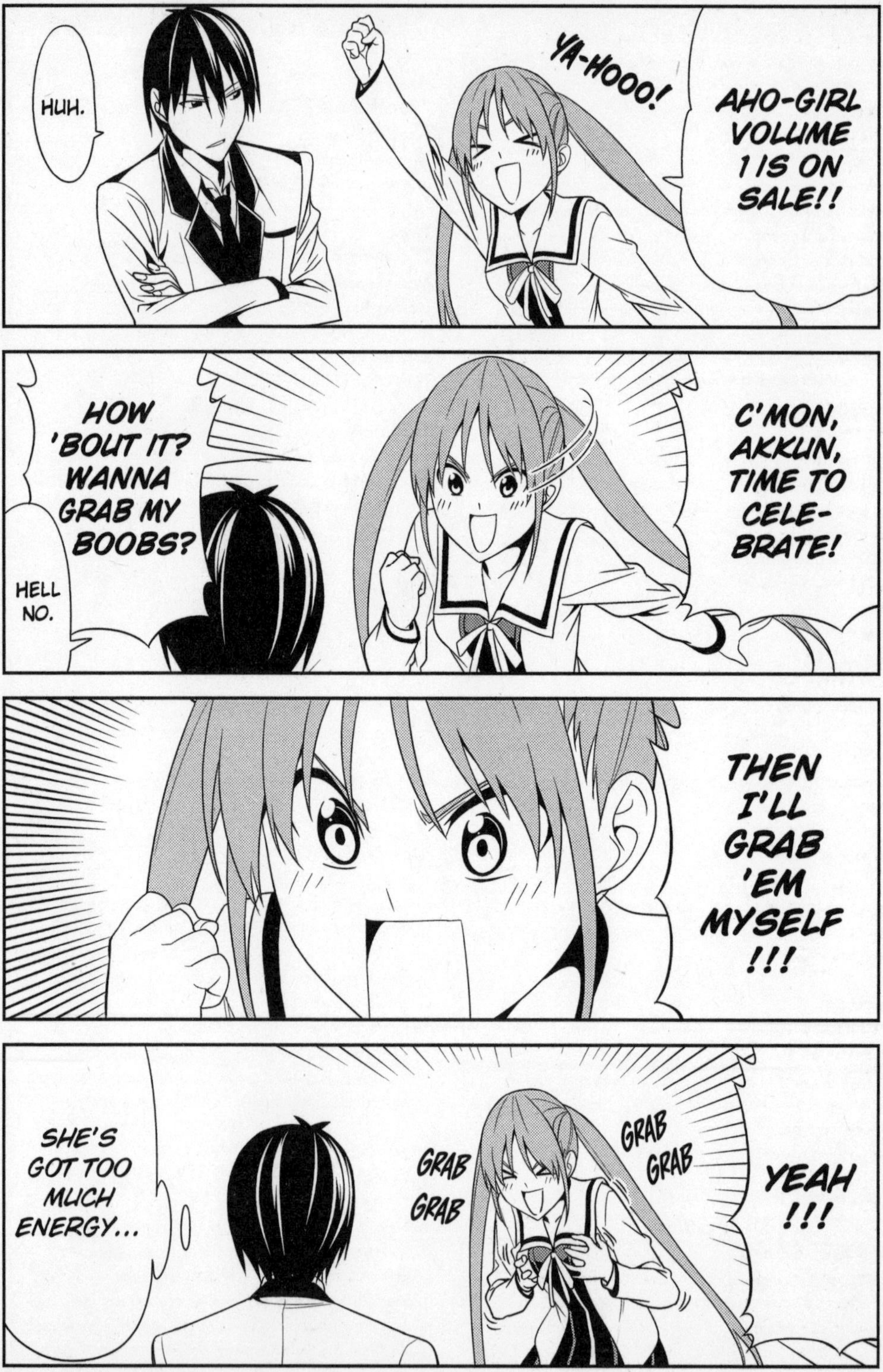
AHO-GIRL VOLUME 1 IS ON SALE!!
YA-HOOO!
HUH.
C'MON, AKKUN, TIME TO CELE-BRATE!
HOW 'BOUT IT? WANNA GRAB MY BOOBS?
HELL NO.
THEN I'LL GRAB 'EM MYSELF!!!
YEAH!!!
GRAB GRAB
GRAB GRAB
SHE'S GOT TOO MUCH ENERGY...

Translation Notes

Page 4
"But Then We Would Never Get Published"
Aho-Girl is serialized in *Weekly Shonen Magazine*, which publishes every Wednesday, a schedule incompatible with Yoshiko's proposed Sunday-only calendar.

Page 9
"Sometimes Prickly, Sometimes Sweet"
Manga readers familiar with Japanese slang may already have figured out what the title of this strip is referring to. The words translated as "prickly" and "sweet" are *tsuntsun* (prickly or short-tempered), and *deredere* (sweet, sentimental, or bashful), which combine to form the neologism *tsundere*. Tsundere in turn describes a person whose personality is outwardly hostile or gruff while being inwardly sentimental and sweet. A classic tsundere move would be choosing to attend school where your crush goes while claiming it's for practical reasons, as Yoshiko insinuates Akkun is doing.

Page 14
"The Banana (-Loving Idiot) Next Door"
"Tonari no Banana" ("The Banana Next Door") is a song from the repertoire of the idol group AKB48. It's a duet sung between two women. The younger woman insists that she's actually very sophisticated, mature, and adult, while the older explains all the ways in which the younger remains childish, and is therefore like a green banana, who will only ripen with "various kinds of" experience.

Page 31
"You're gonna poop"
Ryuichi, the "punk" character introduced on this page, is squatting in a pose called *yankii-suwari* ("Yankee-sitting"). Loitering in this particular fashion is considered unmannerly and indicative of poor moral fiber, such as would be expected of "Yankee"-style Japanese delinquents, whose name comes from their use of an exaggerated mid-century American fashion aesthetic. Yankii-suwari is quite close to another position, *unko-suwari*, "poop-sitting," hence Yoshiko's observation.

Page 32
"Power Level's Only 5"
This is a reference to the arrival of Raditz in the very first episode of Dragon Ball Z. Upon exiting his crash-landed space pod, the villainous Raditz uses his scouter (a green-tinted monacle) to evaluate the power level of a hapless farmer, the first human he encounters. The scouter reports a power level of "only 5," which leads Raditz to conclude that humans pose no threat to him. (Some readers may be very familiar with a another use of scouter-reported power levels: Vegeta's surprise, later in the series, at seeing Goku's power spike to "over 9000!")

Page 33
"Newtype Sensitivity"
The term "newtype" comes from the famous mecha SF franchise Gundam—specifically from the Universal Century timeline, where "newtypes" are hyper-evolved humans better adapted to living in space, with heightened senses, perception, and mental acuity. (Newtype is also the title of a well-known anime magazine in Japan, whose title is also meant to be a Gundam reference.) If Yoshiko is indeed some sort of newtype, it raises questions regarding the environment to which she's adapted.

Page 39
"Monitor"
The head monitor's armband reads fuuki, which roughly translates to "moral order" or "discipline." She would not be merely checking for hall passes the way a hall monitor in a Western school might, and would be more broadly responsible for reporting anything in violation of the moral standards of the institution.

Page 49
"Boss Lady"
The term that was rendered here as "boss lady" is *anego*. Taken literally, anego is a respectful term of address for one's elder *sister*, but its more common connotation is as the term of address a low-ranking gangster would use for the boss's wife. This is appropriate given Ryuichi's criminal, ne'er-do-well affect.

Page 60
"G Cup"
Going by Japanese bra sizing conventions, the head monitor's "G cup" bra would be roughly equivalent to an American DDD.

Page 61
"A Happy Time"
Shiawase no Jikan, which here is translated as "A Happy Time," was a manga by Yasuyuki Kunitomo that ran in Manga Action from 1997 to 2001. It chronicles the descent of a prosperous family into deceit, infidelity, and ruin, and was adapted into a daytime drama in 2012.

Page 72
"Don't Touch My Mustache"
What Yoshiko imagines to be English involves no English words. Instead, she merely continues to use Japanese, mangling it in a caricature of how a Western accent stereotypically sounds. In the final two panels, Sayaka originally said *"Aimu soorii"*—i.e., "I'm sorry" in a thick

Page 116
"Fun Fun We Hit The"
This is a fragment from the nonsensical opening line for "Choo Choo TRAIN", a pop single first released by the J-pop boy band ZOO in 1991. It found new popularity when it was covered in 2003 by another J-pop group, EXILE, a member of which had also been in ZOO. The smooth R&B-ish tune has seen recordings from many other groups, including the K-Pop boy band CODE-V. The complete line reads "Fun fun we hit the step step."

Page 136
"Slime Knight"
A slime knight is a recurring monster in the Dragon Quest series of video games. It typically appears as a dwarfed armored knight riding a green slime. Slimes, in turn, are blob-like, gelatinous monsters that appear in a variety of colors and sizes.

Page 136
"She's Getting Turned into Butter"
The eponymous protagonist of Helen Bannerman's 1899 children's book *Little Black Sambo* tricks four ravenous tigers into chasing each other in circles around a tree until they churn themselves into butter. *Little Black Sambo* has long since fallen out of favor due to its racist caricaturing of dark-skinned people.

Page 148
"Miracles and magic"
Episode four of the hit 2010 anime series *Puella Magi Madoka Magica* is named after a key line in the episode, in which the character Sayaka assures the injured Kyosuke that "miracles and magic are real."

Page 156
"She does the stuff we're too chicken to do!"
This (with male pronouns swapped for female) is a line from volume 1 of the shonen manga Jojo's Bizarre Adventure, wherein an onlooker is admiring the series's main antagonist, Dio Brando.

Aho-Girl
\\'ahô͵gərl\\ *Japanese , noun.*
A clueless girl.

Japanese accent. Yoshiko responded with a classic grade-school joke, *"hige sori,"* which means "shaving your face." The joke is meaningless except for the similarity between the words "sorry" and *"sori"* (shaving). In any case, in our version of the joke, Sayaka says *"dou itashimashite,"* which means "you're welcome," setting Yoshiko up for the English version of a similar joke. It doesn't really make sense—but then again, neither does Yoshiko.

Page 77
"Rah, rah, rah"
The original line here is *"Soore, sore, sore!"* which is a commonly chanted refrain in the style of music played in Japanese summer festivals. (See also the next translation note).

Page 80
"A Dancing Idiot"
The song and dance that Yoshiko distracts Ruri with is called, appropriately, "Yoshikono." It's associated with the *Awa Odori*, a summer dance festival held in Tokushima Prefecture. The Awa Odori is only one of many Bon festivals held all over Japan in July and August.

Page 92
"Sturm und"
"Sturm und Drang," literally "storm and stress" in German, has come to mean "turmoil" or "upheaval" in its usage as a loanword in English. It is also the name of the Gundam Spiegel ultimate attack in Mobile Fighter G Gundam, the 1994 incarnation of the evergreen robot anime.

Page 100
"Shooba doobie touch"
This is a reference to the transformation music from the live-action superhero TV series Kamen Rider Wizard, which simply repeats the phrase "shaba doobie touch and transform!" over and over again. The goofy theme has become a minor meme in its own right.

Page 102
"Cutie Cure"
The title translated here as "Cutie Cure" is "Purichua", which is a reference to the Pretty Cure family of magical girl anime series (also known as "Purikyua," or PreCure). A recent incarnation of Pretty Cure, *Smile PreCure*, was adapted into a Netflix-exclusive series under the title *Glitter Force*. Rather than come up with a disguised version of "Glitter Force," it seemed more faithful to the feel of the "Purichua" term to use "Pretty Cure" as the starting point. Hence: Cutie Cure.

INUYASHIKI

A superhero like none you've ever seen, from the creator of "Gantz"!

Ichiro Inuyashiki is down on his luck. He looks much older than his 58 years, his children despise him, and his wife thinks he's a useless coward. So when he's diagnosed with stomach cancer and given three months to live, it seems the only one who'll miss him is his dog.

Then a blinding light fills the sky, and the old man is killed... only to wake up later in a body he almost recognizes as his own. Can it be that Ichiro Inuyashiki is no longer human?

Comes in extra-large editions with color pages!

KC
KODANSHA
COMICS

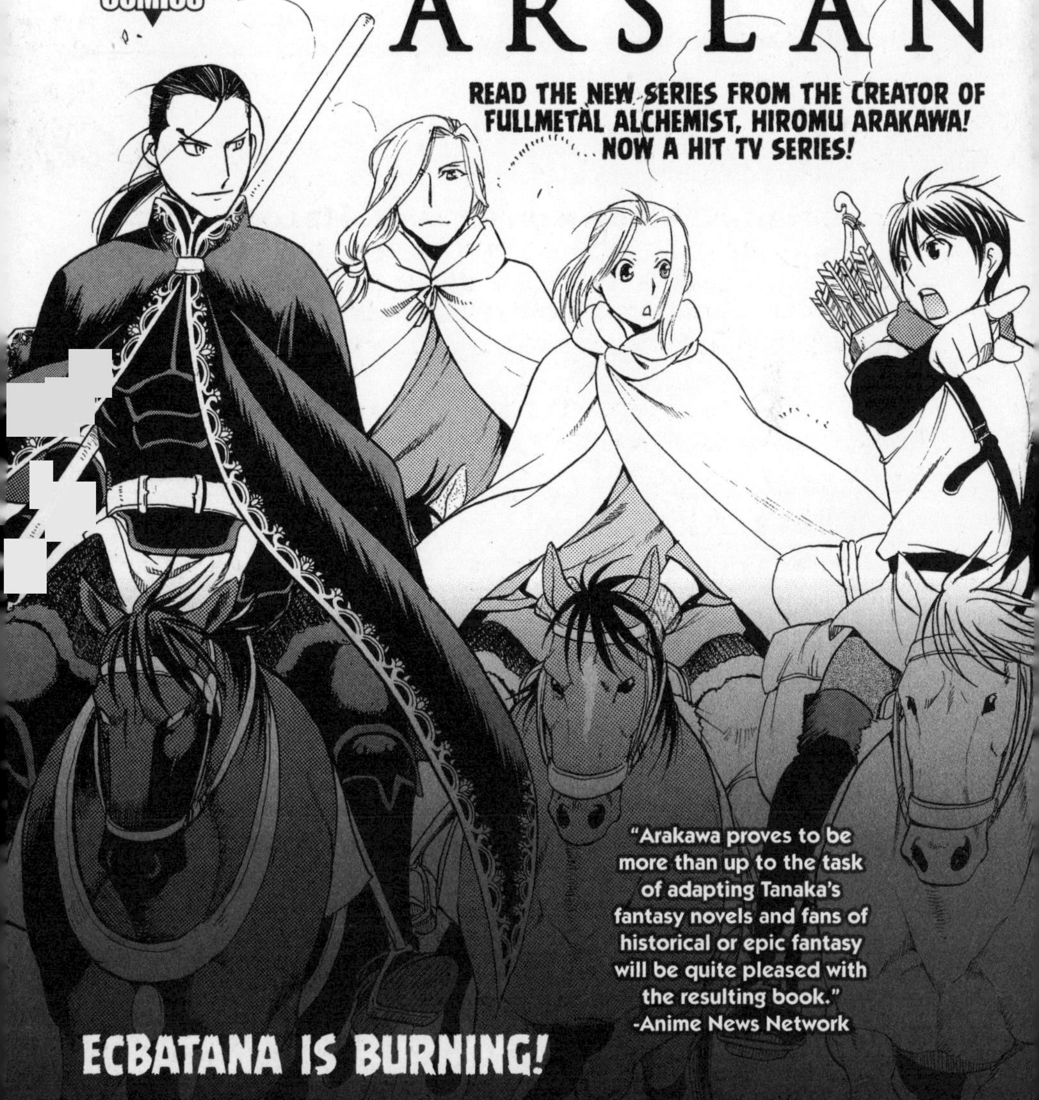

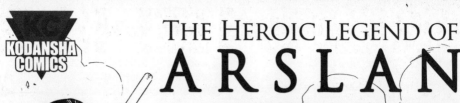

Having lost his wife, high school teacher Kōhei Inuzuka is doing his best to raise his young daughter Tsumugi as a single father. He's pretty bad at cooking and doesn't have a huge appetite to begin with, but chance brings his little family together with one of his students, the lonely Kotori. The three of them are anything but comfortable in the kitchen, but the healing power of home cooking might just work on their grieving hearts.

"This season's number-one feel-good anime!" —Anime News Network

"A beautifully-drawn story about comfort food and family and grief. Recommended." —Otaku USA Magazine

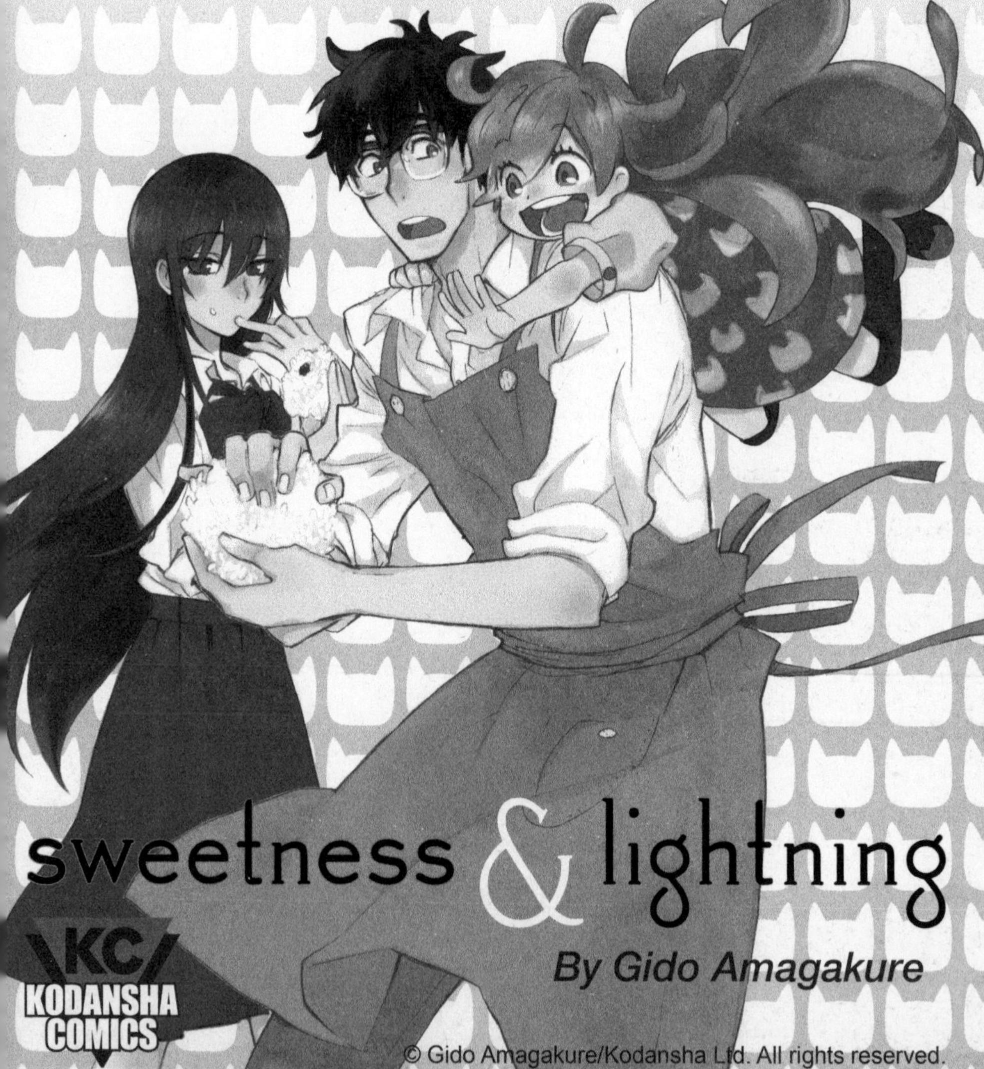
sweetness & lightning
By Gido Amagakure
KC
KODANSHA COMICS

KC KODANSHA COMICS

"I'm pleasantly surprised to find modern shojo using cross-dressing as a dramatic device to deliver social commentary... Recommended."

-Otaku USA Magazine

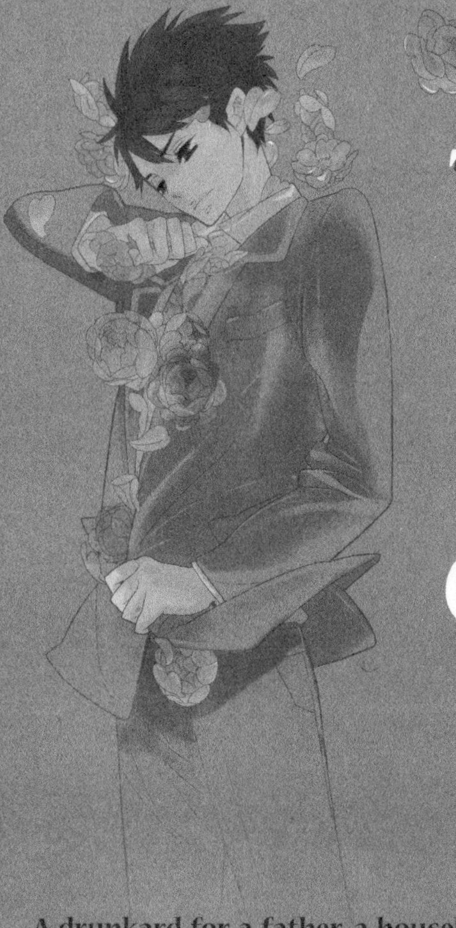

the prince in his dark days

By Hico Yamanaka

A drunkard for a father, a household of poverty... For 17-year-old Atsuko, misfortune is all she knows and believes in. Until one day, a chance encounter with Itaru-the wealthy heir of a huge corporation-changes everything. The two look identical, uncannily so. When Itaru curiously goes missing, Atsuko is roped into being his stand-in. There, in his shoes, Atsuko must parade like a prince in a palace. She encounters many new experiences, but at what cost...?

"An emotional and artistic tour de force! We see incredible triumph, and crushing defeat... each panel [is] a thrill!"
—Anitay

"A journey that's instantly compelling."
—Anime News Network

WELCOME TO THE BALLROOM

By Tomo Takeuchi

Feckless high school student Tatara Fujita wants to be good at something—anything. Unfortunately, he's about as average as a slouchy teen can be. The local bullies know this, and make it a habit to hit him up for cash, but all that changes when the debonair Kaname Sengoku sends them packing. Sengoku's not the neighborhood watch, though. He's a professional ballroom dancer. And once Tatara Fujita gets pulled into the world of ballroom, his life will never be the same.

KC
KODANSHA COMICS

"Parasyte fans should get a kick out of the chance to revisit Iwaaki's weird, violent, strangely affecting universe. Recommended." -Otaku USA Magazine

"A great anthology containing an excellent variety of genres and styles." -Manga Bookshelf

Based on the critically acclaimed classic horror manga

The first new *Parasyte* manga in over 20 years!

NEO PARASYTE *f*

BY ASUMIKO NAKAMURA, EMA TOYAMA, MIKI RINNO, LALAKO KOJIMA, KAORI YUKI, BANKO KUZE, YUUKI OBATA, KASHIO, YUI KUROE, ASIA WATANABE, MIKIMAKI, HIKARU SURUGA, HAJIME SHINJO, RENJURO KINDAICHI, AND YURI NARUSHIMA

A collection of chilling new *Parasyte* stories from Japan's top shojo artists!

Parasites: shape-shifting aliens whose only purpose is to assimilate with and consume the human race... but do these monsters have a different side? A parasite becomes a prince to save his romance-obsessed female host from a dangerous stalker. Another hosts a cooking show, in which the real monsters are revealed. These and 13 more stories, from some of the greatest shojo manga artists alive today, together make up a chilling, funny, and entertaining tribute to one of manga's horror classics!

KC
KODANSHA
COMICS

New action series from Hiroyuki Takei, creator of the classic shonen franchise Shaman King!

In medieval Japan, a bell hanging on the collar is a sign that a cat has a master. Norachiyo's bell hangs from his katana sheath, but he is nonetheless a stray — a ronin. This one-eyed cat samurai travels across a dishonest world, cutting through pretense and deception with his blade.

NekogaHara

STRAY CAT SAMURAI

By
Hiroyuki Takei

Japan's most powerful spirit medium delves into the ghost world's greatest mysteries!

Story by Kyo Shirodaira, famed author of mystery fiction and creator of *Spiral*, *Blast of Tempest*, and *The Record of a Fallen Vampire*.

Both touched by spirits called yôkai, Kotoko and Kurô have gained unique superhuman powers. But to gain her powers Kotoko has given up an eye and a leg, and Kurô's personal life is in shambles. So when Kotoko suggests they team up to deal with renegades from the spirit world, Kurô doesn't have many other choices, but Kotoko might just have a few ulterior motives...

IN/SPECTRE

STORY BY **KYO SHIRODAIRA**
ART BY **CHASHIBA KATASE**

H·A·P·P·I·N·E·S·S
——ハピネス——
By Shuzo Oshimi

From the creator of *The Flowers of Evil*

Nothing interesting is happening in Makoto Ozaki's first year of high school. His life is a series of quiet humiliations: low-grade bullies, unreliable friends, and the constant frustration of his adolescent lust. But one night, a pale, thin girl knocks him to the ground in an alley and offers him a choice. Now everything is different. Daylight is searingly bright. Food tastes awful. And worse than anything is the terrible, consuming thirst...

Praise for Shuzo Oshimi's *The Flowers of Evil*

"A shockingly readable story that vividly—one might even say queasily—evokes the fear and confusion of discovering one's own sexuality. Recommended." —The Manga Critic

"A page-turning tale of sordid middle school blackmail." —Otaku USA Magazine

"A stunning new horror manga." —Third Eye Comics

KC
KODANSHA
COMICS

The Black Museum The Ghost and the Lady

By Kazuhiro Fujita

Deep in Scotland Yard in London sits an evidence room dedicated to the greatest mysteries of British history. In this "Black Museum" sits a misshapen hunk of lead—two bullets fused together—the key to a wartime encounter between Florence Nightingale, the mother of modern nursing, and a supernatural Man in Grey. This story is unknown to most scholars of history, but a special guest of the museum will tell the tale of The Ghost and the Lady...

Praise for Kazuhiro Fujita's *Ushio and Tora*

"A charming revival that combines a classic look with modern depth and pacing... **Essential viewing both for curmudgeons and new fans alike.**" — Anime News Network

"**GREAT!** The first episode of Ushio and Tora captures the essence of '90s anime." — IGN

new
eries
om the
eator
f *Soul*
ater, the
egahit
anga and
ime seen
n Toonami!

"Fun and lively...
great start!"
-Adventures in
Poor Taste

FIRE FORCE

By Atsushi Ohkubo

he city of Tokyo is plagued by a deadly phenomenon: spontaneous uman combustion! Luckily, a special team is there to quench the ferno: The Fire Force! The fire soldiers at Special Fire Cathedral 8 re about to get a unique addition. Enter Shinra, a boy who possesses e power to run at the speed of a rocket, leaving behind the famous devil's footprints" (and destroying his shoes in the process). an Shinra and his colleagues discover the source of this strange pidemic before the city burns to ashes?

KC KODANSHA COMICS

The award-winning manga about what happens inside you!

"Far more entertaining than it ought to be... what kid doesn't want to think that every time they sneeze a torpedo shoots out their nose?"
–Anime News Network

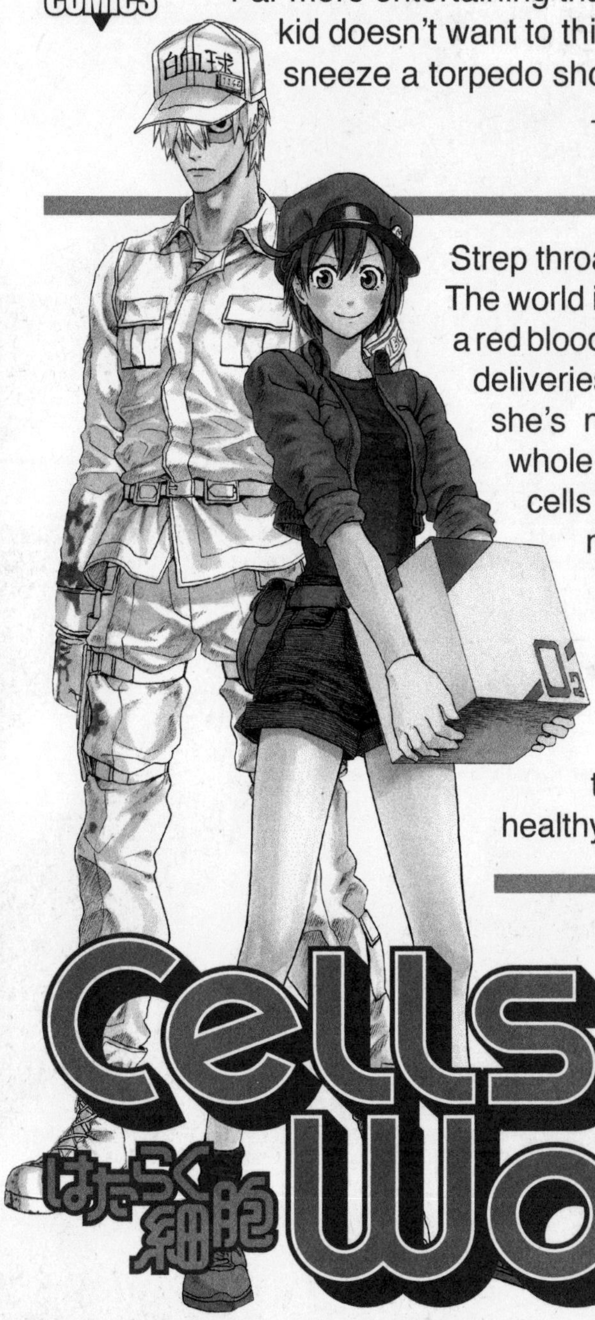
はたらく細胞

Strep throat! Hay fever! Influenza! The world is a dangerous place for a red blood cell just trying to get her deliveries finished. Fortunately, she's not alone...she's got a whole human body's worth of cells ready to help out! The mysterious white blood cells, the buff and brash killer T cells, even the cute little platelets—everyone's got to come together if they want to keep you healthy!

Cells at Work!

By Akane Shimizu

Aho-Girl volume 1 is a work of fiction. Names, characters, places, and incidents are the products of the author's imagination or are used fictitiously. Any resemblance to actual events, locales, or persons, living or dead, is entirely coincidental.

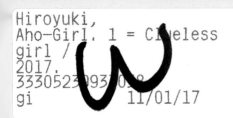

A Kodansha Comics Trade Paperback Original.

Published in the United States by Kodansha Comics, an imprint of Kodansha USA Publishing, LLC, New York.

Publication rights for this English edition arranged through Kodansha Ltd., Tokyo.

First published in Japan in 2013 by Kodansha Ltd., Tokyo, as *Aho Gaaru* volume 1.

ISBN 978-1-63236-457-9

Printed in the United States of America.

www.kodanshacomics.com

9 8 7 6 5 4 3 2 1

Translator: Karen McGillicuddy
Lettering: Maggie Vicknair
Editing: Paul Starr
Kodansha Comics edition cover design by Phil Balsman